CONFRONTING THE THIRD WORLD

Also by Gabriel Kolko

ANATOMY OF A WAR:
Vietnam, the United States,
and the Modern Historical Experience

MAIN CURRENTS IN MODERN AMERICAN HISTORY

THE LIMITS OF POWER:
The World and United States Foreign Policy,
1945–1954 (with Joyce Kolko)

THE ROOTS OF AMERICAN FOREIGN POLICY

THE POLITICS OF WAR:
The World and United States Foreign Policy,
1943–1945

RAILROADS AND REGULATION, 1877–1916

THE TRIUMPH OF CONSERVATISM:
A Reinterpretation of American History, 1900–1916

WEALTH AND POWER IN AMERICA:
An Analysis of Social Class and Income Distribution

CONFRONTING THE THIRD WORLD

UNITED STATES FOREIGN POLICY, 1945–1980

GABRIEL KOLKO

PANTHEON BOOKS
NEW YORK

Copyright © 1988 by Gabriel Kolko

All rights reserved under International and Pan-American Copyright Conventions.
Published in the United States by Pantheon Books, a division of Random House, Inc.,
New York, and simultaneously in Canada by Random House of Canada Limited,
Toronto.

Library of Congress Cataloging-in-Publication Data

Kolko, Gabriel.
  Confronting the third world.

  Bibliography: p.
  Includes index.
  1. United States—Foreign relations—1945–
2. United States—Foreign relations—Developing
countries.   3. Developing countries—Foreign relations—
United States.   I. Title.
E744.K63   1988   327.730173′4   88-42600
ISBN 0-394-57138-X
ISBN 0-394-75933-8 (pbk.)

Manufactured in the United States of America

First Edition
Book design by Beth McNally

TO JOYCE

CONTENTS

PART THREE

THE DEMOCRATIC PARTY AND THE THIRD WORLD, 1961–68

PART FOUR

THE DECADE OF PERPETUAL CRISES, 1969 THROUGH THE 1970S

PREFACE

WE LIVE IN AN AGE OF SUSTAINED PO-
litical tension and social conflict, continuous warfare, and upheaval. Never-end-
ing crises shape profoundly the quality of life in our civilization, defining the
daily lot of a large section of the global population, particularly those in the
Third World. News of this chronic state of crisis bombards those of us who
do not directly confront the hunger, loss of life, uprooting, and trauma that
are part of it. The very intensity and magnitude of this contemporary situation pose a challenge to our ability to comprehend it in its enormity and
complexity. Further, because there has been relatively little effort made,
given the importance of the problem, to blend discrete events and facts into
coherent patterns, most outsiders lack an intelligible scale against which to
understand the significance of what occurs daily throughout much of the
Third World.

Since 1945 the United States has played a decisive, though by no means
exclusive, part in shaping events everywhere on the globe; to varying degrees in many places, postwar history has been inextricably linked to the
nature and conduct of American foreign policy. Poverty and the transition
from colonialism to national independence have made the Third World the
most crisis-prone, and it is here that the U.S. role has grown almost without
interruption. Even if one accepts the contention that the difficulties of the
Third World would be monumental even if the United States had played no
role there, far less debatable is the fact that dealing with these problems and
the issues they have generated has increasingly dominated American foreign
policy. Indeed, it is only in these regions that the United States has engaged
in violent military activities since 1950. To come to grips with the U.S. relation-

ship to the Third World is also to analyze the single most important aspect of the international role of the United States in modern times.

For purposes of this book, the term "Third World" is used to include all of Latin America, Asia, Africa, and the Middle East, even though I focus on only those nations that the United States actively sought to guide or in whose affairs it intervened. By the 1970s some of these states were no longer poor, as in the case of the oil producers, but their vital economic importance to the United States continued. Although this economic factor was by no means always the sole or principal cause of American involvement in these countries, the role of these nations as exporters of raw materials generally defined their structural relationship to the United States. The explanation of how such economic and structural considerations influenced American behavior and goals will require analyses transcending any one nation or region but applicable in certain ways to all of them. I have not discussed China because of its sheer size and importance and because the triumph of the Communist Party there occurred very early in the postwar era.

I have also excluded Vietnam from my account, though I often cite its relevance to the global priorities and domestic economic and political contradictions that were to reshape the context of U.S. relations to the Third World after 1964. The Vietnam story is well known, in any case, and I have a full-scale account of it in my *Anatomy of a War: Vietnam, the United States, and the Modern Historical Experience* (1986). In fact, though the Vietnam War became the main event in the great postwar drama of American intervention in the Third World, until 1965 Vietnam was no more important to the United States than many other nations. Almost by chance it became the place where a policy that was preordained to lead to a military crisis somewhere came to its logical end. At social, economic, and even political levels, experiences there resembled those in numerous other nations, and the Vietnam War illustrated the great unpredictable risks, given the assumptions of U.S. strategic thinking, of any intervention with American soldiers. Vietnam, even more than the Korean War, exposed America's inability to fight decentralized wars in the Third World successfully. I have left most of the details of this fundamental military dilemma to my *Anatomy of a War* as well as *The Limits of Power* (1972), written with Joyce Kolko. But I include here my general analysis of the larger American premises that made the Vietnam debacle virtually inevitable.

Just as American policy is complex in its formulation and application—notwithstanding a certain simplicity in defining its goals and interests—the nations to which the United States has sought to relate are astonishingly diverse, even though structurally they are all societies based on sharp class inequalities. Despite the many similarities among these countries that one can never ignore, the differences among them can often have as profound an influence on the problems the United States confronts in the Third World. Such distinctions may define the focus of U.S. efforts and determine the possibility of their success. If sorting out these critical differences has been the major challenge to American policymakers and analysts—who usually fail in their efforts to do so—such comprehension presents a no less imposing responsibility to the historian.

I have, therefore, included a considerable amount of essential information in this book on the social and economic conditions in various Third World nations, and on their class and political systems, as well as on land and peasant questions. Such information will allow one to transcend those mystifying Cold War shibboleths that describe America's difficulties merely as part of a struggle with Communism. It will also enable one to comprehend far better the real nature of U.S. goals. For out of these social structures and class forms in the Third World have come those forces and issues that have challenged U.S. goals and interests, challenges not simply from the Left and those who are poor but also from the Center and from those many national-ist-middle-class and even rightist-elite elements in the Third World with whom the United States has also been in conflict. How the United States has responded to all these dilemmas is a major focus of my book.

Writing social histories of political movements is no small task, although in my Vietnam War book I undertook such a detailed survey, one that can serve as a model for studying other nations. It will suffice in the following pages merely to suggest the general nature of the economic and social components essential for such assessments. But even this brief summary will convey a sense of those larger relations between the United States and the countries of the Third World and of those unifying patterns and problems that emerged to define both the nature of modern history and the complex economic and political difficulties facing the United States today—many of them the outcomes of initial U.S. policy successes or of the actions of U.S. business interests, as in, say, Central America or the Philippines. Indeed, to prevent these more analytic issues from taking on an excessively abstract or theoretical quality, I will also examine them in the context of the experiences of various countries, of which the most important is the Philippines. Precisely because it had been an American colony and has assumed a special signifi-cance in the U.S. relationship to the Third World since 1945, the Philippines is the one nation I deal with throughout the entire postwar period. The U.S.-Philippine relationship illustrates better than any other the nature and goals as well as the frustrations of the U.S. postwar policies.

Purely as a literary convenience, I employ such terms as "the United States," "Washington," or "America" as interchangeable designations for the most important policymakers in Washington in various administrations, those people with the power to create and implement foreign policy. Despite current fashions in the social sciences, I have not considered it worthwhile here to go into the detailed steps by which these men reached their decisions, basically because I have yet to see convincing evidence that bureaucratic politics among various tendencies in government, which has existed since time immemorial in all nations, really alters the substance of basic national policies. Most of these larger policies can easily be predicted in advance, and to assume that their continuous recurrence is simply the outcome of capricious or arbitrary bureaucratic processes is grossly to beg the fundamental issues of power, interests, and purposes that underlay all U.S. government decisions. The astonishing continuity in U.S. foreign policy since 1945 points not only to the very small size of the homogeneous world from which U.S. decisionmakers are drawn—a community of mobile lawyers, industrialists, bankers, and officials I have described in my book *The Roots of American Foreign Policy* (1969)—but also testifies to the total socialization of all possible candidates for participation in the foreign affairs decisionmaking system. Styles may change, but the parameters of possible choices within which ambitious or vain men function do not—and this explains the uniformity of policy. For purposes of this book, then, unless I designate specific men or organisms, any reference to "the United States" and similar abstractions should be understood to mean the policy as defined by those at the highest levels dealing with the issue: usually the White House or the National Security Council, or both, but sometimes the most senior specialist official dealing with the country or problem. In any event, it is generally those at the highest levels of state who concern themselves with the broader context in which decisions are made and who transcend those parochial concerns that preoccupy, say, assistant secretaries of state or defense who concentrate on regions or topics. But when I have found divisions within Washington affecting basic policy in a significant manner, I have so indicated.

This book was written during 1986–87 while I was a York University Research Fellow, and once again I am deeply grateful to York University for its scholarly encouragement and vital support. Without York's exemplary understanding of how creative knowledge is best sustained, this book surely would not have been completed at this time. I am most indebted to the university, and I take pleasure in acknowledging what has for many years been an ideal environment for fruitful research, writing, and teaching.

Renato Constantino aided me in so many ways over fifteen years, the aid ranging from the inspiration his own great works on Philippine history provided, to his expressions of warm friendship, to his frequently providing materials one cannot find in North America, that I am unable adequately to express my profound appreciation for his generosity and patience with an eager novice. I am most grateful for all he has done. Michael Tanzer has kept me in touch with the oil and raw materials world for many years, much to my benefit, and he and Chester Hartman will be happy to see that I have systematically mined the Cuba press digest they helped to edit. Michael Klare generously shared his documentation on arms and military aid, and Jules Benjamin kindly supplied me with several important letters on U.S. policy toward the Cuban revolution. George McT. Kahin and Albert L. Michaels helpfully clarified some key issues regarding Indonesia and Chile, respectively. André Schiffrin of Pantheon Books has been immensely supportive and a pleasure to work with, playing the roles both of ideal publisher and friend. The York University interlibrary loan office fulfilled my many requests with unflagging good cheer and efficiency, and the Faculty of Arts secretarial service typed the manuscript with expertise and grace.

My wife, Joyce, once again played a very special role in the writing of this book, posing the right questions and drawing my attention to lapses in research and analysis—plus a great deal more. I have benefited immensely, far more than I can express here, from her comments and support.

Needless to say, I assume sole responsibility for everything contained in this book and for any errors of fact or interpretation.

CONFRONTING
THE
THIRD WORLD

INTRODUCTION

A MAJOR PITFALL CONFRONTING ANY writer on the history of U.S. foreign policy is the impulse to portray it much more systematically and coherently than America's political leaders and diplomats were able to at the time they were making decisions or when later reflecting upon them. Both the Vietnam War and the Iran-contra affair surely reinforce the need for historians to assign an important role to haphazard, even irrational influences that arise when those who determine America's role in the world act impulsively and in ignorance of either the challenges they confront or the consequences of their own actions. There have clearly been times in the United States' relationship to the Third World that surrealist poetry would have been much more appropriate to describe the relationship than the relatively stale prose of social science. But the fact remains that much of what we perceive as disorder and inconsistency in American foreign policy is far less the result of its goals and motives than of the United States' leadership's inability, in an astonishingly diverse and complex world, to predict the total effects of its actions or the costs of these actions to the nation's global interests. Those who read the daily news, or write about it subsequently, can easily become bewildered by information with which they are confronted ceaselessly if they fail to see the crucial distinction between the predictable regularity in the causes of policies and the frequently surprising and unintended disorder in the outcome.

Notwithstanding my concern for the uniqueness of events and nations and the foibles and miscalculations of American leaders, I have sought in this book mainly to describe those consistent larger patterns that emerged during the United States' postwar relations with the Third World and the nations in it. I intend to focus primarily on those many similarities found among seemingly discrete initiatives in American policy and the common assumptions, motives, and objectives that underlay them. While these policies have similar institutional as well as ideological roots, in various parts of the world they have had a very different impact. Many excellent accounts of the U.S. role in specific nations exist, but analyses of the relationship between U.S. policies in one country and those elsewhere remain a great gap in current writings, and making such vital connections is essential. My emphasis here is on the whole rather than the parts of American policy toward the Third World since 1945, on those repetitive factors that unify it. My focus is much more on the forest than on the trees within it—though ultimately the trees do make up the forest. Without such a broader perspective, the sheer mass of individual cases and the cacophony of facts in the daily news will submerge the essential coherence that has defined U.S. policy toward the Third World since 1945. More important yet, a general focus is essential to grasp accurately how American policy toward the Third World has evolved in reality as well as intent.

While area-specific elements of that global policy have their own distinctive character, American conduct in one area has frequently affected its involvement elsewhere, and decisionmakers invariably include such interactions in their calculations. Distractions in one nation or region impinge on goals and interests in yet others, producing conflicting demands on U.S. resources as the universal aspirations of its foreign policy assert themselves. To understand this tension, we must comprehend the causes as well as the goals of this policy as unified, the whole becoming the key to understanding the parts to a much greater extent than has been presumed in the literature on American diplomacy. Such interrelations have grown persistently since 1945 and have more and more defined the calculations that went into the making of specific as well as general plans. And precisely because the attainment of foreign policy goals has increasingly eluded America's leaders, it is necessary to give respectful attention to those local forces and conditions that have confounded their desires and taxed their comprehension.

Explanations of difficult problems such as these exist on several levels. First there is the purely objective and reasonably obvious level involving the United States' explicitly stated goals and interests regarding the kinds of political, social, and economic orders it wished to see in various Third World nations. While particular U.S. policies may have varied in each region insofar as Europe's role or the possibility of Communist influence was concerned, America's leading spokesmen made clear the same overall goals in these regions countless times. By no later than 1960, America's ideals and assumptions regarding institutional issues, above all foreign investment and raw materials exports, had been repeated so often, both in its policy guidelines and its routine diplomacy, that one can fairly say that for those ready to read the quite unimpeachable public printed and manuscript sources, there remains no mystery whatsoever regarding American formal premises and aims.

On a second level, far more challenging to explain are those essentially nonmaterial and symbolic elusive considerations that increasingly entered into the United States' decisions in the Third World after its failure to win the Korean War. The credibility of American military power and the emergence of geopolitical analogies and linkages in the form of the domino theory soon subjected U.S. behavior and policies in many areas to new influences that paralleled and sometimes outweighed the more traditional narrower assessments of the economic and political stakes involved in success or failure, action or inaction, in some nation or region. No less important to our explanation was the impact of the growing number of de facto and formal alliances with Third World surrogates the U.S. entered into in this period, raising for the first time the United States' increasing dependence on inherently unstable men and regimes.

Since official decisionmaking circles have never rationally articulated or coherently justified their reliance upon these fluid and seemingly intangible factors, historians of American foreign policy must do so themselves wherever it appears that these factors were decisive in shaping U.S. conduct in a particular nation. If Vietnam remains the most obvious case of this, it is nonetheless far from being the only one. Plunging into such a difficult area of study may be far more daunting than, say, estimating U.S. material needs, but to fail to do so is also to miss out on some of the main dilemmas and tensions of American foreign policy in the modern era. Have, for example, the failures of past U.S. military and strategic policies produced the extreme responses transcending rational calculations we find today, explaining why the United States appears to be leaping into ever higher risk situations that only compound its problems? Does the United States seem to be increasingly ignoring its oft-repeated ideas on the desirability of certain kinds of economic and political forms for the world, and, if so, can it be because these ideas mean something different in the late 1970s than they did in the decade after World War Two? Or have U.S. goals remained constant, with only the means for attaining them having changed dramatically in the postwar era? In fact, whatever their relative weights at various times or places, the explicitly stated U.S. foreign policy goals and those less fully articulated factors that have also shaped foreign policy objectives have through this period existed in tandem and been inextricable—posing a constant and formidable challenge to analysis.

Given Washington's belief during the early postwar years that not only had it the obligation to intervene actively in any country or area in the world in which it thought its interests warranted such intervention but, above all, also the power to do so successfully, the motives and behavior of U.S. foreign policy grew increasingly complex as its ability to impose its desires diminished. The Korean War especially caused American leaders to fear that the gap between their desires and their ability to attain them was wide and might continue to increase, and it stimulated an intense activism that did not abate. Not until the Vietnam War dramatically altered political and economic conditions within the United States and ended Washington's ability to gain its European allies' toleration of costly, dangerous policies was there even a pause in its growing interventionist momentum. The persistent search for an effective, relatively inexpensive means for using military power and force to attain political objectives emerged as a central theme in America's relationship to the Third World after 1950, and doctrines of limited war, counterinsurgency, and much else developed in response to it.

The assumption of activism was always tailored to Washington's regional priorities and options as well as to the extent of its deference to its European allies' interests. Many of its difficulties evolved out of its willingness or desire to replace its allies as the dominant regional power, as in the case of the British in the Middle East or the French in Indochina. Once it did so, the symbolic question of the United States using its military capability to impose its will in those places began to arise with increasing frequency. Coping with such challenges, whether they were real or were merely perceived to be so, became major events in postwar history, often involving scarcely more than a U.S. belief that simply because it *wished* a particular person or party to remain in power it had the duty to bring about its wish.

But even when Washington did not act directly, it increasingly did so indirectly. In order to understand the U.S. relationship to the Third World, it becomes essential to chart U.S. arms aid, its growing reliance on covert action, and its support for ostensibly friendly military elements in many countries. What were the risks and complications of aid and assistance to proxies and friends? Was Washington able to strengthen the role of the military in the political life of the Third World? And, perhaps above all, was the growing U.S. reliance on local officers as the instruments for protecting its interests counterproductive to the accomplishment of its original goals, carrying with it risks that might later require more direct forms of U.S. intervention? Given the enormously diverse problems of nations in the process of dramatic changes, could military officers guarantee the stability so essential to the attainment of America's tangible economic and strategic goals, or would they undermine its realizing its objectives over the long run? These issues were discussed in Washington as its leaders sought to avoid the more obvious dangers of direct American troop involvement, and increasingly they were to emerge as fundamental challenges.

Just as the average Third World nation has its own distinctive qualities, touching everything from its culture to economic organization and social dynamics, so too does the United States have both ideologically and institutionally defined reasons for its actions. How did U.S. objectives in such vast, rich nations as Brazil, which were relatively insulated from the Cold War strategically and politically, differ from those in the Philippines and Indonesia? What weight did the United States assign to strategic and military factors in the various regions? And what was the extent of its economic goals and interests? The nature of the U.S. material relationships to the Third World and its objective position in a global economy that was changing over time provide a crucial context for assessing American behavior. But was this setting a sufficient as opposed to a necessary explanation? How did such factors influence its general policies in the major Third World areas, and how and why did they differ? The manner in which U.S. interests and policies interact and clash with institutional, political, and cultural forces in various nations, shaping as well as reacting to them as part of an integral process, poses fundamental issues for analyzing events and the dynamics of change in the Third World since 1945.

PART ONE

LAYING THE FOUNDATIONS, 1945-50

CHAPTER 1

The Wartime Image of the Future

*T*HE UNITED STATES' WARTIME VISION of the future of the Third World after hostilities ended was far less the result of a conscious policy focused on the poorer and colonial regions than the by-product of its grand design for the entire global political and economic structure. It also reflected its attitudes toward postwar relations with its colonialist English and French allies. Washington planners did in fact articulate broad principles that applied incidentally to the colonized world, from Asia to Africa, as well as to the mandated countries the Paris Peace Conference had distributed to Britain, France, and others after World War One. But never did they divorce these aims from America's relations to Europe or its own postwar political and economic objectives. The United States always assumed that these goals were far more important than colonial self-government or independence, and that once they were attained, solutions to the problems of the Third World would also fall into place. America often proclaimed its anticolonialism in formal policy declarations, but it was always subordinate to far more urgent priorities.

Because of the complex considerations influencing U.S. policy toward colonialism during and immediately after World War Two, the wartime ideological assertions of America's stand on the Third World appear in retrospect more significant than they frequently were in fact, depending on the region involved. Anticolonial rhetoric came easily to American politicians, but in practice the whole panoply of specific U.S. goals and responses at various times and places combined to create incrementally an eclectic strategy that was far less lofty and that explains more precisely both the operational theory and practice of U.S. foreign policy. And while one should not casually dismiss genuinely felt ideas—for they often produced obvious paradoxes in Washington that were the source of much debate—the ideology itself also touched many concrete issues of interests that allowed various powerful constituencies repeatedly to define them to their own needs. The main problem in attributing a greater causal role to ideology in explaining U.S. behavior in the Third World after 1944 was that America's leaders assiduously avoided dealing with the political details of the future of Third World nations. One has to look to its articulated economic goals to locate sufficiently exact notions that can be adapted to reality without attempting to fathom unknown or debatable inner meanings in declarations of belief that were all too often scarcely more than public-relations exercises. And where the problem of colonialism did not complicate U.S. relations to a region, as in Latin America, proposals on political and economic development it advanced in the European spheres of influence it ignored entirely within the vast hemisphere it assigned explicitly to its own domination. Dual standards were integral both to Washington's theory and practice insofar as Latin America or its own colony in the Philippines was concerned.

There was nothing devious or contrived in such pragmatic inconsistencies, and it was scarcely a characteristic exclusive to the United States. American foreign policy leaders have generally been divided between universalists who stress the role of international organizations and collective responsibility, and those who emphasize the direct pursuit of national interest without encumbering alliances. While the universalists, beginning with Woodrow Wilson in 1912, have in reality defined the tangible mechanisms of world organizations in such a manner that they have principally served U.S. national interests, the unilateralist tradition largely associated with Republican presidents has in practice also been promoted by domestic political and economic interest groups found in both parties at any given time. No administration has been able to ignore the pressure of such organized elements, which have often mobilized regionally based bipartisan support in Congress. More importantly, apart from the ability of such domestically oriented constituencies to modify or block Executive strategies has been the fact that even American advocates of universalism have always regarded the Western Hemisphere as a special domain largely exempt from the jurisdiction of international bodies like the UN. It was for this reason that the Truman Administration lobbied successfully to have the UN Charter grant special status to "regional arrangements," which it understood would apply only to its hemisphere.

More than any other branch of the government, the State Department under Cordell Hull, who was its secretary from 1933 to 1944, defined the U.S. vision of the ideal relationship of the colonized and poorer nations to the world order. Hull was a disciple of Wilson and his "Open Door" concept of an integrated world based on free trade that Wilson took from the Democratic Party's traditional policies and raised to a higher level of abstraction. Hull was, as well, both an ideologue and a pragmatist, ready to confront aggressively America's allies, particularly Britain, but also not to press issues too far with them if something tangible could be gained in return. He regarded the breakup of the world economy into isolated trading blocs after the 1929–31 Depression as the single most important cause of the Second World War as well as the most likely source of future wars. Restrictive trade cartels, which had especially inflated the price of the United States' increasingly essential raw materials imports, were integral to this distorted world economy, and it was the British sterling bloc and empire that most epitomized these challenges to an open world economy based on free trade. From 1941 onward the United States never tired of stressing that "raw material supplies must be available to all nations without discrimination" after the war, and this in turn required complete access for U.S. capital to enter any nation to accelerate "the sound development of latent natural resources and productive capacity in relatively undeveloped areas."[1] But while there was a consensus on these essentially anticolonial objectives among key American decisionmakers during the war, they disagreed how and with what speed to apply them, especially because Britain, more than any other nation, was the object of the U.S. program, and the British after 1943 made no secret of their fears that America was trying to advance its interests in Asia and the Middle East at their expense.

But it was not only Washington's desire to keep Britain as an ally in Europe after the war that inhibited its pressing its anticolonial sentiments too far and too fast. The radical nature of many of the local political forces aspiring to replace the colonial powers especially disturbed American leaders, and particularly after 1945 they increasingly feared local Left parties that might presumably be friendlier to the Soviet Union or even aligned with it. But even in India, the United States supported British policy in repressing a thoroughly anti-Communist Mahatma Gandhi and the Congress Party because Gandhi was opposed to the war and because the British successfully demanded that the Americans respect their jurisdiction over India. In the Middle East, at least during the war, Washington retreated when Britain objected to its issuing a declaration favoring steps toward independence for Syria and Lebanon. The implicit recognition of British spheres of influence in the colonial world was extended to Africa also, where the United States kept silent on the future of mandated areas even though it insisted that it retained a residual right under the 1919 Treaty of Versailles to have its trade interests there protected.

The United States did not pursue its nominal anticolonial ideology too ardently also because it expected the British to support American claims for the transfer of Japanese-held Pacific trusteeships to the United States after the war. Indeed, as the Cold War intensified after 1945, keeping Britain firmly on the United States' side quickly submerged any latent doubts Washington felt about the continuation of its imperial power in various forms. Both the U.S. Navy and the War Department wished to establish permanent bases on the formerly Japanese-controlled islands. The State Department, too, sought bases, but with UN sanction and theoretically under UN control. Simply to annex the islands, as the military urged, would allow the British to claim the same right elsewhere, particularly in the Middle East, and endanger, as Secretary of the Interior Harold Ickes put it, "our great stake in Middle Eastern oil."[2]

At the April 1945 founding conference of the UN in San Francisco the divided Americans hammered out a common position and reached a quid pro quo with the British that was to define and limit U.S. foreign policy in much of the Third World for the next five years. All the territories transferred from the mandate system were divided into strategic or nonstrategic areas, with the Security Council, where the U.S. has a veto, in charge of the former. To placate the British, the far larger and populous nonstrategic areas under the new Trusteeship Council could also pass to Security Council jurisdiction should the situation require. Then, over the objection of the Soviet Union and some of the smaller states, the new UN accepted the U.S., British, and French position that an administratively impotent Trusteeship Council endorse "progressive development toward self-government or independence as may be appropriate to the particular circumstances."[3]

Few Americans involved in this debate believed independence per se was desirable as a goal, but they regarded it as a cosmetic word to placate critics, one sufficiently hedged in by contingencies to retain control over what they considered inherently unstable areas and to preserve Britain's confidence in the future reliability of its American ally. The American and British governments understood explicitly that they had reached a quid pro quo touching all the formerly mandated territories. But both in April 1945 and over subsequent years the United States insisted that neither Britain nor any other trustee had the right to deny commercial equality in the trusteed nations. Whatever its political form, Washington unswervingly advocated an integrated world economy open to American interests. Independence, when and where it came, would be for states capable of playing a role in an integrated world order congenial to U.S. designs, a paternalist attitude that further subordinated anticolonialism to American needs. Self-determination as an absolute principle had no vocal spokesmen in Washington.

Precisely because the United States entered the postwar era with its earlier experiences and obsessions profoundly coloring its perceptions of the future, there was a continuity between its policies after 1945 and its earlier problems. Indeed, while its fear of the Left increased dramatically after 1944, culminating in its Cold War fixations, the United States prewar definitions of its goals and needs remained, so that it was not at all surprising that they later deeply influence its policies and action in various nations where the Left was either weak or nonexistent. And because it believed profoundly in the efficacy of its institutional proposals for an integrated postwar world economic and political structure, it assumed that the implementation of this program would prevent the growth of the radical Left everywhere in the world, the Third World included. If one looks at the plans for the World Bank or International Trade Organization (ITO) formulated and made public during 1945, one is immediately struck by the fact that they subordinated the problems of the Third World to the reconstruction of a world economy in which the United States and Western Europe are the principal partners, while the needs and problems of Asia, Latin America, and Africa were incidental and, implicitly, to be dealt with as a by-product of solving difficulties elsewhere.

For the United States, given its official belief in the allegedly complementary nature of national economies that are open to each other and trade freely, this indifference to developments in the poorest regions was logical. The United States was not, in reality, concerned chiefly with either the economic or political problems there. Its explicit assumption was that although the difficulties of the war-torn industrial nations might require a temporary dependence on government funding along with a simultaneous reduction of barriers to freer trade, "It appears obvious that Latin America and other underdeveloped areas must rely primarily upon private foreign capital and business to assist in their development."[4] The creation of the ITO and the International Monetary Fund (IMF), U.S. officials believed, would go a long way toward eliminating the British system of empire preference and opening colonial commerce to the United States. In most of the areas of the Third World, Washington assumed that there was something like a "normal" order of things for which its wartime program for international economic cooperation would be quite sufficient.

The United States continued to hold its sanguine view of the future of the Third World not merely because of its Eurocentrism but also because its leaders had no valid concept of the roots of change in much of the world. Convinced that revolutionary movements were by definition somehow linked to the Soviet Union, the absence of a visible Russian role in nearly all the nations of the Third World tranquilized American leaders into believing they had little to worry about in most of it. That radicalizing local social and economic processes have autonomous origins and subsequently generate a revolutionary opposition was a notion with no serious following in higher circles. That local Communist parties might indeed not be under Russian control, but pursue their own needs and strategies, seemed too farfetched, with the concept of polycentric communism being altogether foreign to American analysts. And because the United States did not comprehend the diverse sources and forms of social change it was, compared to later years, relatively unconcerned about the Left's potential for success throughout the Third World. Nor did Washington ever consider that it might be even more dangerous free of Soviet influence, and thereby beyond the reach of bilateral diplomatic efforts or the cautious advice that Moscow was giving to those parties that it could discipline.

European Priorities in Theory and Practice: From Africa to South Asia

*F*AR MORE IMPORTANT THAN ITS myopia regarding the Left in the Third World was Washington's overwhelming concern after 1945 with European reconstruction. This perspective completely subordinated most African and Asian issues to the success of its plans for Europe's economy and rearmament. The United States always sought to define the relationship of its specific problems in the Third World to its global foreign policy, and for the five years preceding the outbreak of the Korean War in June 1950 Western Europe's political and economic fate and the growing exigencies of the Cold War with the USSR not only greatly overshadowed Washington's concern for the Third World but also largely shaped its policies there.

Key U.S. leaders believed that their power to determine the postwar world's political and economic future was very great but also that it possessed a number of economic, military, and political constraints that only a careful set of priorities and the prudent application of its resources would allow it to overcome. Such a sense of limits was never a permanent abdication of its role in the Third World, and in the Middle East its inhibitions began to wane quickly, but was rather part of a larger American design first to consolidate its power in Europe. If required, it could then exploit that base in order later to address itself to whatever Third World issues had to be resolved. "We cannot scatter our shots equally all over the world," Secretary of State Dean Acheson typically put it in May 1950. "We just haven't got enough shots to do that. . . . If anything happens in Western Europe the whole business goes to pieces. . . ."[1] Although these priorities reflected Washington's ordered sense of its international interests and goals during the first five years of the postwar era, after 1950 its failure to foresee and control the magnitude and complexity of its policies caused military and political events, and the symbolic importance American leaders attached to them, to modify gravely its post-1945 desire to manage efficiently the application of U.S. power overseas.

Several factors eroded Washington's initial intention to use its calculated priorities as a basis for allocating its time and resources. The sheer scope and forms of instability in the Third World transcended its ability to cope with them all by working primarily through its British, French, or Dutch colonial allies, who in many nations only exacerbated local crises and isolated the United States politically. In such instances the United States was never to resolve this dilemma completely, which often left it unhappy with its alliances with European powers in various countries so that, ultimately, it was to waver between support and criticism of the legacies of colonialism that largely defined the most visible Third World problems in the decade after 1945. If this rarely occurred in sub-Sahara Africa, elsewhere the coalition with European colonialism was often troubling. Even more important, however, was the fact that the U.S. collaboration with Europe's colonial powers was not merely based on Washington's desires to see European economic reconstruction and cooperation with its plans for an integrated international economy. It was also strategic and political, involving the desire to rebuild Europe's military power against the USSR as well as to keep Communists and the more militant Socialists out of power in the NATO states themselves. For while Western Europe and the United States shared a consensus on political and military matters that was to prove remarkably durable for the next three decades, the economics of the American-led alliance were far more unstable and subject to tensions. It took only a few years for these contradictions, many inherited from the prewar decade, to assert themselves and reveal that the NATO bloc was comprised of complex elements that could not long cohere, forcing the United States and its nominal allies to deal with fundamental conflicts of economic interests as well as their broad base of political-military agreement.

To varying degrees this dilemma was to color American policy in the Third World with increasing intensity throughout the postwar era as an aspect of a process in which the United States first strengthened the European colonial systems by helping to rebuild the metropolitan economies but then later proceeded to undermine them in large, although by no means all, areas of the Third World as it moved to claim economic and political assets the former colonial nations possessed. What American leaders failed to anticipate was that they would also end up with European colonialism's responsibilities, a process that inevitably engaged U.S. power in open-ended commitments that quickly undermined those priorities Washington had hoped to impose on its foreign policy after 1945.

The U.S. wavered between its need to cooperate with Western Europe and its inherited colonial systems out of consideration for its dominant European priorities, on one hand, as opposed to its hegemonic impulses to define the operating rules for the global economy on the other. The theme of ambivalent tension most aptly describes U.S. policy toward the European-controlled Third World before the Korean War. Only in Latin America and the Philippines, where it had no rivals, did the United States uninhibitedly attempt to impose exactly those social, political, and economic forms it preferred.

Rapid decolonization of the British and French empires risked not only weakening the economic reconstruction of Western Europe, the large majority of Washington planners believed, but also opening the door to instability from which Communists might profit. The failure of America's informal protectorate in Liberia to come close to the British colonies for efficient, honest administration and development helped to put U.S. officials on the defensive in black Africa. During the war the United States had ritualistically called for Africa to be opened to noncolonial nations for trade and raw materials development on equal terms, but by 1947 most of Washington had concluded that while the Open Door in Africa was still a valid goal, immediate political independence was not. In French North Africa, the CIA warned, continued French control enhanced U.S. security interests and forestalled a local Communist takeover. The gradual, carefully regulated transfer of power to moderate elements would also allow America to retain its bases there—a position the State Department also endorsed.

In black Africa the United States consistently supported the British after the war, despite its residual claims on economic rights, because it explicitly demanded Britain's quid pro quo for U.S. interests in the Pacific. As the importance of its colonies' raw materials and dollar earnings exports to Europe's economic reconstruction became more evident, some U.S. officials, like George Kennan, even proposed strengthening Western Europe's domination over Africa, particularly its "economic development and exploitation."[2] This synthesis of anticommunism and an essentially European-focused view of world economic reconstruction defined the practical foundations of U.S. policy in one vast continent, although it supported some movement "where conditions are suitable, toward independence"; but the complementary nature of American and European objectives was clearer in Africa than in any other major region of the world.[3] Elsewhere, however, the situation was far more complex.

THE MIDDLE EAST: THEORY AND PRACTICE

It was in the Middle East, more than in any other region after 1945, that the profound ambiguities in U.S. relations with its closest military and ideological allies were revealed in a continuous dispute over control of the region's vast oil reserves. Caught between a desire not to weaken Britain excessively either economically or militarily but also to increase greatly America's access to the region's oil, both the U.S. government and American oil firms pressed the British as a rivalry that has been simmering, often bitterly, for years burst into a full-scale struggle almost as soon as the bonds of common wartime interests terminated. In five short years, all of the tensions and contradictions in the Middle East, with its many political and military dangers as well as economic assets, emerged to shape profoundly the subsequent long-term position of the United States as a world power.

At the political level, the United States throughout the period before the Korean War sought to support the British military and political presence in the area lest American arms be required to enter any vacuum of power their departure might create. The French, on the other hand, deeply annoyed Washington with their ambition to continue their prewar mandates over Syria and Lebanon, and the United States actively helped to remove French influence from the area. Loans to England after August 1945 were justified partially by the danger of an impoverished England's retreat from the Near East removing a barrier to Soviet influence, which might then sweep without resistance to the Indian Ocean, and the continuation of British power there was always one of the United States' major concerns. Britain's warning to the State Department in August 1946 that it would be forced to reduce its economic aid and troop backing to the wobbly reactionary Greek regime confirmed American fears that any weakening of Britain's regional role would compel a corresponding increase of U.S. involvement—with all its attendant risks. The Truman Doctrine crisis of March 1947, with its vision of dominoes falling from Greece to India, was in part a response to the waning of British power in the area as American money and military advisers replaced the British role in Greece. The "fundamental cornerstone of our thinking," London was informed in September 1946, "is the maintenance of Britain's position to the greatest possible extent."[4]

From the British viewpoint, however, what counted most was to get from the United States a unified economic as well as military strategy in the Middle East "based on an agreed appreciation of the strategical position" in which, as Washington urged, "the British should continue to maintain primary responsibility for military security in that area."[5] Specifically, the State Department explained, "they must have from us economic concessions with respect to the area which will make it worth their while to stay there," although it also understood that even without them the British interests were so great that they would not in any event leave voluntarily.[6] U.S. support for Britain's beleaguered position in Palestine was forthcoming, for the most part, until the 1948 election forced the Truman Administration to waver temporarily from its initially mainly hostile policy toward Zionism. What the British wanted most, and what they had unsuccessfully striven to obtain during the war, was a guarantee that their strong position in Middle Eastern oil, which they largely dominated save in the fabulously rich Saudi Arabian fields, would remain immune from the attacks of American oil firms possessing State Department backing. This assurance they were never to get, for it touched the fundamental dichotomy in U.S. policy in the Middle East between cooperation and rivalry. And this dualism led a decade later to America assuming the responsibilities as well as the rewards of British imperialism in the region, becoming its successor.

Given U.S. objectives, interests, ideology, and the balance of political forces within the country debating the issues involved, there was scant chance for the British to avoid a massive attack on their control over Near Eastern oil. The United States was a net exporter of oil before the war, but by 1946 it had begun the pattern of imports that was by 1960 to require it to buy nearly one-fifth of its oil needs from foreign sources. While it still controlled 59 percent of the world's known reserves in 1946, it was only in the Middle East—where the British dominated—that massive new reserves available for export remained to be discovered. By 1946, even before extensive exploration, the Middle East's reserves were already almost equal to those of the entire Western Hemisphere, and while the Middle East's output tripled between 1940 and 1947, it was to more than double again over the next three years. The future of the world's oil industry, everyone acknowledged, was in the Middle East, not the least because it also cost far less than American oil to locate and extract.

Whatever Washington's sincere desires about collaboration on other regional matters, which would have left Britain with the costly military overhead charges of maintaining Western influence, every factor worked against continued British domination of the area's oil. Ideologically, the United States was for the "Open Door" in Middle Eastern oil, and throughout 1945 it aggressively asserted the doctrine even as it sought to reassure the British by endorsing a proposed Anglo-American petroleum agreement, one implying a condominium over world oil as well, which was then being negotiated. "We have been supporting the policy of the open door in the Near East with regard to investments and commerce," the State Department's Near Eastern office head wrote in November 1945, and "we have no intention of becoming again a mere passive spectator in the Near East."[7] This Open Door principle, which was the foundation of the United States' statement of economic war aims, was reiterated incessantly in the Middle East over the next three years.

Given Britain's inability to spend the money essential to compete effectively with American firms, the doctrine was a poorly concealed justification for replacing Britain's domination over the region's oil, which had been formalized in the 1928 "Red Line agreement" allocating U.S. firms 24 percent of the vast Iraq Petroleum Company concessions, which included every important producing area save Iran and Saudi Arabia. In August 1946 the American oil companies that had signed it notified the State Department that they considered the accord invalid, a position reflecting both the new balance of forces in the region as well as the industry's insatiable desires for new reserves to replace increasingly expensive and insufficient American wells and that would guarantee their mastery over world oil output over the coming decades. Since both Iran and Iraq were enticing U.S. firms in order to counterbalance Britain's predominance, the temptation before the American giants was irresistible. And because most key American leaders also wanted access to the region's vast reserves, with scant concern for British interests, Washington secretly encouraged the U.S. oil giants to take the lead in unilaterally ignoring the prewar restrictions they had earlier thought acceptable. At the same time, the U.S. government pretended to be ready also to defer, to some extent, to British oil interests.

Whatever its verbal concessions to British protestations, accompanied invariably with advocacy of an Open Door ideology at the same time that it was in the process of closing the region's resources to other nations and striving for American hegemony, the net effect of Washington's official policy by the beginning of the Marshall Plan in 1948 was to condone the private actions of U.S. firms and to accelerate the decline of Britain's Middle Eastern power. With the "Red Line" compact dead and U.S. firms rushing into the region, the Anglo-American petroleum agreement, with the tacit approval of the State Department and White House, died in the Senate. Decisive in killing it was the opposition of domestic oil producers who wanted a guarantee that expensive American oil would not have to compete with cheap oil freely flowing through an open door to an American economy practicing principles the State Department was urging upon the rest of the world.

For the next two years America pressed Britain to continue to assume primary responsibility for the military security of the Middle East but now insisted that an economic accord between the two nations on the future of oil would undermine its "liberal principles of international economic relations."[8] And for the first time it began cautiously to explore influencing political as well as economic developments in various Middle Eastern nations directly, though in fact both were inextricably linked and success in one could only affect the other. It was in Iran, which I detail in Chapter 8, that Washington was first to relate to nationalist forces in the region in a manner that was to test to the limit the ostensible Anglo-American regional security system.

In the period preceding the Korean War the United States was less and less deferential to a Britain whose power in the Middle East it was nibbling away at both economically and psychologically. Even in Southwest Asia, with India, Pakistan, Burma, Afghanistan, and Ceylon, by 1949 it began to concern itself with the formidable vacuum that independence and its stormy aftermath of communal strife between India's Muslims and Hindus, or civil war within Burma, had created. Keeping the region, its vast population, and its important raw materials out of the hands of Communists as well as those whose "political and economic principles [would not be] compatible with our own and would thus adversely affect our future trade and investment relationships" was by 1949 the principal U.S. goal in that region.[9] Specifically, the United States criticized the trend toward nationalization and a mild socialism it believed was emerging among the new nations of South Asia. Collaborating with Britain to influence the vast region was also policy, but again on the basis of the Open Door rather than spheres of influence. Whatever the minimal resources Washington was ready to devote to the area, it appeared that here, too, the Americans and British were incipient competitors as well as allies. U.S. vision and ambitions were becoming increasingly global.

CHAPTER 3

Confronting Turbulent Asia

THE FILIPINO DEPENDENCY

It was in the Philippines that the U.S. policies in the Third World, with their complex tensions and ambitions, rhetoric and interests, were revealed most clearly both in theory and practice. As America's only true colony in the twentieth century, the Philippines is the single best example of its impact on the political and economic life of any nation, because only there could it freely impose its desires. And it is the one case I shall systematically examine throughout the postwar era to translate the ambiguities of American ideology and proclamations into realities that reveal best the complex interactions among local social forces and economic changes, U.S. interests, and the needs of the Filipino people.

It was in the Philippines, too, that America's colonial domination produced an economic and political structural legacy that was profoundly to define all of the important issues of Filipino life after 1945. The United States built upon the landed oligarchies it found in place after its conquest of the islands in 1899–1901. Regional politics, with its largely family-based local alliances, became the hallmark of the American-imposed political structure after 1907 as United States-style boss politics and patronage merged naturally with the existing social order, co-opting some new members into the local ruling class but leaving its basic institutional role unchanged. In most of the fifty-one provinces, many isolated by the sea and languages, oligarchies with economic and political power entrenched themselves permanently so that the only significant political party, the Nacionalistas, constituted little more than ever-shifting coalitions of regional political machines with scarcely any commitments save to their own immediate economic needs and the control of power. Patron-client relations mitigated some of the exploitive edges of such a system for the masses, as family and patronage ties or outright vote-buying provided for a few of the urgent economic needs of the politically loyal poor in a highly stratified social and economic structure; but while residues of this system persist even today, it began to break down in a number of strategic provinces during the 1930s.

The main factor eroding the paternalistic, oligarchical political order the United States chose to call democracy in the Philippines was the commercial transformation of the overwhelmingly dominant agricultural economy on which the oligarchy's power was largely based and that employed the vast majority of the nation. From 1909 onward the United States imposed reciprocal free trade on the Philippines and greatly stimulated the production of export-oriented commodities geared to the highly profitable American markets. To satisfy the demand for sugar, coconut products, and the like, capital investments transformed labor and land utilization in ways that made the new rural social conditions far more exploitive and eliminated many small farmers. In central Luzon, in particular, growing population pressures also produced land shortages, and the collapse of the U.S. market for Philippine commodities during the 1930s began to radicalize large sectors of the poor peasantry as purely commercial considerations replaced the agricultural system's paternalism. Usury, excessive dependence on cash crops with unstable prices rather than production for family consumption—all the typical forces that sharply reduce living standards and transform peasants from being acquiescent beasts of burden into angry activists—were already in motion before the Second World War.

These structural changes created increased mass pressures for social and economic reforms in the years prior to World War Two, when "with few exceptions," to quote a CIA report, the normally highly opportunistic economic and political elite chose to protect its interests by collaborating as loyally with the Japanese as they had with the Americans, thereby delegitimizing itself both in the eyes of the people with social grievances as well, potentially, as those of their colonial masters.[1] The most important puppet, the consummately ambitious Manuel A. Roxas, had been the chief prewar rival of President Manuel Quezon and Vice President Sergio Osmeña, both of whom went into exile. But a large majority of the Japanese-controlled National Assembly were former senior political figures, and Quezon's prewar cabinet simply continued to work for the new occupiers. While some collaborators also tried to hedge their interests by maintaining discreet contacts with the guerrillas who formed throughout the country under both U.S. and Communist leadership, most played their new roles loyally, made fortunes, and survived as comfortably as possible the exceptional ravages the war and occupation imposed on the nation.

The question of how to treat these collaborators was, in essence, one that touched fundamentally the future of the traditional ruling class, the nature of those who might replace them, as well as the Philippines' postwar role as a bastion of American power in East Asia. General Douglas MacArthur, commander of the campaign to recapture the Philippines, had lived there for decades and knew the elite well. While he preferred initially to rely upon those who had worked with the guerrilla groups directly under U.S. control, they were too inexperienced and small in number, and he was determined above all to keep the Hukbalahap guerrillas, comprised of radicalized poor peasants concentrated in central Luzon and with important though not exclusive Communist leadership, out of power. Whatever official Washington's position for removing collaborators from authority, MacArthur ignored it when he disagreed with it, and he was allowed to define and implement the policy. As American forces began to return to the islands after October 1944, they fired most collaborators, and eventually fifty-five hundred were charged, though wealthier ones were freed on bail, and their trials were to be the responsibility of the Philippines government, whose independence was then being negotiated. Meanwhile, at the beginning of 1945, the Americans used their local allies to attempt to disarm the Huks, and in February arrested their leaders.

On April 18, 1945, it was announced that a "liberated" Roxas had been released from prison while his colleagues remained behind bars. Restored to his prewar brigadier generalship in the United States-controlled army, the close friend of MacArthur now had his highly dubious wartime secret contacts with Americans used as an excuse to impose a United States-approved political solution on the dangerously fragmented and unstable struggle for power and legitimacy in the Philippines then taking place. Roxas won American approval because in 1945 he confided to key U.S. officials that he was not for the basic principle of independence. As Paul V. McNutt, who had been U.S. high commissioner during 1937–39 and who was reappointed in 1945 reported, "Roxas has indicated by word and deed his desire to follow American pattern of government and retain closest ties with us in all matters. . . ."[2] Signs of America's benediction quickly won the ever-accommodating Roxas the support of ambitious politicians and members of the economic elite who regarded him as a winner, and soon he was restored to his position as president of the Senate. In April 1946 he was elected the first postwar president and, parenthetically, two years later was to grant amnesty to all accused collaborators. It was in this political context, so completely under U.S. control, that the United States negotiated the ostensible legal independence of the Philippines to which it had committed itself a decade earlier.

These negotiations had to take into account the economic interests that had been built up by both sides during the entire colonial period. On one hand, 73 percent of prewar trade had been with the United States, nearly all of it with tariff preferences, and much of the local economic oligarchy had for years resisted independence without guaranteed access to the American market for agricultural commodities whose very profitability was dependent on it. And direct U.S. investments in the Philippines before the war were larger than in any other nation in Asia, being especially concentrated in public utilities and export-oriented agriculture, sectors they largely dominated. In a word, what both the local oligarchy and American traders and investors now sought was nominal political independence with continued economic dependency. McNutt shared their viewpoint. In addition, the U.S. War Department wanted long-term base rights. Within these decisive constraints, the Philippines was given its formal independence.

The problem was that some powerful Filipino businessmen as well as much of the public wished to see more nationalist economic strategies pursued, opposing such monumental compromises on future sovereignty; in the United States, competitive economic interests, involved mainly with Cuban sugar, also wanted a greater share of the market that otherwise would be guaranteed the Philippines should a special economic relationship continue. Perhaps more significant was the State Department, which feared that Filipino and American economic constituencies, working through powerful congressional allies, would make a mockery of its stated global program for an Open Door world trade system, especially in the European-dominated colonial regions, and neutralize its voice "when we protest strongly against such policies which discriminate against Americans in other countries."[3] However important this de facto coalition, the triumphant alliance between the American Congress and military, sanctioned by the Filipino elite and U.S. investors, was to prove that whatever practices and goals the State Department urged on others, it was unable to transcend political pressures at home to apply them in the U.S. colony—a point that was not lost on its European allies, who also knew that Cuba had already succumbed to U.S. pressure to sign a similar preferential-trade agreement.

The U.S. keys to dealing with recalcitrant Filipinos were the rehabilitation bills that a major architect of the bill to grant independence, Senator Millard Tydings, sponsored. The Americans promised $620 million over five years to help repair the massive destruction that the war, and especially U.S. bombing, had inflicted on the Philippines. That U.S. investors were to receive a significant minority share of it was also important. But to obtain this money Congress required the Filipinos to endorse the Bell Trade Relations Act, which created complete free trade between the two nations for eight years, with a gradually increasing tariff over the next twenty—exactly what nationalist economic interests opposed. Moreover, full parity for American investors in agriculture, timber, minerals, and public utilities would have to continue for twenty-five years, thereby protecting their existing investments and leaving far poorer local business interests undefended. This clause required amendment of the new Philippines constitution, a fact that soon produced far-reaching political complications there. The United States also acquired base rights on July 4, 1946, when the Philippines officially became independent, and an American military mission was to continue to guide the army.

The obligation to amend the constitution, which required a three-fourths majority in Congress, almost immediately became entangled with the future of the Huks and the Communist Party (PKP), who began to disagree with each other after the attacks against the Huks had begun in early 1945. The PKP tried to influence the poor peasants who comprised the great bulk of the Huks' followers and who numbered in the hundreds of thousands, but it was itself essentially urban- and intelligentsia-based, and most peasants failed to accept or understand its larger political or ideological perspective—which essentially was to form a united front with the Osmeña wing of the Nacionalistas against Roxas and his American backers and abjure armed struggle. With many Huks under threat of prosecution for their wartime actions, and with the resurrected prewar elite saved from similar fears and eager to reverse all the land reforms the Huks had unilaterally imposed, large-scale repression increased, and many peasants (a portion of whom had never given up their arms) returned to resistance both to protect their gains and to defend themselves.

Meanwhile, the PKP formed the Democratic Alliance in July 1946 and elected six members to Congress, sufficient to block the passage of the constitutional amendment. Roxas then unseated them and one Nacionalista from Congress on the alleged grounds that they had used fraud to get elected, charges that were neither investigated nor proven. And while the constitution was amended, the efficacy of the PKP's political line was shattered and its leadership split over future strategy. Local peasant leaders spontaneously continued to mobilize followers, the Huks grew, and top leaders like Luis Taruc simply ignored the PKP's official majority line, which until mid-1948 opposed armed struggle. With full-scale government military offensives driving more and more former guerrillas back to the resistance, the new nation was now the scene of a civil war throughout central Luzon, one that mounted in intensity over the next four years.

With the Philippines nominally an independent state but in fact still economically and politically a U.S. colony, the Roxas coalition of opportunistic politicians and factions interested in the boodle essential to their machines' cohesion proceeded to reimpose the same exploitive politics that had marred the nation's political life consistently until then. The coalition was completely devoid of nationalist impulses or broader social goals in a war-torn nation plagued with vast human misery and now sinking more deeply into the vortex of civil war. Roxas' first years were characterized by the return to traditional vote-rigging and buying, which began with the Senate election of November 1947, and corruption in the allocation of all-too-scarce government funds. The Huks and its peasants' union were outlawed in March 1948. By the time Roxas died suddenly on April 15, 1948, the exclusion of the Left from the political process and the absence of any reforms to deal with massive poverty guaranteed the spread of civil conflict, and as many as ten thousand people took up arms with the Huks.

The new president, Elpidio Quirino, proved no better than Roxas, and his successful reelection effort in 1949 was the most fraudulent and expensive in the Philippines until then. While senior American officials in early 1948 had hoped that the Philippines would continue as a primary base in the region and take care of its own internal affairs, by 1949 the economic consequences of the existing political leadership as well as the terms of the Bell Act, which in order to tie up bilateral trade had also pegged the peso to the dollar and made them freely convertible at a rate the Filipinos could not alter, had produced economic chaos that threatened also to undermine U.S. security interests. With fully four-fifths of its imports coming from the United States and nearly that proportion of its exports directed to it, the Philippines was still as much of an economic colony as it had been before independence. Rampant inflation and rising unemployment, the excessive importation of U.S. goods, and then massive capital flight were too much to bear, and at the end of 1949 the United States was forced to concede Manila the right to impose exchange controls. "The center of this [Far Eastern] circle is the Philippines," an exasperated Dean Acheson told a closed meeting of senators in February 1950. "The Philippines are our particular interest and ward. We brought them up," but their behavior was still "childlike," their economic problems "very severe," the risks coming less from the Huks, which "I do not think started out" as Communists, than from "disintegration."[4] With the men it selected implementing the policies it imposed, the United States' most ambitious venture in the Far East after 1945 and showcase for its ability to transfer the American way of life to a new nation was heading toward disaster.

THE SOUTHEAST ASIA BALANCE

At the end of World War Two U.S. planners expected the Philippines to be more important to American interests than any other place in Southeast Asia, but it was unavoidable that other countries in the region intrude themselves into Washington's attention if only because Western European recovery, particularly for the Dutch mired in Indonesia and the French in Indochina, partially depended on a resolution of the struggle for decolonization under way in those nations. Moreover, they also regarded the area's vast raw materials riches as vital to not only Europe but also to the United States. However compartmentalized Washington's initial East Asia vision, the linkage of events in Southeast Asia to trends in China and Japan became more obvious as the Kuomintang regime in China began to crumble and stagnation in Japan's economy threatened to erode the power of the conservative politicians on whom the United States was relying. By the late 1940s the problems of all East Asia had become interrelated in Washington's perceptions.

The first issue of the region American officials had to confront was Holland's struggle to defeat the powerful Indonesian nationalist opposition led by former Japanese collaborators under Achmed Sukarno. During the war the United States had vaguely endorsed trusteeships rather than independence for the colonies of the region, but it failed to pursue the point when the French and Dutch had returned with British help to resume control of their possessions. In 1946 the U.S. position on Indonesia was that the Dutch had "primary responsibility" for settling the conflict, although the fact that the leaders of the nationalist opposition were anti-Communist commended some sort of compromise to Washington that would serve the interests of both sides.[5] This effort to maintain good relations with two camps never altered Washington's deference to Holland's primacy, and the United States systematically supported the Dutch in the UN even as it proclaimed its impartiality. When Dutch troops returned in force to the islands in late 1948, the United States objected but continued its full Marshall Plan aid for the Dutch economy and only slightly reduced its funds earmarked for Dutch activities in Indonesia. Without these sums the Dutch, who were also using American arms, could not have afforded their intervention. The United States consciously if discreetly supported the Dutch for the sake of European reconstruction, which benefited from access to Indonesia's raw materials. By spring 1949, as the Sukarno forces' hegemony over the opposition seemed increasingly challenged from the Left because of the stalemate in the struggle for independence, Washington threatened The Hague with a total aid cutoff if it failed to compromise, a strategy that succeeded and temporarily preempted the growth of the Communists. At the same time it urged the Indonesians to allow the Dutch to continue to manage the economy. Yet as the leading authority on this topic has concluded, "the U.S. never pushed the Dutch too far."[6] And once an accord was reached, the United States quickly moved to strengthen the new nation's police and army, a strategy that was successful in containing the Left and that had far-reaching implications for Indonesia's future.

.   .   .

By 1948 Washington still referred to watered-down versions of its wartime rhetoric on the need for changes in the colonial order in Asia, but events in China and Japan caused key American officials privately to discard its nobler sentiments entirely. "We should cease to talk about vague and—for the Far East—unreal objectives such as human rights, the raising of the living standards, and democratization," George Kennan, head of State Department policy planning, urged in February 1948. "The day is not far off when we are going to have to deal in straight power concepts. The less we are then hampered by idealistic slogans, the better."[7]

The reconstruction and reintegration of Japan into the regional economy, in part to abort the Japanese Left's growth and also to create an alternative anchor for U.S. power in Asia as China ceased to play that role, increasingly began to define the United States' larger geopolitical vision of Southeast Asia. American officials calculated that if Japan were ever to cease being dependent on aid, it must obtain most of its raw materials and markets in Southeast Asia. Although but one of a number of factors as its definitions of Asia's problems become explicitly more integrated, it was nonetheless one Washington could no longer overlook. And this fact imperceptibly but irresistibly increased the potential importance of Southeast Asia for America as a world power. Indeed, by the early 1950s, as Washington used the concept of the "domino theory" with increasing frequency to justify its fears for the area, it was scarcely more than another definition of its earlier vision of integrated geopolitical and economic linkages, one it had already applied to the Middle East.

Until the Korean War, U.S. perceptions of the Southeast Asian context were increasingly colored by events not simply in China, where the Communists were quickly taking power, or Japan, but in Europe as well. Such a global perspective explains why Washington chose essentially to work with rather than against European colonialism in this region, for both the success and the cost of the Marshall Plan, U.S. experts knew, was to an important degree linked to Europe's continued access to the area's resources. And events in China throughout 1949 convinced the Truman Administration that a line against the further expansion of communism had to be drawn in Southeast Asia to avert a further shift in the regional power balance and a major crisis there.

At the beginning of 1950 the State Department's public statements of its goals in Southeast Asia remained confusing, but privately it was already wholly committed to maintaining French power in Indochina. A special mission was sent to study the region in February even as it was certain that future United States efforts would mainly be to give the French the economic and military aid they needed to win the Indochina War. "This meant," Acheson later recalled, "supporting the French 'presence' in the area as a guide and help to the three [Indochinese] states in moving toward genuine independence within . . . the French Union."[8] The tragic story has already been told countless times elsewhere, but to gain French cooperation with European rearmament and to preserve the integrated resources of Southeast Asia for its own sake as well as accelerate Japan's reconstruction and protect larger American interests, aid to the French and their puppets in Indochina was formally initiated in May 1950.

Even today it is impossible for a historian to describe the exact importance of each element that entered this regional picture. Indeed, it is far more significant that no senior American policymaker at that time (or later, for that matter) could explain coherently their weighting of the many factors in the whole situation before them, much less how any one might shift in importance and thereby pose altogether new challenges. No one in Washington even remotely imagined how monumental their seemingly quite minor decision in Indochina would become, though in fact the policy of linkages and interdependence used to justify it—the "domino theory"—demanded such acts and left open a seemingly endless chain of future responses like it elsewhere should the conditions require. In this context what looked like an effort to apply priorities in Southeast Asia, with the Philippines at the top of the list, soon began to unravel as every issue of power in Asia, as well as many presumably more important goals in Western Europe, were treated as unavoidably interrelated and America's role in Southeast Asia became potentially unlimited. Yet this very outcome was still some years off, and in 1950 not a single American leader imagined it to be possible.

Latin America: The Nationalist Challenge

*T*HE UNITED STATES' MAIN PROBLEMS in Latin America from the end of World War Two until 1960 differed dramatically from those in the other major Third World regions, for they involved not the alleged menace of Russia and communism but rather the emergence of conservative forms of nationalism—a challenge that has persisted in various guises since then. Precisely because this movement grew out of specific Latin American conditions and was unrelated to the United States' far greater preoccupations with communism, the Left, and the legacies of the demise of European power elsewhere, Washington preferred virtually to ignore its hemisphere during this period as much as possible.

What the United States confronted in Latin America was an alternative concept of national capitalist economic development that rejected fundamentally its historic objective of an integrated world economy based not simply on capitalism but also on unrestricted U.S. access to whatever wealth it desired—hegemony rather than cooperation. Nowhere else were the underlying bases and objectives of U.S. foreign policy revealed so starkly, without the obfuscating intercession of the problems of either communism or socialism. Rather than some amorphous concept of an Open Door accessible to all capitalist nations, power and gain for the United States in economic terms from the inception was the foundation of both its policies and its actions in the Western Hemisphere.

The major Latin American nations had responded to the 1930s Depression by embarking, in varying ways, on policies of economic development that demanded strategic public investments and regulations, especially to stimulate import substitution and industrialization. Often vaguely influenced by corporatist notions prevalent in Spain, Portugal, and Italy, not only the incipient and weak national capitalist class but also frequently the military endorsed this strategy as a way of both building resources essential for armies and to escape the strictures that U.S. domination and priorities had imposed on their economies. Anti-Yankee sentiment was both a cause and an effect of such thinking. In Brazil, Argentina, Mexico, and Chile, these nationalist tendencies generally controlled politics and economic policy after the mid-1930s.

The Second World War reinforced profoundly this impulse toward state-sponsored capitalist industrialization. Because of the collapse of traditional European exports, which had been equal to those from the United States, and the inability of the United States to sustain its normal exports, rapid industrialization occurred, and infant industries demanded protection against primarily Yankee competition. Also stimulating this desire for greater independence was Latin America's reliance on the U.S. market to absorb its exports, which took 30 percent in 1938 but 38 percent in 1948, while its imports from the United States shot up from 34 percent to 65 percent of the total over the same period—making its dependence far greater than ever. The United States, too, found Latin America much more significant as a source of vital materials, and the region accounted for 24 percent of all its imports in 1939 but 34 percent in 1954. In addition, over a third of all its foreign direct investments were found in Latin America after World War Two, accounting for four-fifths of its total investments in the Third World. However much Washington chose to ignore Latin American relations after 1945, these objective economic trends and the ferment within the elites there were bound eventually to make the area much more important in its calculations.

In hindsight it appears remarkable that the most important U.S. leaders were able virtually to ignore the region and to allow relatively junior officials to handle nearly all vital matters within a few broad policy guidelines. Even when they occasionally had to deal with it, they often evinced irritation at having to do so. The first issue those in Washington responsible for the region had to confront was future relations with a number of the "fascist" regimes that had embarked on a nationalist economic program. The well-known case of Argentina involved a U.S. effort to isolate and overthrow Juan Perón's regime, an undertaking that was eventually abandoned because other states in the region objected, and Perón counterattacked successfully with professions of friendship and anticommunism that soon divided deeply the responsible State Department officials over tactics. In Bolivia, however, relatively minor U.S. pressures against the nationalist regime under Major Gualberto Villarroel, which foreign tin interests thought was taxing them excessively, helped to encourage his overthrow and murder in July 1946.

Yet compared to earlier and later periods, the United States still intervened relatively infrequently in the political life of the region's nations. In large part, nonintervention was due to its preoccupation with affairs elsewhere as well as the absence of any perceptible challenges from the Left. It concentrated instead on expounding those principles, nearly all of which were economic, around which it sought to build a hegemonic Western Hemisphere system. When the Inter-American Conference on War and Peace was held in Mexico City in February 1945, the key official who organized it, Assistant Secretary of State William A. Clayton, former chairman of the world's largest cotton merchant firm, was also the principal architect of foreign economic policy during the critical postwar period and a passionate believer in "liberal" Open Door trade principles. The assistant secretary of state for Latin America immediately after the war, Spruille Braden, was himself a major investor in mining there. "Private enterprise is the best and in most circumstances the only really sound means to develop the known or unknown resources of a new country," he stated in September 1946 while attacking nationalist legislation. "The institution of private property ranks with those of religion and the family as a bulwark of civilization." To tamper with it, he warned, "will precipitate a disintegration of life and liberty as we conceive and treasure them." U.S. loans, he made plain, would only be for projects that "blaze the trail for private capital," especially in those nations that were not "exaggeratedly nationalistic." Money, in any case, would not go to any function that private interests, including U.S. investors, were ready to perform, nor would they be expected to make low profits either.[1]

It was this predominately economic perspective that colored U.S. policy and action in the region over the coming years. Latin America was a treasure trove of essential raw materials, and the State Department wanted to see production in private hands not only increase but also with "no invidious distinctions between domestic and foreign capital."[2] "Foreign capital will not venture, and in fact cannot operate, in circumstances in which excessive nationalism persists. . . ."[3] The State Department carefully inventoried the region's minerals before the Organization of American States (OAS) was created in Bogotá, Colombia, in April 1948, and resolved to get more of it out of the ground. Secretary of State George C. Marshall at that gathering simply restated traditional admonitions on "the encouragement of private enterprise and the fair treatment of foreign capital," deflecting Latin American demands for development credits, preferably from a new inter-American bank, comparable to those being given to Europe—appeals that also carried Latin threats of price fixing of exports and trade blocs should loans not be forthcoming.[4]

The United States had the OAS draft a statement of economic principles conforming to its desires, and for the next two years both publicly and privately it unceasingly reiterated the earlier themes on the need to welcome

U.S. private investment on its own terms to develop the continent: there would be no growth unless everything were done to attract U.S. corporations and freely allow them to make high profits with low tax rates. It was official policy, as well, that in case of a world war the region's main function would be to supply raw materials. Such a vision made the crusade to redefine the economic trends in the hemisphere and further consolidate its hegemony all the more imperative to Washington. And here, to repeat a fundamental point, the nationalism of essentially conservative elements was an incomparably greater threat than Communism. Ironically, in the UN the United States consistently relied on these very same groups to sustain its voting bloc against the Soviets, and considered them as close ideological allies for purposes of its global diplomacy.

Of a number of Washington's efforts to reverse the trend toward nationalism, those involving oil were the most important. It was official policy that it would always "encourage and facilitate" U.S. firms' involvement in oil development "not merely because of the readier access which such participation would guarantee to us but also because . . . the technical and managerial skill of the American petroleum industry is preeminently competent to insure the prompt and efficient development of resources anywhere."[5] Whatever the sovereign right of a state to nationalize, it was formally opposed to it in oil as being confiscatory in practice. In Mexico, where the government had nationalized U.S. firms in 1937, Washington persisted relentlessly in attempting to get American producers back into the country, systematically preventing loans or spare parts from reaching the state oil company. And in Brazil it actively opposed the creation of a national oil company.

But it was in Venezuela, whose oil output far exceeded that of the entire continent, that Washington's efforts to protect its oil firms brought to the fore the larger issue of the possible role of the region's military in attaining U.S. objectives and protecting its interests. The Acción Democrática party of moderate liberals had taken power there in late 1945 with the cooperation of junior officers, and it overwhelmingly won the fair December 1947 elections. While thoroughly anti-Communist, it also had a reform program that threatened the U.S.-owned oil companies, the traditional oligarchy, and the army. In November 1948 a junta, with oil companies' support, overthrew the government, and U.S. producers continued to profit handsomely under a dictatorship that was to last ten years. Despite the fact that the State Department had in December expressed concern about military coups against democratically elected regimes, the following month it recognized the new junta.

The relationship of the United States to the Latin American military in this period was made more complex by the fact that in many nations the military was frequently a crucial supporter of nationalist economic strategies, as in

Brazil and Argentina. In such cases nationalism and the absence of basic democratic rights frequently were synonymous. The United States issued declarations against oppressive regimes in the hemisphere and even opposed an Argentine suggestion in August 1947 to make anti-Communist agreements for fear they would be used as a justification by quasi-fascist governments not only to squelch internal dissent and retain power but also to pursue their economic programs. With officers found in both the pro- and anti-U.S. camps, it was inevitable that U.S. policies appear tortured as Washington began to explore after 1946 the possibility of gaining the maximum possible from the Latin American military's growing role as a political mediator as well as its potential for becoming the dominant force throughout the hemisphere.

The issue of relating to the Latin American officers corps could not be delayed indefinitely because the military's importance led many of these nations also to seek to modernize their armies' equipment, and in the period after 1945 the United States was the only possible source. The War Department in 1946 favored allowing such purchases, while the State Department thought most Latin American nations could not afford them. But the War Department argued that if the United States did not supply the arms these states would eventually turn to Europe, which would then send military training missions and would only further undermine existing U.S. influence. Keeping these armies standardized to its equipment and advisers was justified also because it would neutralize a transmission belt for European ideas— ideas that had in the past included, among other things, fascism. More to the point, as a War Department representative explained to a secret hearing of Congress, "In those cases where the army or the navy does not actually run the government, they come so close to it that any influence on them has great national importance to those countries. Our military missions there are working with the most influential people in those governments."[6] And at the very least they were good anti-Communists. Immediately after the so-called Greek-Turkey crisis of March 1947, Acheson reversed the State Department's opposition, and the strategy of integrating and wooing the Latin American military was initiated. While the State Department developed disingenuous justifications for its convoluted recognition policy and de facto support for military dictators, real or incipient, Washington's most senior leaders assiduously avoided thinking about the problems of the region and the paradoxes of their assorted policies.

Latin America was closest to the United States and of far greater economic importance than any other Third World region, but senior U.S. officials increasingly dismissed it as an aberrant, benighted area inhabited by helpless, essentially childish peoples. When George Kennan was sent to review what he described as the "unhappy and hopeless" background there, he penned the most acerbic dispatch of his entire career. Not even the Communists seemed viable "because their Latin American character inclines them to individualism [and] to undiscipline," and he was certain that Moscow regarded them, as he himself did all Latin Americans, "with a mixture of amusement, contempt, and anxiety." In the end, he advised, where popular governments could not cope with the Communists, "then we must concede that harsh governmental measures of repression may be the only answer" from authoritarian regimes, and the United States would have "to be satisfied if the results are on balance favorable to our purposes."[7] While Kennan's brutal analysis caused the department to bury his report, his successor as head of State Department policy planning, Louis Halle, at the same time published an anonymous essay in *Foreign Affairs* arguing for an attitude of noblesse oblige. Pursuing the motif of the "childish" nature of the area, he condescendingly argued that if the United States treated the Latin Americans like adults, then perhaps they would learn to behave like them.[8]

Whether Washington's increasingly petulant mood toward Latin America would be translated into policy remained to be seen, depending as it did on what other issues it had to consider elsewhere in the world. Implied in it, however, was that the hegemony the United States exercised over the economic domain would also have to apply to politics in order to protect the most critical aspect of the U.S. relationship to the hemisphere. In brief, during the first postwar years Washington opposed the main thrust of hemispheric political life toward nationalism, which as yet possessed only a minor leftist, much less Communist, dimension. The fact that large sectors of both the Center and Right especially disturbed the United States and challenged its interests revealed most about its hegemonic objectives in the Third World where neither geopolitical considerations nor nominal European allies constrained it.

The End of Postwar Optimism

*E*UROPEAN PROBLEMS CREATED THE most important postwar obstacles to the achievement by the United States of its goal of a world economy based on free trade. But the Third World was also vital to the restoration of Europe's economic health, which when attained was to increase America's access to its colonies. After a short period of loans and grants, the U.S. government had initially expected that normal trade and private investment would quickly lead to a restructured and healthier world economy based on Open Door principles, thereby eliminating its need to play so costly a role.

It took only a few years to dispel such optimism, and by 1947 American leaders had to devise new solutions based on the assumption, as Assistant Secretary of State for the Near East and former Texas oilman George C. McGhee put it in March 1947, that "Our tradition of free enterprise . . . has become so thoroughly ingrained in our economic thinking that it amounts with us to almost a religion. . . . We are perfectly sincere in our conviction that it would be in the best interests of other nations to follow our example."[1] Nor could the State Department's Manifest Destiny fail, for as one of its key architects pointed out, "We cannot insulate ourselves against the movements that sweep around the globe. If every other major nation were to go Socialist, it would be extremely difficult, if not impossible, to preserve real private enterprise in the United States." Trade and exchange controls by themselves would reduce America's "access to scarce supplies of strategic materials."[2] A $3.75 billion loan to Britain in July 1946 and the Marshall Plan in June 1947 had been justified precisely to avert all these risks to America's values and interests, which were in fact synonymous. The problem, however, was that neither of these costly efforts moved the world much closer toward the desired goals of the United States, and by 1948–49 the distance between America's ambitions and reality was growing wider.

In August 1947 Britain made the pound inconvertible, violating the terms of their loan from the United States, and by late 1947 many nations had imposed additional import and exchange controls. And while the U.S. planners had expected private American loans and investments to lubricate world trade quickly, in fact both were virtually nil in Europe and inconsequential in its colonial possessions. In 1949 nearly half of all U.S. exports were in the form of foreign aid shipments, and in 1945–48 the government provided 85 percent of the United States' capital exports, with the Marshall Plan due to end in 1951. Worse yet, vividly illustrating the decisive disparity between the Administration's ideology and that of other key domestic power constituencies, the International Trade Organization itself was to fail in Congress because of opposition from high-tariff industries, so that both its free trade program for the rest of the world and the structure to implement it now had to be replaced by other means to attain the same goals.

It was obvious to most of the Truman Administration's experts that a quick and sure long-term solution to this multifaceted difficulty was for Europe to earn far more dollars through increased exports to the United States from its present and former colonies. Without such an expansion of mutually beneficial triangular trade, Washington feared, Europe would continue its exchange controls and bilateral and barter trading in a way that reduced the U.S. role in the world economy significantly. And far greater U.S. private investment in the colonies would help them to develop their ability to sell abroad. It was partially for this reason that Washington opposed an accelerated decolonization process that cut the economic ties that bound much of the Third World to European imperialism. Indirectly, as it understood perfectly well, the United States had as much to lose from such a quick rupture because its own geopolitical and economic priorities and needs preeminently required a quickly reconstructed Western Europe.

It was in this context that President Truman announced the creation of "Point Four" in his Inaugural speech of January 20, 1949, a declaration that Acheson later dismissed as "hyperbole" but that unquestionably also had vague reform connotations in Truman's mind—along with his desire to obtain headlines.[3] While the first definition of the program came from Truman's political advisers and publicity staff, who continued to stress its allegedly humanitarian aspects, responsibility for its implementation was immediately handed over to the State Department's most ardent advocates of an integrated world economy, and they were to maintain control over what became a program with inflated pretensions but very little money.

By the time the president delivered a special message on Point Four to

Congress the following June, the State Department had publicly clarified all its objectives, and these merely echoed its traditional litany on the need to foster far greater private capital investment in the Third World. The government's role would remain "residual" and "never replace what private capital is willing to undertake."[4] On the contrary, by helping to build a local infrastructure of roads, power, and essential services it would make far greater foreign private investments possible. It constantly reiterated the need for Point Four aid recipients to give "equal treatment" to U.S. firms, especially denouncing "nationalistic barriers" of the sort that plagued Latin America.[5] Truman's detailed message also promised that the program would result in greater raw materials extraction, though in fact it was the primary goal of the entire effort, but he asked only for a paltry $45 million for the first year, a sum that both Congress and the State Department subsequently halved. While the Administration requested larger sums the following years, reaching a modest $156 million in fiscal 1953, it constantly reiterated that "we put primary emphasis . . . on the need for stimulating an expansion of private investment . . . ," although for the meantime this remained little more than an idle hope.[6]

In principle, Point Four promised many gains for U.S. foreign economic policy. Reducing Europe's dollar gap via its colonies was the most critical function it might have played. Undoing nationalist barriers to the entry to U.S. capital was another objective, but there was nothing in the program to encourage balanced economic development of the sort Latin America nationalists desired. On the contrary, "international specialization along the lines of so-called comparative advantage," which is to say the continued extraction of unprocessed raw materials, was an explicit target of the entire program.[7] But since the program was too small to accomplish any purpose effectively, it is more valuable to see it as a reflection of the accumulated desires as well as frustrations of the United States' emerging relationship to the Third World. And because the Soviet Union and Communism had little or no influence in Latin America, Africa, and the Middle East, the main intention of the United States was to reaffirm and to implement its own goals for the reorganization of the world economy. At the same time that it advanced its own interests, it hoped also to accommodate the needs of its European allies, whom it considered menaced principally by domestic and Soviet communism as well as reluctant partners in America's campaign to reconstruct the world economy.

In the period before the Korean War, European priorities decisively shaped U.S. policies in Asia, the Philippines excepted, and in Africa U.S. concerns over Western Europe's strength caused it to cooperate fully with the colonial powers and to defer to their leadership. In the Middle East, however, although the United States sought to forge a common military policy with Great Britain, the sheer magnitude of the economic stakes there caused the United States after 1947 to equivocate decisively on economic and political cooperation with Britain. The question of whether America would become rivals in some areas with Western European nations that also were its allies elsewhere, thereby replacing European colonialism in parts of the world, depended essentially on whether its practice, as opposed to rhetoric concerning the international economy, was a cooperative one or based on U.S. domination and mastery. It had yet to resolve these tensions, but they were unmistakably evident before 1950. In Latin America it was unequivocally committed, as it had been for at least a half century, to playing a hegemonic role, actively pitting the United States against the rising tide of nationalism of all ideological hues as well as the residues of Europe's traditional influence.

In brief, there was no single American policy toward the Third World but rather several of them, and the global context interacted with them all. This was particularly true in Latin America and Africa, where more pressing questions elsewhere reduced the importance Washington attached to dealing with rising problems on those continents. Degrees of emphasis notwithstanding, America's leaders had a global perspective by virtue of their increasing commitment to participating in all of the momentous issues that were the outcome of World War Two's profound trauma. The sheer magnitude and scope of their goals, the universalism of their pretensions, and the varying degrees of their ambitions all reached fruition during the late 1940s even before the social and political consequences of the war and the collapse of Europe and its empires had fully matured.

The vast complexity and challenges of such a task, which they unhesitatingly approached primarily because they possessed a very clear vision of America's own needs and desires as a material civilization with imperative interests like every nation, even today defies easy description or comprehension. Yet it must also be remembered that those who were called upon to decide and guide the United States after the Second World War frequently could not foresee either the full context of their actions and policies or gauge their total consequences, much less reconcile the contradictions among them. And from this very fact alone greater challenges and even more difficult decisions would emerge to confront them in the future.

FROM THE KOREAN WAR TO THE END OF 1960

The Korean War: The United States Reassesses the Third World

*T*HE GLOBAL CONTEXT FROM LATE
1949 until the outbreak of the Korean
War the following June, especially
Russia's explosion of an atomic bomb in August 1949 and the final Communist
triumph in China, had deeply disturbed the Truman Administration, and it
authorized the National Security Council to prepare a fundamental review of
its policies in order to close the growing disparity between its international
objectives and the military and political resources it had to attain them. That
search for remedies culminated in the top secret NSC-68 report in April 1950,
though the quest ultimately was never to end because the basic contradiction
the United States faced, and refused to acknowledge, was that its goals inherently outstripped its capabilities. The Korean War only increased this dilemma, for just as most American leaders had earlier understood that an
atomic stalemate had been reached with the USSR, Korea then revealed that
limited wars with conventional arms could not be fought either cheaply or
victoriously. Coping with such paradoxes was to obsess American leaders for
decades, for their essential problem became how to relate their immense
military and economic power to the political realities of highly decentralized
agrarian societies in revolt and how to avoid debilitating, and increasingly
costly, land wars that seemingly led only to disaster.

America's involvement in Korea was a legacy of the Second World War and
a direct outcome of the Cold War with the USSR rather than a question of the
U.S. relationship to the Third World, and Washington regarded the conflict
in this way. The fact that American troops had occupied the desperately
poor, largely agrarian south from September 1945 until August 1948, while
Russian forces were in the north some months longer, also warrants my not

including it here. But contextually the Korean War is crucial because of its inconclusive military results and also because it made clear how politically critical U.S. dependence on local leaders, such as the intransigent and thoroughly independent Syngman Rhee in Korea, could become not only in attaining its objectives but also in involving it in conflicts far more often and longer than it deemed prudent.

THE SEARCH FOR NEW STRATEGIES

Korea also revealed that the U.S. fixation with what one may call the symbolism of "credibility" was capable of assuming a causal importance of its own, and from this time onward the need, as Secretary of State John Foster Dulles was typically to put it in 1958, not to "lose the confidence of these countries" became a recurrent justification for America's action everywhere in the world.[1] Even more significant, NSC-68, which had recommended more than doubling military spending and "rolling back" communism in Eastern Europe, was the beginning of the vertiginous growth in outlays that the Korean War made possible. Indirectly, the economic consequences of this trend to U.S. relations with the Third World proved far-reaching within only a few years. Its immediate profound impact on the American economy required the Eisenhower Administration to make critical strategy and policy changes. The effort to correlate policy and costs always defines possible courses of action, and the Korean War revealed that there was a serious fiscal constraint on U.S. behavior. In Vietnam this was later to prove decisive.

NSC-68 and Korea caused U.S. military spending to increase almost four times between fiscal 1950 and 1953, while inflation in 1951 was over three times the 1950 rate and the federal deficit in fiscal 1953 shot up to $6.5 billion—an enormous sum for the postwar era until then. The Republican Party castigated these deficits during the presidential campaign and upon coming to power immediately embarked on the "New Look" policy, cutting military spending by $5 billion each of the next two years and reducing the armed forces by a million people. The famous Dulles "agonizing reappraisal" that publicly began in December 1953, followed by his vague "massive retaliation" speech the following month, which implied that in any future war the United States would fight "by means and at places of our choosing," was less a coherent policy than the search for one that would allow the United States "maximum protection at a bearable cost."[2] Indeed, privately both Eisenhower and Administration leaders freely acknowledged that the "New Look" was not mastering the spiraling costs of weapons but that, as Vice President Richard Nixon observed in July 1958, "we are preparing for the war we probably will never fight and not for the one which will be lost."[3] But while the inadequacy of its weapons cannot be minimized, it was America's virtually unlimited goals in the world, most of them incapable of being attained with arms, that posed the greatest risks and uncertainties to it.

There was a perfect continuity between the Truman and Eisenhower administrations in their definition of U.S. objectives and interpretations of the nature of changes taking place in the world and their relationship to Soviet actions and power. Both privately and publicly, each attributed to the Russians a transcendent ability to shape events in the most remote countries, and even where they did not initiate them they almost invariably knew how to exploit them, so that where Communists were not important, other groups could serve Soviet interests whether or not they intended to do so. Russia "seeks world rule through the domination of all governments by the International Communist Party," as John Foster Dulles typically put it in 1957.[4] Such conspiracies included "extreme nationalism as one of its tools," he reminded conservative Latin Americans. And he found their alleged ability "to get control of mass movements" uncanny.[5] He was convinced, even when as in Guatemala there was "never . . . proof . . . of any contact," Moscow nonetheless exercised a clandestine presence there.[6] The occasional effort of his brother Allen, the head of the CIA, to discourage attributing cosmic powers to the Soviets lest it also demoralize America's confidence in its ability to relate to the world, had no impact.

The risk of such a paranoid vision was that it made almost any significant change unfavorable to U.S. interests a cause for concern in a period where basic change itself, for an enormous diversity of reasons, was the only thing that was certain in the Third World. And since finite funds and other priorities still had to be considered, new and more effective, but above all cheaper, means had to be devised to cope with a turbulent human condition from which an almost endless number of challenges might arise to confront the United States. The Eisenhower Administration sought to face this dilemma in ingenious new ways.

It was integral to the New Look doctrine that although the United States was to use its firepower and technology in future conflicts, it would depend also on its local allies to supply most of the manpower. And to the extent that it was to bank on local surrogates it was now compelled, to an unprecedented extent, also to link its own interests and future to the stability, integrity, and destiny of numerous Third World regimes, thereby risking loss of control over its priorities. America's reliance on local armies required it to increase their size, and it was to strengthen the objective position of the military in numerous states, thereby deeply affecting their social dynamics and political structures—and potentially compounding its own future problems. American power, to some crucial extent, was in the process of becoming no stronger than the critical foreign surrogates on which it was counting. No one in high places in Washington considered these risks, and, indeed, it was Kennan's encouragement of repression in 1950—"harsh government repression may be the only answer"—that soon became typical of official sentiment.

Annual military aid, nearly all outright grants, during the Eisenhower years grew four times compared to the 1949–52 period in Latin America; increased almost as much in East Asia; and began for the first time, albeit a relatively small sum, in Africa. Such a strengthening of officers in local politics was privately always acknowledged as much a fact of life, and an increasingly desirable one, under Eisenhower as it had been under Truman. "We were putting up some money here for hardware," Dulles observed in regard to Egypt the very first week he was in office, ". . . in the hopes it would keep a particular fellow [Nasser] in power and if in power [we] would get something else out of it."[7] Vital contacts were made, as well, by training foreign officers in the United States and by sending missions to maintain foreign military forces, even in many nations whose political leadership was hostile toward the United States—a point that caused some tension with Congress, for example, in Guatemala early in 1954 when the "CIA feels," as Dulles told a potential critic, "we have gotten advantages out of it."[8] If this increasing reliance on the potentially most repressive and least democratic element throughout the Third World flew in the face of America's public professions, no one in Washington's highest levels had any illusions or qualms about it. "One cannot explain everything to our own people," Dulles informed Richard Nixon in April 1954 about the facts of politics, "as it also explains things to our enemies."[9]

With such growing military ties came an impulse to create bases and formal regional alliances to cement and institutionalize the global military network on which the United States was increasingly depending. And a conscious assumption of this system, as Dulles was to acknowledge explicitly, was that were there to be a relaxation of Cold War tensions, "a feeling of need in the face of danger" would end and "The Free World's efforts would rapidly decline. . . . There would be what seems to be a great danger—a tendency to fall apart."[10] Fear had a crucial role in binding together the alliances.

As important as the United States' dependence on officers and armies became, it would be an error to minimize the role of other, relatively less violent solutions, or the Eisenhower Administration's creativity in its efforts "to develop techniques" to neutralize Communists in the Third World.[11] The difficulty in using armies is that most of the problems Third World states had to confront required a much lower level of violence, and a number of major Latin American nations began asking for training in police methods no later than 1953. That the police might serve as well, or even better, than the army in dealing with internal opposition of every sort was obvious. A small CIA course for foreign police was started in 1952, but beginning in 1955, using the

Agency for International Development as a cover, it sent "public safety missions" to thirty-eight nations over the next seven years. The explicit premise of this growing, permanent program was that the police "first detect discontent among people" and "should serve as one of the major means by which the government assures itself of acceptance by the majority. . . . effective policing is like 'preventive medicine.' The police can deal with threats to internal order in their formative states. Should they not be prepared to do this, then 'major surgery' may be required in the sense that considerable force would be needed to redress those threats. This action is painful and expensive and often disruptive in itself."[12]

It was precisely because of this desire to encourage lower levels of violence to forestall a need to use the local regular military, much less American troops, that the CIA's potential as a major arm was quickly brought to fruition under the Eisenhower Administration. Capable of exploiting a huge variety of techniques, it was to become the most flexible instrument of U.S. interventions in the Third World, all the more useful because it was extremely cheap and because its reliance on secrecy had the political asset of "plausible deniability," to American citizens as well as foreign governments, should any of its actions be uncovered. If the premises underlying the CIA's activity and support for local police simplified greatly the nature of social movements in the world, the institutional sources of their conduct, and what is permanently decisive in dealing with them, it nonetheless possessed an incalculable short-run potential for eliminating enemies and helping erstwhile friends for as long as they could perform a useful function. No important American leaders reflected on how the very ease of relying on these new forms of intervention would increase immeasurably the extent to which they might occur, both undermining the possibilities for a less traumatic social evolution in many nations and demanding increased American efforts to save politicians and parties in power by virtue of U.S. aid and incapable of remaining there without more of it. Just as this approach averted the need for massive violence immediately, CIA efforts or more aggressive police also protracted the lives of rotten regimes and thereby intensified social diseases and political instability that might eventually require the very medicine of massive U.S. interventions they were intended to avoid using. What would the United States do once the CIA's actions failed or proved insufficient? Only events over the coming decades would reveal the answer.

The CIA was created in 1947 as part of the fundamental revamping of the military services that replaced the War and Navy departments with the Defense Department. Its mandate was completely open-ended and included "such other functions" as the NSC assigned it.[13] A covert action wing, the "clandestine service," was soon added and from 1949 to 1952 was assigned the Truman Administration's ambitious commitment to the "rollback" of

Communism and had its size expanded twenty times, to nearly six thousand persons. Action-oriented and often operating in Communist nations, under the Truman Administration it still avoided high-risk political destabilization, assassinations, and the like, restricting itself to tasks like espionage, psychological warfare activities, rigging elections, or building anti-Communist unions. Given Eisenhower's passionate desire to avoid a suicidal nuclear confrontation as well his deep skepticism toward the efficacy of expensive limited wars, it was inevitable that the New Look's most original innovation would be to exploit the CIA much more aggressively.

Headed by Allen Dulles, who was very close to his brother John, the CIA flourished under the tight control of the president. Over the next eight years the CIA's "clandestine service" added two thousand members and absorbed the larger share of the agency's budget. It was also to become one of the most important instruments in the U.S. relationship to the Third World throughout the Eisenhower period.

REASSESSING THE STAKES IN THE THIRD WORLD

The Korean War profoundly altered the global context in which U.S. foreign policy was to operate over the next decade. While the effort of the Taft wing of the Republican Party to shift Washington's definition of its major priorities from Europe to Asia was seemingly to fail despite commander in Korea General Douglas MacArthur's impassioned support for it during 1950, the Democratic Administration and its successor nonetheless increasingly lost control over its freedom of choice. Although the Republicans under Eisenhower also believed in Europe's primacy, both the logic of the world situation after mid-1950 as well as a continuous and growing U.S. desire and, increasingly, need to master inevitable developments in the Third World were to erode America's post-1945 primary focus on Europe, altering its priorities in practice as opposed to theory. The net effect was that by 1961 a decisive though unintended change in the Third World's role in U.S. foreign policy had occurred.

If the outcome of this shift was to make the United States far less of a partner of the European colonial powers than it had been, this rupture was never to occur to the same degree in every region. Although the vagaries of politics and social dynamics in the world, combined with America's definitions of its objectives, caused the United States to intrude more overtly into Asia and the Middle East, Washington's concern for its good relations with its NATO allies remained very real. But the logic of globalism and unlimited interests, whatever the formal priorities American planners assigned to them, constantly left open the risk of confusion between the unforeseeable consequences of its efforts in one nation and its possible international commitments, a process that allowed events themselves to impose the real priorities on U.S. foreign policy. The Korean War was the first but not the last event to reveal that the gap between America's desires and its control was becoming wider. But to understand this process of America's loss of mastery accurately we must cope also with its complexity over time. Changes that occurred were often those the United States least expected, and objective forces operated both to constrain and guide its policies—making the emerging U.S. relationship to the Third World the outcome of contradictions as well as planning.

Throughout the 1950s the United States and the major Western European powers were to remain collaborators as well as rivals. Washington's disquiet over its allies' dollar gap after 1949, as we saw earlier, or cooperation on purely European questions, caused it both to want to see colonial economic domination continue and for American firms to share in developing the colonies if they so desired. At the same time, however, the United States also had to take into account that anticolonialism was a key propaganda issue in its struggle with the USSR and that being associated with European imperialism was a major political liability in most areas. In balancing its goals in Europe with its position in the Third World, it had to consider the precise ideological nature of the anti-imperialist forces in each country, and a complex juggling of all of these elements was characteristic of U.S. policy throughout this decade. In Africa, therefore, its essentially procolonialist position was ostensibly to differ radically from its stand elsewhere, but only because it was trying to accomplish many different and seemingly contradictory tasks throughout the world at one time.

The Truman Administration had less difficulty with the issue of colonialism than its successor, arguing publicly that "The grant of premature political independence without adequate economic and social preparation for it can bring to a people untold harm."[14] The Eisenhower Administration was initially more attuned to the fact that such a stance was damaging to U.S. ideological pretensions in the Cold War and made some rhetorical but not substantive changes in it. "We have to be spokesmen for those wanting independence or we will be licked" by the Russians, Dulles confided in June 1954, but at the same time, as a group of highly influential advisers argued the following year, anticolonialism "does not require the West to surrender its own security and its truly vital economic interests in the name of . . . self-determination."[15] And while it was a burden to be associated with colonialism, Dulles believed, should the French or British governments fall because of these controversies there would be a move toward neutralism in Western Europe that would gravely damage U.S. power there.

The result was that while Washington endorsed the principle of a "progressive" movement of the colonies and trusteeships toward independence, it never failed to add decisive reservations.[16] The dangers of "premature independence," for this reason, became more prominent as the decade wore on. "Our policy," Undersecretary of State Robert Murphy accurately described it in October 1959, "seeks to maintain a line which permits of loyalty to our European friends and allies, and understanding and support where possible of the aspirations of the newly emerging nations. We want their friendship. We also do not favor the creation of power vacuums which international communism will exploit if it is permitted to do so."[17] The liabilities of such an extremely ambivalent position on colonialism were to arise during the highly visible UN debates on it, when the United States with great reluctance tried to favor independence more strongly only because it feared that the Soviets would gain if it did not take such a posture. Yet posture it was, and only by turning to specific American policies in various regions can we really understand how and why it behaved as it did.

The Korean War increased the role and importance of the Third World in U.S. foreign policy not merely because of geopolitics but also because the very process of fighting the war, and above all its economic consequences, produced imperative new requirements that altered basically the relationship of the United States to the Third World. The war's demands on U.S. industrial capacity and its huge impetus to European and Japanese recovery, which together compounded the need for raw materials, brought the question of raw materials supplies to the fore in a manner that had not occurred since World War Two. While this consciousness rises and ebbs among policymakers after 1945 depending on scarcity and prices, within that sector of the business community that requires imports it is a constant concern. Korea increased this awareness to a new level, profoundly affecting the United States' definitions of its Third World policies.

The emergence of raw materials as a source of deepening U.S. anxiety after 1950 was the culmination of its growing dependency on imports that began when it became a net importer of raw materials in the 1920s, which even then deeply colored its policies toward the Third World. Excluding gold and iron, the United States imported only 5 percent of its total consumption of metals in the 1920s but 38 percent in 1940–49 and 48 percent the following decade. This deficiency was partly due to the depletion of U.S. sources, but more important was the fact that the rise of modern technology is intimately linked to metals that the United States possesses only in small quantities or, increasingly, not at all. While the bulk or even the dollar value of such metals is not great compared to iron, their qualitative importance is so large that no nation can build many advanced industries without access to them. Even by 1930 the United States was importing 64 percent of its bauxite and copper, and during World War Two, twenty-seven of the sixty minerals it imported came entirely from foreign suppliers. A modern iron and steel industry must have manganese, nickel, and tin, not to mention many other metals, which by 1956–60 were almost entirely imported. Indeed, by that period even a quarter of the U.S. consumption of iron ore was imported. With time, the sheer significance of such materials to electronics, military equipment of every sort, and the sinews of industrialism was to grow—and with it the need for stable sources of supply. Even dollar comparisons are misleading, for in 1945–49 the U.S. outlay for raw materials imports, adjusted for inflation, was only slightly greater than in 1925–29. It was the value of the output of entire industries that were dependent on them that rose enormously. Yet in 1948 the United States, as a share of the world's total consumption, utilized 49 percent of its copper, 47 percent of its lead, 43 percent of its zinc, and 52 percent of its steel.

Access to imported raw materials was increasingly essential to the survival of the U.S. economy as it had developed after 1920 and to its dominant role in the world from 1945 onward. And this meant that the Third World's qualitative significance was also increasing, for most of the critical U.S. imports came from there. Excluding Canada, the Western Hemisphere was the greatest supplier of vital metals (gold excepted) to the United States, and while Africa dominated in a far smaller number of metals, all were critical, and no alternative sources could be found easily, if at all, for most of them. While Southeast and South Asia were relatively the least significant for the United States, Japan literally could not survive as an American ally without their exports. This crucial triangular linkage, as well as the direct dependence of all of its allies on sufficient supplies, also strongly influenced American raw materials policies, if only because it affected the capacity of Europe to reconstruct with less U.S. aid by earning dollars from their colonial domination over many of these sources.

Washington's goal of global economic integration, therefore, was not merely a question of opening channels for the export of investment funds abroad, although it hoped to do so both for the sake of profit and to link the economic and political development of the poor nations to that of the United States and richer countries. Most vital was the task of assuring that sufficient supplies of essential imports were available to American users, which frequently were the same companies that invested in the Third World—for profit, of course, but also to guarantee adequate output so they could sell finished products to American and foreign consumers.

All these considerations weighed heavily on U.S. policymakers in the years before Korea, notwithstanding their far greater concern afterward. Oil, as contrasted to other minerals, had already been assigned a much higher priority, and the way it was pursued is a wholly different story. In July 1946 Congress passed a stockpiling act that not only subsidized inefficient domestic mines but also guaranteed that vital imports would be on hand in case of war. "We are approaching a situation of scarcity in certain minerals," the State Department's Paul H. Nitze warned at the beginning of 1947, "fully comparable to the situation existing during the war. . . . Our concern is . . . whether in the long run we are going to be able to maintain nondiscriminatory access abroad to those minerals. . . ."[18] The Marshall Plan required the Europeans to reimburse 5 percent of the aid received into a special local currency fund that the United States could then use to buy their raw materials, mainly from their colonies, but the effort only partly succeeded. More important, they had to pledge to allow U.S. firms equal access when investing in their colonies—although most American companies were unwilling to invest there on any terms at this time. Point Four made raw materials development in private hands crucial, both for Europe's interests and those of the United States. And even in early 1950, when Washington moved to assist the French in Indochina lest all of Southeast Asia fall like dominoes, the area's "major sources of certain strategic materials" the United States needed became a vital justification for aid.[19]

With the outbreak of the Korean War, what was a serious but relatively subdued U.S. concern became a major national obsession as world prices for all metals by 1952 had risen 39 percent over 1950, while the terms of trade swung sharply in favor of the underdeveloped areas in 1951, and not until 1957 were they again biased in favor of the industrial nations. In a skyrocketing world market, the United States generally outflanked its European allies in obtaining scarce supplies now essential both to their economic recovery and rearmament, creating such serious tensions with Britain and shortages for much of Western Europe that in June 1951 a mechanism for controlling the allocation and price of twelve of the most vital materials was created.

The need for more supplies from Third World sources also gave renewed impetus to Point Four, and in January 1951 the President's Materials Policy Commission, headed by CBS chairman William S. Paley, assisted by a mining industry and probusiness board, began an exhaustive review of the United States' raw materials needs. Its massive report focused on the nation's structural deficit and its import dependency and predicted that scarcity would worsen over future decades. It stressed the importance of creating conditions for greatly expanded U.S. private investment abroad, including active government aid, tax shields, insurance, and the like. The commission heightened government and business awareness of the Third World's vital importance in satisfying American needs. And by pointing out that Europe's demand for raw materials was increasing more rapidly than U.S. demand, it also implicitly raised the issue of how the colonial world's resources would be divided. "I do not believe this country can survive," W. Averell Harriman, one of the postwar era's most influential men, warned a Senate committee early in 1952, "if the sources of the raw materials are in the hands of unfriendly people who are determined to destroy us."[20] In a private memo to Truman he surveyed U.S. interests in the Third World, and in no region did he think it could afford to be aloof—with raw materials providing the only common justification for involvement in all of them. In 1954 a Senate committee reviewing these questions concluded that "To a very dangerous extent, the vital security of this Nation is in serious jeopardy."[21]

This raw materials fever continued as long as there were shortages and prices were high, and not until 1957 did it subside. But a greater awareness of its importance than earlier remained. Such a mood created a general backdrop when the United States confronted its specific regional problems during this decade, and if it by no means explains all the dimensions of its diverse policies it nonetheless is integral to any serious explanation of the sources of its conduct throughout the Third World.

Asia
and the
American System

*T*HE OUTBREAK OF WAR IN KOREA IN June 1950 intensified greatly U.S. anxieties regarding trends in East Asia but did not deepen Washington's comprehension of the problems there, much less their origins. To a vital extent, variations of the interrelated themes of the domino theory, the importance of Southeast Asia to Europe and Japan, and the symbolic credibility of U.S. power were to shape America's policy in the region for the next decade. Its growing involvement in Indochina was far less the cause of this interpretation than its effect. For most of the decade Washington still considered the Philippines as the most important nation to it in the region, but with time its operational priorities inevitably adapted to the scale of fighting, causing the United States to lose sight of its original commitments and definition of its interests.

However integral the domino theory to U.S. policy after the Korean War began, several assumptions reinforced its influence. American decisionmakers regarded events in Asia as the direct outcome of Russian guidance, which gave them a symbolic importance far transcending the region. It was the official NSC view in May 1951 that Moscow was seeking to use China as a base from which to take "control" over mainland East Asia and "eventually Japan and the other principal off-shore islands in the Western Pacific."[1] Unquestionably, it assumed, local Communist parties were all under tight Soviet discipline. This simplistic interpretation not only reinforced Washington's concerns regarding the area but also justified minimizing its unhappiness with France's political policies in Indochina on behalf of its larger objectives of confronting the USSR via the French temporarily in Asia and, later, permanently in Europe, where French power was crucial. France was also essential to the United States, since it was official American policy after Korea not to use its own forces on mainland Southeast Asia. Reform in Indochina could come only through France, not against it, lest alleged Moscow agents replace the French.

The United States assigned even greater significance to the control of the region's raw materials in the wake of post-Korea shortages and spiraling prices. For the next four years scarcely an important analysis or policy statement failed to detail all the considerations, from Japan's reconstruction and Europe's strength to America's needs, that had already figured prominently in its pre-Korea discussions. As Assistant Secretary of State Dean Rusk put it typically in January 1951, "Our vital dependence upon Southeast Asia for tin is almost as great as for rubber."[2] Denying the Soviets access to both the region's huge population and vast resources was essential to the world balance of power—an issue of monumental consequence. It was this larger vision that magnified, as well, the importance of Japanese reconstruction in U.S. plans—and the retention of Southeast Asia was vital to that end.

This concern for raw materials was not simply geopolitical, for while it was firm U.S. policy from the inception that they should be available to itself and its allies, it also stipulated that they be developed in accordance with its plans for a world economic structure based on capitalism in general and access for American investors in particular. "Saving" Asia meant far more than development, security, or stability, much less democracy. U.S. policies in both India and Thailand revealed how it sought to attain this objective.

It was inevitable after Korea that India and all of South Asia would be encouraged to move toward "the expansion of trade along multilateral non-discriminatory lines consistent with U.S. security interests." It was not sufficient to isolate the area from the Soviet bloc, but it required "that we and other friendly countries have access to resources and markets" there.[3] The sheer importance of India's raw materials made this a matter of prime importance in relations with it. Specifically this meant discouraging autonomous national economic policies and, above all, India's experiments with forms of a mixed economy.

India offered Washington a tangible but modest means to shape that nation's internal economic policies because American economic aid in the form of goods or dollars produced an equivalent sum in rupee counterpart funds, which then could be spent locally. Given its general policy throughout Asia that "a real change in the standard of living is achieved when production and distribution are to a maximum extent in non-governmental hands," the United States explicitly opposed "nationalization and socialism." If a government plant "is the type which should be in private hands," then no counterpart funds could be used to finance it, U.S. aid authorities decided in February 1954.[4] Fostering "governmental policies favorable to the investment of indigenous and foreign private capital" became a major objective in India and the region around it.[5] In India this task was not difficult, despite the absence of sufficient U.S. leverage to control policy in such a vast country, because there existed an important national capitalist class and it dominated the ruling Congress Party. It was just as wary of socialistic schemes as the Americans, and its influence was far more decisive.

In Thailand, by contrast, economic nationalism within the army, which ruled the country under a monarchy, by 1950 had begun to define all economic development. Over the next decade official and semi-official agencies operated hundreds of corporations in virtually every field. Partially a consequence of import-substitution notions among a ruling class that was largely uninterested in commerce or industry, the absence of a Thai bourgeoisie meant that the only resistance to such a strategy came from the politically inconsequential but historically dominant Chinese business elite. While the Chinese easily controlled many of the state firms via massive corruption and symbiosis with the key officers, it was scarcely a propitious environment for foreign investors. In 1957 U.S. oil firms and aid officials moved to end this situation, which threatened their future development of Thailand's rich offshore fields.

Given the many Chinese and local interests who were not part of the state-controlled sector, U.S. threats to cut aid, coordinated with pressure from the World Bank, managed to redirect the main thrust of Thai economic development toward a primary reliance on private investment, domestic as well as foreign. Earlier legislation was thrown out in 1960, and private enterprise was guaranteed protection against state competition and nationalization. If the state's role still allowed ample scope for the politically dominant military to obtain a handsome share for itself, so that when Marshal Sarit, who was also prime minister, died in 1963 he left an estate valued at $150 million, the dominant thrust in the economy now favored the Chinese and foreigners—who used their contacts with the political elite to regulate economic affairs as businessmen thought best. As anticommunism replaced the anti-Chinese sentiment that had prevailed among the Thai rulers until then, Thailand proved to be a major success for U.S. policy in the region—and one more domino to guard for itself.

However crucial such economic goals for the United States in East Asia, they were scarcely the only ones, and purely geopolitical and military considerations increased in significance after the May 1954 Geneva Conference on Indochina and the collapse of the American-backed French war there. Whether in a region or globally, American policy is never static, but while its means and emphases often vary, its goals have remained astonishingly constant. Awareness of such changing nuances in its international relations provides analysts with a coherent vision of the overall objectives as well as the problems of managing U.S. foreign policy. Added to the domino theory and raw materials was the Eisenhower Administration's increasingly obsessive concern with "credibility": "The loss of prestige in Asia suffered by the U.S. as a backer of the French"; one that "will raise further doubts in Asia concerning U.S. leadership and the ability of the U.S. to check the further expansion of Communism in Asia."[6]

Given its strong reluctance to employ its own manpower in another land war in Asia, a cardinal principle of the New Look doctrine, the use of proxies became far more important, and a variety of policies initiated under the Truman Administration now reached fruition. Military aid and military training to key nations were augmented dramatically, and the idea of a regional military alliance was revived. The State Department was sympathetic to such a Southeast Asian accord both before and after June 1950 but preferred that it be initiated spontaneously by nations in the region. During and following the Geneva Conference, Washington responded to its impotence there by aggressively sponsoring a military pact in the form of the Southeast Asia Treaty Organization (SEATO), which initially was to have included Japan and Korea but ended with Pakistan, the Philippines, and Thailand as the only Asian members. The same impulse to mobilize as many nations as possible under its aegis led also to a struggle against the alleged "neutralism" that much of the Third World proclaimed in the Cold War.

In its own way, the Manichean ideological premises of antineutralism were more all-encompassing than anything the United States was to undertake in this decade, since implicitly it divided the world into those for and against the United States and advanced a greater demand for political fealty than would have been necessary in purely economic or military matters. And since the posture of neutrality was one even many conservative states adopted because of their nationalist struggles against the West, the U.S. position immediately produced hostility where otherwise none might have existed. India was the greatest villain, but all of the twenty-nine nations that gathered at the Bandung Asian-African Conference of April 1955 were also culpable of the vice of nonalignment. Privately it was policy in South Asia to work with friendly governments ready to "resist communism from within and without," and that surely included India.[7] Publicly, Dulles persisted throughout the decade to excoriate the principle of neutrality as "immoral and shortsighted."[8] However he sought to modify the offense it gave to many nonaligned states, it was clear that formal military ties with the United States would after 1954 become its standard claim on nations, not only in Asia but elsewhere as well. More than ever before, the United States was entering an era of alliances and treaties, not only making demands upon a growing part of the Third World but also putting itself in a position where they could also ask much in return, from arms and political support to, ultimately, troops.

The terms of SEATO, the first of these new-style pacts, were extremely vague but potentially equally open-ended.

THE DILEMMA OF THE PHILIPPINES

Before the Korean War the single most important challenge to the U.S. position in the Far East was in the Philippines, where the politicians it had put in office to implement the policies it designed were plunging the nation into bankruptcy and civil war. The State Department, conscious of its symbolic importance to American power in the region should the chaos in the Philippines continue and open the door to the Communists, in June 1950 sent a special mission under Daniel W. Bell, its leading expert on the Philippines economy, to rectify the situation. He quickly reported that "The Philippines is facing nothing less than a financial collapse" and that the Quirino regime would do nothing to prevent it unless compelled to.[9] And since it had stopped paying many of the government's employees and soon would have to cease paying the army, Bell advised aid linked to the acceptance of firm U.S. conditions on fiscal reform. The problem, as Washington well knew, was that while "The Government is inefficient and corruption is widespread," Quirino was "supremely confident" of U.S. aid whatever he did.[10] The United States did indeed grant Manila $250 million over a five-year period, but it obtained the right to appoint American advisers to all government agencies, allowing them to control aid funds as well as key administration functions. This included giving guidance on dealing with the ten thousand to fifteen thousand Huks fighting the regime.

American decisions in the Philippines after mid-1950 were plagued with doubts. On the one hand they knew all about corruption and that "without our aid, Quirino's regime will eventually be swept away." Even with aid, some State Department officials argued, it might crumble and require the U.S. Army to intervene, and then "The process of recolonizing the Philippines will then be well advanced." Should it fall out of the "American orbit," Dean Rusk warned at the beginning of 1951, it would "more than any other single factor discredit the United States throughout the length and breadth of Asia. . . . it is vital that we hold the Philippines whatever the cost—unless we are prepared to write off Asia." Because of the regional and global context the United States felt it had no choice but "to participate in the defense and administration of the country," but its clarity regarding the venality of its chosen political instruments led it to move actively to replace them with stronger ones, a task it assigned to the CIA.[11] Once again the Americans faced their common dilemma of resolving what to do about one of the puppets of its own creation who had escaped its complete control.

In August 1950 Lieutenant Colonel Edward G. Lansdale was assigned command of the CIA operation, spending his first months revamping the Filipino intelligence and psychological warfare operations, quickly getting deeply involved in political affairs and becoming the intimate adviser to the new defense secretary, Ramón Magsaysay. CIA station officers regarded Magsaysay as dull-witted, but he had tremendous charisma, a winning populist style, and he was virtually the only honest senior member of the Quirino cabinet. More important, he was slavishly loyal to his American advisers, and they soon designated him as their chosen vehicle for coping both with the Huks and the existing regime. The Huks reached their peak strength in November 1951, when they had from one million to two million followers. Lansdale understood correctly that most of them were not Communists but simple peasants who wanted at least lower rents and, in many cases, land reform as well. Magsaysay openly sympathized with their plight and demands, and the combination of American tactics and a post-Korean War prosperity that began to trickle down to the masses caused Huk strength to ebb quickly after 1952.

But the United States did not concentrate merely on suppressing the Huks, and in mid-1951 the CIA began to mobilize a large number of unaffiliated middle-class groups under an umbrella National Movement for Free Elections (NAMFREL) to police the November 1951 congressional elections as a prelude to winning the presidency for Magsaysay two years later. With ample funds and numerous front organizations, its success in 1951 encouraged the United States to discard Quirino, whom the CIA thought "corrupt beyond belief or salvation."[12] With both the embassy and CIA deeply involved in the seamy dealmaking of local politics, in March 1953 Magsaysay won the presidential nomination of the Nacionalista Party after quitting the Liberal cabinet. Apart from his charisma and program, he also had the support of much of the army, but the embassy believed that a no less "Important factor will be high regard felt for Magsaysay by U.S.," for the many opportunistic local politicians were certain to gravitate toward their well-funded candidate in an American dependency.[13] Magsaysay's bandwagon was swollen with key politicos who brought their votes with them, and with the CIA freely passing out funds, eventually to amount to over one million dollars, it was clear that he would win any reasonably honest election. But had Quirino tampered once more with the vote, then Magsaysay planned an uprising, for which the CIA had even begun to prepare. It was no surprise, therefore, that he won 69 percent of the vote, or that, as Joseph B. Smith, a senior CIA officer later recounted, Eisenhower "sent his congratulations to the station via appropriate channels."[14]

The United States' next problem was how to use its direct control of power now that one corrupt regime had been thrown out and a new figurehead, who was surrounded by many of the old-school politicians who had rallied to Magsaysay for their own reasons, was in charge. The Huks were rapidly disintegrating due both to their own failures and the nation's growing if temporary prosperity, so Lansdale and part of his Filipino-staffed CIA fronts were sent to South Vietnam to assist the French and, shortly thereafter, Ngo Dinh Diem—whom Lansdale was to advise next. Before leaving Manila permanently, Lansdale helped orient Magsaysay's new agrarian and governmental policies, and then the CIA station took charge, writing many of his speeches. To a great extent, however, the United States also exploited the situation to use Filipinos, as Smith described it, "as our alter egos to spread democracy throughout the SEATO security area" because Dulles believed they would be more effective than Americans as "political advisers and liaison officers with local intelligence services." When the CIA was not exploiting Magsaysay's time to carry the anti-Communist message to other Asian nations it worked on "activities designed to build up future political leaders upon whom we could count." At the level of changes in Filipino life, however, the deep American involvement altered almost nothing, and Magsaysay, as Smith ruefully recalls, "spent most of his first term fighting with the old bosses of the Nacionalista Party" who had helped to elect him.[15]

There was no chance that Magsaysay would embark on serious land reform because the politicians of both parties were integrally linked to the oligarchy. The first recommendation for reform, by a hapless American expert who in 1952 proposed a measure modeled on postwar Japanese legislation, was shot down as radical by everyone with power in Manila. The bill that finally passed was so full of loopholes that landlords openly welcomed it. The United States, no longer worried about the Huks, ceased to urge reform involving redistribution. It did sponsor and pay for the development of new rural communities in underpopulated areas, which made excellent propaganda outside the country, but in 1959 they had only 5,175 inhabitants in a nation of 27 million. "Magsaysay's program failed," as the AID later admitted, in part because of "fraud and mismanagement."[16] Meanwhile, between 1948 to 1960, even official data reported the tenancy rate among peasants actually increased from 37 to 40 percent, though unofficial figures fixed it as high as 50 percent. Few tenants had written contracts or a minimal home lot for their own use, as the new reform required. In a word, the rural life of the nation remained essentially untouched throughout the decade. Magsaysay retained his unquestionably great popularity with the people, but his program was implemented badly and corruptly, much like those of his predecessors.

Given the demise of the Huk movement, which had only twenty-five hundred troops at the beginning of 1954, and the United States' growing distractions elsewhere in the region and world, with the end of the Philippine economic and political crisis the American role after 1954 was confined to managing its own interests in less adventuresome ways. "Magsaysay is a great friend and was elected on the American ticket," Eisenhower assured Dulles at the end of 1953, and their belief that they now had an effective example of the virtues of the Western democratic system for the rest of Asia consoled them, encouraging their complacency.[17] Economically, the 1946 Bell Trade Act, whose duty-free clause was due to expire, was renegotiated in the Laurel-Langley Agreement of 1955 in such a way as to continue the basic interlocked economic ties, while modest technical changes pleased U.S. investors in the Philippines as well as Filipino manufacturers who wanted some protection against American goods. The peso ceased to be tied to the dollar, a rule that had practically wrecked the peso in 1949, but no dramatic changes were made in the legal structure of what continued a master-dependency relationship. In the military domain the Philippines were to remain a vital strategic link in U.S. planning, and it intended keeping its bases, which had ten thousand men in 1957, there indefinitely.

On March 17, 1957, the United States' good fortune ended when Magsaysay's airplane crashed while he was campaigning for reelection. His successor, Vice President Carlos P. García, was as yet an unknown factor, although the CIA had approved him in 1953 as "a sop to party regulars" who backed Magsaysay. It did not take his equally dishonest opponents long to charge him with corruption, but while the CIA also confirmed that "he was a crook," Washington did not believe he would greatly alter relations with the United States. The problem was that of the four candidates running for president in November, all seemed equally shifty. One of them, however, was Claro M. Recto, who after a long and politically ambitious career of dealmaking with everyone, the Japanese included, emerged as a spokesman both for a nationalist strategy that would remove the country from American economic tutelage and promote a neutralist foreign policy. Only the Liberal vice-presidential candidate, Diosdado Macapagal, had solid links with the CIA, so the United States decided to concentrate its efforts on soundly defeating Recto and, thereby, nationalist politics. García was reelected, while Macapagal won the impotent vice president's office, and the Americans discovered that "we had now no power base around which to center our operations."[18] Worse yet, under García the entire postwar edifice the United States had constructed soon threatened to crumble.

The important changes altering Filipino politics and society throughout the 1950s once again required Washington seriously to regulate Filipino affairs or risk losing its mastery over the nation—with untold implications for its power in Asia as well. While it had mastered the challenge a rebellious peasantry posed, it had now to confront the emergence of an anti-American middle class of small entrepreneurs and industrialists who were rallying around nationalism in an effort to break their colonial economic links in the form of special U.S. privileges. Also attracted to its platform were some landed oligarches ready to diversify into industry and utilities but unable to do so as successfully as they would have liked, as well as sectors of the intelligentsia and leftists who were anti-American for cultural and political reasons. Recto, almost against his will, became the symbol of their common cause, even though as a hardened old-school politician he played the role in a circuitous fashion. What was both new and permanent about this constituency was its growing economic basis: from 1949 to 1960 the share of the national product accounted for by industry rose from 8 to 18 percent, and thousands of manufacturing enterprises that had risen in the interstices of the Bell Act now demanded strong government protection and aid. Questions of currency regulation and exchange controls were vital to these businessmen, who also lobbied with some success in 1959 to obtain government participation to build an integrated steel industry and other concessions to accelerate economic development. Ready to struggle in the political arena to strengthen their interests, Recto was this national bourgeoisie's spokesman.

García, while thoroughly corrupt in the manner of traditional Filipino politics, was constantly striking deals with existing and potential rivals, including Recto, whom he appointed to his Council of State and saw frequently from early 1958 onward. Recto's party soon entered a coalition with the Nacionalistas, with modest political rewards in return. The most important of these, the "Filipino First" policy promulgated in August 1958, did little to undo existing U.S. and Chinese domination of the economy but it became the focus of intensified nationalist agitation among local business elements. American business spokesmen, naturally, were horrified, and official opinion in Washington through 1960 was that the policy was undermining the Laurel-Langley Agreement. While García's nationalism never went as far as Recto desired, it was much more than the United States could tolerate, and García presented it with an unprecedented challenge of unknown dimensions.

Reviewing the entire range of Philippine-U.S. relations in June 1958, the National Security Council reaffirmed all of the traditional reasons why the nation was important but concluded unhappily that everything was wrong with the García government: it was corrupt, opportunistic, and represented "a sharp retrogression from the Magsaysay period, and its prospects for improved performance in the future are not reassuring." Especially worrisome was "a small but important group" around Recto, supported in its "chauvinist," "emotional," and "ultra-nationalist sentiment" "by an influential and vocal segment of the Filipino elite." Pressure for "a more independent foreign policy" in the form of neutralism could be the only outcome of its alliance with García. With the remainder of the García term written off, the

NSC decided to "encourage" alternative political leaders of the Magsaysay variety to run for the eight Senate seats in the November 1959 bi-elections as a prelude to forming a coalition capable of recouping the presidency two years later.[19]

Putting together a winning group of politicians in the Byzantine milieu of Filipino politics, with its deep tradition of total opportunism, was far more difficult in 1959 than in 1953 because no one as pliable and unintelligent as Magsaysay could be found. Working with only $250,000 to redress what Smith called "the total collapse of the showplace of democracy that had been the pride not only of [the] CIA but [also of] the Eisenhower Administration," he soon learned it was impossible to succeed in the internecine world of ambitious local politicos. Macapagal, in particular, wanted total backing for his own candidates as a step toward obtaining the presidential nomination two years later. It was in this context that Ferdinand Marcos, then Liberal leader in the House, first became deeply involved with the Americans. Macapagal, whom the CIA had courted for some years, was particularly worrisome because while the agency was certain that he was ambitious, it had "never heard from Macapagal any ideas about what kind of a country he wanted the Philippines to be."[20] García, on the other hand, moved closer to Recto's followers during the campaign and together they rallied more than ever around nationalist slogans. In the end, Macapagal ran alone, obtaining one-fifth of the CIA's funds, the value of which it had doubled on the Hong Kong black market, and the remainder went to a "Grand Alliance" that included three of its other favorites.

The outcome was dismal from America's viewpoint, for it lost its postwar control of the Filipino political process, although Macapagal won a seat and, in the American estimation, "the right to lead them all" in 1961.[21] Marcos, too, won, with the largest number of votes of any senatorial candidate despite the fact that he was not in the Grand Alliance. The United States' power in the Philippines was threatened at the end of the decade almost as much as it had been at its inception—but now from an entirely different ideological direction.

CHAPTER 8

The Middle East: From Collaboration to Control

*R*ECONCILING ITS DESIRE FOR COOPER-
ation with the British in political and
military affairs in the Middle East with
its increasingly aggressive efforts to win mastery over the area's oil was the
Truman Administration's principal dilemma in the region before and especially after the outbreak of the Korean War. Given its coolness at this time
toward Israel, which pursued a neutralist foreign policy and still purchased
arms from the Soviet bloc, there were none of the political barriers to closer
relations with the Arab states that emerged in the 1960s. Since 1947, London
and Washington had explicitly pledged that their Near East policies would not
only be mutually supporting but also that they would cooperate to exclude
political or commercial challenges from other nations—in effect, to close the
open door through which the United States was walking. At the beginning of
1950 this alliance was again renewed formally.

The Korean War strongly reinforced the centrifugal tensions inherent in
the Anglo-American alliance because the subsequent world economic boom
and rearmament greatly increased oil's economic and strategic importance,
and the British in July 1950 drastically diminished their potential military
utility when they informed Washington that in the event of a war with Russia
they would concentrate their defenses in and around the Suez Canal and
Egypt—writing off most of the region. This made its relations with Egypt the
key to its future power in the area. More vital yet, by 1950 the Near East's
oil reserves were already equivalent to all the rest in the world combined and
double those in the United States—and this vast wealth was largely in British
concessions. "Control of this source of energy," the State Department's experts advised in September, "important in peace and war, is a desirable goal

in itself. . . . The U.S. Government should seek maximum development in U.S. owned concessions."[1]

The single most important issue during the early 1950s to determine who would control the region's oil was the difference between competing oil interests over the division of profits and royalties among themselves and the key oil-producing nations. In 1948 U.S. companies in Venezuela were compelled to pay fifty-fifty, an unprecedented share, and Saudi Arabia soon demanded the same from its American firms—upsetting the area's stability in ways that were to prove far-reaching to the British, who were paying much less. The State Department endorsed the fifty-fifty split for the entire area and thereby gravely undercut their ally's position. Should there be a sharp diminution of Britain's role, the State Department's experts concluded at the end of 1950, "The Arab States are all oriented towards the West in varying degrees, opposed to communism, and generally successful at present in minimizing or suppressing existing Communist activities. . . ." The main risk to the West came from "ultra-nationalist elements."[2] This force was primarily hostile to the British and French, they reasoned, and it was the United States' association with them that also risked isolating it, leaving the nationalists masters of the area. How much longer the Americans could afford politically, economically, or even militarily to cooperate closely with Britain was very much in doubt as the liabilities of the alliance began to outweigh an independent strategy.

At the end of 1950 the NSC began a study "possibly to reorient somewhat our political, economic, and military programs in the . . . area." Britain had abdicated the primary defense responsibilities in the region, it felt, leaving U.S. bases and interests in Saudi Arabia and the Gulf exposed. Roles and obligations had become very confused because, as the NSC concluded in February 1951, British power was "declining" politically and in every other domain as well.[3] During early 1951 both the CIA and all U.S. diplomats working in the region agreed that Britain had been fatally weakened, could not defend Western interests adequately, and was less devoted to genuine equality with America than assuming the role of a "senior" partner.[4] "Oil is the most important single factor in United States relations with the area," the diplomats concluded, and most of the internal Communist problems required only stronger "police controls."[5] Stability would come most quickly if British oil firms would raise royalties to U.S. standards with the Saudis.

This growing general confrontation between the United States and Britain for hegemony in the region continued simmering throughout 1951, the inexorable logic of U.S. power and ambitions and Britain's eclipse, but Dean Acheson is nonetheless partially justified in his later recollection that "in an unplanned, undesired, and haphazard way American influence had largely succeeded French and British in that part of the world."[6] Abstractly, Washington unquestionably opposed the total elimination of Britain's strength and authority and still preferred a regional alliance. The problem was that every one of its concrete steps undercut the British so that their ability and incentive to play their assigned role diminished with every year. During 1951 the increasingly tense allies quibbled over whether an American should be appointed NATO commander in the Mediterranean, swinging the Pentagon behind those who believed Britain's value was sinking. As the British "diddled," in Acheson's term, their adamancy infuriated America's leaders, and at the end of 1951 the NSC began groping for "a new basis and a new kind of relationship with the Middle Eastern states" that took into account "the declining ability of the U.K. to maintain and defend Western interests in the Middle East."[7] The dilemma, as U.S. advisers argued from this point onward, was that America by itself still retained much goodwill in the region, and restive, largely middle-class and officer-led nationalism was anti-British but also anti-Soviet. The rapid demise of British power and the hesitancy of the United States to help fill the vacuum created instability that might lead to a loss of American access to oil and to neutralism—all without any Russian action. Whatever the short-term gains of the alliance with Britain, they concluded, in the long run the U.S. would be best off not identified with it. With the gap between its initial postwar premises and realities too wide to ignore, the Truman Administration now began to move more aggressively into the space Britain's weakness had created.

While it left the final resolution of the crisis emerging in Iran to its successors, in Egypt, the very place the British planned to concentrate their regional strength, the Truman Administration actively defined events when fighting broke out between British and Egyptian forces at the end of January 1952 after the British dismissed Cairo's demand that they withdraw their troops from the canal zone, thereby threatening to create uncontrollable xenophobic anti-Western upheavals. The immediate object of its efforts was the key nationalist officers, who were ready to deal with Kermit Roosevelt, head of the CIA operation, for their own ends. Roosevelt convinced King Farouk, whose past role as Britain's vassal was more of a liability for the United States than his notorious corruption and orgies, to fire the ministers on whom his power depended and replace them with General Naguib el-Hilali as prime minister. But Farouk could not be reformed, and in May the U.S. embassy and the CIA decided to help remove him, the last bastion of British influence, in order to reorganize the chaotic, corrupt nation. On July 22–23 a coup took place, with Naguib as its nominal head but in reality as a front for a group of colonels led by Gamal Abdel Nasser. The United States always knew that Nasser would be the true power behind the throne, but in Acheson's words, the "change appeared to us as mildly encouraging."[8]

The United States immediately began to deal directly with Nasser and helped him to consolidate power by sending him advisers, including former Nazi generals to assist him to modernize his army. A "private understanding that the preconditions for democratic government did not exist and wouldn't exist for many years" had been reached with Nasser beforehand, since the United States wanted a period of discipline to purge the nation of inherited faults, a State Department consultant on Egypt later recalled, and for several more years Washington felt satisfied with its first major action in implementing its new Middle Eastern policy.[9] For practical purposes, the United States had virtually displaced British influence in the nation strategically most important to it in the Middle East. It had also helped decisively to bring Nasser to the head of a vital state, the consequences of which Americans scarcely predicted.

THE IRANIAN CRISIS

All that Britain had left of major significance in the Middle East after the Egyptian coup was its claim to the control of the Iranian oil fields, and by 1951 even this had become tenuous. Indeed, from Britain's viewpoint it was soon to become apparent that the United States was intent on pushing it aside there as well, though in fact U.S. policy and actions were exceedingly convoluted because in that extremely complex local environment the Truman Administration sought to apply its increasingly schizophrenic policy of both fostering Britain's military presence and supplanting its influence in the region.

Iran after 1945 was a thoroughly anti-Russian state, and the young Shah was committed to encouraging a greatly increased U.S. role in the area both to offset British and Soviet strength and to modernize the army, on which his power depended. More important, Iran was going through a deep political and economic crisis that pitted the Shah against rising urban middle-class elements who also wished rather vaguely to modernize Iran along conventional Western bourgeois lines. Whatever their differences, both tendencies agreed that money was essential to bail Iran out of its nearly bankrupt condition and that the Anglo-Iranian Oil Company (AIOC), which had the concession on its oil and was owned by the British Admiralty, should provide much more of it. This national consensus transcended the immediate political rivalries in the long run, but after 1949 politics obscured this reality as factions sought to exploit the nationalist euphoria the oil issue provoked. From the U.S. viewpoint, however, both sides were anti-Communist, and the only real issue initially was the future of British power—which, in any event, it increasingly saw as in eclipse.

When the U.S. oil firms during 1950 agreed to give Saudi Arabia a fifty-fifty split on its oil, American officials had predicted that the Iranians, who had been negotiating terms with the AIOC since mid-1949, would increase their demands also. A coalition of nationalist groups in the Majlis (parliament), led by Dr. Mohammed Mossadegh, throughout 1950 made oil the all-consuming issue in Iranian politics—one the wily, opportunistic Mossadegh was prepared to exploit. He was a European-educated, aristocratic landlord who was both an anti-Communist and devoid of any social reform program. The fact that he wished to aid mainly the urban middle classes also meant that Mossadegh had no mass base unless he could appeal to a nationalism whose main obsession was English domination. It was for good reason that Americans on the scene thought he was capable of playing a useful role. By November 1950, when Mossadegh's committee in the Majlis called for nationalization of the AIOC, the State Department was furious with the British for ignoring its appeals to make concessions and defuse the issue. When the British in early 1951 finally agreed to fifty-fifty to forestall nationalization, it was too late, and after the assassination of the moderate prime minister on March 7 the Majlis proceeded to nationalize the AIOC, the next month electing Mossadegh prime minister.

The British responded haughtily to Iranian demands from the inception, spurning even their right to have simple information on AIOC's operations, and by March 1951 the U.S. ambassador in Tehran, Henry F. Grady, thought their representatives "self-righteous and arrogant."[10] Their aloof disdain, cast in the purest imperialist tradition, continued until the end, but the entire U.S. government was hostile toward the British, and it was only the loyal support of the American oil companies for the AIOC that prevented an even sterner official policy. The Pentagon, above all, feared that Iran would be pushed into neutralism. The geopolitical implications of this as well as the loss of oil seemed far more crucial to the military than Britain's interests. No American official favored allowing what they saw, in Acheson's words, as "the unusual and persistent stupidity" of the British to damage the United States' standing in the region, and after the AIOC nationalization Washington advised London to accept the principle but to be certain they controlled the new company's administration and output.[11] By May U.S. priorities, in order of importance, were to prevent armed conflict between the British and Iranians, which might then bring the Russians into the north of Iran but at the least destroy the position of the entire West in the region, to keep Iran on the side of the West, sustain the flow of oil, and, last, protect the sanctity of concession rights in Iran and the world. Mossadegh, the State Department knew, was anti-Russian, and they moved to shape his policies in ways the British justifiably deemed hostile. In July, Averell Harriman was sent to Tehran and London to mediate, which the British quite correctly saw as encouraging the Iranians to remain adamant until U.S. pressure forced them to make concessions. But American action was calculated, above all, to prevent Britain from using boats and land forces it had positioned in the gulf, and in this it succeeded. Mossadegh himself came to the United States the following fall and convinced Washington that a compromise was possible and that the failure to reach one was largely Britain's responsibility.

Its options exhausted and the British adamant, given the context of other regional problems the United States resolved to move toward a more independent Middle East policy, but it was reluctant at the same time to undercut the British completely in Iran as well as in Egypt. Increasingly unhappy with this stand, for much of early 1952 the United States publicly supported the British position, reducing its economic aid to Iran and halting military aid entirely. By July, with the Iranian economy in disorder and discontent strengthening the following of the Communist Tudeh Party, the United States was ready to press again for a compromise. During protracted negotiations it offered Iran a one-hundred-million-dollar advance if it accepted an arrangement that would have allowed U.S. firms to handle its oil, thereby convincing Mossadegh that he could play America against Britain—and causing the British to complain bitterly to Washington. As antitrust impediments to the U.S. oil giants entering Iran were removed, smaller U.S. companies were allowed publicly to buy Iranian oil to buoy up the bankrupt nation slipping quickly down a precipice that carried, in Acheson's words, "the gravest risk of having Iran disappear behind the Iron Curtain and the whole military and political situation in the Middle East change adversely to us."[12] In November a thoroughly worried White House decided to make available one hundred million dollars to buy Iranian oil, in addition to American loans and private purchases, if Britain would agree to a settlement. Mossadegh, no less afraid of the turmoil within his nation and eager to hold on to American goodwill, seemed in Washington's opinion most conciliatory, but the British refused to consider the matter and so no progress was made.

The British, as the Administration feared, would make no concessions to Mossadegh because they wished to see his government removed, a goal they fixed upon no later than the fall of 1951. They believed that Mossadegh had no mass base and that rather than head off the Tudeh he would increasingly have to rely on it for support in the streets as he rode roughshod over opposition, which was precisely what his opportunism caused him to do. The British solution was for the Shah's position to be strengthened, along with that of the military, which was his main base of power. In November 1952, certain the Democrats would be defeated in the election and that nothing more should be done before they could determine the Republican mood, the British approached Kermit Roosevelt of the CIA and proposed a joint effort to overthrow Mossadegh. Roosevelt informed them the Democrats would reject the idea but that the Republicans might prove receptive, and so London bided its time.

For the new Republican Administration the question of Iran posed two challenges. The most obvious one, to which most attention has been paid, was the nature of the Mossadegh regime, which was in early 1953 both politically and economically in a grave internal crisis. By that time he had managed to alienate many of his earlier middle-class followers and, isolated, he did indeed turn to the Tudeh for support in the streets—where a great deal of activity was now occurring. Mossadegh was unwilling to compromise with the British but unable to bring them to heel, so the Eisenhower Administration, which favored an activist CIA policy of preventive measures against deviant regimes, had no hesitation tentatively to authorize a joint project with the British to overthrow Mossadegh.

Even more important, however, was the new Administration's plans for Britain's future role in the region, and here the president shared completely the view of his predecessors that collaboration as equals was no longer useful. The partnership of World War Two could not be reactivated, Eisenhower noted in his diary in early January 1953 after berating Churchill personally on his handling of Iran. Nationalism was on the march, and for the United States to be associated too closely with British resistance to it would allow Russia to exploit the movement. Whatever the outcome of prior consultations, Eisenhower believed, "It will be far better for us to proceed independently toward the solution of knotty problems."[13] It would be one thing to work with the British to throw Mossadegh out of office but quite another to give them what they wanted afterward.

While plotting for a possible CIA coup went forward, the United States and Britain continued to disagree on the same Iranian problems that had separated them under the Democrats, and for exactly the same reasons. The renewal of aid, sending U.S. technicians and equipment to maintain Iran's refineries to supply their new Japanese and Italian customers—all these possibilities kept the Anglo-Americans divided until June 22, when Washington gave the coup scheme its final approval. The decision to act was based on the fact that Mossadegh in his bid to take total power was losing followers, had alienated deeply the military, and in order to create leverage for his new goals had set loose street mobs whom he could not, ultimately, control.

The coup itself succeeded not because of the CIA's cunning but because Mossadegh had managed to alienate most of those with power while remaining incapable of organizing those, principally the masses, who had none. For while the relatively small Tudeh could bring numbers out on the streets, it was unable to defend a demagogic aristocrat who had no social program. The coup scenario began on August 12 when the Shah, who was already on his

way out of the country, issued a decree firing Mossadegh, which merely led
to the arrest of a few of the Shah's supporters. While Mossadegh's forces
hesitated, the army spontaneously took over the Tehran streets in a pro-Shah
coup of its own even as the CIA was ordering its plan aborted as a failure.
The Mossadegh regime had been a house of cards, likely soon to fall in any
case, and when the CIA reactivated its operation the demise of Mossadegh
was a matter of a few days—he ending in jail while the Tudeh's leaders were
rounded up for execution or prison. But it was one thing for Washington to
help the British throw Mossadegh out of office, quite another to help them
to get back their oil.

The problem was that no one in Iran favored Britain's return, the Shah
above all because the keystone of his foreign policy before and surely after
this period was to align Iran with the United States. Mossadegh's failure was
not due to his anti-British stance, much less to his advocacy of nationalization, but to his political style and ineptness. The British saw all this quite
clearly, realizing that America could easily replace not only its future influence in Iran but also, more important, its control of oil. As early as November
1951, to forestall these risks, they had offered the United States participation
in Iran's fields once they were returned, but Washington demurred and
waited for a more opportune time. The issue involved the basic question of
the ambiguous relationship between the two nations as friends and rivals in
the Middle East, and since the Democrats and Republicans shared one view
on it, it was a matter of prime significance when the need to negotiate the
oil dispute arose after August 1953.

Roosevelt, acting officially, had told the Shah that his cooperation in the
coup left him "under *no* obligation. Not on petroleum, nor on anything
else."[14] The State Department, which had removed antitrust obstacles to
American firms participating in Iranian oil, in September 1953 began approaching U.S. oil giants to discuss a new company that might buy out AIOC.
The oil companies hesitated, and the British complained. But neither the
Iranians nor the British would settle, and a forty-five-million-dollar U.S. grant
to Iran in September allowed the former some leverage. At the end of 1953
the NSC, aware that the new regime looked to America for "counsel and aid,"
concluded that the danger of communism in Iran would return should the
oil revenues not start flowing.[15] It gave the British until July 1954 to settle, or
the Americans would arrange to sell Iran's oil independently. The United
States was ready to consult with London but not to allow it to veto essential
action.

The Iranians wisely hired the former chairman of Texaco to advise them,
while Washington's own representative to the negotiations, Herbert Hoover,
Jr., had worked for major American oil firms. The talks went badly, and by
early spring Dulles was furious, and both he and the Administration believed

the British "do not have [a] very good title."[16] They thought the British were attempting to get twice as much as was fair, but after bitter disputes and threats an accord was finally reached in August. Its main provisions left a nominally nationalized oil company that granted a new Western firm full rights to manage its output and prices with a fifty-fifty split in profits. Even the Shah disliked this arrangement, but he could do nothing about it. Ostensibly to provide the new firm with access to a world market from which Iranian oil had been barred and supplanted for four years, five U.S. giants were each given 8 percent interest in the firm—or 40 percent combined—in return for 32 million pounds immediately and 182 million pounds over the next twenty years. It was the best that the British, who came close to ending with nothing from both Mossadegh and then the Americans, could get—and they appreciated this full well. As for the Iranians, their fragile interlude with parliamentary politics had come to an end, with an absolute monarchy emerging in its place. The Americans, for their part, now had political hegemony in Iran and a large interest in its oil. A major shift in the overall balance of power in the region had occurred, and the extent to which it would continue remained an open question in Anglo-American relations. Unresolved, too, was the issue of what obligations as well as rewards for the United States came with its rapidly evolving replacement of British power.

THE MIDDLE EASTERN CONUNDRUM

The Middle East after the Second World War was undergoing a profound and accelerating transition away from its diverse traditional political and social orders, which made it not only inherently unstable but also exceedingly complex for the United States to relate to. These changes generally undermined Britain's historic domination of the region and were inevitable regardless of anything America might do. No portion of the Third World was as socially and politically complicated as the vast zone stretching from Iran to the eastern Mediterranean. Ultimately these dynamics had far less to do with the role of internal Communist parties—which were mainly inconsequential—than in any other area. This fact alone meant that U.S. policies focused much more on the positions and interests of its British and French allies than elsewhere, making Anglo-American, rather than U.S.-Soviet, relations far more significant. Within this context American decisionmakers had to deal with the social dynamics of the very real but still uneven pace of change in each of the zone's countries. And while the United States was able to gain successes for itself, eventually it, too, was to discover that the labyrinthine forces operating in the region transcended its ability to control.

The Middle East's political and class structures alone guaranteed instability. The traditional elites of the area comprised the monarchies, which ruled ten of the seventeen nations from Morocco to Pakistan in 1951, and a commercial bourgeoisie that was overwhelmingly made up of ethnically marginal elements: Jews, numerous Christians from diverse sects, Greeks, Palestinian Muslims who were recent migrants, and the like. These local capitalists had no loyalty to the nation in which they lived, were highly mobile, and both their commercial basis and intrinsic marginality made them incapable of introducing major industrial economic innovations that might modernize the agrarian societies they exploited. British power, to a great extent, depended on such traditional political and economic constituencies, and by 1945 what Manfred Halpern has called a "new middle class" had begun to challenge the inherited orders in most Middle Eastern states.[17]

The class origins of this rising new element guaranteed that its dominant ideological expression would be nationalistic, and while this made largely anti-British sentiment axiomatic, at the same time it also assured that unlike the rest of the Third World, Marxism's influence would be negligible. Generally the children of professionals, state functionaries, or officers rather than the petit bourgeois or landed elite, they, too, pursued these occupations. Ready and capable to exploit the masses politically, the latter remained as unrepresented and invisible in the changed politics of the area as under the traditional rulers. While many from this new middle class entered the officer corps, whose growth was more rapid than that of the civilian sectors and whose ranks did not attract sons of the traditional elite, their ideas merely paralleled those of their peers not in the army but of the same social background, and the military was the product and instrument of the new elite rather than the reverse. Both were well trained, administratively talented, and proponents of modernization in ways that undermined radically the power of the traditional rulers. Their access to guns made them capable successfully to aspire to power, and despite the failure of most of the thirty military coups since 1930, by 1962 the military already ruled five of these countries and the monarchies had been reduced to six in number. This admixture of tradition, embodying Islam as well as monarchial societies, anti-Marxism, and a rising middle class's syncretic ideologies all defined the development of the region in ways that were altogether unique.

Perhaps most disorienting to the United States was this ascendent class's rhetoric, which concocted doctrines that were often both confused and confusing. Ultranationalist, it also tended to be committed to a strong state economic sector because the ephemeral nature of the local commercial bourgeoisie historically had required, even in reactionary states, that capital investments come primarily from the government—or no one. But whatever the rhetoric, such middle-class leaders were and have been eminently conservative in administering various forms of state capitalism. At the same time, their relationship to Islam has been uncomfortable and often ambiguous, not the least because Islam alone had the potential to reach the masses in ways that Marxist parties have been incapable of doing.

In the 1950s, such dynamic changes in the Arab world were quickly undermining the historic monarchial and traditional foundations of British domination, thereby opening the way for the entry of American influence. During 1951, indeed, State Department Middle East analysts had begun to study this new middle class, and many regarded it as a positive element against the atavistic forces that Britain had sustained for generations. The fact that it was both anti-Soviet as well as anti-British made support for it enticing, but other American experts doubted that aligning unreservedly with them was the best way to advance U.S. interests, if only because Washington also was ready uncritically to sustain royalist regimes in Saudi Arabia and the Gulf that acceded to its desires. In the end, as Iran demonstrated, American policy proved almost as convoluted as modernizing Arab nationalism itself, opportunistically exploiting nationalism and the new middle classes against the USSR and Britain while never precluding working with reactionary elements. Such self-serving pragmatism explains why virtually every British leader who has written about U.S. policy in the region in the 1950s has bitterly portrayed it as primarily anti-British both in motive and in consequence.

It was in this context that the United States backed Nasser during his first years in power and avoided a too-close identification with British plans in the area. American approval did not include significant economic and military aid until November 1954, immediately after Egypt made a statement of support for the West and signed an agreement with Britain governing the removal of British troops in the Suez Canal Zone but also allowing them to return in case of war. Nasser had also removed Naguib from the presidency during November, and Nasser was desperate to consolidate his domestic following lest he, too, lose a grip on power. Foreign aid was indispensable toward that end. But he refused to get drawn into the diverse proposals for a regional military pact the British began to sponsor and that Washington regarded with mixed feelings.

The British themselves saw a military alliance of "northern tier" states bordering the USSR as a way of bolstering their interests in the region at a time when their forces were being reduced dramatically. A treaty between Turkey and Iraq was signed in February 1955, and London tried to get the United States to join, believing that the success of what was to become the Baghdad Pact required it. While Pakistan and Iran joined the wholly innocuous symbolic gesture on Britain's part, the United States adamantly refused to become more than an observer.

Dulles was extremely irritated at the aggressive, unilateral British leadership in producing the alliance, however hopelessly impotent it was, though in principle he favored anti-Soviet treaties. Nasser, on the other hand, had made it abundantly clear that while he was pro-Western he also intended being neutral in the Cold War insofar as pacts were concerned. The British-led alliance of the region's reactionary states offended his mounting national-istic pretensions in the area. At this time Dulles and the Administration were convinced that he was justified. As British foreign secretary Selwyn Lloyd later described it, Dulles did not want "to incur the hostility of Nasser and those in other Arab states who thought as Nasser did."[18] It had become clear after 1950 that the mounting economic and political tension between Britain and the United States would also lead to profound differences on how to relate to rival factions within states as well as to the larger forces of an exceedingly fluid nationalism and middle-class-inspired change growing in importance throughout the region. This emerging Anglo-American conflict of interests and strategies in an increasingly unstable setting produced the context for the final elimination of British power in the Middle East that was to occur with the Suez crisis of November 1956.

THE SUEZ CRISIS AND THE END OF BRITISH POWER

By 1956 U.S. policy in the Near East was firmly committed to replacing British hegemony over the region with its own, and the Administration's immediate estimates of how they might help to accomplish this primary objective tended to color profoundly its responses to the emerging forces of national-ism, the new middle class, and even neutralism. Notwithstanding a division within the American government on how to react to these destabilizing factors in the Arab world, even those who were hostile toward the ideas Nasser best typified—and they were the majority in high places—were ready opportunistically to deal with them whenever a gain could be made. The question of Russia, much less Communism, within the Arab nations was not a major concern to the United States before 1957.

Everyone in Washington from late 1954 until the spring of 1956 knew that Nasser was most concerned with consolidating his precarious domestic posi-tion, and they repeatedly (and correctly) interpreted his foreign policy and efforts to obtain aid in this light. Nearly all of the United States' specialists wanted to see Nasser survive, and its ambassadors to Cairo throughout this period shared the view that if American aid was not forthcoming the risk of a return to the old order—and British supremacy—was reasonably great. They also understood that the large majority of the region's educated Arabs and the new middle class were neutral in the Cold War, the implications of which were initially far greater for Britain than for the United States.

Nasser's confidence that he could parlay a neutralist foreign policy, mainly anti-British in emphasis, to get both aid for his domestic goals as well as to buttress his pretensions to lead the Arab world's foreign policy was greatly reinforced when he received a desperately needed $40 million American economic aid grant in November 1954 despite his refusal to meet U.S. demands on regional defense matters. He knew, too, that the new American ambassador in Cairo, Henry Byroade, was urging the State Department to give him military aid on his own conditions and indeed represented him as the best bet in the long run against both Britain and Russia. Washington was less certain of this and delayed a twenty-million-dollar military aid grant. In the summer of 1955 Nasser let it be known that unless the United States acted quickly he would get arms from the Soviet bloc. However angry the Administration was when Egypt announced a large purchase of arms from Czechoslovakia on September 27, given Saudi Arabia's political and financial support for Nasser at this time it could not turn against him. Both the British and American governments understood perfectly well that Nasser was attempting, in British foreign secretary Harold Macmillan's words, to "induce both the West and the Soviets to bid up each other's price."[19] Dulles, too, shared the view that "it is a risk we are taking but . . . we have to."[20]

The outcome was that both Britain and America decided to up the ante by funding the huge Aswan dam irrigation project to forestall rumors that the USSR might sponsor it if they hesitated, and London was especially eager to do so because it thought that Russians working on the Aswan enterprise might extend Soviet influence to Africa for the first time. In mid-December the British and Americans, in conjunction with the World Bank, offered Egypt four hundred million dollars for the Aswan scheme—a gesture that not only greatly assisted Nasser in consolidating power at home but also confirmed his belief that an independent foreign policy and playing the East against the West paid far greater dividends than slavish support for either.

Thus encouraged, Nasser overextended his hand and deeply offended the U.S. government, which nevertheless retained an ambiguous attitude toward his regional nationalist aspirations. On one hand, as Selwyn Lloyd accurately described it, "there was in many American hearts a dislike of colonialism, a resentment of any authority left to us from the great days of our Empire, and a pleasure, only half-concealed, at seeing us done down."[21] On the other, as Dulles confided, "we are sympathetic with whatever action Nasser reasonably takes to emphasize genuine independence of Egypt," but there was a limit, and it was reached when Cairo recognized China on May 16, 1956.[22]

Egypt's gesture alienated the Administration deeply, but even more important it galvanized the Taiwan and Israel lobbies in Congress into a common bloc able to halt the funds for Aswan. The Americans had never been enthusiastic about Aswan, the British had pushed them into it, and with a presidential election just four months away, the United States on July 19 unilaterally canceled the Aswan Dam loan. Dulles, Robert Murphy later recalled, "never told explicitly why he acted so abruptly," and "the effects of summarily withdrawing the Aswan offer had not been weighed carefully in advance."[23] It was the British, who were informed officially of the decision only a few hours before the public announcement and never consulted as to their advice, who now had to confront the quite predictable consequences, the least of which was that the Soviet Union agreed to fund the project. For Nasser could not afford, either at home or in the Arab world, to remain passive. Quite predictably, he seized and nationalized the Suez Canal a week later. The British reaction, as Anthony Nutting, who was to resign as minister of state for foreign affairs over Suez later wrote, "bordered on panic and hysteria."[24] Suez was essential to Britain's lifeline to the Persian Gulf, Asia, and the Pacific, and given Britain's dramatic decline since 1945, it simply could not afford patiently to absorb such a decisive blow to its position in the world economy. Having already begun aggressively to undermine the remaining governments in the region friendly to it, Nasser had militarily and politically assaulted Britain's imperialist pretensions as well.

Many participants have already produced detailed accounts of the Suez crisis, but Prime Minister Anthony Eden's judgment that "The course of the Suez Canal crisis was decided by the American attitude toward it" is unquestionably accurate.[25] From its inception, the British problem was that they did not know what Washington's policy really was, and they naïvely misread its initial opposition to the nationalization of the canal as approval for the increasingly forceful actions they and the French were to consider. But even before Dulles flew to London on July 31 and gave the British and French encouragement that Nutting called "unwise and dangerous," and appeared ready also to isolate Nasser, Dulles and Eisenhower had concluded that the Anglo-French desire to act strongly was symbolic: for the French it was their worries about its "grave repercussions in North Africa," and for the British "their position in other countries."[26] Given the election pending, the Republicans were also resolved not to appear as defenders of "French colonialism."[27] Dulles, by contrast, never felt he had committed the United States to joint action with its allies. Until September 3, in any case, the British believed that Washington would support eventual Anglo-French use of force if peaceful efforts failed, as they consistently did during August in large part because of lackadaisical American support for all the alternatives being offered. U.S. insistence on a negotiated resolution of the dispute from that time onward, the British justifiably argued, reinforced Nasser's obduracy—but by early September Dulles was ready to downplay the Suez's importance and in early October publicly admitted there were fundamental differences between his government and its allies. The White House would not identify too closely with colonialism. The alliance, Dulles stated in so many words, would be united on purely European questions only.

As the election drew closer, the Administration created more and more obstacles for its allies, the effect of which was to harden Nasser's position. When Israel attacked Egypt on October 29 as the first stage of the Anglo-French invasion of the canal zone, Eisenhower and Dulles were furious and reiterated, more forcefully than ever, that they do "not want to be associated with them in the Arab world," unanimously condemned the attack, and presented a UN Security Council resolution against the use of force that the British and French vetoed.[28] The election aside, the Administration feared that Nasser would be driven into the Russian camp in some vital way at the very moment the Soviet invasion of Hungary had caused Moscow's international prestige to collapse. No less important, they were angered that their European allies had failed to consult them, thereby challenging U.S. hegemony over them in matters crucial to itself, a point Eden was made to understand explicitly. America's cynicism after a long chain of unrelated actions, Eden recounts, had ended a true partnership, leaving "only the choice of parting, or a master and vassal relationship. . . ."[29]

The British had been all too slow to learn about their American associates, whom they had distinctly underrated, but Suez was the final lesson in their decade-long schooling in the Middle East. On December 3, they, the French, and the Israelis were compelled to agree to withdraw their forces from Egypt. The last half of 1956 represented the nadir of Anglo-American relations in the postwar period and the final demise of Britain's historic position in the Middle East. It meant also that the United States would define the West's role in the area without the intermediary role of Britain to insulate it from those unstable new forces of nationalism now coming to fruition. Everything the United States had done in the Near East since 1945 had worked toward imposing its hegemony, and Washington always comprehended the direction of its broad policy; it did not, however, envision its ultimate consequences for its own obligations—and risks.

The American position, Britain's leaders believed then and afterward, was treacherous, having created a crisis without consultation. They saw the U.S. diplomats working on the region as "anti-British" in some cases, with a "mixture of anti-colonialism and hard-headed oil tycoonery," or as callously concerned only with their own interests—which in 1956 meant, at least for Eisenhower, not doing anything that could cost him the forthcoming election.[30] Dulles, at best, was neutral toward the fate of his closest allies, and he and Eden, who resigned as prime minister because of the crisis, "were to end up"—as Nutting phrased it—"as the bitterest of enemies."[31] American leaders, for their part, believed that Eden "had not adjusted his thoughts to the altered world status of Great Britain," and many regarded him as "slippery." "The material interest of the United States was not identical with that of either France or the United Kingdom," Murphy later observed, and "Eisenhower was determined not to have the United States used as a cat's paw to protect British oil interests."[32]

THE EISENHOWER DOCTRINE AND THE NEW MIDDLE EAST EQUATION

The Suez crisis led to the termination of the already tattered Anglo-American alliance in the Middle East and the U.S. assumption, for practical purposes, of the virtually complete Western self-appointed responsibility for regulating the affairs of the area, and it was the first time since 1945 that a major Third World region shed European domination entirely and allowed an open field to the Americans. Neither in Asia nor Africa had such a fundamental transfer of authority yet occurred, and the main explanation for it was both the triumph of the United States' aggressive oil policy, which gave it a unique incentive to succeed, and widespread forces of nationalism, which by undermining British power greatly eliminated the main barrier to America's triumph. U.S. priorities still stressed a Europe-first, NATO-oriented global policy. But while this vision was an inhibition to its ambitions in Asia and Africa, in the Middle East it chose to ignore the restraints that such a commitment might have created in order to exploit the weaknesses of its most important European ally. And since the stakes were economic rather than strategic, for the Soviet Union in no way threatened the area, the materialist foundations of Washington's policy were revealed in a quite incontrovertible manner.

The problem after Suez, obviously, was that just as Arab nationalism had earlier posed a threat to Britain, the United States now had to attempt to control and shape Arab nationalism's and Islam's complex, diverse, and mercurial nature and avoid assuming the role of its new principal enemy. This task became, and remains more than ever, one of the great postwar challenges confronting the United States, one that was the inevitable outcome of its own desire for economic domination and initially had virtually nothing to do with countering the USSR.

At the end of 1956 both Dulles and Eisenhower perceived the magnitude of the new power equation in the Middle East, and without consulting the experts in the State Department, the Pentagon, or the CIA, who later deemed it an incomprehensible error, decided to proclaim the so-called Eisenhower Doctrine. During January 1957 the president discussed it with members of Congress and then asked them to pass a joint resolution. In it the president was authorized to assist nations of the region economically as well as to use

U.S. armed forces "to secure and protect the territorial integrity" of any nation requesting help "against overt armed aggression from any nation controlled by international communism."[33] "The United States appears as the self-appointed policeman and patron of the Middle East," as a staunch defender of its mission explained it.[34] The problem, which greatly embarrassed those in Washington dealing with the region, was that the resolution was aimed at Nasser, who was not by any criterion a Communist. The only challenge the U.S. confronted in 1957 came from the very same forces it had exploited to remove Britain's influence.

"For a variety of reasons," Dulles coyly told the Senate, "certain Western European nations" could no longer deter Communist aggression. When pressed, the State Department had to admit that no state in the region was under "international communist" domination, nor was there any imminent danger of a Communist coup. There was, nonetheless, Dulles warned, now "the most serious threat that we have faced over the past 10 years." Nasser and Arab nationalism, the Administration's principal concerns, were the real objectives of the new doctrine and the main obstacles to the consolidation of U.S. power. Toward the end of the hearings, when former ambassador Jefferson Caffery testified, he wryly noted that Nasser had outlawed the Communist Party and put its leaders in jail. Nasser was ambitious, of course, but "when I was there, he was extremely, extremely cooperative."[35] The Middle East, obviously, was a very complex place.

For much of 1957 and 1958 the United States worked energetically at making an enemy out of a former friend. And for the first time, in a self-fulfilling prophecy, it produced a political vacuum that indeed now made it possible for the Russians to play a much more important role in the area's geopolitics. If stability were the criterion of success, neither Nasser nor the U.S. Army could provide it, for virtually every nation in the region with any degree of literacy was in the process of change, internecine political struggles, cabals, and much else. In Lebanon there was no end to the age-old struggle among the many Christian and Muslim sects, which was intensifying again. Even in Jordan, the British were cut off as arms suppliers and Egypt, Syria, and Saudi Arabia became King Hussein's protectors. At the beginning of 1957 a pro-Egyptian element in the Syrian Army and in the middle-class, socialist, but very anti-Communist Baath Party came to power, soon to be challenged once again by the antireform, conservative Independent Party, which began successfully to outflank it by calling for better relations with and aid from the USSR—initiating a successful policy in August 1957 of exploitation of the Cold War that has kept Syria well supplied, and thoroughly non-Communist, to this day.

Nasser's influence in Syria and the entire Arab world mounted precisely because he had defied the Anglo-French and profited from the Cold War to augment aid to Egypt enormously. As the leadership of these Arab-speaking nations found that their domestic political struggles could not be resolved, they increasingly began to search for allies among their neighbors, and while pan-Arabism was one expression of this, collaboration among rightist regimes was another. While Syria represented the main challenge to the United States in 1957, causing Turkey and Iraq to threaten to partition it, the Eisenhower Doctrine did not prevent a continuous imbroglio within and among most of the Arab states: wars between Muscat and Oman in July 1957, Buraimi and Saudi Arabia at the same time, the rupture of the Jordan-Egyptian alliance in November, the mythical merger of Syria and Egypt into the United Arab Republic by February 1958, to be followed by an equally fictitious confederation of Jordan and Iraq the following March.

In a word, Britain's demise with Suez, the triumph of Nasser (with American aid), and the subsequent outpouring of Arab nationalism—and intrigues— created a far greater instability than the area had ever known. The vacuum the consistent American undermining of the British position since 1945 had created in the Near East had to be filled quickly or the U.S. victory would be chimerical at best and finally open the region to much greater Soviet participation in its geopolitics. The United States won its primacy in the Middle East at a time and in a fashion that presented it with incalculable problems and challenges, not the least of which was the perpetuation of its image as a nation with the power and wisdom to achieve the hegemony that had eluded its predecessors. But the sheer economic importance of the region guaranteed that Washington would make every effort to succeed in this vaguely defined and elusive objective.

The Eisenhower Administration convinced itself by the spring of 1958 that it must act soon to reverse the disorder spreading throughout the region. This time, because King Hussein of Jordan was among those Washington considered threatened, the British were consulted, and after serious sectarian fighting broke out in Lebanon in early May, largely in response to Christian president Camille Chamoun's effort to consolidate his power in the precariously balanced country, the United States announced on May 17 that if asked it would send troops to Lebanon. Planning for the operation with the British began immediately. Assurance of American salvation removed the incentive for Chamoun to negotiate with his numerous domestic rivals and guaranteed that turbulence in Lebanon would continue. As Dulles freely admitted, the "political situation in Lebanon is not simple. . . . it is extremely confusing."[36]

While the political troubles throughout the region were far more of a concern to Washington than the Lebanon crisis, more important yet was the Administration's intense, morbid obsession over its credibility in the area should friendly regimes, as Dulles put it, "think we lost our nerve and those govts will probably run to cover" by compromising with Nasser. Indeed, by mid-June Dulles had come to the pessimistic conclusion that "If we go in it will turn Arab sentiment against us. If we don't all the Arab countries which have pro-Western governments will be overthrown. . . . they will in any rate."[37] On July 14 there was a military coup in Iraq that destroyed the pro-British monarchy, and Eisenhower concluded that "it looks now as if you have a solid Arab world against us because Jordan can't stick."[38] To save the non-Arab nations on the edges of region, in his opinion, was perhaps as much as could be attained.

In a situation where its political objectives were extremely vague and from which the United States could only lose politically, when the first of its fourteen thousand troops landed peacefully in Lebanon on July 15, accompanied by atomic artillery, many in the Pentagon were skeptical about the outcome of such a palpably quixotic undertaking. Both Eisenhower and Dulles constantly reiterated that the political goal, at least primarily, was "to demonstrate in a timely and practical way that the United States was capable of supporting its friends."[39] The Iraqi revolution provided a politically necessary justification as a convenient afterthought, but it was entirely a coincidence rather than a cause. Credibility was the cause, and as U.S. soldiers found there was no one to shoot at and settled down comfortably on the beaches, the Administration's reasoning began to appear both highly dangerous and politically irrelevant. Dulles immediately had second thoughts and worried that the United States might "get bogged down like the Br in Suez and have to pull out."[40]

While British troops entered Jordan on July 17 and reinforced Hussein's power, events in Iraq escaped both America's and Nasser's control. Meanwhile, as the first U.S. troops were being withdrawn, by late August Dulles concluded that "the heart of the Arab world" was being lost to the United States.[41] The remaining soldiers were out of Lebanon by the end of October. The United States had not quite reenacted Suez, but it left Lebanon with its credibility far more tarnished than it had been at the beginning of the adventure, its position in the Arab world seriously damaged, and its capacity to guide events there in the manner it had hoped fatally undermined. Ultimately the most important lesson of its Lebanon debacle was that "credibility" as a symbolic mode of calculating its actions indeed had a powerful hold over America's leaders even in a situation where it knew that political realities preordained any action to be ridiculous or profoundly dangerous. In Lebanon it proved to be the former, but the fact that it possessed both unlimited weapons and political ambitions became an almost hypnotic fixation from this time onward, with credibility requiring extremely high-risk American policies and actions lest the leaders in Washington had to acknowledge that in a world of dynamic social, political, and economic forces, U.S. military strength and foreign policy goals were somehow pathetically irrelevant. Lebanon revealed this, but also that America's aspirations contained a demonic, irrational capacity consciously to ignore realities on behalf of obsessions such as credibility, which now had a life and force of their own in shaping its foreign policy.

The problem, which the Administration soon acknowledged in private, was that the complexity of Arab politics, whether within each nation or among them, transcended any outside state's capacity to master, and that the United States might be just as much a victim of the region's social and political dynamics as the British had been. It was obvious, too, that while Nasser's influence had risen, largely because British and American actions made him the region's only hero, he too was incapable of dominating the area's political currents. This was graphically revealed when Egypt's relations with Iraq began to deteriorate dramatically, so that on March 12, 1959, Nasser denounced General Abdul Karim Kassim's regime as "a Communist reign of terror."[42] Kassim, as the CIA itself admitted publicly in April 1959, was surely not a Communist; he refused to allow Communists in the government, and Russia itself seemed to have no control over them and was urging Kassim, who was now demanding economic and military aid Moscow could scarcely afford, to pursue a much more cautious line on oil nationalization than the local Communists were advocating. Iraq emerged as one of many national political mutations in the Arab world, each with its specific character and originality and quite beyond the control of either the United States or the Soviet Union, much less Nasser, who was merely the first and most charismatic leader of the army-backed new middle classes coming to power in the Arab world. All the two superpowers could be certain of doing was to pay handsomely for their pretensions to meddle into the affairs of the most mercurial, and dangerous, of all the Third World's regions as the Arab states began with mounting success to play one against the other while pursuing their own independent foreign policies.

The confusion and folly of its position soon compelled the Eisenhower Administration to return discreetly to its earlier strategy of treating Nasser as a useful, potentially cooperative force in the region. In March 1958 he intensified his repression against his own Communists, and on July 1 the first U.S. aid agreement since Suez was signed, for a mere eight million dollars. By the time the Eisenhower Administration left office, however, Nasser could boast of having received three hundred million dollars in American aid from it. Nothing more revealed the sheer pragmatism and opportunism that guided American policy throughout the 1950s, for Nasser was in fact a barrier to a Communist movement that loomed immeasurably larger in American imaginations than in reality. He had served Washington's purposes well against Britain. If he was a frustration to its mastery of the politics of the region, he was nonetheless only one of many in a part of the world in which instability and politics were synonymous. The Administration sensed full well that it could go no farther in the Middle East after 1958, despite the elimination of British interests, and that the better part of wisdom was to exploit the handsome advantages it had gained for its oil companies—and hope for the best.

Eisenhower later recalled that the region stabilized after 1958 and ceased to distract him, and Communists took power nowhere. In one crucial sense, however, the transfer of the dominant role in the Middle East from Britain to America throughout the 1950s, with all of its rich assets as well as obvious liabilities, was possible so quickly and easily because the Republican Administration was not friendly to Israel, and privately it was hostile—a fact the entire Arab world both understood and greatly appreciated. Congress, despite Dulles's and Eisenhower's resentment, was quite ready to give Israel modest amounts of economic aid in the form of grants and loans, largely because of the Zionist bloc's skill in mobilizing both Congress' ethnic voting coalition and the Democrats. But having triumphantly projected U.S. power into the region, it remained a very open question whether the Democrats, who were for political reasons obligated to be much friendlier to Israel, could avert the shoals of the Arab-Israeli conflict in the same manner, and if the U.S. policy in the region, after such great successes, could avoid becoming hostage to the quixotic fluctuations in American politics.

NORTH AFRICA AND AMERICAN PASSIVITY

In the western Mediterranean, where the United States had no direct interests comparable to those in the Near East, its position on French colonialism and the nationalist movement in North Africa—Morocco, Tunisia, and Algeria—conformed to the same Eurocentric priorities it applied throughout Africa. Unlike in the Middle East, Washington did nothing to undermine the French and British positions. But because North Africa was part of the Arab world, the issues there both embarrassed and frustrated the Eisenhower Administration with increasing frequency as they undermined its efforts in the Middle East.

The United States' main concern on the North African littoral, including Libya, was to keep its nations out of Communist hands, which became synonymous with preventing any radical nationalist groups from coming to power. The NSC's August 1953 policy was against "premature self-government" for Morocco and Tunisia, or anything that would undermine France's responsibility for the area. Reforms that "do not threaten essential French interests" were desirable.[43] In Libya, too, sustaining the British-French mastery of that kingdom was also firm policy. A year later, however, the CIA pointed out that protracted French resistance to nationalist demands in Morocco and Tunisia would only radicalize the independence movements, increasing France's reliance on military repression. It was troubled by the fact that if the United States encouraged the more moderate nationalists they would alienate the French, but should it remain silent, U.S. prestige in the Third World would suffer—and America's base in Morocco might eventually be endangered. This increasing concern over French intransigence and growing nationalist militancy caused the NSC to tilt slightly in late 1954 to more self-government in Morocco and Tunisia, but still within the framework of French hegemony. In the UN it loyally sustained France, despite considerable reservations. France was America's ally in Europe, and that relationship dominated its calculations. In Algeria, where a million Frenchmen lived, the United States consoled itself in 1954 that nationalism posed no threat, and it had no position on the French policy there beyond implicit support for it.

Events in Indochina and Suez had made the French exceedingly sensitive to American advice on North African affairs, and they were convinced that the United States would gladly supplant them there as well—if France permitted it. By late 1956 the Algerian rebellion had become France's preoccupation, until it deployed nearly three-quarters of a million soldiers there in a futile, brutal war that bled its economy and destabilized its political structure at home. France did accord Tunisia and Morocco a degree of autonomy while retaining economic and other controls, but the United States was deeply concerned that in Algeria a truly radical nationalist force, with both Egyptian and Soviet backing, might not so much take over as undermine France's usefulness to NATO and Europe's defense.

Whatever its mounting reservations over the French policy in the region, the Eisenhower Administration soon learned that even the slightest involvement or criticism drove the French government into paroxysms of fear and anger. In November 1957, when the United States offered Tunisia some rifles on condition they take none from Egypt, the French became enraged and warned the United States against "creating a grave crisis in Western solidarity" that might force France out of NATO.[44] What was a minor question of French prerogatives and symbolic domination now became for Dulles "a crisis of the first order," one that caused him to back down entirely.[45] The Eisenhower Administration privately criticized France's obstinacy, which it believed was radicalizing the nationalists and ultimately would endanger the West's position in North Africa, but it remained a docile hostage to France's threats on NATO. Publicly, while in Paris at the end of 1957 Dulles deplored the allegation "that we might replace French interests with American commercial interests. . . . the United States has no intention or desire whatsoever to interfere in the slightest with the normal relationships of France to North Africa."[46] The region was in fact assigned to the now much reduced French sphere of influence. Although the U.S. alliance with Europe in the eastern Mediterranean had been smashed definitively in 1956, on the western rim of the Arab world Washington's European priorities continued to determine its policies.

Latin America and the Challenge to U.S. Hegemony

*U*NTIL 1950, LATIN AMERICA WAS THE best example of how U.S. global preoccupations could relegate the Third World region most vital to it to scarcely more than a peripheral concern. Objectively, its southern neighbors were of incalculable value to its international position and power, but as long as the Left in the region was of marginal significance, the Truman Administration preferred to assign the numerous tensions and difficulties in relations with its neighbors to lesser State Department officials. Acheson's rare utterances or participation in meeting with the Latins always stayed, as he recounts, "within the conventional limitations of policy statements" and were "mostly for the purposes of reassurance" so that hemispheric issues could once more be discreetly shelved.[1] The Administration's continued adherence to the Good Neighbor Policy of nonintervention, for practical purposes, was largely the outcome of its indifference and distractions rather than an articulate commitment to the policy motives that had led to its creation in the early 1930s. The fact remained that until the Korean War the only serious challenges to U.S. hegemony in the hemisphere came from nationalist forces on the Right and Center, including much of the officer corps, and in Washington's view these hardly warranted great concern.

The Korean War forced Latin America into the U.S. vision to a slightly greater extent because it increased its dependency on its southern neighbors' resources, and throughout the decade troublesome social and economic trends in the region began to reinforce nationalism's political importance not only on the Right but also, for the first time, on the Left as well, for the 1950s became a decade of rapid transition in Latin America. If no major challenges or dramatic, difficult decisions confronted it for most of the period, save in Guatemala and Cuba, there was no doubt by the end of the decade that multiple challenges to its historic hegemony would require the United States to relate more actively to hemispheric issues.

THE MATERIAL FOUNDATIONS OF HEMISPHERIC RELATIONS

It was the economic basis of its relationship to Latin America that set the critical context for Washington's political and military policies, for in no other Third World area were reciprocal material linkages so comprehensive and important. If one seeks to estimate the importance of economics in U.S. interaction with the Third World during this decade, it is preeminently, although surely not exclusively, Latin America that justifies assigning it such great significance. This nexus was to intensify throughout the 1950s, not the least because as U.S. dependence on imports grew, so, too, did Latin America's value to it; for a far larger variety and quantity of essential raw materials for its industry came from there than any other region.

By the end of the 1950s primary products—agricultural products, metals, oil, and such—accounted for over 90 percent of Latin America's exports, and in 1958 sixteen of the twenty Latin nations were dependent on two or less products for at least half of their export earnings, thereby making their economies extremely vulnerable to fluctuations in world prices. While only 6 percent of Brazil's gross national product came from its exports, Venezuela's 40 percent was much closer to the norm for the region. The U.S. market during this decade, far more than before the war, absorbed from 42 to 50 percent of Latin exports, while generally over half of its imports came from the United States. Indeed, throughout the 1950s over a fifth of all U.S. world exports went to Latin America, while about a third of its imports came from there. Economically, it was more important to the United States than all the rest of the Third World combined.

U.S. officials dealing with the hemisphere at the beginning of the 1950s appreciated fully the region's value, which they believed would grow. Initially, their primary concern was to get it to produce more raw materials, but its role as a major outlet for investment was also very much on their minds—although these were interrelated in their calculations because U.S. firms operating there produced about a third of all Latin American exports sent north. Between 1950 and 1960 the book value of U.S. private investment in Latin America doubled to $9.2 billion, with minerals extraction attracting more of it than before, though the far more rapid growth of its investments in Europe and Canada reduced the region's proportion of total U.S. world investments from 39 to 28 percent over the same period.

Venezuela, rich in oil, was the most important investment target for U.S. firms, which accounted for fully 16 percent of its net national product in 1955. Cuba, generally the second biggest outlet, had U.S. companies producing 12 percent of its net national product. Major U.S. investments also existed in Brazil, Mexico, and Chile. The problem, economically as well as politically, was that what was called U.S. direct investment was scarcely that, for most of this capital comprised locally mobilized funds, reinvested retained earnings, and the like. In 1958 only 20 percent of the investments of U.S. manufacturing affiliates in Latin America that year consisted of funds sent from the United States—the average for later years also. Depending on the nature of their funding, profits for some companies were extremely high, far more for the typical firm than had they invested their money in the United States itself. Kennecott Copper's profits in Chile reached 40 percent during 1947–49, while Anaconda's was 12 percent. Postwar net earnings of U.S. manufacturing firms in Brazil as a percentage of book value peaked at 28 percent in 1951, averaging 15 percent during the 1950s. Profits on all U.S. investment in Latin America were 13.9 percent during 1951–55, 12.0 percent during 1956–58. But corporate profits in the United States during this eight-year period were only 7.8 percent.

Given such rewards and the imperative need for the region's raw materials, successive U.S. administrations expected private investors to develop essential industries in Latin America, precluding significant governmental aid. During 1949–52 the twenty Latin nations received $100 million in economic aid and $496 million in Export-Import Bank loans, but in 1953–60 Export-Import Bank loans amounted to $1.8 billion while another $1.3 billion, two-fifths in the form of loans, went for economic aid. Even military aid comprised only $317 million during 1953–59, a sum less than went to South Vietnam alone in the three years beginning in 1956. Economic aid to Latin America comprised less than 5 percent of the world total the United States distributed from 1949 to the end of the Eisenhower period. It was the one area of the Third World where U.S. business was to have a free field, with no place for sentimentality, and where nations were strongly encouraged to borrow at, or close to, commercial terms.

The result was that by 1955 Latin America had developed a substantial debt burden and loan servicing problem. In 1955 its $4 billion public debt comprised two-thirds of the Third World's total, and by 1960 it had reached $6.6 billion. Its debt service obligations, however, more than doubled, from $455 million in 1956 to $1 billion in 1960. Unable to gain the forms of aid that were given to other Third World regions or incapable of earning higher prices for their exports that would preclude the need for loans for development purposes, Latin America was in the process of falling into an economic pattern involving both growing debt and a greater dependence on the world export market that was unique in many crucial regards for the Third World. This trend guaranteed predictable social and political consequences that the United States would later be compelled to confront.

American policymakers understood fully the economic and political implications of the web of economic ties that bound the United States to its southern neighbors, and the Truman and Eisenhower administrations were of one mind on them. To attempt to substitute other sources of raw materials for Latin supplies, a State Department study concluded in October 1953, would double their cost to the United States, and loss of the hemisphere's output would be "a major security blow to the U.S."[2] Every NSC policy statement during the decade accepted this premise and argued that "adequate production . . . and access by the United States to . . . raw materials [was] essential to U.S. security." In vital ways all of its policies in the region, despite some variations, were to revolve around this central theme.[3]

As a result, we see Washington's litany in both its repetitive public statements and closed deliberations on private investment's crucial, essential role in developing Latin America's economies. And these ceaseless homilies not only proclaimed the absolute need to keep the door open to U.S. investors but also for local businessmen to be allowed full rein within the framework of systems that were capitalist in the classic sense of minimum government intervention; for Washington also saw the region as a giant arena for the application of its economic theories, the one place in the Third World where they could be implemented in a pure form without expedient concessions it was compelled to tolerate elsewhere because of the putative menace of the Left or the Soviet Union. And this vision, while ideological, was also eminently practical. For it was designed to guarantee the United States, both as a nation and as part of a hemispheric economy that integrated local private entrepreneurs, a vehicle for its interests in the form of a system that gave the United States access to an immensely rich continent, both greatly strengthening its prosperity at home and its ability to apply its power abroad.

Political difficulties that arose in the region were to a critical extent a by-product of the fact, as Assistant Secretary of State John M. Cabot phrased it in December 1953, that "our problems in our inter-American relations are largely economic, and they largely boil down to the question of how we are going to cooperate in the economic sphere to our mutual benefit." The United States did not deny the legal right of a nation to expropriate U.S. firms if it paid "prompt, adequate, and just compensation," Cabot put it starkly, but such nationalization was equivalent to the "undeniable sovereign right to declare war on any other nation. . . . the question of the treatment of foreign capital is not essentially one of right. . . . it is a question of what is fair, what is wise, what is practical, what is in the national interest, what will preserve the international comity."[4] Six months later this brutal definition found its first expression in the United States-organized overthrow of the Guatemala government.

For it was also the logic of the United States' hegemonic vision that, as an NSC report put it, "the self-interest of the Latin American countries is generally best served by cooperating with us."[5] And in the context of the entire decade, by far the largest obstacle to U.S. attainment of this relationship came not from the Left but from those nationalist political coalitions on the Right and in the Center that actually controlled state power and that had begun to disturb Washington after World War Two. For the U.S. vision was not based simply on preserving private property as the central institution of the area's nations, since that was also the goal of the diverse nationalist parties, but to create an integrated hemispheric economy to which the United States had essentially uninhibited access. Given the fact that the Left held little power throughout the decade, the primary issue was one of rival capitalisms—locally based as opposed to Yankee-dominated. In practical terms it was the difference between economic development oriented to the export of raw materials or toward diversified domestic economic growth and consumption.

Nationalism in Latin America assumed numerous forms, but the two most important expressions of it, in Argentina and Brazil, had a clearly elitist, largely urban leadership that in turn mobilized with populist slogans an essentially powerless mass base to resist challenges to it from the traditional oligarchies, who produced for the export market and whom they were displacing. Free trade had been the oligarchy's ideology, and the import-substitution strategies the Vargas regime in Brazil and Perón in Argentina promulgated required far less emphasis on exports in order to industrialize their nations and, at least for the middle class, expand the domestic market. Any latent radicalism from the masses, who appreciated the employment that came from these developments, was submerged in government-dominated unions, which became crucial vehicles for manipulating the people. Such nationalist strategies sponsored state-controlled sectors, but they also stimulated the growth of a national bourgeoisie that was symbiotic on the new economic structures—and eager to perpetuate them. In the many variations of such economies that emerged, sections of the military could often be found on the nationalist side. Anti-Yankee sentiment was both a by-product and a cause of the diverse nationalist movements, and it was on this issue alone that the populist Right and the relatively much smaller Left shared a consensus.

This growing nationalism agitated greatly those in Washington charged with hemispheric responsibilities, and their concern rose with the nationalist tide. The Truman Administration began to link "the siren song of extreme nationalism" to Communist agitation after 1952, a theme its successor continued, but everyone also knew that while the Communists endorsed it, they were scarcely its cause.[6] "To arrest the development of irresponsibility and extreme nationalism and their belief in their immunity from the exercise of United States power," in the words of an NSC report, increasingly became Washington's main policy objective as it concluded that "There is a trend in Latin America toward nationalistic regimes maintained in large part by appeals to the masses. . . ."[7]

But since these troublesome governments were also extremely anti-Communist, they supported the United States quite loyally in the United Nations on nonhemispheric questions, in return for which they frequently demanded economic concessions in the forms of aid, loans, and much else, greatly annoying Washington in the process—which gave them very little and insisted they place their confidence in U.S. investors. Largely to placate such pressures and counteract the trend away from the United States' free trade design, President Eisenhower sent his brother Milton touring Latin America in mid-1953, and for the next eight years he advised the president on regional issues. His report upon his return also focused on the "rising tide of nationalism" and the need for internal reforms that would open the door to greater U.S. investment, deploring the "danger of excessive industrialization . . . for it own sake, at any cost."[8] His main impact was in increasing slightly the time and attention the White House paid to the growing irritants and conflicts in the hemisphere. But Milton did serve as a conduit through which Latin leaders could express their many grievances. Nonetheless, in a period when the Administration's economic program for the Third World stressed trade rather than aid, there was no possibility of satisfying Latin demands, and when it shifted somewhat to increased aid for the Third World after 1954, it was intended primarily for those regions where Communist and national liberation movements were powerful and least interesting to U.S. businessmen.

U.S. activities south of the border sought to influence many institutions, depending on their significance to its overall goals. One of the best known was a much greater effort to control the Latin trade union movement. Less publicized was the commitment to strengthen the police departments of various nations with missions and technical assistance. In the case of Brazil, which while nationalist was nonetheless militantly anti-Soviet, it carried on a protracted discussion over loans that increasingly alienated the Brazilians, who got funds for a manganese project that U.S. steel firms strongly supported but saw more money dry up when they passed a nationalistic petroleum law in 1954. Washington's crude handling of the most important Latin nation gradually deeply alienated even its traditional friends, so that by 1958 Brazil was ready to embark on a far more comprehensive nationalist economic strategy.

No less alienating was the United States' opportunistic stand on commodity associations to stabilize the prices and output of the key exports on which most Third World nations, but especially Latin America, depended. After the post-Korean War raw materials price boom subsided, the terms of trade—the prices received against the prices paid out—turned against the region and became progressively worse over the course of the decade. The Paley Commission on raw materials had endorsed creating commodity associations at a time when their prices were spiraling and causing U.S. industrial consumers to complain. If this stance violated free market principles Washington advocated for others, the inconsistency nonetheless promised greater profits. After 1954, with prices falling and again in favor of the United States, the Administration again opposed commodity associations. At the same time, its stockpiling program subsidized the politically well placed but inefficient U.S. zinc and lead producers, protecting them from foreign competition and violating free market practices. Throughout the decade, Latin demands for agreements in tin, coffee, sugar, and many other commodities forced the Administration to circumlocute countlessly to justify or conceal its hostility, further alienating the Latins who had most to gain from such accords as well as other Third World nations. These Latins were unable to earn satisfactory prices for their exports after 1954 or to obtain economic grants, and the pressures on the region's Center and Right parties to adopt even stronger nationalist economic strategies insulated from the world market only intensified.

Even as it advocated an open door outside the hemisphere, the United States renewed its postwar campaign to suppress not just Communism and nationalism but to prevent a restoration of European influence as well, an undertaking that was the culmination of its historic pretensions since the Monroe Doctrine in 1821 to dominate the hemisphere. Europe's lessened trade role was hardly sufficient for the United States, and it persisted throughout the 1950s with its earlier policy of attempting to control weapons supplies for Latin American armies and the training of its officer corps.

This effort was hampered after the outbreak of the Korean War because of the enormous demand for arms elsewhere in the world. Until then the Latins had received mainly surplus U.S. arms, and after June 1950 their low-priority assignment for future supplies once again raised the threat of European sales and training missions. The only way to fulfill the goal of standardizing Latin armies to U.S. weapons and to close off the hemisphere, the NSC knew, was to divert more to them. Yet this was not done, and Latin officers were both irritated and alienated. Despite the initiation of a modest military aid program in mid-1952, the Latin armies wanted yet more arms, and purchases of far cheaper European supplies seemed only a matter of time. By 1956, much to the Pentagon's consternation, they had begun to buy weapons primarily from the British but also from the French, Canadians,

Swedes, and Italians. For reasons of goodwill as well as keeping European missions away from the politically crucial officer class, the NSC in September 1956 decided to intensify its struggle to control the hemisphere's arms flow, employing cheap credits and flexible pricing to win back the monopoly, for profits were not its concern; they largely failed in this effort. In this domain, too, events in the region had begun to escape Washington's mastery.

OVERTHROWING DEMOCRACIES: BOLIVIA AND GUATEMALA

Only by analyzing their application to specific nations can one understand both the motivation and practice of U.S. policies in the hemisphere, and the best-known case in this decade was Guatemala. As important as it was, Guatemala must also be juxtaposed against Washington's response to the more radical Bolivian revolution of 1952, which it co-opted with little difficulty. In the Bolivian case, as I described earlier, the United States had been hostile to the Villarroel regime after it came to power in December 1943 with the backing of the Nationalist Revolutionary Movement (MNR). Its social program included Rightist, Centrist, and Leftist ideas, and it was less a party than a coalition of very diverse elements.

Villarroel was killed in July 1946, his government overthrown, and reactionaries took over. "The whole land is now wide open for free American enterprise," the U.S. ambassador in La Paz reported proudly at the end of 1950.[9] This congenial situation ended abruptly in October 1951 when the Bolivian government, with prodding from the largely non-United States-owned tin companies that accounted for most of the nation's exports earnings, stopped tin sales to the United States in the hope of exploiting the serious wartime shortages to obtain far higher prices. Since the U.S. government had constructed and operated in Texas a large smelter that could refine only Bolivian tin, the rightist regime was challenging it directly. Negotiations to fix a new price not only managed to alienate American officials dealing with Bolivia, but also the absence of tin sales and essential foreign exchange devastated the already impoverished Bolivian economy. Worse yet, Bolivia threatened to charge the United States as an "economic aggressor" before the OAS, turned to Argentina for aid, and held out the menace of creating a regional coalition of anti-Yankee rightist regimes of the sort Argentina had long advocated.[10] When the MNR on April 9, 1952, with the support of many urban conservatives, overthrew the military-backed regime and put Víctor Paz Estenssoro in power, the United States was ripe for its blandishments. Privately assured that nationalization of the tin companies would be its only antiforeign act and that it would encourage foreign investment in other sectors, on June 6 the United States recognized the revolutionary regime.

Marxism's influence in the new Bolivian government was far stronger than in Guatemala, and its ability to take full power was surely much greater. The strategically placed minister of mines and second most important person in the government, Juan Lechin, was also the militant leader of the large mine-workers' union and very close to a quite significant Trotskyite party, if not a member himself. The yet larger pro-Soviet Communists supported the government even more uncritically and received posts in it for some years. Given the population, these two groups were at least as large as the Guatemala Communists.

Far more crucial, the army had been disbanded after April 1952 and guns distributed to a popular militia that numbered twenty thousand to thirty thousand by early 1954, some commanded directly by the unions. In the fifteen months after Paz came to office the United States could not even think of overthrowing his government but successfully insisted on a compensation scheme for all tin owners linked to its resumption of purchases at prices favorable to itself, as well as the reconstitution of the army. The first U.S. investors were ostentatiously welcomed to Bolivia at the end of 1952, and they were granted important sulfur and oil concessions from this time onward. In light of this complex situation and especially the fact that workers had most of the guns, the United States rallied to Paz's support after Milton Eisenhower visited there in mid-1953, shipped emergency economic aid to the country from the end of 1953 until 1956, and reinforced middle-class pressures on Paz to keep enlarging the army—which reached its pre-1952 size by 1958.

Washington understood that in the short run the option to Paz's unusual regime was either a leftist one, probably under Lechin and most likely to attempt to install socialism, or the rightist Falange, an ultranationalist group also backed by ex-officers and former tin-mineowners. Given the choices and the two Marxist parties' caution, it preferred successfully to control the Paz regime with aid—which allowed it to impose a comprehensive financial program after 1956—and selective tin purchases, and to bide its time until the army was able to resume its traditional role as the arbiter of power. Until then it had no basis for a more forceful policy. Allowing itself to be co-opted, the MNR was able to survive until 1964, when the army responded to U.S. encouragement and once again took over Bolivia.

The Bolivian experience was unique: a rightist government and private tin interests had damaged U.S. consumers, and a united front party that favored nationalization of tin, and later introduced extensive land reform, aided U.S. interests while remaining incapable of acting in a consistent or decisive manner—quite like many others in the hemisphere with similar pretensions. More significantly, Bolivia also avoided hurting important U.S. property interests, and it was too distant from the United States, and too close to a solicitous Argentina, to overthrow it easily. Most important of all, the Bolivian experience revealed that with adept aid, loans, and the intercession of international banks, even ardently nationalist governments could be tamed when U.S. covert or overt military intervention was not feasible.

In the far better known case of Guatemala, we can best understand it in the broader context of U.S. Latin American policy objectives and their frustrations after 1945. This framework, to some crucial extent, predetermined Washington's responses to developments in this small and exceedingly poor but typical Central American republic. As with its neighbors, its poverty was the result of the concentration of over half the cultivable land in 0.3 percent of the farms, with United Fruit the largest of these. Export agriculture concentrated in coffee and bananas also meant less production of food for local consumption. In 1944 a revolution led by young army officers under Juan José Arévalo, who the next year won the first democratic election in the nation's history, proposed to ameliorate the country's miseries. This typical group of middle-class officers was, like many others in the hemisphere, anti-United States and for mild but long overdue reforms. Arévalo was anti-Marxist but also a committed reformer and idealist. But labor codes, the right of workers to organize, and minimum-wage laws greatly disturbed the U.S. firms that controlled the export sectors, transport, and utilities, and partial land reforms in 1948 deepened their hostility.

In March 1951 Jacobo Arbenz Guzmán, an officer who had been defense minister, succeeded Arévalo and embarked on a comprehensive land reform program that directly struck at United Fruit interests. Farms under 100 hectares were exempt from reform, those between 100 and 300 hectares were excluded if they were at least two-thirds cultivated, and those over that were not affected only if fully cultivated. The measure was directed against those companies, like United Fruit, that left vast tracts of prime land fallow for future exploitation. Worse yet, compensation to those expropriated was to be calculated on the basis of their land's declared taxable value, which United Fruit and others had reported at far lower than its real worth in order to avoid taxes. The land was given to some 100,000 peasant families, who eventually obtained about 1.5 million acres, 234,000 of which had belonged to United Fruit. Compared to Mexico, Taiwan, and Japan, the reform was a modest one. But the problem was that it affected U.S. companies, whose wrath knew no limits and who began actively to lobby in Washington for the overthrow of the government.

In mid-1952 the CIA and United Fruit, with cooperation from the Somoza regime in Nicaragua, Trujillo in the Dominican Republic, and Pérez Jiménez in Venezuela—the three most reactionary states in the hemisphere—almost implemented a plan to overthrow the Arbenz government. But the plan was amateurishly organized, and the State Department convinced Truman to abort the well-advanced scheme, leaving the problem to the Eisenhower Administration.

Every writer with access to the essential documents has shown that there was an intricate web of personal and political relations between United Fruit and many of the Republican and Democratic officials dealing with the Guatemala issue, the most direct being the former president of United Fruit's brother John M. Cabot, who was Eisenhower's assistant secretary of state for Latin America. That United Fruit mobilized a highly effective lobby of former New Dealers, liberals, and the establishment press is an excellent illustration of how pressure groups have an impact, but given the context of official U.S. concerns and priorities, which identified corporate interests with its own, the most one can say is that while United's efforts probably advanced the timing of the U.S. overthrow of Guatemala's democratic, reformist government, it certainly would have occurred in due course in any case. For Guatemala was systematically violating all the economic criteria for the hemisphere that the Democratic and Republican consensus had articulated since 1945, and it was a dangerous precedent. Most decisive, however, was the fact that it was extremely easy to overthrow because the army, while loyal to Arbenz himself, also had many senior officers personally linked to the oligarchy and hostile to land reform. The military still retained the balance of power, and Arbenz had been neither able nor willing to alter its traditional composition or views. The United States, fully aware of this, kept a training mission with it throughout this period to maintain vital contacts.

The principle of overthrowing the Arbenz government received the Eisenhower Administration's blessing immediately upon coming to office, and from this time onward it mounted a vast, sustained public-relations campaign to convince the U.S. public and the world that Guatemala had been taken over by Communists. As before, United Fruit was involved in every phase of the Administration's efforts, yet they remained a useful convenience rather than a principal cause. But neither Dulles nor Eisenhower wanted a mere coup, which could have been accomplished as readily in early 1953 as in June 1954; rather, they sought to exploit the occasion to inhibit nationalists in the other nations of the hemisphere, many of whom had supporters and programs comparable to those in Guatemala, and to deepen U.S. political control of the Organization of American States in order better to be able to utilize it in the future. Given the actual political situation within Guatemala and the army's monopoly of weapons, the United States could be patient.

The NSC decided in March 1953 that it would operate through the OAS to avoid the appearance of taking unilateral measures or abandoning the Good Neighbor policy, which would only have fanned anti-Yankee feelings in the hemisphere. Had the OAS not given the United States the two-thirds required vote approving its action, however, it intended to act alone as a last resort. This opportunistic attitude toward the OAS's role continued for the next eight years. But it was not until the OAS conference in Caracas, Venezuela, in March 1954 that the Administration obtained the legal façade it thought essential, and after "two weeks of very intensive work," involving both threats and promises of aid, Dulles was able to get the OAS to pass a resolution, one that, he confessed, "was certainly not adopted with genuine enthusiasm." It was also less than he had initially demanded. Most of the Latin nations regarded the Caracas declaration that "international communism" constituted intervention in the hemisphere, one requiring strong countermeasures, as "a pretext," as even Dulles admitted, "to permit American [U.S.] intervention in the internal affairs of other republics in the Hemisphere." Their real anxiety was linked to "the commercial and financial policies that the Administration was following in Latin America." Dulles's own broad interpretation of the Caracas resolution, which did not specifically mention Guatemala, was that it "was an extension of the Monroe Doctrine to include the concept of outlawing foreign ideologies in the American Republics."[11] Events over the next months were to confirm the fears of many Latin nations that it was precisely U.S. opposition to independent economic development that was behind its attack on Guatemala. In a sense the United States at Caracas had laid an all-encompassing foundation for confronting directly all those increasingly important reform and nationalist ideas in the region that challenged its hegemonic aspirations. Guatemala was but a major chapter in its larger struggle for hemispheric mastery.

Caracas gave the United States the legal façade it thought desirable, and it quickly proceeded to overthrow the Arbenz government. The label of "communism" it imposed on it was wholly contrived, though in the broader sense Arbenz's reformism was tantamount to the same thing insofar as U.S. interests were concerned. Arbenz himself, in the words of the later CIA-sponsored account of the entire episode, was "an enigma."[12] Had he been a Communist, the army, which the United States never claimed was under any Communist influence whatsoever, would have overthrown him much earlier. Arbenz never made a Communist a cabinet minister, but he allowed them to work very hard for him at lower-level posts, particularly in education and in the land reform ministry, where they comprised under a tenth of its personnel. The Communists themselves, who never numbered more than four thousand, were deeply divided on how to deal with him, and the Party's most important leader and head of its labor union had several times argued for an end to the Party's support for an unconventional nationalist reformer like Arbenz. The Party had only four of fifty-one seats in the 1953–54 Congress's ruling coalition. Arbenz did not fear it because in the hope of influencing him they had largely abandoned their own ideology and organization. It was precisely for this reason, again to quote the CIA-sponsored postmortem, that "The events of the last week of the Arbenz regime showed that Communism in Guatemala had not developed into a successful popular movement. . . . the Communists had not found sufficient time to build a broad base or to sink their roots deeply."[13] Notwithstanding its public statements, Washington never produced proof that Arbenz's government was Communist, and when dealing with Latin nations it never tried to. Privately, the United States admitted that it had never found evidence of any Soviet contacts with the Guatemala party.[14]

The army, in fact, still retained the ultimate power over the nation's future, and Arbenz was an ex-officer who was rapidly exhausting the patience of its more conservative wing. His purchase of arms from Czechoslovakia in early 1954, which the United States used to corroborate the deliberate falsehoods it and United Fruit publicists had been producing, in reality showed Arbenz to be a wholly naïve man. He had failed for years to obtain arms from the United States and Western Europe, and to purchase arms from a Soviet bloc nation created the worst of all possible worlds: it provided the United States with the propaganda it needed, and it gave weapons to the only force in the country able to remove him easily.

It was for this reason only that the chaotic CIA-controlled invasion to overthrow him, which began on June 14 as an opéra bouffe by three hundred poorly equipped and poorly trained men, with three old bombers to exaggerate their strength, was to succeed within two weeks. Had he or the Communists been serious or important, the assault could easily have been liquidated, but Washington's strategy was to force Arbenz's army to cease being passive and to take over. After some hesitation, the army acceded to U.S. demands that they transfer all power to Castillo Armas, the leader of the invasion whom United Fruit had personally selected, and a new regime was installed. Neither Arbenz nor the Communists chose to fight.

The terror that followed was merciless: unions were banned, parties suspended, a majority of voters disenfranchised, and at least nine thousand persons arrested and an unknown number killed. The new regime abolished the post-1945 reform legislation, and United Fruit had its huge estates returned. As the pre-1944 order was fully restored and the government sank into corruption, Guatemala became the leading example of the kind of hemisphere the United States sought to create.

LATIN AMERICAN DILEMMAS

The events in Guatemala shocked many Latin American nations, although they were also partially responsible for them insofar as they had conceded reluctantly to the United States at Caracas a global juridical and ideological rationale for action it would have taken in any event. The United States had proved that it was now willing and able to have the CIA also do in the hemisphere everything it was undertaking elsewhere, removing once and for all the constraints that the Good Neighbor policy had presumably imposed on its resolve to dominate the hemisphere's economic life. But while in September 1956 and later the Eisenhower Administration privately reaffirmed its readiness to use covert or overt means against any nation warranting it, the mere fact that such efforts were also potentially embarrassing and exceedingly time-consuming compelled the Administration to rely also on other means—namely, greater support for congenial dictatorships. Given the low priority it still attached to becoming involved in Latin affairs, opting for acceptable and presumably stable regimes that knew how to eliminate dissent appeared more advantageous to it than tolerating many of the reform forces increasingly active in the relatively democratic nations.

The Truman Administration had also been moving toward a reliance on military regimes, but its successor privately carried this bias to its logical conclusion. In late 1953 the State Department decided that democracy of the United States variety was not likely in Latin America in any case and that its major goal in the region should be political continuity—as long, of course, as it was also pro-United States and fostered congenial forms of economic development. Dictators, an NSC estimate observed in mid-1954, "present themselves as guarantors of stability and order and of cooperation with the United States," while reformers believe the United States has a moral obligation to support them—taking U.S. ideological rhetoric at face value.[15] In November 1954, to make the message clear, Eisenhower presented Legion of Merit citations to two dictators who had overthrown civilian-elected governments. As Adolf Berle, one of many liberals who were also involved in Arbenz's overthrow noted in his diary in February 1955, Dulles's "instructions are flat: do nothing to offend the dictators; they are the only people we can depend on." "Dulles had laid down the policy with vigor," a State Department official assured him.[16] In 1954, however, military men ran thirteen of the twenty Latin American nations, but by 1960 their number had fallen to four, so that for the remainder of the decade Washington was persistently, stubbornly to swim against the hemisphere's political tide.

Publicly, the question of its support for dictators embarrassed the Administration, just as it alienated the growing number of civilian governments the military threatened. It tried to deflect criticism by arguing that "We try to conduct our relations . . . with the government which is, in fact, in power"—as Dulles claimed in May 1958, making an exception for China. In the hemisphere this meant "the doctrine of noninterference in the internal affairs of other countries"—save, he did not have to add, when they came under the Caracas resolution as he defined it.[17] Yet out of deference for Latin opinion it drew the line in January 1959 when Luis Somoza, the Nicaraguan dictator, asked to come to the United States for medical reasons; while the State Department said it expected he would not pass his power to his family, which had ruled Nicaragua since 1936, it also appreciated his support for the United States in the UN and the OAS, and "we continue to remain favorably disposed towards the present Government."[18]

Even more important to the hemisphere's larger nations, which were increasingly committed to nationalist economic programs that deeply concerned Washington, were quite technical economic issues that especially affected those middle-class sectors that supported autarchic economic strategies. The United States had consistently opposed commodity associations to sustain the prices of Latin exports, arguing instead for a pure free market, but after 1956 intensified U.S. protection of its own markets with quotas and tariffs, along with its dumping of subsidized exports abroad and similar efforts to improve its balance of payments, greatly intensified nationalist sentiments in Latin America. The United States imposed import quotas on nine agricultural commodities and import fees on three others. Latin America's exports of some of these, particularly cotton, were vital to it. After 1955, United States-subsidized exports of grain, cotton, beef, and such began seriously damaging Latin sales to Europe as well. Import quotas on zinc, lead, and oil further hurt Latin participation in normal world trade. When Milton Eisenhower tried to explain to Latin officials that his brother was under strong internal political pressures, he received mounting complaints from conservative Latin leaders, especially in the key nations of Brazil and Argentina, who were increasingly forced to shift to nationalist alternatives.

Given these circumstances, ceaseless hypocritical U.S. admonitions for greater trade and against "nationalist" economic programs deeply alienated the Latin middle classes, and the United States made no concessions on such matters, either publicly or in private. Latin desires to create an effective regional common market that would by necessity have excluded the United States intensified as a consequence of such trade disputes, but rather than oppose it categorically, U.S. representatives agreed to support a common market only if it adopted tariff and currency rules that would have made it impotent. An international free trade system remained Washington's unwavering goal, despite its own growing deviations from it. "I think the principal divisive issue between the United States and Latin America today," a State

Department senior official in the field told a closed Senate hearing in March 1959, "is the issue of economic development."[19]

Such seemingly obtuse economic questions nonetheless had profound political implications, and these became clear when Vice President Richard Nixon visited Latin America in May 1958 and was greeted everywhere with demonstrations and even riots. And the triumph of the Castro-led revolution in Cuba in January 1959, the details of which I treat in Chapter 13, transformed the hemisphere from a peripheral U.S. concern to one of considerably greater significance. While the Administration worried far more about coping with the rising tide of nationalism and anti-Yankee feeling, its sole significant gesture was finally to create the Inter-American Development Bank (IADB) in December 1959, yet even the IADB was just one more attempt to head off the tide of nationalism about to engulf the region.

The trend toward economically policing the Third World through so-called multilateral banks was well advanced by 1954, when U.S. officials understood that a nation wishing a loan had also to take " 'house-in-order' actions to attract it."[20] Export-Import Bank and World Bank loans were consistently earmarked for countries "which have taken measures which would reasonably encourage private enterprise."[21] As Eugene Black, the World Bank's president, explained it, "The desire for autarky will not be tempered until there is an awareness how, by underemphasizing exports, the leaders of these nations are prolonging the poverty of their people. . . . aid must be a means of promoting 'the right kinds of decisions' in terms of development. . . ."[22] It was in this light that Milton Eisenhower and other U.S. officials defined the purpose of the IADB, which had the virtue that "if loan conditions were deemed to be intervention, at least it would be in a collective form and not intervention by the United States."[23] The IADB's additional asset was that U.S. control of 41 percent of its votes allowed it to block any loan, which required a two-thirds vote for it, if it did not meet its standards. The bank's initial capital of one billion dollars of mainly non-U.S. funds was not significant in any case, given the magnitude of the challenges Latin America faced. The IADB was far too little, far too late, and it was more of the same policy in multilateral guise.

When President Eisenhower traveled to Latin America in early 1960, in response to the Cuban revolution's popularity and the growing hostility toward the United States, there was no possibility that his statements would waver from the strictures and goals that had characterized U.S. policy toward the region since 1945. Brazil's president had urged him to embark on a struggle against Castroism by stressing genuine economic development, yet Eisenhower lectured him and others on their obligation to oppose Castro under U.S. leadership, and he issued homilies on the need to create conditions that would attract U.S. private capital. The net effect was to deepen the regional leadership's orientation toward those autonomous economic strategies the United States so deplored.

That Washington's hegemonic objectives would generate a political response as well as an economic one, bringing it into conflict with much of Latin America after 1950, seemed, in retrospect, inevitable—and for Latin Americans necessary if they were ever to develop their nations. The extent to which the United States managed to alienate social classes who were also opposed to the Left was itself not surprising because its hemispheric objectives were so pervasively and aggressively economic. That its position produced such broad opposition was disagreeable to the United States but, ultimately, also incidental. If its economic goals and raw materials requirements were perfectly comprehensible, given the U.S. economy's specific needs, what its leaders could not anticipate was the extent to which their monomania would eventually force it to confront virtually all of the hemisphere's political forces committed to lifting the area out of the political and economic miasma that had so distorted its social development. Yet here, too, the United States was impervious to the immense human costs to the people of the hemisphere; far more crucial, it so welcomed and aided dictators in such an overt fashion as to intensify profoundly a general hatred toward it. To be anti-Yankee in thought and deed became a precondition of the region's emergence from its suffering and sloth.

Given all these circumstances, it was certain by 1960 that the United States could no longer continue to remain so oblivious to Latin America, and that the rising storm there would compel it soon to cope with the monumental political consequences of its past policies and greed. But that was a legacy that the Eisenhower Administration was to bequeath to its successors.

Africa
and the
European System

*U*NITED STATES POLICY DURING THE
1950s relegated Africa south of the Sa-
hara to the place of least importance in
the Third World and assigned it, despite certain reservations, to the European sphere of influence. Washington did not introduce a single fundamental
policy innovation toward Africa throughout this decade, and not until 1958
did the State Department create an assistant secretaryship devoted exclusively to this vast continent. The Eisenhower Administration adopted whole-
heartedly its predecessor's policy of opposing political independence,
favoring the use of African resources to strengthen Western Europe's recovery, and asking in return only an Open Door for the relatively modest American business interests involved there.

This European-oriented perspective defined Washington's policies completely, and while a small group that saw Africa as a problem in its own right
emerged toward the end of the decade to create relatively minor internal
differences in its discussions, policy itself remained firmly in the hands of the
Europeanists in the State Department; for Western Europe controlled three-
quarters of Africa's population in 1950 and economically benefited greatly
from colonialism. Britain and Belgium gained the most, and their colonies'
dollar earning from exports to the United States greatly reduced Washington's need to aid them directly. Africa's exports to Europe in 1948 amounted
to half as much as those from the United States. Its African possessions' dollar
surplus during the early 1950s paid for one-fourth of Britain's imports from
the United States, and American experts fully appreciated the significant
market this created. The franc bloc in Africa also aided France's economy
until the mid-1950s, while 15 percent of Portugal's entire trade was with its

African colonies. Despite its Open Door objectives, which were irreconcilable with such imperialist economic relations, the dominant U.S. concern during the early part of the decade was the "restoration of a sound European economy," which would then be strong enough and confident enough to cooperate with the larger American design for an integrated world economic order.[1] Colonial Africa was an important pillar of that strength.

Both publicly and privately, U.S. spokesmen stated that they did not want direct responsibility for managing Africa's affairs and that Europe's colonial domain had the advantage of guaranteeing both tropical Africa's stability and its integration into the broader United States-led world economy. This meant there was to be no shift in its earlier policy of supporting whatever its allies chose to do regarding local demands for greater independence. "The metropolitan powers need reassurance from the United States," the State Department decided at the end of 1950, "that we are not purposefully working to bring about a premature according of political independence to the peoples of Africa."[2] "Premature independence for these peoples," Assistant Secretary of State Henry A. Byroade indicated in October 1953 while extolling all the benefits the white man's burden had brought to Africa's benighted people, "would not serve the interests of the United States."[3] In the case of South Africa and its apartheid policy of white supremacy, the Truman Administration discreetly but firmly supported it during the increasingly embarrassing UN debates, minimizing Pretoria's racial policies to emphasize its decisive strategic and economic importance as well as its active support in the Korean war. Its policy of voicing opposition to racist dictatorship, yet refusing to vote for UN resolutions condemning it, continued until 1958.

American spokesmen discussing Africa in 1952 described the people there as, for practical purposes, hardly more than primitive savages in coping with "twentieth-century problems which they scarcely understand and for which they are quite unprepared."[4] Five years later, the NSC's policy assumed "the African is still immature and unsophisticated with respect to his attitudes towards the issues that divide the world today."[5] Posing "as friends of both sides" during this decade, Washington's frequent affirmations "that basic advantages were brought to the African territories" by the colonial experiences often made it sound more royalist than the king. To remove the white man's burden suddenly would not only "seriously weaken our European allies" in the "worldwide contest" with Communism, but would also end colonialism's enlightening function.[6] "To proceed at too rapid or too slow a pace is to risk the extension of areas of disorder," became the consistent American position on the growing independence movements.[7]

Such caution was due more to implicit racist disdain American officials had for Africans, which created a sympathetic attitude toward Europe's role, than to fears of communism which were so influential elsewhere. "Communism has made no real progress in the area," Washington had decided earlier, although it did not exclude that this, too, might change.[8] Their main concern was that the removal of European hegemony would lead to local and tribal conflicts, not so much opening the way to Communism as depriving the West of Africa's great economic and strategic resources. Whether nationalism would find expression in "an orderly channel or through a sudden floodtide of destructive energy" concerned the few American officials preoccupied with Africa, and they counseled European caution in granting self-determination lest their haste create "areas of disorder" in Africa.[9]

Its loyalty to its allies, very different from their relations elsewhere, nonetheless did not preclude the United States from defining its own economic objectives that impinged on Europe's colonial prerogatives, but one can seriously overestimate the importance of the incessant references to the Open Door and classic American trade principles that lard its internal discussions. On one hand these goals were intended to encourage U.S. private investment and access to Africa's rich raw materials. But in practice Washington's commitment to Africa as a complement to its European allies' power and as an incentive for their maintaining the military strength there that could guarantee Africa's strategic integration invariably overrode its instinctive desire to impose a true Open Door system on the region's economy. In 1960 the NSC's policy resolved that "it is important that the traditional economic ties which bind Western Europe and Africa be maintained," and this by necessity meant ignoring trade arrangements that violated the Open Door.[10] Indeed, given the exceptions the United States was making for itself in Latin America, the Middle East, and the Philippines, and for Europe in Africa, it was clear that abstract ideological principles would play second fiddle to pragmatic divisions of the Third World into spheres of influence.

In any case, what the United States wanted and needed most in Africa—raw materials—it freely got. Its frequent listings of Africa's essential riches never included complaints that it was not able to obtain them at prices it was willing to pay. It was tension and unrest alone that threatened supplies, and this only reinforced its commitment to its allies' hegemony. U.S. exports to Africa throughout the 1950s far exceeded prewar averages, while its imports, which counted most, were much larger also. A total of 4 to 6 percent of all its world imports after 1954 came from Africa, and while this made it the least important Third World region statistically, the significance of the metals involved cannot be overemphasized. All this it obtained within the framework of a European-dominated system.

Moreover, U.S. direct investments in Africa, which in 1950 amounted to $286 million divided equally between South Africa and the rest of the continent, also increased without significant business grievances about restrictions. By 1960 they had grown to $925 million, but the fact that South Africa now held under a third of this sum carried with it certain implicit constraints on future U.S. policy toward apartheid. The great mineral and oil potential in Africa appeared to exist in those black countries undergoing the greatest political transformations and most opposed to racism.

While the United States was not to increase the importance it attached to Africa in the world or alter its basic policy, political changes both there and at home after 1956 required the Administration to nuance and sharpen its focus. Vice President Nixon's Africa tour in April 1957 did not affect thinking in any way but drew attention to the continent; more significant was the Democratic Party's criticisms of its rival's slavish support for colonialism, which made African issues more politically sensitive. Most important, Britain and France embarked on programs to loosen their grip on their colonies, and this required Washington to adapt to them. The Gold Coast became independent Ghana in March 1957, and under the pan-Africanist leadership of Kwame Nkrumah created a center of nationalist agitation. France's political crisis in 1958, which produced the Fifth Republic under Charles de Gaulle, also led the French to reduce greatly their colonial pretensions, and over the next three years its fourteen colonies gained varying degrees of nominal political independence within the framework, for nearly all, of continued economic dependency. The immediate U.S. reaction was to decide that most nationalist leaders were moderates and that with a small effort Washington could help keep them that way. Some American officials were concerned that Portugal's exploitive policies risked producing dangers in Angola and Mozambique, although the Belgian Congo received fairly high marks at this time. But in general the Administration was gratified to know that reforms France and Britain were sponsoring in Africa had been channeled in directions it considered positive.

Africa's significance in American policy after 1957 increased slightly, but within the framework of its by now well-worn positions. The changes that were occurring had to be kept gradual and orderly to prevent a vacuum into which Russia could move, and while Washington pretended to be a mediator, it really attempted to perpetuate European continuity. It sought the creation of federations wherever possible, with formal associations to the metropolitan powers. While it acknowledged that its public problem was how to handle African insistence that it oppose colonialism, the NSC felt it imperative that NATO preserve its hegemony over Africa after making nominal concessions to demands for independence.

Given mounting political pressures at home, the Eisenhower Administration ultimately felt compelled to make some adjustments in its South Africa policy. Moreover, in February 1958 a key Dulles adviser on the region warned him that it was potentially the most dangerous place on the continent as well as the most important, and reforms so far had been wholly inadequate. The

United States had opposed or ignored all UN resolutions attacking apartheid until then, but in return for "condemning" being watered down to "expressing regret and concern" at the end of 1958, it voted against South Africa for the first time.[11] From this point onward it opposed apartheid publicly, but "intemperate or strongly condemnatory resolutions" as well.[12] When the Sharpeville massacre of sixty-nine blacks occurred in March 1960, however, the entire Administration disavowed a moderately critical statement that low-level State Department officials released without authorization. At stake, the White House decided, was access to its raw materials and the U.S. fleet's increasing use of Capetown, and it was wholly unwilling to sacrifice these.

While France and Britain had managed decolonization to the Eisenhower Administration's satisfaction, Belgium and Portugal came to disturb it deeply by 1960. In addition, given the absence of an important middle class in the colonial states, it was increasingly apparent to U.S. African experts that the creation of something that resembled capitalism would be far more difficult than in other regions and that large governmental functions would be inevitable. Indeed, they felt that perhaps the best that might be attained was for such a state sector to create the infrastructure essential for greater foreign private investment in the extractive industries. The NSC conceded in Africa, as it did nowhere else in the world, that in addition to a strong state economic role the new governments would have neutralist as well as authoritarian tendencies. The key to containing them was perpetuation of metropolitan influences and responsibility, including Europe's provision of most of the economic aid essential to tame Africa's new leaders.

For all these reasons, the Eisenhower Administration preferred at the end of its mandate to continue avoiding the growing challenges in Africa. In Angola and Mozambique, where the Portuguese held absolute sway, it hoped they would pursue more enlightened policies, but it did nothing to persuade them to do so, and publicly it supported them against the independence movements in both those nations. In the Belgian Congo, where there were important American interests in copper and cobalt, it endorsed Belgium's granting of independence on June 30, 1960, but it hoped to see close ties between Belgium and the Congo continue. It therefore subordinated its Congo policy to Belgian needs and desires, entrusting the U.S. embassy in Brussels primary responsibility for the problem. The Congo was the major African legacy it was to bequeath to the next administration.

In this and many other crucial ways, Africa was distinctive in U.S. policy in the Third World. At the end of 1960 it was as firmly assigned to Europe's sphere of influence as ever, serving as yet another exception to Open Door ideology in practice if not in theory, and the internal social forms the new African states adopted neither pleased it nor galvanized it into taking action. Its compromise with what it perceived to be the unavoidable realities of

Africa was essential as well, because Washington's Africa experts concluded that while there was slight danger of the Soviets and Chinese helping the inconsequential local Communist parties, the leaders of the new states would gladly accept aid directly, thereby opening a new route for Communist pene-tration. Working with them on their own terms became necessary as the United States worried that the Cold War in Africa might take the form of aid competition. It hoped that its effort to combine change with order, making certain that anticolonialism and independence moved in conservative direc-tions, would continue to succeed in the future as it had in the past. As long as there was no real Left on the continent to challenge Western power, it could look at the strategic implications of such modest political changes with equanimity.

The Eisenhower Administration preferred to remain as passive as possible in Africa, the continent least important to it, and it was its preoccupation with what it considered far more momentous tasks elsewhere that also led to its pragmatic acquiescence on what would have been vital questions of princi-ple and national interests in other regions. It felt relieved to pass the neces-sity of dealing with all these turbulent forces and changes involving decolonization, the growing confrontations involving racism and national-ism, and so much else to its successors to cope with as fate and circum-stances might require. But it was reasonably clear at the end of 1960 that Africa would become a far greater challenge to America in the future than it had been in the past.

Institutional Bases of the United States' Role in the Third World

*T*HE CAPITALIST CREDO THAT U.S. leaders applied consistently in dealing with the Third World was a reflection of the fact that America was preeminently an economic civilization, and all those who succeeded in it were products of its culture, absorbing its instinctive values and premises without reservations. Their identification of freedom of choice in economic affairs with freedom in "intellectual or spiritual life," as Dulles argued typically in May 1954, cannot be dismissed as merely conscious propaganda, for it was deeply and genuinely embedded in the minds of those who led America both politically and economically.[1] And that it was also a premise that aggrandized U.S. economic power abroad does not alter the fact that this beneficial reality was both a cause and an effect of its profound commitment to the deeply rooted traditional idea, as Eisenhower put it in January 1955, that "the United States holds forth the ideals of personal freedom, private property, individual enterprise, and open markets."[2]

What is unquestionable is that this overarching belief invariably led to predictable policy conclusions that then had to be implemented, and that just as invariably aided U.S. interests in the Third World at the same time. While there were many varieties of capitalism consistent with the anti-Communist politics the United States also sought to advance, what was axiomatic in the American credo was that the form of capitalism it advocated for the world was to be integrated in such a way that *its* businessmen played an essential part in it. Time and again it was ready to sacrifice the most effective way of opposing Communism in order to advance its own national interests. In this vital sense its world role was not simply one of resisting the Left but primarily of imposing its own domination.

Influencing the transformation of the Third World "to render its outcome at least compatible with Western values and vital interests," as a group of influential consultants put it, was the consistent keystone of U.S. efforts in the Third World after 1945.[3] The extent to which the economic component of this mission predominated over all strategic and political considerations depended on the region, but only in parts of Asia did noneconomic factors eventually become equal to, or more significant than, material causes in American policy. Only by separating the importance of such determining elements by continents can we gain an accurate perspective of the diverse and changing sources of America's policies in the Third World as well as its objectives.

U.S. economic goals required that Third World nations avoid various forms of autarky and import substitution, and above all both welcome outside investors and forgo creating an important state economic sector. "A major task for U.S. foreign economic policy," a senior State Department policy group argued in May 1954, "is to get across to other countries an understanding of our conception of the role of government in economic affairs." Specifically, the "normal function of government . . . is to provide an environment in which private enterprise can flourish free from artificial restraints."[4] It was this message, with its axiomatic corollary of free access for U.S. investors, that America carried to the world throughout this decade. In the UN as well as in the countless demarches of its officials, it never ceased to argue that "where private capital, both domestic and foreign, is encouraged, the nation's economic and political health and stability are strengthened."[5]

This meant, as an International Cooperation Administration directive put it in September 1957 shortly after Congress had voted a new development loan fund, that it would "employ U.S. assistance to aid-receiving countries in such a way as will encourage the development of the private sectors of their economies."[6] In effect, it was the constant U.S. assumption that the internal economic policies of many nations, but especially the major ones and above all in Latin America, were legitimate concerns for its foreign policy. And since local politics determines the choice of economic programs, the obligation for America to shape it, too, soon became an unavoidable concomitant. For however much it hoped that the economic parameters for development it defined would also shape the political character of Third World regimes, by the end of the 1950s a relatively small group of important American officials realized that this was not happening in the way they had hoped for. They had expected that a middle class, one with congenial politics, would emerge throughout the Third World, but it did not in Africa, the Middle East, and much of Asia, and even where it occurred, as in Latin America or the Philippines, that class's penchant for economic nationalist strategies proved to be a great challenge to U.S. hegemony. Whether the local economies conformed to the American formula or not, some officials and key businessmen began to reason, was less crucial than U.S. interests gaining access to extractive industries geared to export. From the viewpoint of most potential and actual U.S. investors, all the rest was quite incidental, and a relatively small but growing number became more tolerant toward an important economic role for the state in Africa and the Middle East. Indeed, even providing such countries with U.S. aid was acceptable and perhaps desirable if it was politically essential or if it aided the extractive sector.

Moreover, despite the intense and unwavering ideological consistency of most senior officials in Washington or U.S. business leaders, some became defensive as they considered the extent to which the United States violated the canons it expounded to others. After 1956, particularly, this became impossible to ignore in Latin America, as Milton Eisenhower reported how irate Latin businessmen were over the United States' subsidized dumping of its surpluses abroad and import quotas. "The agricultural export sales policies and the import quotas on minerals," Lamar Fleming, head of the giant Clayton, Anderson cotton firm reminded the president in 1958, "put the United States in the role of perhaps the world's greatest violator of the principles that it advocates in international competition and tries to sell to others through GATT."[7]

This obvious irony was to increase throughout the 1950s because of the Administration's balance-of-payments problems and the political leverage of the farm bloc and interest groups. From 1954 through 1958 from a third to a half of all U.S. agricultural exports, which competed most with the Third World, were government-subsidized. Three-quarters of all U.S. rice and 57 percent of its cotton production in 1957 was exported. Over half of its foreign aid was being shipped in much more expensive U.S. boats, while over two-thirds of all its aid was tied to U.S. goods—which were far dearer than its competition. And by 1957, U.S. loan policy shifted even more emphatically to harder terms requiring repayment in dollars.

The extent to which its aid policies made a mockery of the trade principles it advocated for others was not completely lost on American planners, whose aid strategy was inconsistent and often counterproductive. In part because of the $1.2 billion the USSR gave to poor nations in 1953–57, American aid was distributed primarily for political reasons, so that the many official review committees found that aid often lacked purely economic coherence. Washington had preached export-oriented development to the Third World but then closed its doors to many of their products, saturated many of their best markets with its own governmentally subsidized goods, and then gave the kinds of aid that most satisfied U.S. rather than local interests. With neither trade nor aid as its real strategy, it gyrated between both.

During the last years of the Eisenhower Administration its economic policies toward the Third World were in disarray, save insofar as they responded unvaryingly to its own domestic needs, and all that remained constant was the ideological principles that it demanded others implement. Yet given the fact that from the inception the United States had expected its private investors to play the critical role in extending American power overseas, underneath this superficial disorder there still remained a foundation of consistency around the deeply held conviction that the continuing expansion and prosperity of U.S. corporate interests would greatly help the Third World also.

TOWARD MULTILATERAL SOLUTIONS

By the late 1950s most of America's officials were aware that the challenge of managing its economic relationship to the Third World was beset with growing difficulties, not the least of which was that its own protectionism was undermining its capacity to impose its ideal norms on the economic policies of poor nations. Opposition from Congress and even within the cabinet to bilateral economic aid was mounting, and the worsening position of the budget deficit and balance-of-payments situation reinforced its pressure. For this and other reasons, the United States began to shift toward a greater reliance on multilateral development banks.

A preliminary step in this direction had been the creation of the International Finance Corporation as a branch of the World Bank in 1956. The IFC was designed to loan funds at lower interest than its parent only to private investors in the Third World, but by 1960 its capital remained negligible, and some of its loans went to U.S. and European firms. Yet it was certain for a variety of crucial reasons that the United States would use the Washington-based World Bank and International Monetary Fund far more extensively in its effort to confront its increasingly difficult economic relations with the Third World. First, the management of the bank was firmly in its hands, not only because it controlled 31 percent of its votes plus a bloc of others, but also because the bank's presidents were always Americans: Eugene Black, a former Chase banker, during the 1950s, and before him John J. McCloy, a top Wall Street lawyer. Both concentrated on building a market for the bank's bonds, and this meant charging stiff interest and avoiding risky loans. Nearly two-thirds of its loans went to power and transport infrastructure projects essential to investments in extraction and with potential quick returns, and over half the proceeds of its loans were spent buying equipment in the United States.

Even more important was the World Bank's philosophy of "promoting 'the right kinds of decisions,' " to quote Black again, directing poorer countries to specialize in exporting primary materials that could earn hard currencies with which to pay back loans and create the international division of labor that U.S. development planners, both in and out of government, so enthusiastically endorsed. The bank's unwavering effort "in promoting sound policies" congenial with U.S. opposition to state economic enterprises or nationalist protectionism was much appreciated in Washington during the late 1950s.[8] Its relentless demand that borrowers "have taken measures which would reasonably encourage private capital" made it obvious that Washington would be better served getting multilateral banks to force its goals upon reluctant nations than assuming the politically highly delicate task directly.[9] The creation of the Inter-American Development Bank was the first expression of this awareness.

It was in this context that the Eisenhower Administration sought to resolve some of its difficulties in the Third World after 1959 by shifting many of its activities toward the multilateral banks. One of the arguments for such a move, as well, was that they would permit it to reduce bilateral aid and to help lower budget deficits. The president's high-level aid advisory committee under William H. Draper, Jr., in July 1959 strongly recommended precisely such a shift toward a multilateral approach, including, in addition to the IADB, the creation of a higher-risk soft-loan section within the World Bank, the International Development Association, which would grant low-interest, long-term loans. Ironically, the very fact that the IDA was necessary to supplement the World Bank's functions testified to the bank's incapacity to solve development problems in the poor countries, but rather to aggravate them. In reality, the main value of the bank and the IMF was in their ability to act on behalf of the United States to impose "conditionality" clauses on loans to control the economic policies of borrowers.

Extremely stiff World Bank and U.S. Export-Import Bank loan terms had by 1960 begun to cause mounting difficulties for other Third World economies, in addition to those in Latin America. While the net inflow of resources to the borrower was great at the inception of the loan, paying it back caused a net outflow of funds for Export-Import loans after nine years and for World Bank loans by twelve years, so that the long-run effect was to create a mounting drain on resources as well as a debt-servicing problem that kept nations bound to those exports able to earn the dollars essential for repayment. The public debt of the entire Third World doubled between 1955 and 1960, but debt servicing grew substantially faster. The IDA, which was capitalized at one billion dollars when it came into existence in 1960, was far too small to cope with this emerging problem. In a word, the multilateral cure was beginning to prove worse than the illness, subjecting many nations to external dictates.

For both domestic and international political reasons, the Eisenhower

Administration initiated the important shift toward multilateral approaches to the Third World's economic problems, its principal motive being to use an ostensibly neutral body to get the poor nations to conform to economic policies that the United States itself was increasingly abandoning, thereby avoiding exacerbating its bilateral political relations. But while Washington's goals were clear, the methods it formulated for implementing them had been haphazardly concocted, and it barely contemplated the potential costs to the Third World. Multilateralism momentarily solved the United States' problems, but it created others America would eventually have to confront.

THIRD WORLD TO CENTER STAGE

The U.S. position in the Third World at the end of the Eisenhower era was both substantially weaker and more complex than it had been at the inception of the decade, and the attainment of its original goal of an integrated world economic and political order conforming to United States-defined norms was much farther from realization than ever. Washington's own role had itself altered dramatically in the Middle East and in important and increasingly irreversible ways in Asia. From a position of partnership with Britain in the Middle East it had become the chief foreign presence, now primarily responsible for the military and political security of the area as well as dominant over its vast oil riches. In Latin America its hegemonic ambitions remained constant, but the challenges it faced from local forces of nationalism and, to a lesser but growing extent, radicalism, were unprecedented and disturbing. Only in Africa was the United States to continue to depend on its European allies to manage an important continent, largely because they carefully deferred to America's economic needs and the Left was as yet of no consequence. In these three great regions of the world American policy was primarily economically motivated, and only in Asia—the Philippines always excepted—were strategic and political considerations also so important as to make a dissection of the diverse sources of American conduct incapable of facile generalizations.

Despite the fact that European affairs and relations with the Soviet Union remained its main preoccupation in 1960, as in 1950, objectively the Third World was becoming more crucial to the United States, and its many new and potent means for coping with it, ranging from the CIA to innovative forms of economic domination, failed to keep pace with the scope, speed, and complexity of the problems that were emerging to confront it. As countless social, economic, and political developments gathered momentum in villages and towns of the dozens of nations in transition, the United States' operational as well as articulated assumption that it had not only the historic mission and responsibility to guide them in directions it thought desirable, but above all the capability to do so, began to impose increasing demands on America's most important leaders. They could not continue, it was clear by 1960, to relegate continuously these momentous issues to lower-level officials who were incapable of making decisions involving massive expenditures of money or commitments of force, whether in its overt or covert forms, sufficient to resolve growing difficulties. The Third World as a focus for U.S. global ambitions was moving irresistibly toward center stage, American leadership's desires or awareness of them notwithstanding.

The challenges it confronted were all the more redoubtable because in many areas of the Third World the barriers to U.S. hegemonic aspirations came not from Communists or leftists but from centrist and even rightist elements, revealing that its habitual Cold War definitions notwithstanding, nationalism in its classic forms as an obstacle to the American-defined schema for a new international order was not only still alive but also growing. In Latin America and the Philippines, as well as all of the Middle East, Washington's preferred explanations of a world divided into communism and those against it made less and less sense. And it was its clash with nationalist elements, as diverse as they were, that revealed most about the U.S. global crusade, for had fear of Communism alone been the motivation of its behavior, the number of obstacles to its goals the United States confronted in the Third World would have been immeasurably smaller.

The obvious paradox that the economic and social forms it sought to impose on others, much less the Open Door ideology it endlessly reiterated, bore no relationship to its own conduct and policies is not at all surprising if one discounts greatly the significance of the Open Door doctrine. That most leaders genuinely believed it while consistently pursuing very different courses only forces upon one the conclusion that successful American politicians should never be trusted as social theorists, for useful inconsistencies were prerequisites to their personal success. The only constancy in their actions and U.S. policy was their desire for power—economic, political, and military, in that order—and they were increasingly prepared to utilize whatever means were essential, to the extent it required, to attain it. That the United States in the modern era has not had thinkers capable of giving theoretical and intellectual coherence to its role and practice makes it far more difficult to comprehend if one treats its ideas at their face value. In reality, the notions of the Open Door, internationalism, or anti-Communism it utilized at its convenience were sometimes sincere, sometimes ritual afterthoughts, but generally quite misleading when the overwhelming pursuit of its national interests, economic above all, was involved. While it confronted dilemmas and tactical choices throughout the postwar era, and constantly had to improvise new responses with often unpredictable consequences when dealing with failures, the overarching objectives of the entire effort themselves were clear in the various Third World regions, notwithstanding the significant nuances that were to operate in each of them—and above all in Asia.

America's problem in 1960 was not the perceived goals and interests of its policy in the Third World, which no one was to contest before or after, but the very viability of its gigantic ambitions. For in Asia and Latin America, above all, the economic and political tools it was employing were failing on their own terms, and many in Washington by 1960 possessed a gnawing realization of the growing inadequacies of their efforts. It was this legacy that the Democratic Administration would inherit, and how it might seek to remedy the immense challenge to America's increasing postwar commitment to regulate the many corners of the world, incorporating them under its leadership, was one of the most momentous decisions that the United States was to face in this century. Dependent on it was both the future of its power in the world and the stability of its society at home—and the very prospects for social change in much of the Third World. In 1960, however, American leaders did not regard the issues of the Third World as so imposing—or dangerous.

PART THREE

THE DEMOCRATIC PARTY AND THE THIRD WORLD, 1961–68

The Democratic Administration Confronts a World in Change

*T*HE EISENHOWER ADMINISTRATION greatly advanced the belief that the United States had both the right and the obligation to intervene in any region or nation whose domestic affairs it thought had international significance. Whether the reason was symbolic and involved credibility, as in Lebanon, or touched the sanctity of U.S. business interests, as in Guatemala, the basic assumption that it could arrogate to itself the authority to approve or disapprove the politics of any nation was by the end of the 1950s a firmly implanted conviction, and the Democrats also shared it. But America's problem was not the principle of its global mission but the functional question of its priorities and capabilities, and how best to regulate the larger contours of the world's political and economic evolution in ways congenial to the overall U.S. international design. The Eisenhower Administration had developed new means for doing so, as with a greater reliance on covert action and friendly dictators, but as the diversity and intensity of challenges for it to resolve exceeded even the United States' vast resources, it had to seek other, more effective means. It was this troubled search that was to prove its major legacy to the Kennedy Administration in 1961.

The interrelated vision of the world's difficulties that had emerged after 1945, which both physically and symbolically linked problems in one nation to the fate of its neighbors, projecting them onto the vast region around them, had begun under Truman and by 1961 was a firmly shared assumption in all American foreign policy discussions—a virtual categorical imperative. The domino theory was only a simplified analogy for justifying a far deeper conviction that its international role demanded an American policy every-

127

where, and for every contingency, and even if the degrees of activism the United States committed itself to in advance were tailored to its formal definition of priorities and interests, its constant dilemma was to find and effectively employ means capable of maintaining its larger commitments by quickly attaining its objectives in this or that nation.

The Kennedy Administration, like its predecessors, came to office nominally dedicated to emphasizing European affairs and the larger issues of the Soviet position in the world. The articulate intellectuals who comprised his advisers were far more aware of the dilemmas of administering U.S. power globally, and their unlimited self-esteem convinced virtually all of them that with a proper application of their thought and U.S. resources they could accomplish far more and far better, not just in the Third World but everywhere. One can make too much of their hubris, but in a milieu where ideas counted for much it remains a fact that their self-confidence was a spur to experimentation unlike any known in the period until then. If the Vietnam War was the eventual capstone of this mentality, in the early 1960s Indochina was still only one of many places, and far from the most important, to which the Kennedy circle turned its attention. Vietnam's ultimate significance, indeed, is as the culminating conjunction and reflection of the new Administration's more global concerns, and it is best understood in this context. For the president and the men around him, the war there was one they always set in a regional and world setting, not only symbolically, involving the question of credibility, but also physically, including the belief that they were also encouraging the states around Indochina, particularly Indonesia, to resist Communism.

The importance of events in the Third World during the early 1960s was magnified especially for the Kennedy circle because it became persuaded that the USSR and especially China were shifting their challenge to the United States from Europe, where they believed American resolve and nuclear power had stalemated alleged Soviet expansion, to the Third World. Even those like Harriman who were reticent about the extent of the Administration's eventual commitment to the Vietnam conflict shared this conviction well into the decade. The Moscow conference of world Communist parties in January 1961, the same month that Kennedy took office, nominally endorsed wars of national liberation in the Third World. But Washington never considered seriously the extent to which such rhetoric was merely ammunition in the deepening Sino-Soviet struggle for ideological mastery of world communism, much less the degree to which each side would subordinate their state interests to those of a quite diverse, if not amorphous, global collection of causes and parties. It was presumed to be the Sino-Soviet line simply because it was on paper, though the fact that the USSR also endorsed "peaceful coexistence," and China negotiated away its support for armed struggle in the 1962 Laos agreements to better ensure security along its southern border, did not strike the Cambridge ideologues as revealing more about the substance rather than the rhetoric of Sino-Soviet policy. "We are determined to help destroy this international disease," Kennedy adviser Walt Whitman Rostow stated in June 1961, "that is, guerrilla war designed, initiated, supplied, and led from outside an independent nation."[1] Southeast Asia was by no means alone, in the Administration's internal estimates, "as a symbolic test of strengths between the major powers of the West and the Communist bloc."[2] Hapless peasants in the most remote parts of the world might very well have to answer to Washington, whatever the reasons for their actions.

Rostow was especially active in arguing for the critical importance of the Third World in defining the United States' future problems and position. He succeeded to an extent that would have otherwise been impossible because even those who wished to continue to emphasize European priorities—and they were the large majority—nonetheless shared a consensus involving the symbolic interrelationship of European and world issues. This accord among key decisionmakers made it impossible for them to disagree on presumably minor involvements, which they believed could be kept sufficiently small to remain compatible with their overall commitments, and even strengthen, as in Africa, the useful role Europe could play in the world's military and economic balance. Given their global pretensions and ignorance of the risks involved, there was no effective barrier to the United States' deepening intervention in one place overwhelming its original intentions and assuming a dynamic and importance of its own—as was to occur in Vietnam after 1965. The Korean War first revealed the dilemma of being a global policeman, and even the staunchest Europeanist in Washington, Undersecretary of State George Ball, ardently believed it essential that the United States prevent the emergence of power vacuums everywhere in the world into which Communists might march. When those who advocated a European-centered orientation later attempted to reimpose an ordered sense of priorities on U.S. actions, they found that the universalist perspective they shared left them no coherent basis for arguing for a reorientation.

By the early 1960s most officials in Washington were convinced that the consequences of their passivity in some nation whose internal affairs displeased them were potentially more dangerous than the unpredictable risks of action. The symbolic importance of the credibility of power inherited from its less articulate predecessors, and of the interrelated nature of changes in one nation to events all around it and in the world, had become fixations transcending a reasoned assessment of the sources of internal tension and change. Indeed, given the economic considerations operating in tandem with the essentially symbolic, the combination invariably reduced opposition within the ranks of American leaders to a more active U.S. role in some nation when the choice presented itself. In a context where everything became potentially important, for whatever the reason, and past successes removed inhibiting concerns about the repercussions of failures in the future, it was highly likely in 1961 that something like the Vietnam conflict would soon occur somewhere, and only chance fixed on that poor nation rather than another. No less inevitable, also, was that such increasingly adventurous thinking would cause regional issues to threaten to overwhelm the United States' priorities and broad international goals and produce uncontrollable new dynamics in its foreign policy and power.

By August 1962, when the NSC approved national policy on a grand strategy toward the Third World, virtually everyone of importance agreed that confronting internal disorder and insurgency in the Third World—or Sino-Soviet "conquest from within," as opposed to conventional warfare—was essential. The NSC favored a greater readiness to act even when there was no direct Russian or Chinese involvement but where they might gain objectively from "other types of subversion" inimical to U.S. interests. The minute issues of the internal affairs of various nations became more than ever the legitimate concern of the United States, including, if need be, a warrant for action. It was, even more than under earlier administrations, the U.S. purpose to make certain "that developing nations evolve in a way that affords a congenial world environment"; naturally, this required "that strategic areas and the manpower and natural resources of developing nations do not fall under communist control. . . ." But in the even larger sense it meant that the United States had "an economic interest that the resources and markets of the less developed world remain available to us and to other Free World countries."[3]

Here was the basis for a far greater activism in the Third World. It embodied Washington's fears and stereotypes regarding Soviet culpability for the poor nations' problems as well as its residual right, even obligation, to manipulate autonomous trends for which Communists were not responsible and recast them into an integrated world order under U.S. hegemony.

The new Administration believed that its fresh will and far greater wisdom, combined with a superior organizational structure for implementing policy, would allow it to master the elusive threads and contradictions that had plagued its predecessors. All the involved agencies—the State and Defense departments, the CIA, the Agency for International Development, and others—met frequently to analyze in seminars and papers the "problems of development and internal defense" for which they needed common solutions.[4] As Cambridge professors were invited to Washington to supplement local talent in analyzing the vast panoply of social, cultural, and political changes in the Third World, the United States confidently prepared to confront it energetically.

One of its first and most important initiatives was in "counterinsurgency," a rubric that was more a vague philosophy of action than a concrete set of techniques and goals, a typically "can do" vision whose optimism was to carry the Administration along until Vietnam raised profound doubts as to its efficacy. The debacle of the Bay of Pigs invasion of Cuba in April 1961, rather than puncture such sublime self-confidence and produce caution, actually became a goad to further activity. It had revealed its CIA organizers as incompetent and the U.S. confidence in its Cuban exile proxies as naïve, but instead of learning from this failure, the unanimous consensus in Washington favored renewing the effort, in Kennedy's words the day after the invasion failed, to fight subversion with "the new concepts, the new tools, the new sense of urgency" that were still in the process of being articulated.[5]

Frequent references to "Vietnam and Thailand as counterinsurgency laboratories," of Vietnam "as a test case" of U.S. ability to fight wars of national liberation successfully, revealed how experimental counterinsurgency doctrine was from the inception, and it was based mainly on the assumption that American brains and money together would quickly find ways to translate desires into realities.[6] Precisely because of this, Vietnam after 1961 was principally a conjunctural problem for Washington, set in a regional and global context, its symbolism being as much a stimulus to action as the domino theory. The mere fact that the conflict in Vietnam was initially intended to be fought primarily "by those on the spot" rather than with U.S. forces revealed that those who led the world's most powerful nation, and who were also still naïve learners, were also extremely ignorant concerning the huge void they were about to plunge into.[7] The Administration quickly created a special interagency group to coordinate counterinsurgency, broken down into country sections. A Vietnam task force was organized in April 1961 as the first response to the Bay of Pigs disaster, on the mistaken assumption that Vietnamese might prove easier than Cubans to overcome.

Because counterinsurgency was at the beginning a strategy employing surrogates, above all to avoid drawing in American manpower, its first and quickest application was in the form of aid to the police in various nations. The CIA's police training program, which operated under an AID cover, had functioned until that time at a modest level. It doubled its activities in fiscal 1962, beginning in July 1961, over the previous year. Police training schools were opened in both Panama and Washington as well as in Liberia. By 1968, in addition, it had 458 U.S. police experts operating in 34 countries, and by 1973 it had trained over 7,300 foreign police in the United States alone.

This police program was overwhelmingly political in its functions from its inception. In virtually all of the nations it operated in, the police, as in Guatemala in 1956, were, as one American official wrote, "acutely geared to security against subversive activity and communist attack, with the primary police function taking a secondary role."[8] In Indonesia, a U.S. police adviser could report in late 1960, he had left a "pro-Western influence" among a vital force in a disturbingly anti-American nation. Reports the AID's overseas advisers sent back described countless examples of the police's role in the "control [of] social unrest," to "maintain internal security," "investigating and controlling subversives," and the like. All advisers were given systematic political indoctrination to equip them for this function.[9] That the AID's police program provided the status quo in dozens of authoritarian regimes help to retain their power was the explicit goal of the effort, not so much for the sake of various dictators and juntas but primarily to immobilize leftists and other undesirable elements as part of a global assault against national liberation movements.

The police's function, as the liberal luminary Chester Bowles explained to Kennedy in 1961 and as everyone acknowledged from this time onward, was largely to eliminate the role of the military in coping with violence, especially in the cities. Were guerrilla warfare to break out, the military could then use its much larger and more destructive firepower, but that was to be avoided— as indeed it was in most places. Since use of the military against strikers or demonstrations was counterproductive, by 1965 some Pentagon officials argued it was more essential in Latin America to equip the police adequately rather than the military since the police were much more likely to utilize what they received. What the police did in numerous nations was to serve as the basic instrument of violence, allowing the military, with whom it was invariably allied ideologically, the time to assume a much larger role in the Third World's politics during the 1960s than ever before. This, too, was understood and desired in Washington.

THE DECADE OF GENERALS

Just as the Kennedy Administration's action academics came to power animated by notions of counterinsurgency they justified with social science jargon, so, too, did they possess a much more articulate vision of the role of the military in Third World societies than their predecessors. True, the Eisenhower Administration preferred military regimes, but its rationale for doing so—that they kept order—was clumsy even if honest.

The Pentagon itself by 1959 had qualms about such a crude defense of the official NSC policy, and so it commissioned various think tanks, the Rand Corporation being the most important, to develop a more sophisticated rationale. Rand's 1959 conference of experts on the military in the Third World argued, despite a few skeptics gathered there, that in addition to providing a stable alternative to democracy when it failed, the military alone possessed the technical and administrative proficiency essential for more rapid modernization and were in fact the leading carriers of industrial and secular values. Given the semiliterate nature of most of these nations, the officers transmitted vital skills to their largely peasant soldiery and were prone even to be solicitous of the needs of society's poor. Rather than being a menace, the officer class was an integral aspect of solutions for Third World problems congenial to American interests. Similar views came from other analysts, and the articulate minority of consultants who disputed such notions was ignored. "Military modernization" theory was to become a major social science fashion for the next decade and beyond, especially among Washington's large stable of subsidized professors.

In later versions, modernization theorists added that civilian institutions could not direct or control civilian demands but that the military's "efficiency, honesty, and nationalism," as Harvard's Samuel P. Huntington described them, caused it to become true defenders of middle-class order against the impatient masses, and that they were the best friends of U.S. ambitions and needs in most of the Third World.[10] Walt Rostow by early 1962 was employing such analyses in an aggressive campaign to win Administration support for targeting the officer classes as its main allies. He did not deny that in some nations they might not conform to the desired model, but their role in the modernization process was potentially decisive—extending well beyond their task of maintaining internal security. The NSC's official policy on "internal defense" in August 1962 reflected Rostow's influence: "A change brought about through force by non-communist elements may be preferable to prolonged deterioration of governmental effectiveness," it stated, giving approval to those alone who had access to sufficient power to mount coups. "It is U.S. policy, when it is in the U.S. interest," it continued, "to make the local military and police advocates of democracy and agents for carrying forward the developmental process."[11]

From this point onward, with leading Rand advocates of this position incorporated to help define the rationale for the strategy, U.S. dependence on officers and the military for "nation-building" became a standard aspect of the indoctrination of all Americans working on "internal defense" and counterinsurgency.[12] This vision was to shape Washington's political policies decisively, as we shall see, in every major area of the Third World for the remainder of the Democratic Administration. The era of the generals was inaugurated not just in the realm of policy, as under Eisenhower, but in theory as well.

Still unresolved in the early 1960s was whether this use of ideas to influence policy was merely an attempt to justify an existing brutal one and make it appear more respectable in order to intensify it. Did the United States want officers who were truly modernizers conforming to their abstract techno-cratic model or simply pliable anti-Communists who would also sacrifice their national interests if they clashed with American needs? In a word, what would be Washington's response to officers who were genuine nationalists rather than merely anti-Communist, especially when true nationalism also con-flicted with the United States' integrative requirements and ambitions?

This issue was not to arise in many places, much less quickly, and so the theory's impact caused U.S. officials increasingly to regard military aid to many Third World nations as political in purpose, because to varying degrees it strengthened the officers' actual and potential power in the political struc-ture of every state receiving aid, thereby shaping its political evolution. Few needed arms for external defense, in any case, and most had no insurgency to confront. U.S. military missions working in foreign nations were integral to the effort, as a Pentagon official was later to phrase it, "to maintain our relations with the people who are in a position of influence in those countries so we can help to influence the course of events in those countries." Officers are "the coming leaders of their nations," Secretary of Defense Robert S. McNamara argued: "It is of inestimable value to the United States to have the friendship of such men."[13] Between 1950 and 1969, as a consequence, about 128,000 Third World officers and enlistees were given training in the United States, while U.S. missions trained 76,000 abroad.

The political potential of this enormous, costly effort was obvious to all in Washington, including those who dismissed Rostow's attribution of efficiency and virtue to the military as either false or irrelevant—or both. When an aid review committee under retired General Lucius Clay in early 1963 argued for reducing economic and military assistance to inefficient or corrupt regimes in order to save taxpayers' money, the circle of key policymakers around Kennedy thought it excessively naïve. "I daresay if we confined our aid to those countries who would use it 'effectively' (whatever this may mean)," Robert W. Komer told the president, "we could reduce the list of our clients considerably. . . . But in applying such criteria we would be opting ourselves out of shoring up, or otherwise influencing, a whole series of client states which, whatever their own internal weaknesses, it is in our strategic interest to help."[14] Regardless of their character or form, the United States was more firmly committed than ever to working politically with the military in the Third World.

THE ENIGMA OF THE OFFICERS

The nature and role of officers in the Third World defies simplifications—including those used to justify relying on them much more heavily. If it was perfectly clear long before 1961 that while U.S. military aid might alter fundamentally the political balance in favor of the military in many nations, the final outcome of such intervention could not be reliably predicted, save that it rarely led to permanent stability. The innumerable variations among the many military-dominated nations of the world after 1945 made many outcomes possible—as Washington was to discover repeatedly.

The dominant character of military regimes is their internal factionalism. The frequency of coups in military-led regimes as opposed to those led by parties or monarchies was over twice as great from 1945 to 1972. Latin America accounted for nearly half of all coups during this period, but even more significant was that the likelihood of coups was directly proportionate to the poverty of the nation, so that the United States linked the development of the poorest and potentially most revolutionary nations of the world to the efficacy of the military modernization theory. In some states, such as Thailand, intramilitary conflict became the constant concern of an army that had few military duties to distract it. Elsewhere, as in Latin America, military coups were not uncommonly the result of civilian groups convincing the military to mediate in power struggles on their behalf. At least 250 Third World coups between 1945 and 1975 revealed the endemic precariousness of power based on the military and the incapacity of officers to provide leadership in all domains, including those essential economic changes that alone were the precondition of political stability. The Americans, ironically, increasingly opted for the weakest reed of all on which to lean in the Third World. It was the very ease of the process of intramilitary struggle, of coups generating yet more coups, that undermined the long-term interests of the existing local ruling classes—and the United States—as a whole.

Nevertheless, if the military was not in reality an effective agent of modernization, a socioeconomic condition no one in Washington ever defined precisely, the resulting social and political instability would inevitably confront the United States with greater challenges in the future. Implicitly and astonishingly vague, modernization meant a society often designated simply as "middle class." In those nations where the United States most needed armies to perform their strictly military functions competently, such as South Vietnam and the Philippines, their clients were never able to master logistics and maintenance, much less extirpate corruption. In the Middle East, where the military's claim on national budgets was double that for desperately needed welfare, officer-led regimes failed to master the use of their arms or to create efficient armies. And soldiers and officers who returned to the civilian sector were able to perform only the most primitive tasks there.

More often than not, what the military accomplished while controlling power was to accumulate wealth. Indeed, it was far more likely for a military elite to drain a nation economically for its own account than to strengthen it in the long run against radicalism. In Latin America, Thailand, South Vietnam, the Middle Eastern states, Zaire, and many other nations, corruption varied from significant to fabulous in scope, often uprooting the existing and relatively stable elites institutionally and leaving nothing durable in their place—while the displaced rich often plotted their return to power. In some nations, of course, the military had a class basis or was symbiotic on an existing class much larger than itself and thereby able to provide social continuity and a measure of stability. But the greater the corruption, the bigger the void after the inevitable fall of some U.S. client—and the more the risk of sudden and total radicalization. The military was preeminently an agent of grave destabilization, and the extent to which it allowed intraclass rivalries among the traditional forces of order to erode the whole structure of ruling class politics was often vital to the chances of the Left to gain power.

U.S. advocates of reliance on officers as the key agents of modernization claimed that their supposedly overwhelmingly middle- and lower-middle-class origins would reduce their commitment to protecting existing elites. At the time that this theory was adopted there was little evidence on the class origins of officers, and while much more exists today, it only confirms that a far more complex reality exists, though in fact the U.S. shift to the military needed no scientific justification but merely embodied the rougher impressionistic generalities and biases about the world that were usually sufficient to vindicate official predilections.

In the Middle East most officers were from middle-class backgrounds and deeply linked to it. In Asia the picture was different: Thailand's officers tended to be sons of officers and to have wealthier backgrounds, as did Indonesian and Burmese officers. In Argentina the picture was mixed, depending on the branch of the military, while elsewhere it was generally no less convoluted. In Peru, perhaps alone of all the major nations, the existing industrial and landed elites scorned the military as a profession, boycotting it socially, although the higher officers were from better-off families than their juniors. I shall return to the Latin military in the next chapter, but nowhere in the world was the original U.S. assumption regarding the relation of officer-class background to its ideology justifiable. How long a military-based regime could survive autonomously of an existing class, whether upper, middle or lower, without relying increasingly on brutal repression remained a very open question—one whose implications were subtle but also fundamental. And whether such rulers would also choose to make themselves into the new economic as well as political elite posed even greater dangers to the process of presumably rational stabilization the United States ostensibly was committed to.

Power had its own dynamics—and risks—in every nation, and that modernization and stability would be the outcome of passing it to generals was, given the behavior of officers until then, a leap of pure faith on the Kennedy Administration's part. In the long run the real question was how far the military could distort the political, social, and economic dynamics of innumerable nations, and how Washington would cope with the growing traumatizing consequences of its increasingly dangerous dependence on its decadent client regimes. Vietnam was the first test of this dilemma but hardly the last.

The Challenge
of
Latin America

*F*IDEL CASTRO AND THE CUBAN REVO-
lution of January 1959 guaranteed that
the United States would not be able dur-
ing the 1960s to shunt Latin America aside as peripheral to its global concerns, for of the many unresolved legacies in the Third World that the
Eisenhower Administration left to its successor, Cuba was the most pressing.

CUBA SHAKES THE HEMISPHERE

Cuba, more than any place in Latin America, had been virtually a de facto
U.S. colony. Economically, preferential tariff arrangements since 1901 transformed it into a vast dependent sugar plantation tied wholly to the U.S.
market while importing three-quarters of its needs from the north. During the
1950s the stagnant sugar industry still accounted for 80 percent of Cuba's
export earnings and a quarter of its national income, requiring a country with
vast uncultivated estates reserved for sugar to import a quarter of its food
needs. Cuba's trade deficit with the United States in the decade up to 1959
amounted to one billion dollars. U.S. investors owned fully 40 percent of
Cuba's sugar production, 90 percent of its utilities, half of its railroads, and
much else—while naturalized citizens controlled a significant part of the
remainder. The main economic function of the highly Americanized Cuban
middle and upper classes was to service this United States-owned system as
well as the immensely profitable industry that catered to Yankee tourism with
hotels, prostitution, and gambling. Marginalized and with precious little national identity, this comprador bourgeoisie preferred to make and spend

money and left politics, and the army that controlled it under Fulgencio Batista for most of the time since 1933, to déclassé, highly corrupt soldiers with few ties to the established local economic elites. Perhaps more than for any other nation in the hemisphere, the United States' domination had created in Cuba a centrifugal, highly unstable society.

It was the very nature of this ruling class, combined with the economic and social consequences of a dependent export economy with large unemployment and growing land tenure problems, that made the July 26 Movement under Fidel Castro capable of winning power so quickly and with relatively few forces, for the Cuban status quo had few defenders ready to stand and fight for it. The proximity to Florida and the elite's strong personal and economic links elsewhere in the area, where it had diversified a large part of its money, also allowed it to be highly mobile. Cuba was a nation with a society the United States had made over for its own needs and desires, and in 1959 it was to become a challenge to it without precedent.

Ironically, the movement Castro led was also eclectic and an ideologically confused by-product of the fractured Cuban society, with the middle and upper classes providing his most active early followers. Washington's inability to comprehend an admittedly complex and unique cause was to give the July 26 Movement crucial time to consolidate its power. Had Castro been anything close to a Marxist before 1961 the United States would have unquestionably, without hesitation, taken all the steps necessary to destroy him, for the Eisenhower Administration was in no mood to waver on Marxism in the region at any time during its tenure in office. Castro's genuine perplexity also compelled Washington to hesitate, as did his distance from the Cuban Communist Party—which had worked sporadically with Batista and in March 1958 had dismissed Fidel as a potential "middle-class dictator."[1]

This is not to say that Washington was in any way tolerant toward Castro's revolutionaries, whom Dulles in 1957 thought "don't sound too good."[2] But all U.S. officials familiar with Cuba admitted it "has been plagued for 60 years with graft and dishonesty," and they did not feel that defending Batista was as important as the question of who would replace him.[3] They were habituated to change, and justifiably cynical about those with reform pretensions, and this too won Castro time. America knew that anti-Yankee feeling was widespread in Cuba, even among some conservatives, and this was often expressed in demands for nationalization of foreign-owned utilities. Castro distanced himself from such proposals in early 1958, playing down his earlier opinions. When in March 1958, sixteen months after the July 26 Movement began its revolt and a wave of bloody repression had turned, in the State Department's opinion, "some 80 percent of the Cuban people" against Batista, the United States suspended the export of combat arms, although it left its military missions in place.[4] Its new posture, given the U.S. ambassador's continued public friendship with Batista, only managed to alienate both sides. It was certain, however, that Castro was anti-American, and so in the final months of 1958, as Batista's power was reduced to control of the major cities, it made clumsy, partially exposed secret efforts to replace Batista and keep Castro from coming to power. When Batista fled the country on January 1, 1959, Castro was justifiably convinced that the United States was seeking to thwart the revolution's victory, despite Washington's embarrassed recognition of his government a week later.

Castro's program during his first three months in power was persistently vague, and conflict between the July 26 Movement and the Communists for control of the labor federation merely confirms a CIA analysis two years later that Castro's movement at this time was a middle-class-led force completely independent of the Communists and with no exact reform platform. Nor was it especially anti-United States by Latin standards. When Castro accepted a private invitation to the United States in April 1959, he hoped to determine whether Washington would tolerate him even as the NSC was already discussing the question of removing him from power. The closest he came to a meeting with the Administration was an informal session with Nixon, who confirmed the opinion of some Latin experts that Castro was naïve about international communism but not worse than that. The State Department decided that he was "like a child" and "quite immature" about power, and it was this psychological interpretation that also helped delay open U.S. hostility and gave the revolution more time to consolidate itself—and time is what it needed most.[5] Meanwhile, Castro publicly welcomed foreign investment and hinted he wanted the United States to give Cuba a larger sugar quota as well as long-term aid, but official silence discouraged him from pressing for it.

During May the conflict between the July 26 Movement and the Cuban Communists intensified; and before the OAS Castro called on the United States to provide a thirty-billion-dollar, ten-year aid package to the hemisphere to thwart social upheavals that might bring Communists to power, greatly irritating Washington. "This is not a Red revolution," he stated in May.[6] Red or not, when Castro and the July 26 leadership at the end of May announced an astonishingly mild land reform law and took their first hesitant step toward serious change, they inadvertently set their course toward conflict with America. Huge U.S. holdings of 1.7 million acres were affected, and from this time onward American-Cuban relations consisted of a series of escalating actions and retaliations that was to culminate in July 1960 with the Administration's abolition of the Cuban sugar quota. The United States protested the terms of the land reform law and then applied various pressures, including successfully blocking the sale, in October 1959, of British jet fighters that Castro thought essential to his defense. The first use of exile-manned small planes based in Florida to bomb Cuba that same month only convinced Castro that sooner or later the United States would attempt to overthrow him. The British had warned Washington that if they did not sell the jets, Cuba would turn to the Soviets for supplies, but their argument carried no weight because in the fall of 1959, while Washington was moderately concerned about Communist infiltration in the Cuban government, they did not believe Castro himself was a Communist.

Given the Latin American context, Washington felt that, if anything, Castro was even worse than a Communist. A Communist leader could have no real impact in the hemisphere, but a neutralist who was anti-United States might galvanize far more successfully the latent nationalism of the region, and "if emulated by other Latin American countries, [it] would have serious adverse effects on Free World support of our leadership." To tolerate Castro, much less cooperate with him, would create a situation in which "the United States cannot hope to encourage and support sound economic policies in other Latin American countries and promote necessary private investment."[7] Castro's already growing influence in the region was based on his nationalism, and it was this rather than communism that the United States feared most. Indeed, both privately and publicly the United States operated on the assumption that he was not a Communist but a neutralist who was anti-American and for the "confiscation of private property," leading him to take positions that "international communism" could exploit indirectly.[8]

This attack on its hegemony in the hemisphere could not be left unchallenged indefinitely, but had Castro been a Communist—to reiterate a crucial point—the Eisenhower Administration would not have hesitated to act decisively, including with U.S. troops. The State Department early in November 1959 urged support for the Cuban opposition effort to replace Castro. The CIA began to plan an exile invasion the following month, and in March 1960 Eisenhower approved steps to commence the actual training of exiles. Until they were prepared, increased economic sanctions were to accompany smaller CIA-organized sabotage operations and radio propaganda. It was in December 1959, too, that Castro was told that a cut in Cuba's sugar quota was possible, a threat he was to hear often.[9]

The events of the next months saw no basic shift in U.S. policy, which was by then irreversibly committed to Castro's eventual overthrow. This, along with a sharp increase from U.S. bases of small air attacks on economic targets, caused Castro to diversify his economic ties toward the Soviet bloc and prepare to confront a United States-backed economic and military offensive. In February 1960 Cuba endorsed integrated national economic planning for the first time. It also moved to take control of U.S. mining operations, and in June it asked United States-owned companies to refine Soviet oil. Their refusal to do so led to their seizure, followed by a U.S. ban on Cuban sugar in July and a final break between the two countries.

This was the situation the Democrats inherited. The Republicans had attempted to isolate Castro's charismatic impact on Latin America throughout 1960 even as they methodically prepared for an armed assault on Cuba. But the Eisenhower Administration believed that it could fend off immediate hemispheric issues and transfer the responsibility for longer-term problems to their successors, and that meanwhile the very amorphous nature of Castroism would also make it incapable of consolidating power and equipping a loyal army. It was a major miscalculation. No less of an error was its failure to understand that Castro, unlike any other middle-class leader in the hemisphere before him, was able quickly to address the social issues Batista had neglected, thereby winning the support of the masses. It was this success, above all, that had changed the balance of forces between Cuba and the United States and made the Cuban revolution permanent.

The Kennedy Administration eagerly took up the challenge of Castro, though it, too, saw that while the July 26 Movement and the Communists might collaborate, they were still independent ideas and, usually, movements. This made Cuba all the more dangerous. Like its predecessors, the Kennedy Administration also regarded the basic issue as one of a credible challenge to hemispheric solidarity under U.S. leadership—and it was here that the Soviet Union was allegedly gaining, if only symbolically, from Washington's distress. It was this crisis-ridden context that caused liberal Democrats like Adolf A. Berle, who had as much influence over Kennedy as anyone on this topic, to elaborate Republican plans to overthrow Castro while employing reform rhetoric to justify themselves—yet the means were to be the same. "My estimate is that there will be a major climax over Latin America," he confided in his diary at the beginning of March. "The Caribbean will explode. We shall have to act. . . . And the battle is joined."[10]

The Kennedy Administration used the invasion machinery its predecessors had made ready to discover that, unlike Guatemala, the Cubans would fight, and do so with mass support; worse yet, the Bay of Pigs debacle in April 1961 exposed both the CIA and its exile clients as incompetent. It was the Democrats' rude introduction both to the counterinsurgency enterprise and Latin America. Remarkably enough, they learned nothing about either, but were only goaded to push ahead resolutely.

The Bay of Pigs finally forced Castro and the July 26 Movement into a far greater dependence on the Soviet Union than they had desired or thought necessary until then. Above all, it convinced him that he needed sufficient arms to deter an otherwise inevitable direct U.S. invasion. Communists were given far greater access to key posts, but not until April 1961 did Castro proclaim the Cuban revolution to be socialist in character. After the most uneasy unification of the Communists and the July 26 Movement the following July, Castro and his old allies remained very much in the ascendancy, but the distinction between Castroism and Communism that even Berle had acknowledged to be a reality began to erode somewhat, until the following December, when Castro for the first time proclaimed his belief in Marxism-Leninism. This alliance continued only because Russia agreed most hesitantly to accept Castro on his own terms, including all his unorthodoxies regarding the role of the personality cult, coexistence, and the function of democratic centralism as opposed to his individual whims. Most of all, they were ready to pay most of the material price he demanded, including that part directly attributable to *fidelismo*'s often negative impact on the economy.

Only ninety miles from its shores, the Kennedy Administration now confronted what was as close to a Communist state as had ever existed in the hemisphere. Appropriately, it was created in the one Latin nation the United States had most influenced and controlled, for Cuba's evolution from the beginning of this century down to 1959 was the product of American actions and policies, and its final radicalization was the result of the social and economic dislocations intrinsic in that historic relationship—and were entirely the United States' responsibility. At the inception of 1961 Washington found this situation profoundly disturbing, and Cuba made the hemisphere no longer a peripheral U.S. concern, as it had been until then, but one that was central and increasingly challenging.

THE LATIN AMERICAN CONTEXT

Social and economic conditions in Latin America gave the deeply agitated Kennedy Administration no cause for complacency. Statistical indicators, whatever their methodological deficiencies, revealed a troubled region in the process of a structural crisis and with a vast mass of humanity in profound distress.

Latin America has been the most rapidly urbanizing Third World region in this century, in large part due to the failure of the existing land system to provide the minimum livelihood for survival. From 1930 to 1960 the percentage of the population (201 million people in 1960) living in urban areas had doubled, to reach 33 percent. East Asia, by contrast, had only 18 percent urbanized, and the other Third World continents even less. This pattern of growth continued in much the same fashion for the next twenty years. Put another way, in 1960 two-thirds of the Latin population lived in rural areas, while agriculture and mining, the basic economic activities to which they related, generated only 17 percent of the gross domestic product.

The social causes of the misery the masses lived in were diverse, but the inequitable structure of land tenure was by far the most important. In Peru, with the highest rate of urbanization, those owning more than 1,000 hectares of land in 1960, or 0.2 percent of all landholders, accounted for 69 percent of the land. Over nine-tenths of those engaged in agriculture owned no land whatsoever, working as tenants or laborers. In Argentina the 5.8 percent of the holders with 1,000 or more hectares had 74 percent of the land. In Brazil, 0.9 percent of the owners held 44 percent of the land, while in Chile 1.3 percent owned 73 percent. In Colombia, 0.3 percent owned 30 percent of the land, while in Venezuela 1.3 percent held 82 percent.

This basic pattern in land ownership showed up in income distribution statistics. In 1960, the richest 5 percent of the population earned 33.4 percent of the income in Latin America taken as a whole, with 29.2 percent for the next richest 15 percent—or 62.6 percent for the wealthiest fifth. Peru and Colombia had the most inequitable distribution in the hemisphere and among the worst in the entire Third World. Latin America's poorest half of the population received 13.4 percent of the income in 1960. The per capita annual income of those in the poorest fifth in 1960 was $60, while those in the wealthiest 5 percent received $2,600. Latin America was, above all, a class society with a vast gulf—economic, social, and political—between the rich and the poor. Indeed, the statistical gap between them was significantly greater in Latin America than in any other Third World region.

RULING LATIN AMERICA

Politics in Latin America both reflected and reinforced the highly inequitable economic structure, and even those civilian parties that disturbed the United States, with the exception of the relatively unimportant Marxist groups, never challenged a system of distribution that favored them. As complex as civilian politics in the region was—and the distinctions among the many countries in this regard discourage excessive generalizations—beliefs in egalitarianism never influenced it. The general rhetoric of reform, on the other hand, was far more important because the huge congregations of displaced peasants in the cities, most without appropriate skills and living precariously, made labor-absorbing economic development a key issue for them, reinforcing the political strength of those sectors of the middle and upper classes who for their own reasons and interests wanted economic, and particularly industrial, growth. Elite-dominated populism created a distinctive political dialogue in many Latin states, but it scarcely shaped economic policy beyond the crea-tion of employment—a goal for which most of the masses were grateful. Nor was political democracy in the formal, institutional sense an important issue in civilian politics in Brazil, Argentina, and elsewhere. Civilian elites were ready to manipulate the masses for their own purposes, but not to give them real power, for the continuation of their own privileges precluded that.

Latin politics comprised, in essence, intraclass rivalries, complicated by the fact that in many countries there were no strict lines separating the various sectors of the civilian upper and middle classes. In some nations, such as Argentina, the older landowners, financiers, and industrialists were often socially connected members of the same families. What they had most in common was their interest in maintaining the existing distributive struc-ture, although their conflicts over their own relative positions within it, while softened by personal ties, were nonetheless sharp.

The principal issue dividing rival factions in Latin politics, and the one that most involved U.S. interests as well as goals, was the relation of the state to economic development, and politics became the crucial vehicle for resolving this dispute and determining, to some great extent, the distribution of wealth among contesting elites. It was the United States' misfortune to embark on its economic program for the hemisphere at a time when the main thrust of Latin politics—above all, among relatively conservative elements with great economic ambitions—was toward a far greater role for the government in the economy. Whatever the nuances in conservative civilian politics in the various states, Washington was out of touch and sympathy for its most dynamic sector, and Latin civilian-led politics proved the most frustrating for it.

Every Latin nation was different from the rest in important regards, but the divisions within the middle and upper classes in each and their relation-ship—whether friendly or hostile—to foreign interests was generally *a* (if not *the*) central political issue. Nationalism was an expression and reflection of this struggle but only infrequently its real cause, serving mainly as a powerful tool in political debate. Yet over time the political alignments and economic strategies of the various key sectors—technocrats from more affluent profes-sional and middle class backgrounds, industrialists producing for the domes-tic market, export-oriented landowners, those servicing either one or another of these burgeoning sectors—also frequently altered as surplus capi-tal led to diversification within each of these groups and the possibility of making deals with foreign interests on terms acceptable to each opened up. In no place in Latin America did a purely national capitalism led by a national bourgeoisie emerge with the goal of industrializing an autonomous economy; nor were there any important states where foreign capital could operate as freely as the United States wished. The essence of each situation, and the key to comprehending its politics, was in the marked gradations between these extremes. And however crucial foreign (which is usually to say U.S.) capital was in defining each nation's economic evolution and its relation to a world market, the outcome of intraclass political struggles, with or without coups, was generally at least as critical.

Industrialization in each nation was to some extent a by-product of pragmatic responses to the 1930s depression and the Second World War's shortages, but combined with more deliberative policies it thereafter produced its own momentum as state funds to develop basic heavy capital-intensive industries allowed networks of privately owned lighter industries in consumer goods and metalworking to become symbiotic on the state sector. The masses who gained employment, nonexporting larger landowners, and the service structure linked to such state-stimulated growth comprised a formidable and often politically dominant section in many nations, particularly the more populous. The technocratic bureaucracy managing this system was highly educated and self-confidently committed to an expansion of their own roles in society. In many nations these administrators had the basis, and often the need, to relate to foreign multinationals that could provide technology, and they were also quite ready to do so if it was to their own interests. In Mexico the state's control over the gross domestic product grew from 8 percent in the 1930s to 25 percent in the 1960s and 45 percent and over in the following decade, while its social structure was as inequitable as ever, its politics authoritarian, and it was open to many kinds of foreign investment. Comparable patterns existed throughout the hemisphere.

While this fracturing of the already ambiguously defined upper and middle classes was to produce fluid political coalitions, and the consumption habits of these groups made their nationalist pretensions a sham as their rising living standards opened the door to foreign investments and imports to meet their distinctly internationalist bourgeois tastes, they usually shared a consensus on keeping the masses in their place should co-optive populist demagoguery fail, an accord that bound them together as a class with an elemental sense of its own role in society. But the risk of populism being used in intraelite struggles in ways that threatened inadvertently to open the path to truly radical measures was a tension with which Latin politics lived. It was a danger, too, that struck many U.S. officials as excessive. Neither the form of much of mainstream Latin politics, with its populist rhetoric, or the substance, with its mercurial and opportunistic commitments to mixed state and private economic development, pleased Washington.

Given the doleful state of Latin civilian politics and the dominant influence of military modernization theory on the Kennedy Administration, it was no surprise that for the next eight years the United States preferred generals to civilians at least as much as its predecessors. The Pentagon, with its innumerable contacts among Latin officers, was unwavering in endorsing them, and congressional committees often described them as pillars of stability and reform. Delesseps S. Morrison, whom Kennedy designated ambassador to the OAS in May 1961, was an ardent exponent of supporting officers, and over the objections of Latin spokesmen who feared it would become a breeding ground for military cabals, he had the United States create the Inter-American Defense College in Washington, which gave primarily political indoctrination to senior Latin officers. He successfully isolated the few remaining White House liberals who were queasy about the alliance with generals and who especially opposed the Administration's acceptance or quiet welcome of those coups for which it was not directly responsible. "The military *could* be a force for stability," he argued.[11]

In May 1964 a combined report of the State and Defense departments alleged that "The potential for advancing U.S. interests and objectives through effective U.S. influence upon the Latin American military is great," attaching the "highest" priority to direct contacts with them.[12] Military modernization theory aside, the strongest consideration increasing U.S. reliance on generals was the essentially conservative civilian elites with strong nationalist bents, opportunistically prone to anti-parliamentarian means on behalf of their own interests, and indigestible in the United States' grand plan for the hemispheric economy. Its integrative economic goals, rather than anticommunism (on which both civilian elites and generals were in accord), defined whom the United States would support in the convoluted Latin political spectrum. It made eminent good sense in Washington to affect the power balance in various key states by backing officers who alone had the resources for maintaining stability against such radicalized masses that might exist but above all against the nationalist Center-Right that defined civilian politics in much of Latin America.

Submissive, authoritarian, and socially regressive regimes that catered to U.S. investors and local constituencies ready to work within the boundaries it defined meant an end to the vestiges of Latin parliamentarianism, but Washington had no difficulty justifying them. The Latin system operated its own way, senior Pentagon officials argued, and "democratic constitutional" government on the "Anglo-Saxon model" was not likely to flourish, warranting toleration for authoritarian states and reliance on the military.[13] When Lincoln Gordon was made assistant secretary of state for Latin American affairs, he argued that as a "pragmatic idealist" he believed that economic growth would have to precede social justice in order to have something to distribute. Only North America and Western Europe had a sufficient consensus on the institutional framework for political democracy, and "much of this continent" did not.[14] But whatever the reasons for it, the United States deepened its dependence on the Latin military to regulate the region's affairs in a way it expected to find far more congenial to its interests.

This commitment was made despite the fact that although U.S. officers were acquainted superficially with many of their Latin peers, both the State and Defense departments in 1964 admitted privately that there was a great deal that they did not know about the military in each Latin nation, especially their positions on socioeconomic issues, their class origins, and how they related to political dynamics. And like the infinitely complex matrix of civilian politics, the officers, too, defied simple descriptions. Indeed, the United States had already turned so irrevocably to the military, essentially in a leap of faith reflecting its predilections, only because it could no longer control the civilians.

Latin officers were a very mixed collection, and their access to the levers of the state, which the United States, in varying degrees, often aided them to attain, altered the context of class and economic power in every country they ruled. Military juntas directly made rapid class transformations and alterations in the structure of domination possible when they confiscated national wealth for their own purses, and indirectly by changing the framework and rules of economic activity and capital formation.

The military in some states, such as Argentina, had precious little ideology save *antiperonismo,* and were divided into countless cliques that were scarcely more than vehicles for careerism. Their main role was to keep their civilian allies from their own conservative middle- and upper-class backgrounds in power, and it was the latter who largely defined programs. Prosperity that brought stability and social passivity was for them a good thing, yet this alone was not a program. Growth became a goal for others, and in several nations the ruling generals when in power transferred economic leadership back to civilian technocrats and local industrialists. In this sense, officer corps were frequently more ready to act as mediators than leaders, at least until they were overthrown by other officers with their own ambitions. Yet the vast majority of Latin officers ran regimes that were corrupt and incompetent as well as repressive, usually putting the civilians to shame in this domain. And it would eventually become clear that military-led regimes might also have anti-Yankee nationalist residues that months of training in the United States could not expunge. Of this, more later.

When Kennedy came to power, generals ruled only four Latin nations, yet when Nixon took office there were nine—and these in the largest, most important countries. The Republican succession accepted, *in toto,* the Democratic legacy on the nature of the military and the wisdom of relying on it. The decade of generals was to be extended.

CREATING THE ALLIANCE FOR PROGRESS

It was in this context that President Kennedy proclaimed the Alliance for Progress on March 13, 1961, a month before the Cuba Bay of Pigs invasion. Milton Eisenhower later claimed that the Alliance was the outcome of his brother's Latin policies, and he was correct in the sense that it, too, reflected a troubled Washington's search for means to cope with both conservative nationalism and the advent of Castroism in the hemisphere. Yet it was the decision to implement the CIA-backed invasion of Cuba that unquestionably determined both the Alliance's timing and rhetoric as the new Administration moved down a dual track in Latin America of employing a big stick along with what was to prove, despite much verbiage, a quite modest carrot. The struggle against the Left also created the vital context in which the Alliance was implemented.

Kennedy's speech was energetic rhetoric in favor of social and economic progress and reform, crafted mainly by liberal White House speech writers and, above all, by Berle—who synthesized liberal shibboleths with the values he acquired as a legal adviser to U.S. corporate interests operating in the hemisphere. For this small band, the Alliance was to fight the extreme Right opposed to change as well as communism—presumably in the form of Castroism. Yet the Administration's Latin American specialists, in translating the stirring but vague message into numbers and conditions, ignored Berle's original emphasis on support for the so-called democratic Left in the region, and on politics rather than economics. Vital details of the program had to be honed at the Punta del Este meeting of the region's nations in Uruguay the following August, where the head of the U.S. delegation, C. Douglas Dillon, a Republican Wall Street banker who was now secretary of the treasury, was not in the least inclined to stress an excessively reformist approach. Instead he speculated publicly that if the Latin nations made the right kind of domestic changes they might expect twenty billion dollars in aid and investment from the United States over the next decade. In fact there was no specific U.S. aid commitment beyond one billion dollars the first year, with the fiscal assumptions of the plan quite confused, not the least because Dillon had unilaterally chosen the twenty-billion-dollar number, and soon American officials suggested that 80 percent of the Alliance's total program would be financed out of Latin domestic savings. In the end, the Latins were to get half of Dillon's amount and pay for 87 percent of Alliance costs.

If numbers remained vague, so too did the reform goals in the Alliance's charter. Annual economic growth at 2.5 percent per capita, a fairer distribution of income, increased industrialization and employment, better education and housing, and land reform were lofty aspirations, but the means for attaining them were left both elusive and discretionary. Naturally, the need for foreign private investment was mentioned often. Detailed discussions revealed, however, that the United States wanted monetary stabilization essential for foreign investors, while the major Latin nations futilely pressed Washington to commit itself to pay higher prices for Latin exports so they could attain the Alliance's goals via equitable trade as well as aid. The Alliance's charter, clearly, was directed toward neutralizing Castro, whose influence on the region was rising, and the Cubans justifiably took full credit for its creation.

The Punta del Este promises began to tarnish very quickly because, despite a few lone voices in Washington, the United States and the major Latin nations disagreed on the same questions after the Alliance's creation that had divided them since 1945. The most important remained the terms of trade between U.S. and Latin exports, which persistently favored the United States after 1957; the need to stabilize prices for their exports via commodity agreements; and eliminating the United States' protective measures and subsidies to assist its own farmers, which had aggravated relations since the mid-1950s. The Latins welcomed aid, but as Colombian officials pointed out in early 1962, their losses from the declining price of coffee exceeded their Alliance credits by about three times. A modest coffee stabilizing agreement did win U.S. support for two years because it also allowed the United States to impose a ceiling on prices, but by the summer of 1964 Congress not only withdrew U.S. participation in it but also cut back on imports of foreign meat, mainly from the hemisphere, and reduced foreign sugar quotas. Throughout this period the United States continued to compete aggressively with Latin exports on the world market with its subsidized wheat, cotton, and meat. U.S. aid and loans via the IADB were still tied to its own goods, and continued to be carried mainly in expensive U.S. boats. By 1964, as well, servicing its foreign debt alone offset 30 percent of all external assistance Latin America received.

Latin response to the Alliance at its inception had ranged from skepticism to a mild though cautious receptivity, precisely because they understood the decisive significance of such economic issues, and the United States evaded a commitment to change its long-standing trade practices from the inception of the program. United States-Latin trade relations remained as lopsided in the United States' favor as ever, so the Latins did not waver from their pre-Alliance economic strategies. The Kennedy Administration and U.S. investors strongly opposed their efforts to create a regional trade market, LAFTA, since it would have excluded many foreign goods, and it regarded such schemes as part and parcel of the nationalist sentiment growing in the hemisphere.

The Alliance charter endorsed the central role of private enterprise, both local and foreign, in implementing its broad if vague goals, and Washington emphasized it as much after 1961 as it had before. References to it studded virtually every U.S. statement and report, public and private, like a ritual incantation. But during the first years of the Alliance there were no barriers to either increased local or foreign investment continuing in the future as it had in the past, local nationalist legislation notwithstanding. Save for Cuba, no political change occurred in the hemisphere to cause it to decline or dry up, yet the Alliance was inaugurated at the moment of a crisis of nerves among the Latin rich and U.S. corporations. Cuba caused a panic that, along with the difficulties of normal trade between the United States and the Latins, guaranteed that the Alliance's economic goals would not be achieved.

Capital flight by local businessmen out of the region, by its nature, was impossible to measure exactly, but informed estimates in May 1962 fixed it at ten billion dollars to possibly more than twice that—a huge sum given the ten-year projected cost of the Alliance plan. U.S. direct investment in the Latin republics, on which Washington was counting so heavily, actually fell over six hundred million dollars in 1960, and while its book value tended to increase from two hundred to three hundred million dollars each year through 1964, the growth came largely from locally borrowed and reinvested profits. Despite a large increase in the value of U.S. capital in the region in 1965, in 1966 it dropped by over eight hundred million dollars. From 1966 to 1972, indeed, funds from the U.S. comprised only a fifth of its direct investment. In real terms, U.S. private investment's role was declining, and the Latins were not getting the local or foreign investment Washington planned upon. The AID, which coordinated the Alliance program, came under pressure to expand its investment guaranty program for U.S. corporations afraid of risk, and in 1964 it did so—with no measurable impact on investment.

From its inception, the Alliance did not alter in any significant manner the political assumptions and objectives of U.S. policy regarding Latin politics, the military, and dictators, nor did it modify in any way those classic economic principles it had tirelessly reiterated since 1945. The Alliance's reform rhetoric, in a word, is a wholly misleading basis for understanding U.S. goals and actions during the first half of the decade, which one can comprehend only by examining its bilateral relations with specific countries. The Latins had relatively slight interest in the program, and many of its conservatives feared a close association with the United States for economic rather than political reasons. Despite the Kennedy speech writers, who tried to read something into the Alliance that simply was never there, both Democratic presidents of the decade, Kennedy and Johnson, entrusted basic policymaking in the region and its implementation to men whose vision was aggressively hegemonic. Indeed, their Latin policy was nothing more than the classic assertion of U.S. economic interests along with, for the first time, a response to a serious leftist menace in the form of Cuba. Politics was a means to advance these goals, and therefore cooperation with dictators and generals both continued and intensified. On the first anniversary of the Alliance, the United States' soon-to-resign representative to its inter-American committee dolefully admitted that the Latin Right, dictators included, would not accept the program's reform rhetoric and would obtain aid in any event.

In no important way did the Democrats alter traditional U.S. policy. The appointment of Thomas C. Mann as assistant secretary of state for Latin American affairs in December 1963, after having served in the same post under Eisenhower, was a purely administrative shift. Mann's convocation in March 1964 of all the U.S. ambassadors in the hemisphere to review policy, which later critics claimed to represent a new direction, merely codified the NCS's long-standing commitment to work for U.S. private investment, oppose communism, cooperate with undemocratic regimes, and foster economic growth while minimizing reforms. In 1964, however, the main concern for the United States in the hemisphere was the fact that, the Alliance notwithstanding, "the economic outlook in the area," as the CIA put it in April, "is generally gloomy."[15] Most political parties advocated statist economic strategies, and local business elements supported variations of it. Argentina, Brazil, Peru, Chile, Venezuela, and Mexico, the key nations, it thought especially infected with such ideas. Insofar as there were difficulties in much of the hemisphere, Mann reported to the president in February 1965, they were "mostly trade and investment problems."[16] For the United States, what it also called political challenges only reflected such economic factors, because it remained on a collision course with every political expression of Latin nationalism.

CRISIS IN BRAZIL

Washington's policy in the Western Hemisphere revealed itself most vividly in its bilateral relations with specific nations rather than in its general statements, and in no place was this clearer during the 1960s than in Brazil and the Dominican Republic. And as the most populous Latin nation in the hemisphere, Brazil had special significance for the United States.

Brazil's commitment to economic growth carried within it the seeds of its internal social and political contradictions as well as conflict with the United States. To generalize on Brazil's ideology and the logic of its relentless thrust to modernize is not simple because Brazilians themselves rarely explained coherently their hybrid and quite pragmatic merger of state economic planning, socially regressive policies toward the masses, national capitalist expansion, and foreign investment. In certain ways, Brazil's growth had its own imperatives, and the conjugal relationship between business and the state reflected a consensus among the political parties that the government's distinctive role, which created opportunities and prosperity for the bourgeoisie and employment for the people, should continue. Few principles were evoked; the key was success in material terms, and the relatively fragmented entrepreneurs, many of them *nouveaux riches,* endorsed the state economic sector. Nationalism was as much an afterthought as a cause of this synthesis, for all welcomed foreign capital—but in its place. The public economic sector accounted for 16 percent of the fixed capital formation in 1947 but 46 percent in 1960, a share of the latter also going into mixed private-government enterprises. At the same time, the state financed its role mainly through indirect taxes and inflation, both of which penalized the masses much more than capitalists, so that real labor costs fell sharply from 1947 to 1960. Tightly controlled unions were co-opted into this system as passive instruments of national policy.

The military accepted this arrangement as desirable, since it built industry and an infrastructure that it, too, favored; its many personal links with the ruling economic elites and surprisingly nonideological technocrats in charge of the state economy deepened the national consensus among those who ruled—and the military had been the essential arbiter of politics since the late 1930s. An increasingly homogeneous professional caste, even the military had a small minority, perhaps a fifth of its officers, whose nationalism made their views on social questions relatively progressive in an otherwise distinctly conservative milieu.

Yet the precarious, frequently opportunistic politics sustaining this state capitalism made it intrinsically unstable. The vast rural areas, where two-thirds of the people lived in impoverished regions under the political control of large landowners indifferent or hostile to the basic changes occurring in the cities, were also politically greatly overrepresented in a Senate based on regions rather than population. While the remarkably constrained urban masses had traditionally been grateful to the state for creating employment, the rising toll the elitist postwar economic policies imposed on them turned the poor toward the mildly reformist Labor Party, whose share of the vote rose from 8 percent in 1945 to 27 percent in 1962. It was this growing discontent, inevitable given the way the economy neglected the vast bulk of the population, that made economic development without social progress inherently fragile, for much of the import-substitution economic development consisted of producing consumer goods for the middle and upper classes, only making existing economic inequality much more visible. It was also to make a merger of populist appeals and programs of national economic growth inevitable.

The United States was overtly unsympathetic toward all these trends, and its hostility, in conjunction with the Eisenhower Administration's trade and aid policies, drove conservative Brazilian leaders farther toward the nationalist, state capitalist position. Politically, the Kubitschek government and the military were staunchly anti-Communist, but Kubitschek refused to allow IMF supervision of the Brazilian economy in ways that would have reversed state economic planning, and after October 1960, when Janio Quadros was elected to the presidency, the United States and Brazil were already on a collision course. Economically, moreover, although Brazil had been extremely profitable for U.S. investors until 1955, profits fell sharply after then and by the early 1960s there was a net foreign capital outflow, further stimulating nationalist economic ideas.

Quadros took office in January 1961 as the candidate of the conservative, middle class, and while very pro-American, his first error was to adopt a neutralist foreign policy in the hope, as Douglas Dillon reported it, that he would "strengthen his position against the Brazilian left in the battle over his domestic program."[17] When Berle saw him in early March and offered him a one-hundred-million-dollar loan that Quadros considered a bribe to support the United States on Cuba, Washington had already decided that Brazil's growing economic problems would indeed allow it to use money to define Brazil's foreign policy. And despite his initially rightist position, Quadros refused U.S. funds and conditions and set out to win labor support with social reforms. His own party then disowned him, and the military, which had not been consulted, also disapproved. On August 25, 1961, he resigned the presidency and after obtaining the military's sanction handed the presidency to the vice president, João Goulart of the Labor Party, whose power was formally circumscribed at the same time.

Goulart took office under a dark cloud insofar as Washington was concerned. Allen Dulles immediately disapproved of him but expressed confidence that the military would keep the Left from taking over. Yet the United States was willing to accept Goulart if he abandoned neutralist foreign policies and supported the Alliance. By the end of 1961, Goulart's cautious economic actions reassured the Administration, and he was considered less offensive than Quadros on foreign affairs matters—though not yet ideal. Communist infiltration of Goulart's government, the CIA believed, would increase but not get very far. When Goulart visited Washington in April 1962, Lincoln Gordon, the U.S. ambassador, regarded the situation as "far more optimistic": Goulart was courting Brazil's conservative parties, despite the fact the United States deemed them excessively nationalist on economics, while the Communists were internally divided on how to relate to him.[18] Goulart was much taken with Alliance rhetoric, and although tolerable relations between the two governments continued, no later than August 1962 Gordon established contacts with Goulart's domestic enemies, in particular Carlos Lacerda, governor of the state of Guanabara.

Given the broad support within Brazil for the state's economic role, his own party's unfulfilled reform commitments, and the sheer scope of the economic problems the inflation was producing, Goulart's naïve efforts to win significant U.S. economic backing were destined to fail. Goulart decided that he could do nothing without the return of full presidential authority, and a legal plebiscite in January 1963 by a vote of four to one allowed him to embark on his program with a strong mandate. Implicitly, he took back the power the military had denied him when he came to office, frightening both conservatives and officers.

Goulart first attempted to come to grips with mounting inflation and a foreign exchange shortage, and the only way he believed he could do so without imposing the cost on his supporters was to try to get both U.S. and IMF aid. Goulart's program was essentially conservative, but the price the United States demanded for its support was huge. It insisted that Goulart accept IMF conditions that would have undone much of the nationalist economic legislation, that he purge Communist infiltration that the State Department openly alleged was taking place, and that he cease making occasional neutralist statements. At the same time, negotiations over compensation for United States-owned utilities one of the states had nationalized had to be settled, and on this point alone Gordon told Goulart on April 9 that the United States would be prepared to "bring Brazilian economy to [the] brink of abyss."[19] Goulart assured the ambassador, who later described the president's intentions at this time as both modest and constitutional, that he could handle those to his left but that the main danger was from Lacerda and antireform elements. The United States refused to help him except on terms they knew he could not accept.

Goulart realized that he was in a race against the military, and the CIA reported no later than May 3, 1963, that key generals and civilian elements in six states had begun plotting a coup. Indeed, the AID began to give funds directly to governors like Lacerda and others whom it deemed for the Alliance and the United States but against Goulart. Washington in the meantime wrote off Goulart as an uncontrollable leftist opportunist, though not a Communist, who also had the makings of another Vargas or Perón. What both it and the military feared most, however, was that Goulart would attempt to appoint his own officers to the army and alter its command. In June he dismissed his entire cabinet and methodically moved to defend his government against the coup attempt he saw coming.

Goulart was anything but a Communist, and it was this fact that made him so dangerous, for Communists in the Latin context were, in the CIA's estimate, less threatening than the "non-Communist, ultranationalist, extreme left."[20] The CIA regarded Goulart as a power-hungry politician who would not align Brazil with the Soviet bloc but pursue a much more independent line, which in the region was increasingly menacing because it created such a plausible precedent for others. Indeed, the left wing of Goulart's party, the

CIA informed Washington, feared that his opportunism would allow the Right and the United States to get him under control, and they opposed any conciliatory gestures to either. Finally, at the end of August the CIA reported that the USSR was telling the Communists to "go along with the United States" because "the Soviets cannot afford another Cuba. They are not encouraging any new naïve adventures such as the Castro experience."[21]

While the United States had contact with conspirators well before then, no later than September 30, 1963, it made the decision to support a coup. But it would be one, it hoped, that would not merely produce a new regime free of the "extreme left" but which would also oppose "the reactionary proposals of the extreme right."[22] The latter's ultranationalism was nearly as much a villain as radicalism, and the United States insisted that foreign investment had to be welcomed again. Brazil would be encouraged to ask the IMF to take over its financial problems so that it might impose all of the measures Brazil had resisted for over a decade. When Goulart at the end of 1963 made another futile conciliatory effort to get U.S. aid, ostensibly to head off pressures from his party's radicals to move more aggressively on reforms, he was once more kept hanging with urgings that he create "a framework which removes unnecessary barriers to trade and investment."[23]

Goulart spent his last months seeking to insert friendly nationalist officers into key army slots as well as win noncommissioned officers away from their superiors, and he finally proclaimed a national-laborism reform program that never went beyond paper but only provoked the military and the Americans farther. It was clear to many that not only his removal was imminent but also that the direction of Brazil's post-1945 political and social development would be reversed. In this context the United States did not have to do much, since unlike the Dominican Republic there was already a firm social foundation for a reactionary regime, and Goulart was inept, indecisive, and had no united political following. Had all this not been the case, then there was precious little that the United States, by itself, could have done.

The most important factor working against Goulart was that his wholly democratic reversal of the conditions the military had imposed upon him when he received the presidency had challenged its historic role as arbiter of the political process. Equally infuriating were Goulart's feeble efforts to neutralize its political role by appointing friendly or at least impartial officers and to take the military out of politics. In effect, the military was no more inclined in Brazil than elsewhere to concede its ultimate control of the political process. Nearly as disturbing to both the military and the middle and upper classes was the legal growth of the Labor Party, a trend that could only lead to social issues being inserted into the political debate and threaten to make parliamentary politics both vital and dangerous. It was for this reason that the nationalist ideological consensus that had bound all the parties together after 1950 shattered so quickly, and those who were against both the U.S. design for their economic development as well as democracy prepared for a coup. They, certainly, had too much to lose not to act. But it remained to be seen whether this alliance of convenience between conservative nationalism and American imperialism could endure.

The United States sent General Vernon Walters, later deputy director of the CIA, as military attaché to Brazil, and he immediately established contact with the many officers he knew there, and especially Castelo Branco, who became the coup's leader. Since the United States had trained fully 80 percent of the officers involved, and its police missions had their own contacts, there was no shortage of willing accomplices. Yet the principal role of those Americans who were involved in the coup was to reassure the Brazilians of their support, thereby encouraging them to persist—though it was scarcely necessary to do so.

U.S. officials expected the military, in Gordon's words, to be a "stabilizing and moderating factor" in the future, and they fully endorsed the coup plans as its organizers presented them.[24] They did, however, accept the conspirators' belief that it would take time and be bloody, and so when some of its leaders asked on March 30, 1964, that a U.S. fleet be positioned off the Brazilian coast, Washington immediately authorized a fast carrier task force—"Operation Brother Sam"—"to establish a U.S. presence in this area when so directed and carry out such additional tasks as may be assigned," not the least because the position of the Brazilian navy toward a revolt remained unclear.[25] Other boats also carried U.S. arms for the plotters. When the coup finally began on April 1, a special Washington committee organized an array of generous economic concessions and credits the new junta would need to solve its immediate financial problems. With the majority of the state governors behind them, the military met no resistance, and the revolutionary Left the United States had conjured proved a myth. So on April 2 its naval task force, though not arms deliveries, was recalled. Moderate reform and a "greatly improved climate for private investment" would be the outcome, the CIA cabled Washington the glad tidings.[26] A revision of the constitution to prevent independent conservative nationalists from being reelected was likely also, Gordon informed Washington, as "Operation Clean-up" began searching for the junta's opponents. As thousands of unionists, political leaders, and members of Congress—Communists and anti-Communists alike—were arrested, Gordon advised Rusk that "Stretching Constitution at this point would seem to be a rather small price to pay for rapid apolitical solution. . . ."[27] As the repression became more brutal and the first legislation to continue it was issued, Gordon suggested that the State Department inform the concerned press off-the-record that the Communists had planned a bloody coup in about a month and that "A substantial purge was clearly in order."[28]

CONSOLIDATING BRAZIL'S REPRESSION

Brazil was the first and single most important expression of the Johnson Administration's Latin policy, and it had to renew fundamental decisions on its political and economic goals—thereby revealing the substance as opposed to the rhetoric of its hemispheric policy. The issue of dictatorship versus democracy was the easiest because there was an essential consensus on it between Washington and the generals in power. In May 1964 Branco decided to stay in office for three years, annulling the scheduled 1965 presidential election and thereby transforming the military from the mediator of politics to its direct controller. American officials working on Brazil supported this continuing authoritarian trend and resolved to relate to its new possibilities with greatly increased economic aid. Over the next four years Brazil received over $1.5 billion from the United States, much of it in the form of flexible program loans that Washington negotiated in tandem with the IMF and the World Bank, who imposed the standard orthodox conditions requiring emphasis on exports able to earn desperately needed foreign exchange.

But the problem of Brazil's future political and economic course was never settled because although conservative civilians shared a consensus with the military on eliminating the Left, they agreed on precious little else, and it did not take long for them to become disenchanted. The April 1964 coup was the Right's answer to democracy, yet although they were suitably anti-Castro they differed profoundly among themselves on economic issues. Nationalism, in brief, was still very much alive, and this was best revealed when Carlos Lacerda toward the end of 1964 split with Branco on his concessions to the United States and IMF on foreign investments and a tight-money economic policy, beginning an opportunistic trajectory that by 1966 took him to a Center-Left political position remarkably similar to Goulart's. Throughout 1965 conservative industrialists, especially in São Paulo, and military nationalists formed a coalition to stop Branco's United States-dictated economic program and began planning another coup. Moreover, the nomination of several anti-Branco conservative nationalists in gubernatorial races in August 1965 and their victory the following October made it clear that the regime's repression of the Left alone would not suffice. Kubitschek-led forces would have taken over if the generals' control over the political system had not been further tightened. At the end of October Branco abolished the existing political parties and proclaimed the power to recess Congress whenever and for as long as he liked. The mandates of elected officials could be suspended along with the political rights of citizens. Brazil was now a dictatorship, and Washington supported the move unequivocally.

By this time the real income of workers had fallen sharply, and many marginal businessmen were being squeezed; foreign investors were not rush-

ing to exploit the favorable laws, while exports stagnated and inflation remained very high. The IMF program, especially lower protective tariffs, was
not working, and the military was compelled to bring back many of the
technocrats and begin listening to the advice of dynamic São Paulo industrialists who still regarded the state sector in purely opportunistic terms. Greater
public outlays soon returned, and Brazil partially veered back to its eclectic
nationalist economics, but without fear of the masses opposing its economic
consequences. In January 1967 the military designated General Artur da
Costa e Silva to replace Branco, and while he was equally anti-Communist,
he was also more of a nationalist on economic questions. Technocrats became yet more important, and by June Washington was again concerned that
there was a clear trend toward neutralism in Brazil's foreign policy.

Using the IMF and the World Bank to present its demands, the United States
postponed disbursing its own loans until essential conditions were met, a
divisive issue that dragged on for the remainder of the Democratic Administration and deeply alienated the Brazilian regime. Brazil was "our major ally
in the hemisphere," as Rostow described it, but in the end it proved too large
and too independent to control in any form, democratic or authoritarian.[29]
Costa e Silva's December 13, 1968, abolition of Congress and complete clamp-
down on the press and courts institutionalized the military dictatorship irrevocably because it had too small a political base, but its polyglot economic
strategy still failed to meet U.S. desires.

The United States could not reverse Brazil's mixed economy because it
satisfied the interests of too many powerful local interests whom even a
dictatorship could not eliminate without plunging the entire society into a
chaos that would have made the victory of the Left probable. Brazilians
welcomed foreign investors but found that dealing with them through the
state greatly increased the bargaining power of private interests, affecting the
final division of the profits. The state bureaucracy's willingness to coordinate
with local capitalists in this fashion only strengthened the so-called national
bourgeoisie's historical symbiotic relationship to the dynamic government
sector. It was the U.S.-IMF plan for a noninflationary export-oriented economy, which stressed agriculture and minerals rather than industry, that most
offended Brazil's rulers, so U.S. control over the economy was to decrease
under the dictators also.

Ironically, it was the very integration of Brazil into the world economy that
accelerated the decline in U.S. hegemony. U.S. investment, while it increased
sharply after 1966 and proved highly profitable, did not keep pace with the
flow from Western Europe and Japan, so that the U.S. share of foreign direct
investment in Brazil fell from 48 percent in 1950 to 33 percent in 1974. With
this division of foreign interests, Brazil's leverage increased along with it, and
the growth of state enterprises in manufacturing and oil from 17 percent of

the assets of the top three hundred corporations in 1966 to 32 percent in 1974 augmented it further. In 1971 government firms concentrated in mining, metallurgy, chemicals, and petroleum accounted for 20 percent of all manufacturing and mining assets, leaving the remainder for foreign firms, which had 34 percent, but especially the national interests who were linked to both these sectors and profited enormously from the mixed system's dynamism, particularly after 1971. The state also owned nearly all public utilities and over a third of the banking, finance, and service sectors. In this context, while U.S. interests grew, Brazil became less rather than more integrated into the United States-led hemispheric system.

Brazil also remained a repressive class society, and the state-business alliance transferred its social costs to the people, for while its Right rebelled against United States-imposed conditions that would lead to foreign hegemony, they successfully sought to perpetuate their own. Given the state's control of wage rates, real income was forced down, and the real value of minimum wages fell 15 percent from 1964 to 1967. By 1970 the richest 5 percent of the population received 36 percent of the income compared to 27 percent in 1960. Brazil became a consumer society par excellence for middle- and upper-income groups, one resting on a sea of deprivation and social misery.

THE DOMINICAN REPUBLIC: DICTATORSHIP AND INTERVENTION

U.S. Marines installed Rafael Trujillo to run the Dominican Republic in the 1920s while they occupied it, and he ruled one of the hemisphere's poorest countries as America's loyal servant. His corruption was legendary and his repression comparable. Not until the advent of Castro did Washington begin to doubt the wisdom of relying upon him, and an OAS condemnation of his regime on June 8, 1960, goaded it further when several weeks later there was a Trujillo-sponsored assassination attempt against President Rómulo Betancourt of Venezuela, who had led the criticism against Trujillo's incarceration of many thousands of political prisoners, murder, and torture. The Eisenhower Administration then reduced its purchases of Dominican sugar, essential for the island's economy, and later attempted to cut it entirely. In response, on August 25 Trujillo's radio began to defend Castro and announced it would broadcast Soviet news agency reports. By that time the CIA had established contact with various opposition groups and begun to provide them with guns fitted for assassinations.

On May 30, 1961, one of them killed Trujillo. With his vice president and the dead dictator's longtime ally, Joaquín Balaguer, nominally in control,

Trujillo's eldest son assumed power with the backing of the army. Yet the United States remained undecided what to do as the military, a conservative middle-class party, and a democratic Left party, the Dominican Revolutionary Party (PRD), under Juan Bosch, emerged as the main contenders. Finally, despite Balaguer's reimposition of repressive measures, the Kennedy Administration resolved to try to liberalize the existing regime and proposed that the OAS lift its economic sanctions. It demanded, however, that the Trujillo clan, which was seeking to hold on to power, leave the island, and threatened an invasion should they refuse. On November 17, 1961, the Trujillos departed, taking an estimated two-hundred-million-dollar fortune with them and leaving behind four times that in property. Balaguer and the army took over, and at the beginning of 1962 U.S.-Dominican relations were normalized, the sugar quota restored, and large amounts of economic aid given the impoverished country.

Meanwhile, riots and aborted coups forced Balaguer to leave office, and the island remained in suspense pending the outcome of elections in December 1962. A new U.S. ambassador, John Bartlow Martin, arrived to keep all the contending factions in order until then, while a council of former Trujillo officers provided a transitional government, but he quickly resolved that the Left should be suppressed, and he assiduously cultivated the military. The four deeply disunited and small radical parties disturbed him greatly, but he later conceded that "None of the Castro/Communist parties seemed to me prepared to try to overthrow the government by force," but instead would try to infiltrate larger groups—though how they could do so while divided remained unclear.[30] When Bosch, however, won the December 20 election by a two-to-one majority, what Martin feared most appeared to him about to come to pass.

Martin was hostile toward Bosch from the inception, and especially resented the freedom he gave to the smaller leftist parties to function, suspecting he had secret ties with them himself if he was not actually a "deep-cover Communist"—a claim that found echoes in Washington.[31] Almost as ominous, Bosch pressed his social and economic reforms, canceled an Esso contract, and then stopped delivery of sugar under the U.S. quota because world prices were far higher and the Dominicans had already lost six million dollars in potential income thereby. On September 20, 1963, seven months after he came to office, a rightist-led strike against Bosch caused the State Department to wash their hands of him just as an inevitable coup seemed days away. Martin himself opposed Bosch but feared abandoning the constitutional process even more, making a feeble gesture to keep the Right from taking over, but five days later a military coup installed a pro-American civilian junta while generals remained in the background, supervising it. After several months of feigned distress, the State Department recognized it.

The new junta took office with no concessions to the modest U.S. demands that it return to constitutional processes while also excluding Bosch and the Left, and it refused to broaden its membership because it realized that in the existing hemispheric context Washington would not challenge it. Until April 1965 it ran the Dominican Republic in a way that alienated virtually everyone: the masses, who suffered as much as they had under Trujillo; the middle class parties, who disliked the return of rampant corruption; reformers within the military itself; and even some officers who had served Trujillo and wanted to see Balaguer's reinstatement. By that date Bosch had managed to wield together an alliance that demanded a restoration of the 1963 constitution, and when it initiated an uprising on April 24 a large part of the army rallied to its side, as well, of course, as the masses. The junta fell the next day, and on April 26 the army distributed guns to from three thousand to ten thousand people in the capital, Santo Domingo, where the combat was confined. Within three days it was virtually in the constitutionalists' hands, and only a few pockets of resistance remained.

Following the crisis, State Department officials convinced themselves immediately that guns passed out to the population might end up in the hands of the deeply divided leftist groups, who could then take leadership away from the pro-Bosch officers. But they did not believe it was certain to occur if they did not act, for the CIA estimated that there were about fifty-five disunited Castroists and Communists among the rebels, and from three hundred to three thousand in the entire country. American officials urged the remnants of the military to continue resisting, but on April 27, when their local allies' defeat appeared imminent, they made a unanimous decision to recommend the use of U.S. forces. Their immediate concern was that pro-Castro nationalists would take power, but to reach this conclusion they had to number Bosch and his party among them; and while risk of a leftist takeover appeared dangerous enough, even more persuasive was the credibility of American power in the world—since at least that, Washington believed, seemed certain to be at stake. President Johnson made it plain that he did not propose "to sit here with my hands tied and let Castro take that island. What can we do in Vietnam if we can't clean up the Dominican Republic?"[32]

On April 28 U.S. troops began landing in the Dominican Republic, reaching twenty-three thousand on May 9. Ostensibly to protect the lives of American citizens and arrange a cease-fire, their obvious objective was to keep Bosch and the Left out of power. They complied with none of the ostensible OAS procedures for actions such as this, and indeed the Dominican invasion was, and still remains, the most massive U.S. direct hemispheric intervention in this century. Press opinion in Latin America ran ten to one against it, and Mexico, Chile, Venezuela, and others protested formally. The sham pretensions of inter-Americanism were laid to rest, but the message that the United States had both the will and the capacity to act decisively was unmistakably clear to the entire world.

The rest was foredoomed, since foreign troops were there to fight against real or alleged Communists, and this meant restoring the pro-American military to complete control of the army. U.S. forces were reduced, but enough remained to make it possible for Washington to dictate settlement terms, which culminated in June 1966 in an election between Balaguer and Bosch that, not surprisingly, brought Trujillo's intimate back to power. While the United States' defenders insisted that the election was genuinely free, the point would be irrelevant even if true. With all the arms in the hands of Balaguer's allies, and U.S. soldiers still present and Washington's position on Bosch unmistakably known, the population's option of a resumption of the war or a vote for the U.S. candidate alone would have been sufficient to determine the outcome.

Balaguer restored many former Trujillo officers to military service and brought back the old regime. "The terrorism, corruption and misery that marked Rafael Trujillo's 31-year dictatorship . . . are even more widespread today under constitutionally elected President Joaquin Balaguer," a *Wall Street Journal* reporter said in summing up his reign in late 1971; "So say some friends as well as most foes of the U.S.-backed Balaguer government, and evidence is mounting to support their view."[33]

In the end, Washington far preferred to save the dictators of its own choice to tolerating the array of democrats, demagogues, nationalists, and reformers that the people of Latin America chose to lead them.

THE RESULTS OF THE ALLIANCE FOR PROGRESS

The Democratic Administration pursued a policy of support for the Alliance for Progress in Latin America's economic domain and sponsorship of officers in the political. Such a strategy was essential to cope with the increasingly unwieldy role of the civilian middle and upper classes, who favored nationalist economic development, and, more tangentially, the rising social consciousness among the poor and dispossessed, who formed the great majority of the region.

The Alliance never achieved its original reform goals because Washington's specific economic objectives and the political framework it preferred preordained genuine reform to failure, for there was no way that needed basic changes could occur in the context of perpetuating reaction, foreign domination, and inequality. And this meant that the deeper socioeconomic currents eroding the hemisphere's stability continued to operate.

The annual volume of U.S. funds during the Alliance exceeded by surprisingly little the $851 million the Eisenhower Administration had allocated to the region in its last year in office. Only in 1967 and 1968 did it approach $1.5 billion, but by then inflation also reduced its real value. What was most striking about the Alliance was that from half to two-thirds of its aid in any year was mainly in the form of tied loans that had to be repaid eventually. The Alliance could not redress the economic balance between Latin America and the world, so from 1961 to 1970 the region's per capita gross domestic product as a share of that in the OECD nations fell by a tenth. Per capita growth in income under the Alliance was smaller than it had been in the period preceding it, and far less than targeted. In terms of education, in 1960 a total of 52 percent of the children five to fourteen years were not enrolled in primary school, and while it fell to 43 percent by 1967, most of this change was the result of Mexican, Brazilian, and Argentine literacy efforts that had been under way before the Alliance.

If Latin America's economic performance during the Alliance era was scarcely better than its postwar average and essentially static in per capita terms, politically it was demonstrably the decade of the generals—a trend the United States endorsed strongly. From 1962 to 1967 there were nine coups against civilian constitutional presidents, seven of whom had been elected by majority votes. By mid-1967 the military directly ran eight countries with over half of the region's population, and indirectly ruled five others with 14 percent of the population; only six Latin nations with 28 percent of the population escaped the blessings of military modernization Washington thought desirable. Both economically and politically, the structural preconditions for social change in Latin America compatible with the perpetuation of U.S. interests did not exist either at the beginning, much less at the end, of the Alliance period.

This reality is best measured in terms of food, agriculture, and land issues—the most elemental domains for reform and human betterment. Agriculture had both to feed the region and export commodities, and it did neither as well as the Alliance originally projected, much less human needs required. Per capita agricultural production of food and fiber was lower in 1965–66 than before World War Two, and the region passed from being a net exporter to a net importer of wheat and feed grain over that time. Its food and farm imports continued to rise significantly more rapidly during the Alliance period than its exports did. This per capita food deficit increased during the Alliance era partially due to the birth rate but at least as much because of the shift in agriculture from food for local consumption to commodities for the world market, and while the volume of its exports grew markedly, its value was a scant sixth of this increase because of the worsening terms of trade. The Latin nations geared themselves to international commerce, as the U.S. insisted, but their social and economic problems mounted as a consequence. While this export trap was especially grave in Central America, it affected other nations critically also. In brief, Latin America's structural problems worsened throughout this period.

The land distribution system, as all knew in 1961, was the origin of social misery for the peasants who comprised the vast majority of the region. While the United States had acknowledged this at the Alliance's inception, it abandoned this definition of the problem immediately because virtually all of the political forces it might identify with—and above all, the generals—opposed changes with far-reaching implications to the existing framework of wealth and power. But U.S. policy in Latin America was identical to its position throughout the Third World, and for the same political reasons. While it paid verbal obeisance to reform, its land experts understood clearly that "Land reform is perhaps first and foremost a political phenomena," one that affects "in most cases the political structure of the rural areas and perhaps the country at large." The real issues "thus revolve around what type of a political and social structure the country wants."[34] As the perpetuation of its client regimes in virtually every nation of the world became its dominant concern, the United States invariably opted for the status quo.

It was for this reason, as well, that the AID, which had nominal responsibility for land reform but had to accept the political guidelines given to it, switched from land reform as a question of land distribution and tenure to one of the productivity of the existing land system via credit, information, and technical inputs—which also benefited the large-scale, capital-intensive agricultural export sector most of all. The barriers to greater production within the status quo absorbed its attention throughout this decade and beyond, and this was one of the reasons why food, which was so important to small peasants as opposed to larger cash-crop producers, was neglected—with predictable social and political results. Where governments permitted, it also participated in setting up peasant small holdings on public or unclaimed lands, usually located in poorer frontier areas, but this was a minor aspect of its overall activity. The AID quickly grew cynical about such efforts because so often, as in Guatemala, it found local projects, in the words of one of its reports, "too internally corrupt to carry out a worthwhile program in any case."[35] Such experiences throughout the world reinforced its natural inclination to stress "productivity." It was obvious that real land reform required radical politics, and this was precisely what the United States opposed everywhere.

The land tenure structure throughout Latin America either remained static or became more unequal during the Alliance period. In 1968 about half of the eighteen to nineteen million rural families were either tenants or farm laborers. In Colombia, for example, large landlords helped to write the so-called land reform law to forestall the reemergence of the post-1948 poor peasant upheavals that had traumatized the nation and resulted in tens of thousands of deaths. U.S. officials found that not only had its per capita agricultural production fallen since 1957–59, but also 71 percent of the landowners with under five hectares had 6 percent of the land while those with over a hundred hectares, or 2.7 percent of the total farms, had become yet larger and now held 59 percent of all land. Excluded entirely from such data were the tenants and landless laborers. Unemployment in Colombia stood at 20 percent in 1968 and was growing rapidly, partially because of labor-saving techniques United States-sponsored reforms helped to introduce. And by the late 1970s, some four thousand to five thousand guerrillas were operating mainly among the rural poor.

Such trends in land tenure continued to shape income distribution as well, and in 1970 the richest fifth of the Latin population received no less than they had in 1960, and considerably more in a number of countries. Taxes as a share of the GNP, which the United States had said it wished increased to alter this pattern, were 11.4 percent in 1961 and 12.1 percent in 1967. The economic structure of inequality and oppression, the seedbed of revolutionary activity, was no different at the end of the Alliance than it had been at its inception.[36]

Indeed, in certain crucial regards, to the degree the United States succeeded in integrating the Latin economy into a world economy it hoped to dominate—and to a lesser extent still did—the region developed new and potentially grave problems that would eventually interact with an economic system already full of tensions and unable to support yet more without the risk of even greater social crises. The most important of these, in the long run, was the debt service trap and its concomitant imperative that nations tailor their economies to maximize exports capable of earning hard currencies and conforming to the world financial system's strictures.

Between 1961–65 and 1966–70 the average annual flow of official grants or loans and long-term private capital more than doubled, to $2.7 billion, while short-term private capital, which was negligible before 1966, was $317 million annually. During 1971–75 it rose to $8.2 billion annually, private direct investment now constituting less than a quarter of this amount. No later than 1967, with the service on its external public debt already absorbing three-quarters of its gross capital inflow, it was obvious that, as an IADB report phrased it, "Latin America could be approaching a virtual bottleneck in its foreign financing."[37] Since much of this sum was owed to the United States and, increasingly, official multilateral banks that could dictate economic programs to the indebted states, Latin and other Third World nations that fell into the debt trap had to appeal to their creditors for a renegotiation of terms, generally linked to more borrowing. Argentina, Brazil, and Chile were compelled to do so before 1968—usually having to go through the IMF first to negotiate terms. As a World Bank analysis in 1969 put it, "they could rely on a certain amount of good will on the part of the international community because of their willingness to avoid default and to undertake economic and financial reforms or because of political changes which increased the confidence of creditor countries."[38] Principally, this meant that the United States utilized official multilateral banks as vehicles for pursuing its own objectives more than ever, a topic I detail in Chapter 19. Suffice it to say that these banks gave the United States important new leverage and even made a sector of the generally opportunistic Latin elites more comfortable in continuing in another form the dependency into which they had fallen both out of necessity and, insofar as the infusion of foreign resources brought the luxuries they craved, choice.

Such a situation required more exports, which alone meant that the financial context in which the Alliance operated would make social reforms impossible—though few dictators and oligarchies wanted them anyway. Even more dangerous for the long run was the incentive loans placed on the key Latin nations to borrowing more to try to stay ahead of debt repayment obligations, which they proceeded to do. By 1979 the annual flow of net external resources into Latin America was almost 20 times the 1961–65 average, or $20.4 billion. The ratio of its external public debt service to its exports throughout the 1960s had already been too high, at about 14 percent. By 1979 it reached 28 percent. Latin America was, by far, the most indebted Third World region, and its economy was vertiginously escaping from control as it climbed higher up the debt ladder.

Yet these dilemmas were only partially ones the United States imposed, because at least as important was the Latin nationalist elites' unwillingness to impose those structural reforms essential to create an internal market sufficient to sustain real, durable growth. But the idea of a regional common market, LAFTA, seemed to them an alternative way around this dilemma, so there was an upsurge of Latin interest in it during the latter part of the Alliance period. In the short run it was a plausible solution, but the United States, quite oblivious to the risks in the direction the Latin economy was drifting, resisted a regional common market more strongly than ever. At the OAS meeting at Punte del Este in April 1967 the Latins stressed again the need for the United States to accept a common market, compelling the United States to endorse the principle in 1970 for all Third World regions but none of the specifics the Latins thought essential. The original LAFTA concept was to fail also because smaller Latin nations feared that their larger neighbors would dominate their economies, but U.S. resistance was the principal obstacle. This also proved the case regarding commodity associations. To cope with their debts without borrowing more by 1967 would have required the

Latin Americans' exports to be worth twice their existing value, and getting higher prices appeared easier than increasing output or finding new markets. U.S. officials made it clear that, save perhaps for coffee or cocoa under certain terms, in principle they were opposed to measures that would require their own industries and consumers to pay the costs involved. The essentially conservative Latins, in brief, were compelled either to introduce radical internal measures or to borrow more. This stance produced more anti-Yankee sentiment across the ideological spectrum, and it was a recipe not just for economic crisis in the long run but for political conflict as well.

Structurally, the relationship between the United States and the hemisphere began to change in important ways throughout the 1960s, and this, too, compelled the Latins to borrow more and diversify toward a larger world market. U.S. direct investments in the entire region increased from $8.4 billion in 1960 to $13.0 billion in 1970 and $23.9 billion in 1976, but this was a slower growth rate than elsewhere in the world, so the Latin share of all U.S. investments abroad continued to fall, from 26 percent in 1960 to 17 percent in 1976. This shift was due to the fact that mining and petroleum, which in 1960 had attracted over half of U.S. capital, by 1976 absorbed only a fifth—and other opportunities in the region for U.S. firms were limited. U.S. corporations therefore began decapitalizing after 1960 by repatriating far more capital to themselves than they shipped in, though their unusually high profit rates caused this to be possible. Between 1960 and 1972 the U.S. capital inflow minus repatriated profits was a negative $9.2 billion, an amount equal to all U.S. economic grants and loans in 1961–68, and this huge sum came principally from the petroleum and mining industries, which had annual rates of return in the 1960s of 15 and 23 percent, respectively. This capital outflow only increased the Latins' need to borrow. The investment decisions of U.S. and other multinational firms in the region thereby helped to define significantly the internal economic resource allocation and policies of the various nations in which they operated, a fact local nationalists deeply resented.

Structurally, lower prices for Latin goods and the limited export market this created for the United States, huge Latin borrowing notwithstanding, made the region's economic integration with the United States fall statistically, though in fact it was still enormous. U.S. exports to Latin America fell from 16 percent of its world total in 1960 to 12 percent in 1976, while its imports declined from 21 to 11 percent over the same period. Growth elsewhere had caused the relative importance of the U.S.-Latin relationship to shift. Latin America's shipments to the United States in 1960 absorbed 41 percent of its world exports, while by 1976 they were 32 percent. More important was the decline in its import dependency that burgeoning European and Japanese competition made possible. In 1960 a total of 45 percent of its imports came from the United States, but by 1976 they had fallen to 27 percent. The Latins were gaining leverage in their trading relations to the world economy even as their mounting debt was causing them to lose it in other domains.

Initially, the United States' far greater involvement in the Hemisphere after 1960 was its direct reaction to the political threat from the Left that Castro symbolized. Yet its responses consistently rejected the status quo of conservative nationalism that predominated in the larger states, and it sought, above all, to integrate the region into the classic world economic model it had advocated consistently since 1945. Washington's definitions of reform were but another means of attempting to impose its hegemony, an effort both the nationalist Center-Right and now the emergent Left challenged. Dictatorships seemed the easiest way to circumvent such political forces, and the United States' Alliance for Progress phase raised its dependence on military proxies to the highest stage ever. But as the risks from the Left appeared to diminish, so too did U.S. interest in the hemisphere. By the mid-1960s it was mechanically pressing for the economic and investment conditions it believed in and that the concerned U.S. business community demanded, greatly increasing its investment insurance program, creating boards of U.S. corporate investors to help design new U.S. legislation to protect them, and taking all the measures natural to a nation whose economic and political policies were inextricably linked and often articulated by the same people.

Most U.S. leaders understood by 1967 that relations with the hemisphere had gone awry with much of the Center-Right as well as the Left, which shared a consensus on the need for the positive role of the state in the economy and were most unlikely to be converted to Yankee doctrines. Lower-level officials were to persist in seeking to implement the United States' now-traditional policies and objectives, but the White House's main attention had long since turned to the jungles of Vietnam, and flying back from the April 1967 Punte del Este conference, Johnson resolved, "We would now be a junior partner in Latin American economic and social development."[39] If that was not to be in many important regards, it was nonetheless certain that the Alliance for Progress era was dead. Minor bureaucrats continued to repeat its initial rhetoric, but the White House was no longer interested. In Latin America scarcely anyone on the Right, Center, or Left had ever believed it, and Brazil and the Dominican Republic, not to mention the bevy of generals the United States funded, only confirmed all their earlier skepticism.

Despite a measure of success in the domain of finances and debt, U.S. efforts throughout the 1960s to reintegrate the independent forces in the hemisphere were clearly failing by the end of the decade, creating the basis of an even more profound challenge to its economic and political hegemony than the advent of Castroism in Cuba. The sheer magnitude of the region's multiple human and economic problems more than offset aid as a political lever, and they threatened to generate social and political challenges to U.S. hegemony that not even its client generals and their armies could wholly contain—notwithstanding the extent to which dictators and growing repression scored real, if temporary, successes. Structurally, at the end of the Alliance for Progress period the institutional trends throughout the region were more ominous than anyone in Washington could imagine, for the cumulative impact of years of U.S. exploitation, its support for dictators, and its disdain for nationalist sentiments were producing their own momentum to challenge Yankee paternalism and its many forms of interventionism. The United States was unmistakably still aligned with the forces of reaction and oppression throughout the hemisphere, and its own fate was linked inextricably to the highly exploitive economies and social institutions upon which those forces based their power.

In the end, the United States' manifest destiny merged and made common cause with the oligarchies' and corruptionists' mission to save themselves from the radical Left and the nationalist Center. Its interventionism in the 1960s on their behalf both reflected the independent, autonomous currents of thought and policy sweeping the hemisphere, and which it was trying to contain, and became one of its principal causes. By resorting to covert warfare in most places, or its own troops, as in the Dominican Republic, Washington had tried to rely on its military power to circumvent the failure of its economic efforts to integrate the hemisphere even more thoroughly—guaranteeing that all the advocates of change throughout the hemisphere, whatever their ideological hue, would be required to make resistance to Yankee imperialism a prerequisite for progress.

If the Johnson Administration chose after 1967 to pay far less attention to hemispheric affairs, it was less and less certain that its successors would also have the same freedom to do so.

The Other Southeast Asian Challenges

*A*LTHOUGH VIETNAM WAS TO BECOME the central preoccupation of U.S. foreign policy in Southeast Asia and then the world after 1964, its neighbors continued to possess a significance to America's leaders that was, given the logic of the domino theory, also a major justification for the entire Vietnam enterprise. In purely economic or strategic terms, both Indonesia and the Philippines were far more valuable to the United States than Vietnam, with the official arguments for the war increasingly involving the symbolism of the credibility of American power. Vietnam did not preclude U.S. involvement elsewhere in the region, but it did constrain the forms it might take. The value of focusing on the far less familiar American policies in the key nations surrounding Indochina is that they reveal much that is vital about the regional framework and objectives in which its Vietnam policy evolved, particularly its economic context and U.S. assumptions about politics and change. Even more important, the Indonesian case is crucial because the nation is the largest and best endowed of the region. And while the Philippines is insufficiently understood outside its own borders, its special significance is the fact that no other Third World country has been so intimately and so long connected with the United States. It therefore remains the single most important nation of all for comprehending the United States' role and purposes in the Third World.

INDONESIA: THE AMERICAN FRUSTRATION

Indonesia was potentially the richest state of Southeast Asia, but its people were among the very poorest. It is the most populous nation of the region, and its raw materials made it vital to the long-term prosperity of the Western industrial nations and especially Japan. Sukarno, its president since its creation, was a brilliant orator whose charisma won the adulation of the masses and the military, while his seemingly infallible sense of political tactics reinforced his power and enormous ego.

The United States' consistent policy after the Indonesians won their independence was to aid the police and military with equipment to maintain order against the Communist Party (PKI). In late 1948 Sukarno and his army ruthlessly suppressed a PKI-supported land reform movement in the Madiun region, virtually destroying the PKI leadership, jailing thirty-six thousand, and greatly increasing Washington's respect for him and particularly his officers. Strategically, by 1953 the NSC resolved to encourage those nationalist forces the army especially personified, as well as the very large Islamic parties, to prevent Indonesia from moving toward the Left. The security of Japan, whose access to the islands' vast resources it believed crucial to keep it safely in the U.S. camp, was unquestionably its primary concern, and for practical purposes it assigned Indonesia to Japan's economic sphere of interest. Indonesia was a major link in its expanded geopolitical domino theory for East Asia. No later than December 1954, the NSC decided that the United States would use "all feasible covert means" as well as overt, including "the use of armed force if necessary," to prevent the richest parts of Indonesia from falling into Communist hands.[1] Implicit in its position was a possible partition of the nation.

The Indonesian military was and still remains an extremely complex, heterogeneous organization, deeply divided internally by region and culture, conflicting economic ambitions, and profound ideological differences, as well as traditional bureaucratic rivalries. Functionally, the military ran significant sectors of the local economies in their district, often as virtual warlords but usually in collaboration with the universally disliked Chinese, who dominated Indonesia's economy much as they did those of the rest of Southeast Asia. The seizure of Dutch property in 1957 finalized this evolution toward bureaucratic capitalism when the military was assigned the task of managing it as well. The corruption that emerged from this role seriously eroded the military's public image, but it also increased their absolute power and pretensions to direct the nation's affairs.

The PKI after the Madiun affair related to politics cautiously by avoiding any action that might draw renewed attacks upon it. The Party loyally endorsed Sukarno on his own terms as a counterbalance to the power of the military, whom it especially feared, giving Sukarno the incentive to protect it. It employed the time it gained in this delicate context to build its parliamentary strength and especially its mass organizations among peasants, workers, and others. Given the intense and nigh-universal poverty in the nation of peasants, it was able to overcome deep religious and cultural barriers to gain 16 percent of the votes in the 1955 election. In the 1957 regional elections its votes increased by a third, moving it from the fourth- to the second-largest party and causing D. N. Aidit, the head of the PKI, to predict victory in the 1964 general elections. By 1957 Sukarno had obtained their support for his ruling bloc in return for lesser posts, but they were not allotted cabinet-level appointments before 1962. He used them primarily to offset the military and especially the Islamic parties, which won 44 percent of the 1955 vote and were the main common threat to the military, the Communists, and Sukarno alike. The PKI, especially Aidit, eschewing revolutionary action on behalf of a united front, placed all its hopes on Sukarno and his politics of balancing contending forces to rule them all.

But however adroit as a political manipulator, Sukarno did nothing for the economy, which deteriorated throughout the 1950s and further increased the objective potential for PKI successes. By early 1957 the always-present secessionist threat to the island republic's existence became real with revolts in the outer islands and especially Sumatra, which earned nearly all of Indonesia's export income and resented seeing Javanese politicians and officers who ran the nation squander it. At the end of 1957, anxious "to help keep Indonesia going to the Left," the United States elected to go along with the British, Japanese, and probably Australians in an effort to encourage the independence movements in the raw materials-producing islands most crucial to them all. For Dulles, withdrawing recognition from Sukarno and giving it to dissident elements in Sumatra able "to protect the life and property of Americans" would be "an excuse to bring about a major shift" in Indonesia.[2]

In February 1958, the local Muslim Masjumi Party leadership and officers in the regional army proclaimed a new government in Sumatra, and the next month Sukarno's loyal generals invaded it. The CIA assigned some three hundred to four hundred Americans and foreigners to supply the rebels with arms and supplies in one of the clumsiest CIA operations of all time, a fact that became public when on May 18 a plane piloted by an American in the CIA's employ was shot down. The dissidents did badly, however, and the United States managed to create the worst situation possible for themselves, deeply alienating every nationalist force in Indonesia, including the military.

The United States tried both to deny aiding the insurrectionists as well as extract from the great majority of the senior military leaders loyal to Sukarno pledges to thwart the growing influence of the PKI as the price of stopping support for secessionism. But the net effect of the 1957–58 revolts was to weaken the political influence of those officers most hostile to the PKI as well as that of the national Masjumi Party, which later was outlawed, thereby eliminating the single most important counterbalance to both the PKI and the military.

Sukarno proclaimed a "Guided Democracy," which attained its final form in July 1959 when, for practical purposes, he abolished parliamentary democracy. To offset the far greater power this gave to the military, he brought the Communists into a collaborative relationship but not into the government itself until March 1962. This foreclosed the possibility of continued PKI successes at the ballot box in return for some relatively marginal offices, and the army was now Sukarno's main check on the PKI—facts U.S. officials much appreciated. And while Sukarno had outflanked the PKI but also used them to check the army, the military continued to run large sections of the economy to its own advantage, obtaining a greater share of the budget and many more arms, principally from the USSR. Sukarno, the U.S. ambassador to Djakarta observed, "had no intention of sharing power" with the PKI, and the United States intensified its commitment to aid the military and encourage it eventually to take power.[3] That the military was neutralist also did not overly disturb the Americans, the greater risk of the PKI far outweighing this liability. And while U.S. officials understood Sukarno's co-optive strategy vis-à-vis the PKI, they also feared he would miscalculate and lose control. To others, however, it looked as if Sukarno and the army had made the PKI relatively harmless.

Under Guided Democracy the military's belief in its mandate to help run the nation deepened profoundly at the ideological level, and the army chief of staff, A. H. Nasution, was its key spokesman. In mid-1962 Sukarno replaced him with a slightly less dangerous new chief, and the divided military's interest in politics intensified as a consequence. American officials sustained intensive contacts with those senior officers most likely to resist Sukarno and the PKI. But the military's nationalist support for aggression against Malaysia and its hostility toward U.S. investments, especially the Stanvac and Caltex oil concessions, muddied relations with them also. Indeed, protecting U.S. business with a ferocity that has few equals anywhere took an inordinate amount of the embassy's attention and not only greatly complicated rapport with the very forces the United States was relying upon but threatened to weaken them as well. Interspersed between meetings of Ambassador Howard P. Jones with officials, where Jones broached a military takeover and gave "obvious hints of U.S. support in time of crisis," the Indonesians were repeatedly threatened with aid cuts should its 1963 oil law, which the oil companies considered tantamount to expropriation, be applied.[4] They were also promised increased economic aid if they reversed nationalist economic measures and created a "tolerable political climate," efforts the United States coordinated with Japan and the IMF, the latter taking the main initiative in trying to get Djakarta to accept major economic changes.[5]

Sukarno took over management of U.S. oil and rubber firms in March 1965 with the army's endorsement because of American military aid to Malaysia.

In response Washington finally cut all military assistance to Indonesia. George Ball warned the president that "Our relations with Indonesia are on the verge of falling apart" and that Sukarno was relying more and more on the PKI while the military's "internal cohesion" was being sorely tested.[6] Were Sukarno to die, the CIA pessimistically predicted at about this time, the army would probably take over but the PKI would still continue as an important force. The longer he stayed in power, however, the better the PKI's chances for an eventual victory. Any government, even the army's, would remain anti-Western.

By mid-1964 Sukarno had become seriously ill, leaving the country often for medical treatment, and it was clear that the entire precariously balanced power structure over which he presided would not last much longer. At stake for many officers were careers and fortunes, so the tensions within the military intensified. The U.S. embassy received constant coup rumors from January 1965 onward. That month, those in charge of the army organized a secret committee, which others dubbed the "Generals' Council," to deal with purely political issues relating to Sukarno, and it definitely considered what to do should he become incapacitated or die.* Sukarno fell seriously ill again in early August, and the CIA learned that the Generals' Council convened a meeting in Djakarta on September 30. With rumors of threatened coups from both sides circulating throughout September, any gesture by one side was certain to evoke a response, including a preemptive one, by the other. It was a time, as the second-in-charge of the U.S. embassy later recalled, when "there was a power play going on, everybody was maneuvering to get to the top."[7] Regardless of its truth or falsity, a pro-Sukarno faction of the military was convinced that the Generals' Council was planning a coup against Sukarno on Armed Forces Day, October 5, when many of their troops could be brought unnoticed into the city, ostensibly to parade. Since the army leadership had contingency plans should Sukarno leave the scene, their fear may have been wrong, but it was not implausible. The September 30 Movement was the pro-Sukarno officers' response to this alleged or real danger, and it was not a coup but principally an effort to keep him in command, as well as a struggle between factions of the military.

The U.S. embassy on October 3 was correct in suggesting that the PKI at

---

* U.S. documents for the three months preceding September 30, 1965, and dealing with the convoluted background and intrigues, much less the embassy's and the CIA's roles, have been withheld from public scrutiny. Given the detailed materials available before and after July–September 1965, one can only assume that the release of these papers would embarrass the U.S. government. It is entirely possible that a generals' coup was planned, if not for October 5, then later, a policy that would have conformed to earlier U.S. urgings in any case, and that Washington's involvement in the terrible events of late 1965 was far greater than it has been willing to admit.

that time had no incentive whatsoever to try to take power because it was doing very well as it was. The following year Aidit's alleged special assistant for the September 30 events, whom the government revealed was a double agent, claimed that in August 1965 he had been assigned the task of organizing the September 30 Movement, but even his evidence merely shows it was a preemptive strike against an expected October 5 coup and not a PKI effort to take control. The PKI involvement was concealed, one of the CIA's later studies argued, but at most it was Aidit's unilateral undertaking, and the great majority of the PKI and its leadership were not implicated in any way. In any event, the embassy's and the CIA's contemporary reports will have to serve here as the most authoritative account of the actual events of October 1965 and what became one of the greatest massacres in modern history.

The officers in the September 30 Movement comprised two main groups: The first were younger central Javanese who condemned the corruption, Westernization, and personal laxity of the leaders of the army living in Djakarta; the second were air force officers, including its commander, who had long-standing complaints against the army over allocation of the military budget and whose careers were dependent on Sukarno remaining in power. The first group was anti-Communist, the second apolitical opportunists ready to accept the PKI as a fact of political life, and their initial proclamation was a murky blend of all their ideas—none of which was Marxist in nature. Both were prepared to use the PKI but not to subordinate their own limited goals to them when in the early morning of October 1 they captured and killed six of the key army generals and wounded Nasution, who then escaped.[8]

THE FINAL SOLUTION IN INDONESIA

Many of the causes of the events of September 30 remain unclear even today, but by far the most probable explanation is that it was primarily an internal military struggle with which both Aidit and Sukarno maintained a cautious but essentially opportunistic relationship. Since the September 30 group sought only to protect Sukarno and keep him in power, and since there was indeed a growing risk of hostile officers greatly reducing his control over the nation, both had an incentive to see the September 30 Movement prevail, and had its organizers been successful they probably would have overtly supported it. Sukarno allowed himself to be taken to the air force base near Djakarta, which was the headquarters of the effort, possibly because he feared he was in danger from the generals under Suharto, but did not give the public endorsement its organizers thought so essential; and after the September 30 effort quickly fizzled, he went about his business as head of state as if the event had never occurred. The PKI also hesitated, and nearly everywhere ignored the matter and sought to appease the army for most of October. Aidit most likely provided the conspirators with roughly thirteen hundred PKI militants, many of them women, to beef up their relatively small forces, but the PKI paper's October 2 editorial on the matter treated it as an internal army affair, nonetheless showing a sympathetic willingness to offer aid should it be required. Since by that time General Suharto's far more numerous and better-equipped soldiers were rounding up the September 30 leadership and troops, it did nothing more, and both Sukarno and the PKI then distanced themselves from the doomed rebels, the PKI doing so unequivocally no later than October 5.

The U.S. embassy's and the CIA's interpretation of the facts certainly support this analysis of Aidit's and Sukarno's actions, and they never believed the PKI was attempting to take power for itself or that a coup was involved. The September 30 events, as their reports show, were intended to preserve the status quo in an increasingly fluid situation. At most they regarded the PKI as privy to the affair, probably as a result of Aidit's hurried decision, but of secondary causal importance, and by October 4 they understood that the PKI would disavow those of its members who were involved, many of whom were from its more militant wing and unhappy with the PKI's united front strategy. Indeed, the embassy's experts trying to fathom the event concluded at the end of October that the September 30 Movement was the product of a motley, incongruent collection of elements who had dragged Aidit along with them and that the Communists involved in it—and that excluded the vast majority of its leaders, not to mention members—probably had no responsibility for its planning and timing and likely thought poorly of it. The PKI, in their view, while one of a number of groups involved, was not the principal one. Had the PKI given the efforts its full support, U.S. officials knew, its chances of success would have been far greater. In April 1966 the CIA decided that "The precise details of the PKI's role in the events of 1 October are not known, and . . . may never be," and their later analyses came to the same conclusion.[9] And no U.S. official ever believed that China was in any way involved in the affair.

Indonesia by late 1965 presented U.S. strategy in Southeast Asia with a danger at least as great as Vietnam at a time when its preoccupation there made large-scale intervention in Indonesia impossible. The logic of the domino theory applied to it as much as to Vietnam, but its economic and strategic value was far greater. Relying on peaceful means, the PKI had grown consistently, and could be expected to continue to do so. The United States had depended on the military since 1949 to create a barrier to the Communists, and it understood well that Sukarno's skilled balancing of contending forces to maintain his control would end in the near future with his death. The events of September 30 created a small challenge but also an enormous opportunity to resolve America's dilemmas by directing the military's wrath against the Communists.

The U.S. embassy no later than October 3 thought the crucial issue was whether the army under Suharto would "have courage to go forward against [the] PKI," an obsession they were to communicate to Washington over the next days without any disagreement from the State Department.[10] There is no doubt, either, that they informed key Indonesian officers of their opinions on the need to destroy the PKI, and the latter had similar thoughts even though they, too, believed the degree of PKI culpability was still very much a question. On October 5 the army made the decision to "implement plans to crush [the] PKI," the CIA reported, without indicating when they had been drawn up.[11] With Sukarno and the PKI on the defensive and Suharto's forces firmly in control and backed by the Muslims, the embassy cabled Washington, the army could move against the PKI—"it's now or never."[12] Three days later, the first reports of attacks on PKI offices came in, with mainly Muslim youth acting with army encouragement. Marshall Green, who had been ambassador since June 1965, still worried about the military's "determination" to stand up to Sukarno, but he was not to be disappointed.[13] Indeed, the military allowed Sukarno, ever the supreme opportunist, to claim he was the head of state while they began the vast task of destroying the PKI, each seeking to use the other. "We do think [the] Army will go on trying, possibly not always as directly as we would like, to keep matters moving in direction we would wish to see . . . ," Green cabled Washington on October 14; "Their success or failure is going to determine our own in Indonesia for some time to come."[14] By this point the embassy and the officers were often discussing their mutual needs and plans, and there were no doubts whatsoever that the United States wished the army to act decisively.

Reports of killings of alleged PKI members arrived at the embassy constantly, and its experts correctly concluded that the PKI—which was now being blamed for the events of September 30—was not likely to resist because it had long since ceased to be revolutionary. Since the PKI had neither the arms nor the will to resist, the tide of destruction began to rise by late October as mainly Muslim and right-wing youth, with aid from the army, began systematically to sweep the cities and countryside. Into their hands fell peasants who had asked for lower rents and alienated their landlords, those who were apolitical and denounced by enemies settling grudges, PKI members and those who were vaguely linked to it, religious elements the Muslims disliked—all suffered the same fate.

Washington received all the details the embassy possessed on the army's support for the massacres, and it took consolation that the army had resisted Sukarno's belated efforts at the end of October to stop the slaughter. The cleanup task would go on, Green told Rusk on October 28, and the next day the secretary of state cabled back that the "campaign against PKI" must continue and that the military "are [the] only force capable of creating order in Indonesia," which they had to continue doing "with or without Sukarno." Meanwhile, the generals could expect United States help for a "major military campaign against PKI."[15] A week later Green reported back that while the army was aiding the Muslim youth in Java to take care of the PKI, it was assuming the task directly in the outer islands, and it was contemplating a military state in the future. We have "made it clear that Embassy and USG generally sympathetic with and admiring of what army doing."[16] The army was wholly engaged, as Green described it several days later, attacking the PKI "ruthlessly," and "wholesale killings" were occurring.[17]

It was in this context that the Indonesian generals in early November approached the United States for equipment "to arm Moslem and nationalist youths in central Java for use against the PKI. . . ." Most were using knives and primitive means, and communications gear and small arms would expedite the killing. Since "elimination of these elements" was a precondition of better relations, the United States quickly promised covert aid—dubbed "medicines" to prevent embarrassing revelations.[18] At stake in the army's effort was the "destruction," as the CIA called the undertaking, of the PKI, and "carefully placed assistance which will help Army cope with PKI" continued, as Green described it, despite the many other problems in Indonesian-U.S. relations that remained to be solved.[19]

The "final solution" to the Communist problem in Indonesia was certainly one of the most barbaric acts of inhumanity in a century that has seen a great deal of it; it surely ranks as a war crime of the same type as those the Nazis perpetrated. No single American action in the period after 1945 was as bloodthirsty as its role in Indonesia, for it tried to initiate the massacre, and it did everything in its power to encourage Suharto, including equipping his killers, to see that the physical liquidation of the PKI was carried through to its culmination. Not a single one of its officials in Washington or Djakarta questioned the policy on either ethical or political grounds; quite the contrary. "The reversal of the Communist tide in the great country of Indonesia" was publicly celebrated, in the words of Deputy Undersecretary of State U. Alexis Johnson in October 1966, as "an event that will probably rank along with the Vietnamese war as perhaps the most historic turning point of Asia in this decade."[20]

No one counts the dead in a massacre, and those able to make a reliable estimate afterward had no incentive to do so in this case. On December 4, as they both were clamoring for yet more killing, Green wrote to Rusk that over 100,000 but not more than 200,000 had been murdered in northern Sumatra and central and eastern Java alone, and the destruction was still going on. At the beginning of the following April the CIA estimated roughly

250,000 deaths in a party of 3 million and 12 million front group members. By the end of the month it dismissed the government's claim of 78,000 dead and thought 250,000 to 500,000 closer to reality. But "An accurate figure is impossible to obtain," the CIA concluded.[21] A State Department estimate that year placed the figure at roughly 300,000, a number former ambassador Jones employed when he published his memoirs five years later—though he, too, did not exclude 500,000. Other estimates range up to 1 million dead, and official Indonesian data released a decade later gave 450,000 to 500,000 as the number killed. As stunning as these figures are, not a single official U.S. document dealing with them has ever expressed dismay or regret![22]

The number of people imprisoned is somewhat more precise. At the peak, there were 150,000 to 200,000 of them, the CIA reported. Ten years later, Amnesty International estimated there were still 55,000 political prisoners, though others thought nearly twice that more accurate.[23]

Even as the United States was encouraging the carnage, however, it was to carry on a running dispute with the new military elite, in part because it wished to see Sukarno and all those loyal to him removed from office but primarily because it considered Suharto and his circle also neutralist and expansionist like their predecessors, and hostile to foreign investment in general and U.S. oil companies in particular. A tone of exasperation always accompanied the sense of relief in American dispatches throughout this period, for its goals transcended only murder. The new leaders were told no later than mid-November that the resolution of the disputed oil concessions was the key to future U.S. policy, including aid, although privately American officials thought the military was confused about its future economic as well as political direction, and they favored channeling aid through multilateral aid schemes under IMF leadership. But the United States was never simply anti-Communist, and it did not hesitate aggressively to push its policy of integrating Indonesia and its raw materials into a United States-led world economy. And since Indonesia was far richer than Vietnam, the economic foundations of its anticommunism emerged much more starkly in Indonesia.

During December 1965, the generals and the Americans discussed frankly what they wanted from each other. For their part, the Indonesians in their "Bluntest remark," as Green reported it, "was question of how much is it worth to U.S. that PKI be smashed and trend here reversed, thereby swinging big part SEA from communism."[24] If the basic economy continued to deteriorate for lack of rice and textiles, they warned, all the gains against the PKI might be reversed and Sukarno's position strengthened. Aid via third countries was also preferable to the Indonesians. The United States demanded, as well, a sympathetic posture on the Vietnam War and an end to aggression against Malaysia, but especially protection of U.S. oil firms. In a word, it wanted the new generals to abandon traditional Indonesian nationalist commitments. And it constantly pressed for a total purge of Sukarno and those friendly to him for fear they would use their still substantial control over the state bureaucracies to outflank what Washington considered the rather naïve and inexperienced officers. Green tried to treat Suharto and his circle more tolerantly, but by early 1966 the United States could use the leverage that the destruction of the PKI gave it to press for its other objectives. Neither Sukarno nor those around Suharto were ready to take direct U.S. aid at the price demanded, much less associate with its foreign policy goals. "There has been no basic improvement in U.S.-Indonesian relations," Washington concluded bitterly.[25] But the following March 11 Suharto made himself acting president, and the United States had to reconsider its tough stance.

At the end of March, in an unusually acute assessment that reflected the consensus of U.S. opinion, the State Department outlined both its options and its prospects. It concluded that nationalist rhetoric aside, the profound legacy of personal corruption among the circulating elites would allow outsiders to control them, especially because the government sector of the economy was not a means of development but of personal enrichment. A mixed state-private economy, guided by multilaterally managed foreign aid, might dissolve the state economic sector in due course and tame the political elite. It was, given Indonesia's heritage, the best the United States could hope for at the time. Economically, therefore, it proposed operating in Indonesia under the aegis of an international consortium, perhaps with Japan assigned a special role in it to channel its growing power and ambitions, and it thought foreign investors could best operate under its protection. Such a structure could also apply pressure to sell state-owned firms, though the fact the local Chinese would acquire most of them complicated this goal. The paper clearly favored bringing in civilian technocrats and regarded all officers linked to the economy as corruptionists. Politically, however, it realized that should the generals fail, strong radical-nationalist forces would reemerge. Worse yet, there was the practical question that "after the army has destroyed the PKI" and eliminated Sukarno, were the United States to press the Suharto circle too strongly, "we could sow the seeds of resentment: not only in Indonesia but [also] internationally." "The experience could carry unforgettable lessons for those who may be faced by similar internal political challenges."[26] The generals would collect their reward!

It was this reasoning that led to the American effort to reintegrate Indonesia into the world economic order after a long postcolonial hiatus that had produced only economic stagnation and corruption in the name of nationalism. While the Soviet Union provided the anti-Communist generals with arms just as it had before the slaughter, the Japanese and the United States, working through consortia and the multilateral banks, used aid as a lever to rewrite Indonesia's basic economic legislation. During the remainder of 1966 technocrats trained mainly in U.S. elite universities took charge of the economy and, with the assistance of teams of American and European academics and businessmen, quickly redefined the nature and direction of the economy—at least on paper. Djakarta rejoined the IMF and the World Bank, and at the beginning of 1967 issued a new investment law that made it a haven for foreigners. U.S. aid climbed to over $200 million by 1969, its exports to Indonesia rose by over three times in three years, while its direct investment rose from $106 million in 1966 to over five times that in 1972 and $1.5 billion in 1976, making Indonesia far more important than the Philippines. Surveying its accomplishments in 1967, the Johnson Administration was proud of its only success in Southeast Asia. In nearby Vietnam it hoped to attain yet one more victory like it.

The system that emerged in Indonesia after 1967 was even more centralized around one man than it had been under Sukarno, who at least had allowed a modicum of civil liberties and permitted parties to function far more freely as long as he could control them. Sukarno co-opted many of his potential opponents, but Suharto put them in prison, or worse. He also concentrated all power over the army in the hands of a monolithic clique, which had never existed under Sukarno, and used it as both a mechanism for political control of the state apparatus at all levels and economic aggrandizement via a level of corruption that ranks among the highest in the world after 1945. Politically it created an unstable administrative order subject to arbitrary changes, predictable only in that its primary function was to reinforce the Suharto clique's power. Economically it is far more complex save in one regard: what Suharto and his circle have done for themselves.

Suharto never truly committed himself to an economy patterned along United States- or IMF-endorsed classical lines but rather acted as the State Department's experts in March 1966 predicted he would: He became richer. After 1972 and the massive entry of Japanese capital into Indonesia, Suharto found he had leverage in dealing with the rest of the world and his debtors— which he used repeatedly to borrow immense amounts for the state oil company, Pertamina, and other huge ventures. Local banks loaned massive sums to his political friends or their generally Chinese business associates, who still run most of the state as well as most of the private sector, and the magnitude of the corruption and waste nearly led to Pertamina's bankruptcy in 1977 and a serious weakening of the internal banking system. By astutely playing off foreign interests and milking them all, the political structure Suharto controlled worked with allied national business interests to operate a debt-ridden economy whose stability was as much dependent on a world economy that encouraged and funded such high-risk economic strategies as on Suharto's wisdom or folly. Indonesia's external public debt was $2.4 billion in 1970 but $14.9 billion a decade later, much of which had funded patronage projects. By 1986 Suharto and his family controlled thirty companies dealing in transport, electronics, chemicals, and much else. He had become a fabulously wealthy man.

Less problematical were the conditions of life for the masses, which in Indonesia meant largely the rural areas. During 1963–67, a depressed period, and 1970–74 the nation's ability to supply its own cereals declined, and in 1969–71 per capita calorie consumption was only 83 percent of minimum requirements—making Indonesia the poorest nation in Southeast Asia. In 1969, a total of 47 percent of the rural population lived in the starkest poverty. While data on such trends are uneven, all point to a decline in the rural living standards during Suharto's "New Order." The introduction of capital-intensive agriculture among wealthier peasants reduced employment for the poorer without reversing the national food deficit. Peasants after 1965 were afraid to organize, so landlessness increased and ownership became more concentrated. In eastern and western Java, by the late 1970s the real wages of rural workers was declining sharply, while land ownership also dropped. The percentage of farmers owning less than half a hectare grew from 46 percent in 1973 to 63 percent in 1980. In the end it was the peasantry, as everywhere, who paid the costs of the regime the United States supported, leaving in place all the prerequisites for an eventual renewal of social upheavals—and radical politics.

THE PHILIPPINES: THE CRISIS OF THE TRADITIONAL SYSTEM

When the Kennedy Administration took office the Philippines was still the primary U.S. strategic and economic concern in East Asia, and the nation remained as close to a colony as a nominally independent state could be. Even when the regional context had allowed it to continue as the core of Washington's designs in the area, however, dealing with the question of U.S. interests there was a matter for relatively minor officials, and for those above them the country was a nuisance that periodically, and usually very briefly, inserted itself into their attention. But the fact was that independence had proven an unruly phase insofar as American prerogatives and objectives were concerned, for although its political leaders were acculturated to Yankee values, rising nationalism under the García government had from 1957 to 1961 begun to undermine seriously U.S. hegemony over vital phases of the life of the republic. This trend was to present America with a constant problem and challenge throughout the 1960s—and beyond. If it appeared to diminish in this decade because of the growing Indochina crisis, which eventually consumed all of Washington's attention, its perception of the Philippines was also increasingly to be colored by its relationship to the Vietnam War; but in reality all the problems that annoyed and challenged the United States at the end of the Eisenhower era continued to develop. Economically, socially, and politically, the Philippine nation was heading toward profound crisis. Only the symptoms of this trend confronted the Johnson Administration.

It remained the United States' desire, in the 1960s as in previous decades, to use the Philippines to show the world what it alone could do to create democracy and an ideal society in the Third World. At the same time, it regarded the country as a key market and investment outlet as well as a major supplier, and it insisted that Filipino politics adjust to its needs rather than pursue the nationalist economic policies to which the García regime, despite its traditional corruption, had surprisingly given momentum. Yet the fact that a truly indigenous national bourgeoisie emerged during these years had political implications that greatly exceeded the still relatively marginal economic resources such a class could mobilize. As long as economic development was linked to the control of political power, the main threat to the United States after 1960 came not from the dormant Left but from middle- and upper-class entrepreneurs who by necessity had to expound a nationalism that was synonymous with anti-Americanism.

The United States supported the victorious Macapagal in the November 1961 elections not because the Liberal was less corrupt than García, and honesty was the main campaign issue, but because he favored a restoration of the U.S.-Philippines bilateral trade system to its original form—notwithstanding a formidable nationalist contingent in Congress. His first major act upon taking office was to implement IMF and U.S. Treasury recommendations and lift all exchange controls, in return for which the Philippines, which had earlier been denied IMF and World Bank loans, received $300 million in U.S. and IMF aid. With the peso devalued by about half, the Philippine economy once again became an open hunting ground for U.S. businessmen, most of whom still preferred sending previously blocked profits out of the country rather than investing further—to the extent, in fact, that in no year after 1945 had new foreign investment equaled profits repatriated to the United States. Macapagal's economic program, the price of continued IMF aid, was consciously antinationalist, and the major damage it inflicted on local business interests led to an end of the rapid growth of the manufacturing sector that had occurred during the 1950s. Export interests, in conformity with the standard U.S. and IMF formula, were ascendant once more.

Economically, the results showed up quickly in inflation, which drove down the real income of labor and forced thousands of businesses to the brink of failure or over it. By 1964 a tenth of the labor force was unemployed, while almost a third of the remainder was underemployed—farm labor that worked the smaller part of the year, or the innumerable urban poor who had been forced off the land to live a lumpen existence in slums. The larger structural trends in the economy during this decade were testimony to the ability of the U.S.-IMF program to impose countless otherwise avoidable difficulties on national economic development strategies. By 1965 almost a third of the nation's capital stock was foreign-owned, mainly American-owned, and two-thirds of the hundred largest corporations, dominant in manufacturing, utilities, and commerce, were foreign. By the mid-1960s the repatriation of profits and the amortization of its loans were costing close to $400 million annually, forcing Manila to continue borrowing. The national public external debt rose from $174 million in 1960 to $480 million in 1965, then doubled by 1970. Given the Laurel-Langley Agreement as well as the nature of U.S. investment, Philippine exports still flowed primarily toward the colonial power: 54 percent in 1961 and 42 percent in 1969. But its imports fell dramatically, from 47 percent in 1961 to 28 percent in 1969, when Japan became the nation's largest supplier. The most important political conse-quence of these figures was the intensification of nationalist businessmen's resistance to United States-sanctioned policies.

Growing nationalism also interfered with the White House's desire after 1964 to obtain Manila's aid for the Vietnam War both in the form of an endorsement and troops, thereby allowing Washington to pretend that the intervention was a regional rather than a strictly American affair. Vietnam significantly shifted Washington's focus in the Philippines from purely eco-nomic issues or the prevention of a revival of the Left to its integration into the increasingly important Vietnam conflict. At the same time, because it had few other means of expressing its opposition to U.S. hegemony, large sections of the national bourgeoisie resisted supporting the war. In its own way, the Vietnam War became a focus for a much larger American-Filipino conflict and a nation's search for national autonomy as the issue of imperialism and anticommunism throughout Southeast Asia moved to the fore.

The White House found Macapagal's statements on the Vietnam War "help-ful," and at the end of 1964 it impatiently pressed him to fulfill his pledge to send troops there.[27] It was willing to pay the entire cost of a Philippine force, but Macapagal's prowar position unleashed a storm of opposition, and it soon became clear that an alliance of political opportunists and nationalists of all persuasions might capitalize on the president's lack of resolve to block what became the United States' obsessive immediate goal in its relations with Manila. The war defined the U.S. response to the November 1965 election, in which Macapagal and Ferdinand Marcos, who switched over to the Na-cionalistas to obtain their nomination, were the two major contestants. By that time economic problems had become acute with rising inflation, and informed Manila experts estimated that corruption was consuming about a third of all government revenues. The CIA believed that all the candidates were pro-American and that neither would do much to bring reforms to the nation, making a stronger Left in the future likely. Both would send forces to Vietnam, despite the fact that Marcos had earlier opposed Macapagal's bill to dispatch engineering troops, and Marcos was deemed a "ruthless politician" while Macapagal was flabby.[28] Washington always considered Marcos a cynical opportunist. Many Western papers, tired of Macapagal's traditional corruption, hailed Marcos as the last chance to avert revolution in the nation—but few expected him to be anything more than just another ambitious, corrupt personality so characteristic of the Philippine oligarchy's politics.

Given the fact that it could not lose, the United States remained neutral in the election. Marcos won and immediately assumed the role of the typical Philippine politician, in the United States' estimate, and in July 1966 he helped push through a measure that authorized two thousand engineer troops to Vietnam. Even more important to the United States, which still hoped to get combat forces from Marcos, was a carte blanche from him to use American bases in the Philippines as logistics centers and even, possibly, for combat launches in the Vietnam War. In September 1966, to "Keep Marcos on our side and help him silence his critics," whom the war had made far more numerous, Marcos fulfilled his desire to visit Washington. The Administration knew that it would have to reward him with significant aid and that it would be channeled into Marcos's political coffers—perhaps even his pocket. In addition to eighty million dollars in grants, Marcos received thirty-nine million dollars for the expenses of his Vietnam contingent—part of which was paid in cash and deposited in banks he controlled. It was in this context that the United States also pressed Marcos to "improve general trade and investment climate in the Philippines and find ways to protect American acquired rights after 1974," when the Laurel-Langley Agreement was to expire.[29] However much Vietnam dominated relations between Washington and Manila after 1964, economics was still very alive in everyone's calculations.

Marcos' visit proved to the Johnson Administration that he could be bought and that he would remain a loyal ally in protecting American interests not just in his own country but in Southeast Asia as well. A month after Marcos was in Washington, Johnson visited Manila, primarily to participate in a seven-nation meeting on Vietnam. But the Administration believed Marcos had "rapidly mounting problems," partly because he was "failing to pursue economic reform and development programs effectively" in his "successfully operating Asian democracy." "Demonstrating U.S. support for the Marcos Administration" and his "strongly pro-American" stance was a quid pro quo for "his all-out support for our objectives in Vietnam." Part of the bargain, Marcos expected, was "full U.S. support for various requests for assistance."[30] Not since Magsaysay had a Philippine president cooperated with the United States so completely. When CIA and other analysts noted that Marcos' failure to remedy pressing issues, particularly agrarian, might renew "a major insurgent threat," they were simply ignored.[31]

However central Vietnam in the making of the Marcos-Washington axis, there still remained Philippine nationalism as represented by the Philippine Chamber of Industries, which wanted an end to IMF domination of the economy and a return to exchange controls and protection for domestic producers. The political system allowed them a growing voice via Congress and the media, which local businessmen influenced. In the long run, the overarching question for the United States was what would happen to its many interests after the expiration of the Laurel-Langley agreement in 1974, and during 1967 officials of both nations began to discuss the prospects. For the Americans, "The nature of Philippine nationalism will be a critical element," and while they knew Marcos himself was ready to adopt a desirable investment policy, he could not transcend congressional prerogatives.[32] Their meetings only underscored the probability that the neocolony would claim its total independence. In 1967 Congress passed a law that all companies in traditional industries must be at least 60 percent Filipino-owned, and foreign investment fell dramatically. Given earlier nationalist legislation on retail trade that was being contested in the courts, U.S. firms in the country were now very much endangered. The failure of the IMF-defined program and the massive external debts the nation was accumulating caused the Philippine House and Senate to assert themselves aggressively, and in mid-1969 they issued a comprehensive set of economic goals reflecting the desires of the nationalist business constituency: protective tariffs, exchange controls, Filipinization of the economy, and even an independent foreign policy. The challenge to American hegemony had never been so great, or come from such powerful opponents.

By 1969 and the beginning of the Nixon Administration, politics within the Philippine ruling class had long since reached an impasse, and the existing political institutions and forces no longer had the capacity to resolve the profound contradictions and needs of the contending sections of the elite, much less the larger society. The nation's economic malaise, which threatened to deepen into a crisis with untold implications, was not only making a travesty of the U.S. desire to use its former colony as an example of what it was capable of accomplishing for the world but also reflected the continuing role of the United States in the economy. The election of November 1969 was the turning point, pitting Marcos against Sergino Osmeña, a former collaborator with the Japanese. Osmeña had switched parties constantly since 1945 and was a classic Philippine oligarch who knew everything about patronage, corruption, and violence. He stood only for himself, leaving no one to represent the nationalist businessmen. He was also ardently pro-American, and while neither he nor Marcos threatened Washington, Nixon as much as endorsed the president. Marcos took no chances and simply raided the national treasury, spending from fifty million to two hundred million dollars, depending on the source, on his campaign—more than the cost of all postwar elections combined. The violence and ballot-box manipulation that went with it were also unprecedented. The election's impact on the economy and society, its morale and cohesion, ushered in a new era that at the same time reflected the inevitable logic of politics in the nation the United States had created after 1946.

The Vietnam War, tradition, and much else precluded the Johnson Administration or its successor from dealing with the Philippines as a major issue, so it became one of the many minor distractions that inserted itself periodically into senior Administration circles. But however much those in Washington sought to ignore or avoid thinking about America's colonial legacy, it was certain that sooner or later events in the Philippines would produce a far more serious challenge to the U.S. role in East Asia.

The Problem of Sub-Saharan Africa

*A*MERICAN POLICY TOWARD AFRICA after World War Two had deferred to European interests, and the Eisenhower Administration's desire for NATO unity and its fear of Communist infiltration in the wake of premature independence reinforced this commitment throughout the 1950s. If by the end of the decade it made cosmetic changes in its public statements on African questions to make the United States appear somewhat less supportive of the status quo, neither its European allies nor African nationalists believed them, and when Kennedy campaigned for the presidency in 1960 he attacked the Republicans for supporting colonialism in Africa. Many anticipated that his victory would bring a change in American policy in the vast continent even though the 1960 Democratic platform gave no explicit justification for such expectations.

Whatever their rhetoric and style, there was little likelihood that the Democrats would introduce a new policy in Africa, for the same reasons they failed to do anything fundamentally innovative in all the other domains of U.S. foreign policy. The operating premises and consensus among all those called upon to articulate and implement U.S. foreign policy allowed very little room for basic departures, and to focus on Democratic rhetoric as opposed to practice in this area is, as with the Alliance for Progress, seriously misleading. Given all the United States' other concerns in the world, Africa in the 1960s remained essentially no more vital in U.S. definitions of its priorities than it had been earlier. And just as the Kennedy Administration was to continue the policy of deferring to its European allies and working through them in Africa as much as possible, so, too, did its rationale for supporting military rulers elsewhere in the Third World define its choice of allies in Africa.

G. Mennen Williams, a former Michigan governor with a strong domestic civil rights record, was made assistant secretary of state for African affairs, and while he was often dubbed an idealist, he failed to articulate new departures even when he had the opportunity to do so. His principal argument for a position in Africa less supportive of colonialism was the need to preempt Communist influence there—a danger few American experts in the 1960s thought existed. Chester Bowles, the undersecretary of state and a renowned liberal, had neither the patience nor specific ideas essential to formulate concrete alternatives, and after a year he was pushed aside, while Adlai Stevenson in the UN, another liberal, was too passive and ambivalent to challenge existing policies effectively.

Like its predecessors, the new Administration unquestionably wished to be friends with black Africa, but mainly to get their support in the UN and protect relatively minor American interests on the continent. It also favored self-determination, but as part of an orderly transition that was, vaguely enough, neither precipitous nor too slow, and it, too, did not want to see its NATO allies or existing white-settler rulers withdraw suddenly lest a vacuum open up into which chaos or, less likely, radicals could move. The so-called liberals under Kennedy were insipid in their means and ends, and the differences between the "Africanists" in Washington during the 1960s who wished to treat with Africa for its own sake and those who saw it as integral to the European system were essentially those of degree, not kind, of tactics rather than goals. The basic problem was that no administration thought the vast continent that important, and their policies were formulated primarily in response to tangible problems in individual countries rather than in some general fashion.

CRISIS IN THE CONGO

The Democratic focus on specific issues was inevitable not only because they had no desire or rarely the need to deal with the continent as a whole but also because the crisis in the Congo was at a critical point just as they entered office and least welcomed a major challenge, and in the course of it they were compelled to make choices that revealed that their core commitments and natural instincts resembled those of their predecessors. The Belgian Congo had been given its independence in June 1960, only to see a Belgian-sponsored secession of the mineral-rich Katanga Province and two claimants for control of the central government. One of these, Patrice Lumumba, was a pan-Africanist close to Nkrumah of Ghana and the least tribally oriented of all the contestants and best able to weld the Congo into a nation. Prepared to work with Western interests on his own terms, he was also ready to exploit

Cold War tensions to extract maximum aid from both sides. This position had caused the Eisenhower Administration to order the CIA in August 1960 to assassinate him, but on January 17, 1961, his enemies secretly accomplished the task—probably without direct CIA participation but surely with its encouragement. When Kennedy took office three days later, the Congo was in chaos.

U.S. stakes in the Congo were large, less because of its direct investments in its rich copper, cobalt, and diamond mines or important role in financing Belgian interests but because of the potential impact on Europe and world copper prices were Congo supplies no longer to be available. The Eisenhower Administration had worked with the Belgians loyally until then, fearing a vacuum would emerge in the Congo into which Soviet influence might enter, and since it had always favored a continuation of Belgian control over the former colony, it supported the Belgian troop-backed secessionist regime of Moise Tshombe in Katanga, where the majority of the mines were located.

During the first months of 1961 the Kennedy Administration was divided over its response to the Congo crisis, where UN troops were unsuccessfully attempting to restore order, and although Stevenson tried to placate the Afro-Asian bloc in the UN, the United States refused to criticize Belgium's role or accept the return of Lumumba to power before his murder became known in mid-February. Lumumba's death caused worldwide protests and intense anger within the Afro-Asian bloc, and when for a brief period the United States feared direct Soviet, Egyptian, or other intervention, it sent five ships, along with Marines, off the Congo coast and hinted at its readiness to send tens of thousands of troops to resist any foreign involvement. While a compromise UN resolution was hammered out, Washington backed away from the use of force, preferring to manipulate the UN troops and let them take the risks.

Over the next two years, aided by a new Belgian government less responsive to its mining interests, the United States in a painfully convoluted effort helped to remove Lumumba's radical followers as well as curb Tshombe's secessionists, who threatened the Congo's existence until the end of 1964. It sought a unified Congo but one under pro-Western leadership, and to accomplish this it decided to back Colonel Joseph Mobuto, who had been Lumumba's chief of staff but whom the CIA knew to be anti-Communist, self-serving, and amenable to U.S. influence. Special American military assistance helped to build his strength, and in November 1965 he seized power— where he has remained ever since. While Belgium retained its mines, the United States became the Congo's (now renamed Zaire) main source of military and economic aid.

The protracted, risky, and very costly Congo crisis effectively purged any Democratic Administration inclination to become too involved in African affairs, which in many nations meant choosing sides in civil wars, and it revealed that when it unavoidably did it would opt for authoritarian regimes very much like those it was endorsing in Latin America at the same time. This policy began immediately under Kennedy, and given the same advisers under Johnson it continued through his presidency. Despite the noble rhetoric the Democrats produced routinely, in essence they pursued the same overall policy as their predecessors.

The United States abhorred a vacuum anywhere, and Africa was no exception, and its grand strategy in Africa was based on this explicit premise, shaping its policies in southern Africa when the issue of the future of white settlers arose. "At stake," as a leading State Department planner phrased it in 1962, "is not only justice (for majority and minorities alike) but the requirements of minimal order."[1] The simplest way for it to cope with the enormously sensitive issues of Africa was to leave them to the European powers, and this was as much explicit policy under the Democrats as it had been under the Republicans. They should have "primary responsibility" even as the U.S. role grew, Rostow argued in May 1961, and supplementing rather than replacing the European role remained official policy.[2] The United States objected in principle to the preferential trading system the Europeans imposed on their former colonies, but while they wanted it altered they also opposed dismantling it hastily lest the change produce more unpredictable disorder. On the contrary, in 1962 it considered the "reinforcement of African ties with Western Europe" more desirable than ever.[3] In Zaire, for the remainder of this period, Washington assigned Belgium the primary responsibility, including for any direct action that might be necessary in the event of civil war. Indeed, with the possible exception of South Africa, by 1964 the State Department dismissed the risks of communism succeeding in Africa as very small indeed, and this reinforced Washington's clear desire to maintain only a "residual interest" in the region.[4] Axiomatic with this policy was support for the status quo.

Such equanimity did not end U.S. efforts to strengthen its prestige in black Africa, and in the spring of 1965 the State Department believed that upgrading America's image there would not only be useful to safeguard or advance its interests but also to win greater political support from African states for U.S. policy elsewhere as well, particularly in Vietnam. An effort to inject new life into its aid program in Africa, perhaps even to launch an equivalent to the "Great Society" there that Johnson was seeking to build at home, listlessly moved across desks for a year, and when Johnson on May 26, 1966, made a general policy speech on Africa, it evoked little attention or enthusiasm because he failed to increase aid funds significantly. For just as Vietnam was to lead to the demise of the Great Society within the United States, it also aborted it in Africa.

SOUTHERN AFRICA: RHETORIC AND REALITY

U.S. policy in southern Africa revealed most starkly the vast gulf between the Kennedy Administration's periodic liberal rhetorical flurries and its policies in specific cases. These tangible American responses had to consider the European dimension of its positions, the unfavorable consequences they might have on NATO, and the likelihood of its action—or lack of it—helping to bring to power African nationalists hostile to the United States.

In Angola, where the Portuguese ruled with obstinacy and brutality, this dilemma confronted the Administration immediately because in March 1961 the movement against white rule initiated open, sustained armed struggle. Given the crises in Berlin, Cuba, and Indochina at that time, the new Administration's response was to treat Angola as one factor interrelated to many others in the world—an approach that ultimately pleased neither Africans nor Portuguese. The question was complicated for the Administration because its lease on the Portuguese-owned Azores bases, which the Pentagon deemed vital to future operations in Europe or the Middle East, were due to expire at the end of 1962 and the Defense Department thought their retention far more important than anything else. On March 15 the United States voted for a UN resolution that condemned Portuguese intransigence and demanded "self-determination" rather than independence but did not mention sanctions against Portugal, its moderation being the result of the American role in drafting it. Washington then cut its already nominal military aid to Lisbon. Antonio Salazar, the reactionary dictator who had ruled Portugal since 1932, minced no words condemning his American allies, and he failed to appreciate that Washington was attempting to save Portugal from far greater ignominy.

The challenge facing Washington was how to maintain its ties with Portugal, essentially to guard access to its bases, but also to make certain that Lisbon's intransigence not radicalize the Angolan resistance, a resistance it considered inevitable given Portugal's obduracy and the fact that it was too weak and too poor to win a protracted war. Nor did the United States want sudden independence, but rather a controlled transition in the hands of moderate nationalists also ready to maintain links with Portugal. The Congo crisis only reinforced this desire. While African opinion was a factor of modest importance to some Americans there was never a possibility that the United States would support one party or the other unequivocally. It was essentially this highly cold-blooded assessment of the situation that led the Administration to play both sides of the fence in the hope it could steer events down the middle. It was an exceedingly difficult policy to implement despite its logic, not the least because the Angola task force the White House created at this time resolved that while access to Azores bases and NATO unity would be its first priority, it would also press the Portuguese to reform. And while American officials often disagreed on how such a strategy should be implemented, with the Africa desk bitterly confronting the Europeanists and the Pentagon in a very unequal match, they all agreed on the need to attempt to define both Angolan and Portuguese policies—an effort that promised total success or alienating every side.

While the United States pursued its public strategy of supporting UN resolutions against Portugal during 1961 in order to moderate them, it tried to reach the Portuguese primarily through normal diplomatic channels. After it voted for another moderate UN resolution on June 15, the Administration attempted to bait the Portuguese with promises of large-scale economic aid should they permit self-determination in their colonies, at the same time deciding secretly to sponsor the most anti-Communist and responsive of the liberation groups under Holden Roberto in the hope that when Portuguese repression inevitably failed, a pro-American regime would replace it. Roberto collected significant amounts of money and nonmilitary matériel from the CIA for the next eight years, continuing on its payroll thereafter as well. This effort quickly became public and alienated both Roberto's rivals for leadership and Portugal.

By mid-1962 both sides in the Angolan war were locked in a struggle that was to last over a decade. Although the United States tried to relegate it to a minor concern, those dealing with the issue realized that Salazar had embarked on a potentially suicidal course from which he could not be moved, raising the additional challenge of not only keeping the Angolans from moving leftward but also avoiding the collapse of the Salazar dictatorship itself, "with unknown elements coming into power."[5] Given this new dimension to the Angola issue as well as the expiry of leases for bases at the end of the year, the United States shifted to a more tolerant position toward Portugal, voting against strong Security Council resolutions in December 1962. Salazar, whose public scorn of the United States knew few limits, decided not to renew the Azores lease but to allow the Americans simply to use it—with the threat of expulsion at any time.

From this point onward the Administration played a passive role in what it knew to be a situation fraught with immense dangers both in Africa and Europe. Publicly it favored a gradual transfer of responsibilities to the Angolans over an indefinite time to prevent chaos, opposing immediate independence as well as sanctions against Portugal. In July 1963 it abstained from voting for a UN resolution it had watered down and led the African states to believe it would support. Privately, however, even Portugal's strongest advocates in Washington thought Salazar irrational, threatening his own survival in office on behalf of colonial pretensions Portugal was no longer able to maintain—risking the creation of radical regimes eventually and turning the Afro-Asian bloc against the United States.

In December 1963 the United States again voted for an extremely mild UN resolution, further alienating the Portuguese. Roberto at this time began to accept aid from China as well, though he took CIA funds even as he condemned American policy. Salazar continued excoriating the Americans and left them nervous about their tenure on the Azores, inhibiting their criticism. Essentially Washington continued down this track quietly for the next decade, until its greatest fears were realized in both Angola and Portugal. Meanwhile, although the United States had stated it would neither give nor sell Portugal arms destined for its ruthless and hopeless colonial wars, in May 1965 it secretly sold it seven B-26 bombers fitted for jungle warfare. Its failure in Angola, along with its most pessimistic and presciently accurate foreboding about its implications both to Africa and Portugal's future role in Europe, further intensified the Democrats' impulse to relegate African affairs to the lowest priority.

THE SOUTHERN AFRICAN DILEMMA

South Africa and Rhodesia also reinforced Washington's dour mood. On South Africa the Kennedy Administration allowed those within its own ranks opposed to the apartheid regime to criticize it publicly, but privately it assured the South African government that cooperation on questions of mutual interest would continue. This included not only economic relations, but increasingly military collaboration as well. A U.S. missile tracking station was installed in South Africa in 1960, and overflight and landing rights for U.S. military aircraft, port facilities for the Navy, joint surveillance of Soviet ships, and probably intelligence-sharing also followed. The racist regime quickly learned that it could deal with the new American government, successfully demanding the right to buy U.S. arms in return for continued use of tracking sites. In the UN the Americans opposed mandatory trade sanctions against South Africa, and while it publicly opposed apartheid it loyally defended the whites against constant assaults in the UN. Perhaps no other African issue so alienated a minority within the Administration's ranks.

It was not that the United States opposed change in South Africa, but its official secret policy guidelines wanted to "help to preserve that nation's internal stability," and it did not wish to see it isolated.[6] Those who decided such plans always recognized that U.S. investments there were very large, nor did they want to sacrifice informal military relations. Privately they wanted the separate-homeland concept, which the overwhelming majority of blacks wholly rejected, improved to win their acquiescence. Ultimately the main challenge the United States confronted in South Africa was its public relations in the UN, and since it had stood against the Afro-Asians on a trade boycott in 1963, it acceded to an arms boycott, but with conditions that allowed it to fulfill its existing contracts and sell more in the future—virtually nullifying the resolution.

When Johnson entered the White House, the basic U.S. policy of courting African opinion while maintaining solid business and military relations with South Africa continued. Occasionally it tilted to assuage public opinion on specific questions, but it maintained functionally strong ties with the racist regime. For internal purposes, the Administration opposed violent black resistance under all conditions, yet it also thought majority rule unlikely to be attained by any means, including peaceful. It believed the country too important to the United States to risk it being lost via black armed struggle, so its white rulers obtained what they needed from the Americans, and only when they demanded advanced arms in unnecessary quantities did the Administration impose constraints upon it. This approach had overwhelming support both within the government and from major business constituencies. At the end of 1967 the State Department admitted to itself that "A fully consistent policy is probably impossible at this time," but in practice U.S. policy throughout this decade was overwhelmingly supportive of the racist order in South Africa—for which it obtained major economic and strategic returns.[7]

In Rhodesia, on the other hand, Washington preferred to avoid tarnishing its public image even further and deferred to Britain's primary role there, maintaining the lowest profile possible. Since its economic interests were less significant, the United States hoped it could nuance British strategy where necessary. But it loyally supported London through the twists and turns of its policies even when criticizing them.

THE AFRICAN CHALLENGE

Africa frustrated the United States consistently throughout the 1960s, and as its problems in Vietnam and elsewhere increased monumentally, it sought to relegate the continent to the very bottom of its concerns. All this only reinforced the Administration's natural inclination to employ the ideas on the crucial role of the military in modernizing new nations that it was applying elsewhere, if only to locate sympathetic anti-Communist elements in the hope that they might create stability where none existed. At the inception of the decade its Rand consultants on Africa argued that the military alone might modernize tribal societies and impose skills and a common language on them. In a region where most Africanists influential in establishment circles believed the state had preceded formation of the nation, officials in Washington dealing with Africa were instinctively drawn to supporting the military. There were sixty-four military mutinies and failed or successful coups in Africa in 1963–68 alone, and many American specialists thought that military coups were a healthy response to foreign "alien ideologies" that such civilians as Nkrumah, Lumumba, or African socialists were advocating. These more "realistic" officers, their reasoning went, would be "more receptive to the free world economic doctrine and technology."[8] CIA experts tried to amend this optimistic analysis by pointing out that while officers were becoming the decisive power group in Africa, they shared none of the military's capacity elsewhere to administer nations. They were primarily ambitious and interested in power, but rather than noting the risks in this reality Washington simply accepted the military as a dominant, unavoidable, and desirable fact of life. But in its quest for stability, which by 1966 caused even the small group of reformers among U.S. decisionmakers to regard the African political climate after so many military takeovers as "the best it has ever been," the United States opted for relying on the armies in Africa also.[9]

This American preference was especially the case in those nations where neither the French nor the British were likely or able to control events should they veer in directions the United States thought undesirable. Five thousand Africans were given military training in the United States between 1950 and 1969, plus a thousand abroad. Aid went principally to Zaire in black Africa, but lesser sums were spread around liberally. By the end of the decade it was clear that the CIA's predictions of military inefficiency and avariciousness were valid, but as Zaire also proved, armies kept the centrifugal impulses inherent in tribal societies tightly under control, and they efficiently suppressed radicals.

The political and social order Mobuto imposed on Zaire was possible only because of loyal American support for him after 1965. With all the resources for becoming a rich nation, it declined into one of Africa's most disastrous economies as unbridled corruption was systematically institutionalized until its loans from international banks led to control over its economy passing entirely into the IMF's hands. "Bankruptcy, near-total breakdown of vital services, military incompetence and repression, mass impoverishment, the increasing unpopularity of the Regime, and increased dependence on foreign creditors, technicians, and soldiers" is how the foremost authority on the nation described it in 1980.[10] This pattern of military corruption extended throughout the continent, less spectacular than in Zaire only because there was less to steal. Tribal purges became common, deferring the attainment of true national unity. In this context foreign domination continued easily. Yet whatever miseries it brought to Africa's people, the military to whom the

United States turned so emphatically after 1960, in Africa as everywhere, seemed to promise Washington the stability and protection against radicalism to which it attached such a high priority.

Notwithstanding the United States' deepening desire for conditions in Africa that allowed it to focus its energies elsewhere, at the end of the Johnson era major problems remained that would demand the attention of subsequent administrations. It was one thing to wish to assign as much responsibility for the continent to the British and French spheres of influence as possible, as long as they respected American economic and strategic interests, but the very nature of the corrupt and inefficient regimes the Western powers installed, and the still unresolved outcome of the intensifying struggles in the Portuguese colonies and southern Africa, left open innumerable dangers. These included the European powers being no better able to guide their former wards and possessions toward social systems acceptable to the United States than they had been in Asia. Should the transition from colonialism lead to radicalization, only the United States had the ambition and, it believed, the power to challenge it. Given its still modest but growing economic interests and goals and its strategic definitions of the relation of Africa to the world, only time would tell whether conditions in the future would allow the United States to attain its objectives there without far greater commitments. The American role in Africa was still very much an open question.

THE DILEMMAS OF WORLD EMPIRE

"Never before in human history has a nation undertaken to play a role of world responsibility," George Ball reflected in March 1965 in assessing the United States' global position, "except in defense and support of a world empire." While conceding that "Our actions have not been motivated by pure altruism," he nonetheless differentiated America's motives from those of traditional imperialists to justify its global efforts and argue against any reduction in its vast commitments because "no action by a global power can ever be taken in isolation."[11] It was this refusal to adjust its international role to its priorities and capabilities, as it had nominally sought to do since 1945, that caused Washington after 1964 to ignore the relation of its power to its objective interests in the Third World as well as the material constraints on its resources. In Vietnam the logic of interventionism led to U.S. loss of control over its foreign policy not only in the Third World but in Europe also, fundamentally threatening the future of the informal, de facto empire that men like Ball acknowledged implicitly.

To some vital extent its lack of mastery over its priorities had also frustrated the Truman Administration in Korea, and it became the cardinal goal of all its successors to avoid a repetition of an event that damaged the United States so profoundly politically and economically as well as revealed the limits of its military power. However much they had desired to do so, Vietnam proved that the mixture of its readiness to intervene everywhere, combined with the logic of the domino theory and credibility, produced an intrinsically highly unstable, dangerous basis for conducting a foreign policy that aspired to lead the world yet also to avert crises.

For the two Democratic presidents in the 1960s, even more than the ideologically more defensive Eisenhower Administration, reliance on dictators and military juntas in the Third World explicitly became their preferred mode of relating to political dynamics in the Third World. The problem of such a policy was the risk to U.S. power and credibility when those repressive surrogates created their own opposition, as they invariably did, and American strength, both symbolically and in terms of protecting its tangible economic and strategic interests, became linked to keeping them in office. And capital-intensive interventions had to be won quickly or they produced their own economic and political contradictions, both within the nations it was attempting to control as well as in the United States itself. If Vietnam was the most extreme example of both of these dangers, the likelihood of their occurring again in innumerable other nations also was very high, and U.S. might was ultimately no greater than that of its clients. And since the United States was locked into conflicts not only with movements on the Left but also with essentially conservative but nationalist forces that, as in Latin America, refused to accept its hegemonic economic visions, actively seeking to determine who ran governments in the Third World involved Washington in the complex, constant difficulties of politically managing poor nations everywhere.

This alone, along with a preference for repressive political opportunists whose collaboration with the United States was frequently a means for them to obtain maximum rewards for themselves and their cliques, by the late 1960s left the Johnson Administration with the growing necessity of interceding in the Third World at the very time when Vietnam imposed decisive limits on the means it could choose for doing so. Domestic political and economic constraints precluded, for practical purposes, another conscious intervention that might escalate into an open-ended conflict as occurred in Vietnam. U.S. aspirations in the Third World remained constant, from its unwavering desire for economic systems it could integrate wholly into an American-dominated world order to its determination to see strong Communist and Left parties muzzled. The dilemma of devising more effective means to attain these goals was a challenge it bequeathed to its successors. It was remarkably like the one Truman had left to Eisenhower.

By 1969 the Johnson Administration's priorities in the Third World, especially to optimize its objective economic interests in Latin America and the Middle East, had unraveled functionally, however coherent they appeared on paper. Confronting the myriad challenges that war raised both in Vietnam and at home more than consumed all its resources, and when the Democrats were voted out of office largely because of it, they left more dilemmas to be resolved than any preceding government had ever done. The most important of these was the war itself, but there were also innumerable new difficulties as well as traditional ones: the future of interventions in the forms of counterinsurgency and local war, the rising tide of both nationalist and Leftist forces in many poorer states, the increasing role of Europe and Japan in the economic life of many regions as a counterbalance to U.S. power, and much else. Compared to the late 1950s, the problems confronting the United States' imperialist ambitions had increased far more rapidly than its means for coping with them.

The question was whether the Johnson Administration's successors would be any better prepared to confront these challenges and make the preservation of the U.S. "world empire," as Ball had alluded to it, any more likely.

PART FOUR

THE DECADE OF PERPETUAL CRISES, 1969 THROUGH THE 1970s

The Nixon Administration Confronts the Third World

R ICHARD NIXON WAS AWARE OF SOME
of the challenges his predecessors had
bequeathed to him, but he and his clos-
est advisers were no better equipped to appreciate their complexity and
intractability than they had been. The Vietnam War, above all, weighed
heavily on the new White House's time and resources, and it demanded
reassessments of those methods of relating to the Third World that culminated in the Vietnam debacle. Yet while some of its means might change,
there was never the slightest indication before 1969 that the new president
or his advisers, quintessential adherents of the Cold War's harshest assumptions, would seek to redefine the traditional basic objectives of U.S. foreign
policy in the Third World.

Just as Vietnam in the early 1960s had to some crucial extent been a test
of U.S. ability and determination to respond militarily to revolutionary
change in the Third World, by the end of the decade the Vietnam War had
become the decisive measure of its willingness to sacrifice its relations to
Europe as well as its power to deal with the Soviet Union. The war also
shattered the postwar domestic political consensus on foreign policy, undermining the very health of the American economy on behalf of an increasingly
symbolic and wholly futile campaign in only one intrinsically quite marginal
country. By 1969 Vietnam was primarily a test of the rationality of the U.S.
leadership and mode of reasoning. It was inevitable, therefore, that the new
Administration renew yet once more the postwar search for those elusive
doctrines and means for successfully projecting its power throughout the
world in order to control the main contours of international developments.
For even its incontestably significant successes after 1969 did not eliminate

myriad difficulties with profound implications to the United States' future global role.

The kinds of issues the Administration had to deal with included specific cases, such as policies toward various nations and regions, many of whom resembled each other in form and substance, as well as more abstract, seemingly analytic structural problems involving, above all, economics but also touching the Vietnam War's dramatic influence on American political psychology. Yet while the Nixon White House could grasp many of the traditional problems it confronted, it was unable to comprehend those new larger domestic political and international structural forces likely to impose constraints on its future capabilities and conduct. The most pressing, as well as most subtle and unresolvable, problem facing the new government was the role of economics in undermining American imperialism's foundations.

As in Korea, the Vietnam War proved that when using its own forces the United States could only fight capital-intensive, technologically sophisticated wars and that if it did not win them quickly their economic and political costs would soon become prohibitive. Given the fact that the U.S. share of world trade was 13 percent in 1977 compared to 48 percent in 1948, the dollar's role in the global economy was an anomaly, and Washington could scarcely afford to ignore the desires and growing power of the other major industrial capitalist nations when considering the economic implications of its foreign policy. Europe's pressures immediately before and after the Vietnamese Tet Offensive in February 1968, and its persistent drainage of the U.S. official gold stock from $17.8 billion in 1960 to $10.9 billion in 1968, became decisive factors in imposing a ceiling on American escalation in Vietnam, guaranteeing that at best Washington would be stalemated in the war. Foreign official claims on the United States had been scarcely $3 billion in 1949, but by mid-1971 they had risen to $31 billion—and over four times that sum by the end of the 1970s. Its major capitalist competitors had a far greater growth in manufacturing productivity and gross domestic investment from 1960 through the 1970s. And beyond economics, the United States could no longer ignore the risks of its unrestrained actions fundamentally undermining the American-led alliance against the Soviet bloc in Europe, which remained then, as today, the single most important concern of its foreign policy after 1945.

When the Nixon Administration took office these problems were already very imposing. Inflation had been a mere 1.2 percent annually during 1960–64, jumped to 4.2 percent in 1968 and 5.4 the following year, peaking at a highly destabilizing 11.0 percent in 1974. The federal budget deficit had been $4.2 billion in the early 1960s, hit $25 billion in 1968, and while it was effectively eliminated during the first two years of the Nixon Administration, during 1971 and 1972 it was back up to $23 billion, and then shot up to $44 billion in 1975, and almost twice that the following year—initiating the vertiginous annual budget deficits that have been virtually permanent since then. And these soon spread to its foreign trade and payments balances. As a globalist foreign policy's potentially unlimited costs increasingly corroded the stability and quality of life in America, successive administrations have had to confront, however reluctantly, the growing constraints the nation's very great but still finite fiscal resources imposed on them.

Both Nixon and Henry Kissinger were oblivious to economic questions when they entered the White House, and as such problems irresistibly intruded upon them, they responded with both irritation and ignorance. Of the over 140 policy reviews the NSC completed during the first three Nixon years, only one dealt with international monetary policy. Kissinger later confessed that he was illiterate in international economics when he was first called upon to advise Nixon, and "Only later did I learn that the key economic policy decisions are not technical but political."[1] However self-sufficient and arrogant in other fields, Kissinger was wise enough not to trust his own judgment in this domain, but the White House was also unwilling to rely on others. Nixon quickly excluded the New York Federal Reserve Bank, which had traditionally managed foreign financial questions for the United States, from any role whatsoever—creating a serious break with Wall Street circles that was later to help undermine his presidency. The Federal Reserve System was entrusted to Arthur Burns, who knew and cared little about international finance, as part of a strategy of "benign neglect" of the dollar's role in the world. If this policy reinforced the White House's ignorance at the inception, later it imposed potentially decisive constraints on Washington's options in dealing with its problems in the Third World. While requiring it to reduce the Vietnam War's intensity and costs was the most obvious example, it was by no means the only one.

The president and his obedient assistant Kissinger not only circumvented issues by reducing or ignoring those agencies in Washington better able to deal with them but also eliminated to an unprecedented extent the informal but politically powerful advisory groups that had guided governments for decades, furthering the process of isolating themselves that helped to bring about the Watergate crisis. The self-sufficiency that Kissinger greatly encouraged in order better to be able to define policies himself eventually helped to produce political instability and limitations on the freedom of the presidency—culminating in the War Powers Act in late 1973—to embark on overt adventures of the sort that had been common until then. A far more skeptical and potentially destabilizing Congress's reinsertion into the foreign policy decisionmaking structure also created a new political context for the United States' relationship to the Third World after 1973, especially when interventions costing protracted time and money were involved.

. . .

Upon coming to office, the Nixon Administration initiated a quest for a new basis for its role in Asia. Like all the others since 1953, its effort was far more notable for what it left unresolved than in articulating tangible premises for future conduct. The Nixon Doctrine, as it was to be called after July 25, 1969, tried unsuccessfully to confront a fundamental dilemma but only ended in compounding it. In a casual press conference Nixon spontaneously indicated that while the United States would keep its existing treaty obligations under the vague SEATO treaty and the Manila Pact, it expected internal security "increasingly" to become the task of its local allies, who would have to assume "primary responsibility" in dealing with purely domestic opposition. The United States would neither automatically withdraw nor intervene in the region, but help each nation on a case-by-case basis with military but especially economic aid. "Certainly the objective of any American administration would be to avoid another war like Vietnam any place in the world."[2] Dulles, of course, had made similar declarations after Korea, but at a time when U.S. economic power was far greater and the domestic political consensus was favorable to interventions.

Kissinger was privately dismayed that the president had ventured on a major policy statement with little forethought, and while subsequent expositions of the Nixon Doctrine added emphasis to maintaining U.S. responsibilities to its friends for much longer, and reasserted that "a major American role remains indispensable" in Asia as well, it defied close examination as to what the United States really intended. In fact, the Administration itself was never certain.[3]

The president's musings were paralleled by the Pentagon's own NSC-approved strategic planning. Under Melvin Laird it had moved rapidly to reduce its limited war spending in favor of a resumption of much greater emphasis on strategic weapons aimed at Soviet targets, and in 1969 it articulated a "war and one-half" doctrine that equipped the U.S. military to fight a general war and one major local war, a vague formula it used to justify reducing its military personnel by 1.1 million people and especially to eliminate its ability to fight another Vietnam-type war in isolation from its new global priorities. As obscure as this policy was, both its capabilities and its intentions were to shift its military might away from fighting in the Third World, which Vietnam had equipped it to do, back to confronting Soviet power. The Pentagon became the Administration's leading exponent of withdrawal of U.S. forces from Vietnam until 1973, and later for cutting military aid to Nguyen Van Thieu's corrupt, inefficient army there.

The Nixon Administration's initial intention to avoid another Vietnam never fully adjusted to the new economic and political structural context in which decisions had to be made, or the heritage of interests and attitudes that were inherent to American imperialism. Apart from the relative cheapness of covert interventions, none of which challenged the priorities in its grand strategy at the inception, its deeply rooted Cold War mentality soon reasserted itself, including in new ways that undermined its own initial intentions and increased the dangers to world peace. Moreover, its continuation of traditional policies of support for dictators and corruptionists who were loyal clients allowed all the factors leading to instability and crises in the Third World to continue seething, each containing the necessity of U.S. decisions to save the status quo.

The White House soon also adumbrated for its internal purposes a policy that linked the fate of its allies in wars with its neighbors to the credibility of U.S. power. In the India-Pakistan crisis of late 1971, the outcome of a secessionist movement in East Pakistan (now Bangladesh) that had its roots entirely in local conditions, the White House decided to support Pakistan, despite its acknowledgment that the dissidents had good cause for their actions. The basis of this decision was that Pakistan was an ally fighting with American arms, while India, a friendly but decidedly independent nation, was employing Soviet weapons. To impress especially its Middle Eastern allies and China that the United States was a staunch, reliable friend just as it was withdrawing from Vietnam obsessed the White House, causing it to threaten both India and Russia as well as aid a thoroughly bankrupt military dictatorship in Pakistan that had brought its difficulties upon itself. During the October 1973 War the Administration again assigned important symbolism to the defeat of arms America's allies possessed, in this case Israel, by Soviet armaments in the hands of nations with which the United States had normal relations. This expanded definition of credibility made possible untold interventions, and was as open-ended and dangerous as any administration has ever devised. It revealed that the White House was wholly incapable of translating its initial cautious impulses into policy, whatever the president's public musings.

Although the larger domestic and external structural context in which U.S. decisions were made had altered dramatically since 1964, there were nonetheless countervailing factors likely to increase U.S. involvement in the Third World. The most important of these was the fact that Marxist and national liberation movements were now far more numerous than in any preceding decade, in part the result of the examples that successful revolutions had created elsewhere but mainly due to the accumulated social problems, ranging from land tenure and peasant displacement to the weight of decades of oppression, that finally made the Left far more important in so many more nations. In Latin America especially, the various Marxist parties, despite their great diversities, increasingly supplanted the United States' earlier dominant concern with the nationalist Center-Right and were posing far greater challenges to its hegemony than ever. In a global context in which U.S. dependence on its clients and proxies was increasingly due to political and fiscal contraints the Vietnam War created, the social, economic, and political instability of these nations was also growing, and the United States could scarcely estimate the consequences of its surrogates' weaknesses.

Such challenges meant that the United States would rely more than ever on covert warfare, the most inexpensive and politically least inhibited form of intervention, as well as continue to aid the police in friendly nations "so it can serve," as one of its in-house reviews put it, "as a reliable instrument of constituted political authority."[4] The police's role as the lowest level of necessary violence became an even more articulate notion among those who weighed options, essentially to preclude the need for both the local army and, beyond it, direct American intervention. "The programs of the International Police Academy," Undersecretary of State U. Alexis Johnson stated in August 1971 in referring to the Nixon Doctrine, "are exactly the sort of effort that President Nixon had in mind."[5] Partially because of revelations of its support for police torture, Congress at the end of 1973 banned the AID from conducting police training in foreign countries, confining its activities to its Washington academy and the supply of equipment. The CIA then covertly assumed this responsibility directly in a number of countries. Aid to the military in friendly nations continued as before.

As the domestic political net around the White House tightened in the wake of antiwar agitation and Watergate revelations, the CIA's role in relating to "domestic developments in other countries" of the Third World increased under close Executive scrutiny, a policy Kissinger believed "one's conception of the national interest" justified.[6] And since Kissinger was chairman of a committee of five to determine all covert operations, his definition of interests became crucial. By 1975 Congress mildly circumscribed this activity also, but the CIA's capacity for damage throughout the decade remained enormous. Meanwhile, in addition to destabilizing nations—cases I detail later—it performed myriad functions, many of them long known, in hiring and influencing journalists, academics, and book publishers; disinformation; subsidizing organizations everywhere; harassment of U.S. as well as foreign citizens; mail-opening and personal surveillance; and a variety of activities that later made it vulnerable to congressional and press assaults when the policies it was implementing fell into doubt.

The American role in the Third World under Nixon represented a continuation of those of his predecessors save in one important regard, and it more than undercut the initial constraining premises of the original Nixon Doctrine. Nixon was convinced that the Vietnam War could be won as much through a diplomatic offensive to gain Soviet, and later Chinese, cooperation as any other factor, and his unwavering devotion to this strategy even as it was largely failing led the Administration to believe it could also apply this ambitious global effort to resolve innumerable essentially unrelated issues throughout the Third World. More than any other postwar president, Nixon and his devoted assistant Kissinger treated events and movements in the Third World as mere pawns of a giant Cold War struggle, without concern for their local causes or their real autonomy. They therefore believed that they were quite capable of being eliminated as threats to U.S. interests as part of a global linkage of issues and nations in which alleged Soviet failure to regulate a problem in accordance with American desires in one place would lead to U.S. penalties for it in others. But Soviet cooperation would produce American rewards, especially in trade. Ultimately, when Nixon incorporated China into a triangular global diplomacy, his most ominous threat to Moscow was a de facto U.S.-China alliance that threatened the Soviet bloc on all its borders. The notion of states such as Pakistan and India as mere proxies for American or Soviet arms was only the beginning of this convoluted chain of linkages that defined Republican policy and later also became the keystone of Democratic policy under Carter.

By 1971, official definitions of the Nixon Doctrine noted also "the emerging polycentrism of the Communist world presents different challenges and new opportunities," and it resolved to exploit these fully.[7] Great-power diplomacy reintroduced a buoyant optimism into its vision of the capabilities of American power. It added, above all, a new belligerency to U.S. policy and a belief that a "very dramatic" Soviet action in any area that made the United States appear weak would require an equivalent U.S. response, even when, as in the case of East Pakistan, the United States thought Moscow's evaluation of specific issues similar to its own.[8] In this game, form became more important than substance, and it placed an incentive on a new toughness in U.S. policy everywhere in order to appear credible. This grand strategy of triangulation was soon to subsume U.S.-Soviet-Chinese relations, and it continues in various guises till this day.

If Washington's exact expectations for Soviet conduct were never wholly clear, and many conflicting American desires and needs were to complicate the effort, eventually to cultivate a decisive illusion in the White House on the nature of the peace it was to attain in Vietnam in January 1973, it nonetheless further reduced the United States' already minimal appreciation for the independent roots of innumerable national crises, attributing powers to the USSR in the Third World it never had. While ultimately it made little difference to the United States that the Russians were scarcely the cause of any threat to American interests in the Third World, for what was most vital was to preserve them, its new premise revealed that after two decades America's leadership understood less than ever about the dynamics of change in the Third World.

Managing the political context in which events occurred in the Third World, a traditional U.S. goal, was now even more significant as inherited Cold War calculations suffused many disparate issues and places. While the specific cases of U.S. involvement in the Third World illustrate the workings of this approach far better than its utterances, suffice it to say that a vague Nixon Doctrine reflecting the chastening the United States was receiving in Vietnam was soon supplanted by the geopolitical vision the Sino-Soviet split produced in an Administration seeking ways to reimpose its mastery over a world that in many other domains was escaping it. Ultimately, the persistent American search for a doctrine and method that would allow it to attain its objectives, and overcome the constraints of its resources and priorities, eluded America's leaders after 1968, just as it had done for over two decades.

Latin America: The Limits of Reform

*T*HE NIXON ADMINISTRATION HAD NEI-
ther the inclination nor the ability to
involve itself deeply in Latin American
affairs, essentially for the same reasons that its predecessors had been incapable of sustaining their initial commitment of time and resources to the
Alliance for Progress. Almost as soon as he entered office, Nixon declared
that the "Action for Progress" would replace the Alliance for Progress, emphasizing trade rather than aid, and he abandoned reform pretensions. The
difficulty he was to face was that the hemisphere was too unstable and its
problems too urgent to be ignored or wished away, and stability was the
precondition for U.S. indifference, especially insofar as its own vast interests
were concerned. In no place in 1969 was this more true than in Peru, which
had reached a boiling point in its relations with the United States just as the
new Administration took office.

THE PERUVIAN ENIGMA

Like all Latin nations, Peru had enormous unresolved structural problems,
but the class system confronting them was distinctive, producing a unique
political challenge to the United States. Peru's economic difficulties were
familiar. In 1961 half of the employed population was engaged in agriculture
in a nation with one of the most inequitable land distributions in the world,
and nearly half of the country was composed of Indians almost totally outside
organized society. The rural population was as miserable as any on the
continent, and over them ruled an aristocratic rural elite with immense

economic and political power, deeply involved in export agriculture and allied to foreign interests, but also dominant in banking, real estate, and mining. U.S. investment was concentrated in mining, smelting, and petroleum, sectors it largely controlled, but after 1961 it had begun to repatriate large sums, draining Peru of capital and aggravating its economic problems. Like all Latin nations, Peru's debts mounted quickly after 1955, tripling over the next decade and creating predictable debt service problems that the U.S. capital outflow only intensified.

What was most unique in Peru's development was the nature of the military and its relationship to a class structure that in many ways resembled that of the more advanced Latin American nations. While the upper class in Peru was united on certain issues, depending on how various oligarchs diversified their economic interests or intermarried, there was also conflict within its ranks, for no wholly cohesive national bourgeoisie or comprador elite exists anywhere. More crucial was that the informal grand alliance of export-oriented oligarchs and foreign capital, which together controlled the banks, refused to meet the growing capital needs of those middle- and upper-class elements seeking to industrialize the nation and diversify the economy. There was no alternative source of capital, as in Brazil, and this helped to produce a nationalist, anti-Yankee middle class. And its importance rests in the fact that the army after 1950 was increasingly drawn from a lower middle class with no personal or sentimental ties to the elite that had traditionally wielded all forms of power.

By 1960, the Peruvian officers were largely convinced that an effective socioeconomic struggle against the Left, the main topic studied in officer training schools and their primary preoccupation, required nationalist economic and political innovations to reduce the power of both the oligarchy and the United States. And as the traditional mediator of deeply divided civilian politics, which their intervention in 1962 had tilted to bring a moderate reformer, President Fernando Belaunde Terry, to power the following year, it was inevitable that nationalism and social reform in Peru challenge U.S. interests. Belaunde's first act was to nullify the International Petroleum Company's four-hundred-thousand-acre concession and initiate land reform moves that threatened yet far larger United States-owned holdings. IPC, a Standard Oil of New Jersey affiliate, immediately brought the State Department into the picture in a dispute that was to simmer for the next five years. It was a model case of conflicting U.S. goals during the Alliance for Progress, once again proving that simple anticommunism was scarcely the main U.S. objective and that it would attach greater importance to the protection of its own economic interests.

On one hand the United States wanted some land reform in Peru because it realized that land inequality offered extremely fertile ground for leftists who had begun to work among the Indians. On the other, Washington reminded Belaunde of the "importance of private sector in achieving goals of Alliance and that any move which altered traditional favorable climate of private investment jeopardized these goals."[1] The fear of the Left was shunted aside as the United States cut aid during 1964–65, costing Peru $150 million. A settlement of the IPC controversy favorable to Standard became America's precondition for normal relations, and since the IPC refused to compromise, Belaunde—with the army watching him—could not either. With no aid and with U.S. corporations shipping funds out of the country, Peru's economy fell into a depression, and the CIA warned the Johnson Administration of growing prospects for instability. At the end of 1965 the United States resumed aid for those regions where the Left's prospects were the most favorable. In 1967, however, it cut aid again when the Peruvians bought French Mirage fighters after the United States refused to sell it F-5's. Even the army thought the purchase of planes for the rival air force a waste of money and one more example of Belaunde's incompetence. In October 1968 it took direct control of power, and General Juan Velasco Alvarado became president.

The new military rulers presented the Nixon Administration with a serious Latin headache, for in February 1969 they gave the IPC a bill for $690 million for past tax frauds and effectively confiscated the company. The problem confronting Washington was clear, in large part because it had a far better comprehension of the class dynamics and nature of Peruvian politics and the military than of any other nation in the region. Its experts understood perfectly well that the military rulers precluded a threat from the Left, the United States' putative main concern, and that the elite was too divided to challenge the officers as well as too reactionary to cope with the Left. They predicted that the military would prove cautious and eventually could be redirected toward more traditional policies. The State Department therefore decided that drastic action was unnecessary and that forcing the junta into a corner and having to confront the Left later was undesirable. Moreover, other American business interests in Peru warned Washington that should it press too hard on the IPC controversy they also had over $600 million in investments to lose should the junta retaliate against them.

The Administration struck a balance between support for the new regime as the last line of defense against revolution and refusal to tolerate actions against U.S. investors, engaging in tough negotiations during 1969 that led to a stalemate. Despite threats of cutting off all U.S. aid under the Hickenlooper amendment, which since 1962 had required the Executive to do so (though in fact it had happened only once), or reducing sugar quotas, the United States was not about to produce, as in Cuba, a Left government where none had existed. Instead it had loans from the IADB and other multilateral banks delayed, letting Velasco know that it had ample means to hurt him. This pattern of nonovert pressure via banks continued for five more years. Meanwhile, the new junta proceeded to implement land reform, affecting some United States-owned sugar plantations. "Our revolution is not Marxist," Velasco declared, "It is nationalist and it will go on."[2]

The military regime was able to undermine partially the traditional property base of the oligarchy, which nonetheless retained immense resources in other forms. But without new tax laws there was no change in income distribution, and land reform scarcely affected the Indians. Perhaps one-quarter of the population, mainly the lower middle classes, benefited from the new regime—which proved remarkably conservative. Opposition was suppressed; workers were not permitted to form independent unions, much less obtain higher wages; and the new regime was never popular. While middle-class technocrats welcomed the rapid expansion of the state's role in manufacturing and a variety of steps that made the lower middle class and aspiring national bourgeoisie the main beneficiaries of the new system, foreign investors in 1975 were still considerably more important than the state sector in manufacturing, while private national interests still dominated the economy as before, and the junta never achieved Brazil's mastery over economic development. U.S. preeminence in Peru's imports and exports dropped somewhat between 1968 and 1973, but not enough to alter the decisive link.

Despite its initial anxieties, the United States learned that the junta's rhetoric was far stronger than its actions, and it closely watched the important factions in favor of more foreign investment who were able successfully to stop further nationalization. The junta sought to adjust for its weak economic management by massively borrowing in the private markets, thereby quickly reopening the door to IMF and World Bank influence, though the United States had effectively prevented multilateral loans to it until February 1974, when Peru agreed to compensate the IPC and the official credit blockade ended. With this dispute resolved, U.S. direct investment in Peru rose substantially, by 1976 nearly doubling the 1968 level. By 1974, U.S. officials concluded that while Peru would continue its anti-American rhetoric, it had in fact been completely gotten in hand. From this point onward the IMF, working with private banks, determined the main thrust of Peru's economic policies, with only sufficient concessions to keep the conservative officers who took over the government in August 1975 from provoking more radical officers to challenge them. By 1978, when food riots and strikes became rampant throughout the country in response to IMF-imposed stringency measures that caused real income to drop a third since 1973 and unemployment almost to double, the military agreed to return power to civilian authority. In June 1980 Belaunde was once again elected to the presidency.[3]

CHILE AND THE END OF ILLUSIONS

Chile in many regards resembled the other Latin nations seeking to develop economically, and it posed the same problems for the United States as well. Import-substitute strategies had won support from a rural elite as well as urban middle classes that had both blood and business ties to each other, and the state was assigned an important role in implementing them. Unlike Brazil, however, the effort was less successful in this much smaller country, in part because Yankee-owned firms solidly dominated its copper exports, which earned the large majority of its foreign exchange. U.S. relations with Chile, therefore, operated within a context in which American interests conflicted with those of most of the Chilean political parties. Moreover, unlike Brazil, the Left was far more powerful, partially because of one of the most inequitable land distributions in the hemisphere, and in 1958 the Socialist candidate, Salvador Allende Gossens, narrowly missed defeating conservative Jorge Alessandri for the presidency. After Cuba, Chile by the early 1960s was the one Latin nation most likely to break totally with U.S. hegemony.

Chile's upper and middle classes also possessed the ambiguities that marked conservative nationalist reform movements elsewhere, and their addiction to imports essential for their life-style caused post-1955 governments to run up debts and borrow heavily, periodically allowing the IMF to impose austerity programs requiring more emphasis on exports and reduced internal economic development programs. Politically anti-United States, the elite vacillated between collaboration and hostility toward it. Washington, on the other hand, had to weigh its fear of the Left against its opposition to a conservative nationalism that was the most immediate threat to its interests. Chilean-American relations until 1970 reflected all these conflicting crosscurrents.

Chile received far more aid and loans on a per capita basis than any other Latin nation during the decade of the 1960s, most of it as part of an effort to elect Christian Democrat Eduardo Frei in the September 1964 presidential race. The CIA's direct support for his campaign cost three million dollars, though some estimates run far higher. The United States turned to Frei in 1964 at a time when it preferred officers elsewhere primarily because the Chilean military had been relatively apolitical since 1933, proudly contrasting its professionalism to that of its neighbors. At the same time that Washington chose to support Frei as the man most likely to accommodate its interests yet introduce simultaneously sufficient reform to preempt the Left, it also resolved to politicize Chile's officers, especially regarding the Communist threat within Chile itself, and they became the focus of special strategic intelligence courses organized for them in the U.S. Army's Canal Zone training school. Until that transformation occurred, however, Washington was compelled to rely on civilian politicians—and it was never happy with the results.

Frei became a problem for the United States partially because of his contradictory program, which sought to introduce a measure of reform along with development in the context of collaboration with foreign investment, which he saw as essential as long as copper required export outlets; but Frei's effort to accomplish essentially irreconcilable goals soon increasingly alienated everyone. Two U.S. companies, Anaconda and Kennecott Copper, accounted for 90 percent of Chile's output, and the only way Frei could raise funds for his programs without borrowing was to force up the price of copper and obtain a greater share of its profits. Frei attempted against stout U.S. resistance to increase the price of copper in 1965 by two cents a pound, to thirty-eight cents, and Washington regarded the matter with "most serious concern" and immediately linked future loans and aid to the dispute.[4] In fact Frei wanted greater trade revenues as well as aid, and he guaranteed the United States a hundred thousand tons of copper a year at thirty-six cents a pound even as the world price, under Vietnam War-induced scarcity, reached over twice that. With aid linked to prices, U.S. officials calculated that the savings to U.S. buyers equaled the value of the surplus food it was dumping in Chile.[5] It was not a situation conducive to Frei remaining sympathetic to Yankee advice or interests, yet while his concessions to the United States alienated the radicals in his own party, his impositions on the Americans managed to deepen their mistrust of him, for in his own way, Frei was an economic nationalist.

Frei sought to attain all his social goals without breaking with the United States when he introduced a plan in 1966 to "Chileanize" the copper industry. Essentially an effort to compel the companies to invest and nearly double their output, it increased their revenues along with their taxes. The state purchased a 51 percent interest in the two U.S. firms, but the Americans were permitted to manage them both at home and overseas, a situation that caused their profits to rise astronomically while Chile's income increased sharply also. At the same time, following an economic downturn that began in 1967, the IMF forced an austerity program upon Chile that required a postponement of land reform and alienated both those to Frei's right and left, who objected to such kind treatment of U.S. firms while their needs were either being attacked or neglected. Frei's economic program had become confused and inconsistent, still subject to American control, and the elite began to send its money abroad. Even Washington found Frei's support for its Vietnam policy more than offset by his open opposition to it on all Latin issues, ranging from Peru's and Bolivia's measures against U.S. firms to its invasion of the Dominican Republic and diplomatic isolation of Cuba. In 1969, with his party now well to the left of him, Frei tried to return to total nationalization after the Christian Democrats lost heavily in the 1969 congressional elections. It was Frei who nationalized Anaconda in June 1969, but it was too late. The radical wing took over his party.

In 1969 the Nixon Administration was therefore faced with a possible political defeat in Chile regardless of whether the Left, which now emerged as an Allende-led Popular Unity coalition of Socialists, Communists, and others, won or not. Indeed, the White House's hostility toward the Christian Democrats, who nominated Radomiro Tomic for the September 4, 1970, presidential election on a program of total, immediate copper nationalization, was no less intense. It was obvious that it could lose everything unless it could affect the election outcome.

The United States' deep involvement in the 1970 election was later subjected to massive congressional investigations, so a brief outline here is sufficient. While the U.S. private investments of eight hundred million dollars were surely as important as any reason for its efforts, it was by no means the only one. It was wholly impossible for the Nixon Administration to accept either a leftist or a nationalist victory at the polls. The former was the more frightful because of geopolitics, visions of dominos falling throughout the region, credibility, and all the fixations that had long since become conventional wisdom. But it was Tomic, above all, with his Catholic and middle-class backing, who possessed the greatest and therefore the most dangerous appeal for other nationalist parties in the region and who revealed how fundamental America's economic interests were in its overall calculations. The CIA did not think Chile's loss to either would affect the United States' world military position. What was at stake was both economic and psychological, and the White House was prepared to go to great lengths to hold on to Chile.

The United States moved in three directions: first, it sought to influence the election's outcome via money; next, it tried to have Allende assassinated; and last, it attempted to convince the military to overthrow Allende. These efforts were more or less sequential. The first had been employed with Frei and it was a standard procedure throughout the world, while the last two were frequently utilized as well. "There is a gray area between military intervention and formal diplomacy," Kissinger later characterized this effort, "where our democracy is forced to compete against groups inimical to it."[6] Frustrating the outcome of a free election was a common way of doing so.

The U.S. government itself gave money for anti-Allende activity designed to win the election for Alessandri, the Conservative. The sums actually committed were not large, and probably less than went to Frei in 1964. American firms in Chile, led by ITT, also made comparable contributions, but Washington had convinced itself that Alessandri would win and that huge amounts were unnecessary. When Allende won a plurality of votes, a common event in Chile that meant the Congress would elect him to power fifty days later, the infuriated White House then turned to the assassination and coup options.

The murder of Allende was too difficult for the CIA to organize, though they paid money to at least one assassin, who managed only to get himself arrested. More serious was its effort to urge the military to take power, a thought it had been cultivating since 1964 and that conformed to American practices elsewhere. Here the main obstacle was the commander in chief of the army, General René Schneider, who was a strict constitutionalist and represented the old army traditions. The CIA both armed and paid a small band of rightist officers to kidnap him, and cooperative officers were assured "of continued American military assistance if they moved," in Kissinger's words, to overthrow Allende, but after failing in two efforts, they simply killed Schneider.[7] The United States later claimed it was done without their weapons or authorization, but that it accomplished the task of eliminating a man they thought a major obstruction cannot be denied. Schneider's assassination did not stimulate a coup; rather, those senior officers who had shown interest now pulled back, and an uncontested congressional election made Allende president on October 24. Allende's first major action was to complete the nationalization of all foreign copper companies, a policy Tomic also endorsed. Chile now had a democratically elected Marxist government pledged to create a "republic of the working class."[8] It was the first in the hemisphere's history.

The White House's policy, while it assigned a major role to covert efforts, was essentially to reinforce its relationship to the military and wait for it to act. As long as the military had a monopoly of the arms, the Allende government's freedom to act was sharply constrained. Meanwhile, the United States turned to economic pressures with the goal, as Nixon jotted in his notes, to "make the economy scream." "Not a nut or bolt will be allowed to reach Chile under Allende," the U.S. ambassador had warned Frei. "Once Allende comes to power we shall do all within our power to condemn Chile and the Chileans to utmost deprivation and poverty. . . ."[9] A policy of implacable hostility became official policy. All U.S. aid or loans were cut to a trickle, save insofar as they helped the military, and Washington successfully blocked all new official multilateral bank loans as well. Indeed, the training of Chilean officers in the Panama Canal Zone actually increased, and the White House enlarged the CIA station in Chile and spent over eight million dollars on its work until September 1973. Now it moved systematically and did everything from maintaining constant contact with coup plotters, whom it encouraged in every way, to fabricating documents on Cuban control of the police to drawing up arrest lists and the key targets to take when the coup began.[10]

Allende did nothing to create a counterbalance to the military, whom he courted with increased funding and cabinet posts, and the economy suffered from the inevitable reduction of U.S. aid and the inflationary disorder Frei had bequeathed it. Chile got some aid from the Soviet bloc, but it was not sufficient, and when he went to Moscow at the end of 1972 in the hope of obtaining a hard-currency credit of $500 million, the Russians advised him to come to terms with the United States rather than fight it and face disaster— and they then informed Washington of the fact. He attempted to borrow money elsewhere, with only modest results. Yet despite the innumerable difficulties, the new government successfully introduced land reform and basic social programs that helped the masses, and in the March 1973 congressional elections its vote increased from 37 percent in 1970 to 43 percent of the total despite the fact the United States secretly gave $1,428,000 to the opposition. The middle class, above all, suffered most from inflation and reform, and the United States covertly funded their destabilizing transport strikes against the government's policies, generously aiding the militant opposition.

The officers were almost all from middle-class families and deeply distressed over their plight. After the March elections made it clear that the normal political process would not remove the government, the reticence of a portion of them to act melted and the coup began on September 11, 1973, killing Allende within hours and quickly wiping out what little resistance there was. Americans knew of every detail of the planned coup, and the carefully drafted CIA strategy for an efficient operation was put into practice. A U.S. naval group and air force team quietly positioned nearby in case the progovernment navy reacted was no longer deemed useful and was withdrawn. Meanwhile, at least three thousand people were killed and untold thousands arrested, and interrogation centers employing torture were set up permanently throughout the country.[11]

A brutally repressive regime was essential to America's interests because there was no civilian political option for it to turn to, and Washington had no hesitation in immediately endorsing the new order and aiding it, revealing again its two-decades-long preference for dictators and repressive regimes in the hemisphere. Chile also proved once more that the United States could never gracefully accept the verdict of democratic politics in any nation where anti-Yankee sentiment was overwhelming for fear of seeing not only its local investments lost but also encouraging anti-United States economic legislation elsewhere in the hemisphere. The coalition ranged against it in Chile was centrist as well as leftist, revealing that the historically dominant hemispheric trend toward nationalist economic strategies certain to constrict, if not exclude, U.S. investment was more vital and dangerous than ever. Indeed, the very nature of this nationalist vision created a hemispheric consensus that was politically still far more widespread and effective, and therefore threatening, than conventional Left ideologies. Had it survived, the

Chilean example would have posed an unprecedented, grave challenge to Yankee hegemony. Allende's failure to neutralize the military immediately was his decisive error, however, and that, too, was a moral all those of similar persuasion were certain to understand.

Because of the obvious fact that deep economic ties carry with them inevitable political and military consequences, both direct and symbolic, it was clear by the mid-1970s that hemispheric affairs would increasingly insert themselves into Washington's attention, whatever its desires and distractions elsewhere. The cumulative development and impact of those economic and political currents in Latin America both its ruling classes and the United States had imposed upon it made growing conflict with Yankee imperialism irresistible. Proximity, the sheer weight of vast economic interests, and tradition were all operating to make the region more important than ever as the United States became increasingly isolated—and hated—politically and ideologically.

The Middle East: Toward Protracted Crisis

*T*HE MIDDLE EAST IN THE DECADE after 1958 had moved from being one of Washington's principal concerns to a relatively minor place, largely because the comparative stability in the region gave it little to think about contrasted to its growing preoccupations elsewhere. But none of the basic political or economic elements in the area changed, and U.S. policy also remained constant. No state had become Marxist, the British were still present as a minor but useful partner, and not until Israel's lightning surprise attack against its neighbors in June 1967 did the Middle East once again begin to pose serious challenges to the United States. The Six-Day War rekindled the fires of Arab nationalism and initiated an arms race that permitted the Soviet Union to play a far greater role in the region than ever.

U.S. relations with Israel, friendly but also relatively discreet until then, became increasingly close after 1968, when Washington agreed to supply it with advanced weapons and share intelligence. However complicating this growing intimacy, even more significant was Britain's decision in December 1967 to withdraw all its forces from the Persian Gulf area by the end of 1971, for it raised fundamental strategic and economic issues. After 1950 America had desired to supplant Britain's economic and political domination, but not to the extent requiring it alone to assume all responsibility for policing and directing the entire vast area—an undertaking its intervention in 1958 had shown to be very precarious at best. Now its triumph over the British left it with major concerns and, potentially, obligations it could scarcely afford given its vast distractions in Asia and elsewhere. This challenge confronted the Nixon Administration in 1969.

The White House, fully aware of its vast international commitments and eager to avoid more, resolved that preventing a vacuum of power into which Soviet influence could move should be the responsibility of its key surrogates in the region. Iran and, later, Saudi Arabia were both anxious to play such a role. Although the State Department preferred to view the main dangers as those arising from nationalism and the Arab-Israeli conflict rather than the Cold War with Russia, both Nixon and Kissinger ignored its sophisticated rejection of conventional wisdom and defined policies by themselves, with global politics usually their primary concern. Given the enormous American stakes in the area, one that purely local nationalist forces might also endanger, the assertion of American power was essential regardless of any role the Soviets might or might not play. With the five U.S. major oil companies alone controlling half of the output of the Middle Eastern and Libyan fields, the stakes involved had immense value at a time when world demand for oil was rising far more quickly than supplies and when prices had already begun to climb sharply. Washington never contemplated at the inception of it whether its strategy of relying on surrogates was likely to be a solution to its problems or increase them because of its additional need to defend and stabilize its proxies.

It was the United States' decisive tilt toward Israel after 1967 that made possible the USSR's growing leverage in the Middle East, for the Arab nations that Israel threatened most were unable to obtain all the arms that they desired elsewhere. This fact alone greatly complicated America's policy insofar as it believed, as did Kissinger, that its credibility was also involved whenever Soviet weapons in the hands of non-Communists threatened to defeat U.S. arms in the hands of its friends. This expanded credibility doctrine, which the United States applied during the India-Pakistan crisis in 1971, revealed that while the Nixon Administration would pursue a surrogate strategy, it would be quite as ready as its predecessors also to intervene directly in the area, usually confronting the USSR at the same time, and ultimately remain unable to exercise self-control. This dual-track approach toward conflict in the region was not calculated well in advance but was initially a visceral reaction to immediate events. This was first revealed for the Nixon Administration during the Jordanian crisis of September 1970, and it has remained the fundamental, and dangerous, contradiction as well as the premise of U.S. Middle Eastern policy since then.

Since 1968 Nasser had energetically tried to increase Soviet aid and advisers to his nation, and by 1970 had succeeded to a greater extent than ever before. In the summer of 1970, Nasser and King Hussein decided to move against the radical elements of the Palestine Liberation Organization stationed in both their nations but primarily in Jordan. The now familiar tragic imbroglio in the Arab world broke out when Hussein on September 15 began to stamp out the PLO and when Syria sent tanks and troops to protect them. At this point, in constant touch with and supporting Hussein, Washington announced the dispatch of aircraft carriers and other ships into the eastern Mediterranean and alerted its airborne troops. And while Kissinger warned the bewildered Russians that they would be held responsible should their Syrian "client" not withdraw, the United States also urged the Israelis to prepare to invade if required to save Hussein. Israel in turn demanded and got a U.S. promise to intervene should it become the target of a Soviet or an Egyptian attack. Reassured, Israel mobilized, and on September 23 the thoroughly frightened Syrians, probably under Soviet pressure as well, began to leave Jordan. A major war had been averted. And after trying desperately to keep the conflict from escalating, Nasser died of a heart attack on September 28.

The Jordan crisis, coming just as the British were leaving the region, reinforced the United States' commitment to Iran as its principal ally in the Persian Gulf, and while the containment of the Soviet-armed radical Iraqis was Tehran's primary responsibility, it was also to assure that radicals not undermine the Gulf states. This reliance "on the central importance of Iran to the safeguarding of the American . . . interest in the oil region of the Persian Gulf," as President Jimmy Carter's national security adviser later described it, was to continue until 1978, when the Shah's eagerness to spend vast sums on arms and his pro-Americanism led to his undoing and to a historic new challenge to the United States.[1]

Israel, meanwhile, became the Administration's principal but not exclusive surrogate in the territory immediately surrounding it, and also Hussein's guarantor. But Nasser's death and the emergence of Anwar Sadat as his successor, who expelled all Soviet advisers in July 1972, soon increased America's options. From this point onward, relations with Egypt improved dramatically. Yet until this trend reached its culmination, the White House relied entirely on Israel, whom they began to arm heavily after early 1972. And while neither the president nor Kissinger had ever thought much of Secretary of State William Rogers's December 1969 plan that recognized UN Resolution 242, calling for Israel's withdrawal from occupied territories, they ceased to press it altogether because of Israel's adamant opposition. Israel now exercised a de facto veto on U.S. diplomatic policy in the region as the reward for its obedience in other domains, even though the Administration thought Israel often unreasonable. Washington did not consider the peace process crucial, however, because it persisted in regarding all regional issues as basically aspects of Soviet-American rivalry with few purely local roots, and Kissinger's main goal was to reduce Soviet influence. This was soon to prove a major error, for, as Kissinger was later to confess, the Soviet advisers in Egypt were probably a major constraint preventing Sadat from using his now formidable military power. When on October 6, 1973, the Egyptians struck the completely surprised Israeli army in Sinai, inflicting huge losses on its tanks and aircraft over the next weeks, they also irreversibly changed the entire military, economic, and political situation in the Middle East.

Israel's allegedly invincible army was now shown to be highly vulnerable, and while the White House warned Moscow not to intervene, it also did nothing to stop the Soviets from resupplying the Egyptians when the battle turned against them. Politically the United States was unwilling to range itself against the entire Arab world, including its Saudi and Persian Gulf allies who supported with both words and funds Egypt's surprise attack and who on October 17 increased the price of oil 17 percent as the initial step in their profound transformation of the world oil structure and its relation to the global economy. As the first reverberations of the October War were felt and a massive oil boycott was set in train, the United States and the USSR united in the UN to try to terminate the fighting.

The radical changes that were to occur in the Middle East after 1973 revealed that the United States' two-decade effort to assume primary control over the area had been a chimera based on illusions and false assumptions from the inception. The British had been completely supplanted, and the Arab world had exploited Soviet willingness to provide enormous quantities of arms even though not a single Marxist state had been established. It was perfectly obvious that nationalism was far more potent than radicalism and that the festering Arab-Israeli conflict guaranteed that this would remain the case, making anti-Americanism inevitable. "In retrospect," George McGhee, one of the key architects of Middle East policy, admitted in 1974, "this was always a greater danger in the Arab States than communism itself, which didn't find fertile ground among the Arabs."[2] By 1974 the United States, despite Iran, Saudi Arabia, and Israel by its side, was losing control over Middle Eastern oil—the main objective of its efforts there since 1945.

The quickening cycle of change and crisis meant that the region would never again be relegated to the sidelines, and it would increasingly become a central challenge to U.S. foreign policy. Indeed, by the 1970s the Middle East had become the area most likely to draw America into a major war that ultimately risked direct conflict with the Soviet Union itself. Given the vast responsibilities in the region the United States was prepared to assume and its need both to depend on and protect surrogate regimes of questionable stability, only unresolvable crises loomed before it.

CHAPTER 19

The United States and the Changing World Economy

*B*Y THE END OF THE 1960s THE UNITED States' connection with the Third World was the product of many forces, ranging from deeply embedded symbolic assumptions such as credibility, geopolitics, and the domino theory, to the profound structural interrelationships between America's business interests and economy and those of poor nations. To ignore any of these elements is to simplify the complex matrix of factors that shape events, but just as the Vietnam War experience compelled Washington's decisionmakers to be far more wary about the symbolic dimensions of its actions, so, too, did the United States' weakening material status in the world economy compel it to pay far greater attention to raw materials and its investments and financial position in the Third World. Ironically, at the very point that U.S. military power and its ability to cope with diverse challenges in the Third World were stalemated to an unprecedented degree, its objective need to dominate it became greater than ever—a reality that continues to the present. The economic component, always inextricable with all the motives of U.S. conduct, and often, as in Latin America, its primary impulse, continued to grow sharply in significance. Indeed, by 1970 its sheer weight made the issue one not of what was essential to U.S. interests in the Third World but how far America's leaders would go to protect them.

THE NEW RELATIONSHIP IN OIL AND RAW MATERIALS

In petroleum, the United States' standing fundamentally altered after 1945 as its national share of world output fell from 61 percent in 1938 to 14 percent in 1978, while its domestic proved reserves dropped to 5 percent of the global total in 1979 (at a time when it was consuming 28 percent of the world's oil) compared to 56 percent in the Middle East. By 1960 the United States was importing 19 percent of its supply, then 30 percent in 1972 and 45 percent in 1979, and while the Middle East and North Africa had provided a negligible part of its imports in 1970, by 1980 nearly half of American crude oil imports came from those areas. Authoritative industry sources in 1972 expected the U.S. need for oil in 1985 to be twice the 1970 volume.

By the late 1960s it was clear that the gap between world oil demand and supply was growing wider, and the bargaining position of the surplus producers increased with it. In 1970 Libya broke the unity of U.S. buyers and showed the Middle East that it could use the Organization of Petroleum Exporting Countries (OPEC) to jack up their revenues, which had risen relatively slowly after the organization was formed in 1960. Given the fact that the seven major international companies earned far more in the Eastern Hemisphere than elsewhere, during the period before the October 1973 War the world oil system began to undergo profound changes that the war brought to a head for ostensible political reasons but primarily because the economics of the industry had been shifting in favor of the producing countries, and against the United States, for some years.

In the case of nonpetroleum raw materials, the deep concern among all decisionmakers over the depletion of U.S. supplies that the Korean War had triggered, and that the Paley Commission in 1952 had warned required decisive action, by the late 1950s had declined sharply with lower prices and surpluses. By the mid-1960s there was an equanimity in most high-level government circles that the expansion of reserves and acceptable prices would continue indefinitely. Raw materials as a motivating factor in U.S. policy in the Third World remained a major consideration mainly among American companies and officials involved with specific resource-rich nations. Critics of U.S. policy who still stressed its objective significance were dismissed as neo-Marxists.

While there is no doubt that many of Paley's prognostications were incorrect, U.S. dependence on raw materials imports after 1960 nonetheless grew absolutely as well as in qualitative new ways. Adjusted for inflation, U.S. minerals imports doubled from 1950–54 to 1965–69, and increased by half again over the next five years. As a share of consumption, iron and ferroalloys imports grew from 32 percent in 1950–54 to 44 percent in 1975–79, and all other metal ores, after declining for a time, by 1970–75 were 40 percent of consumption. While world reserves of most metals rose after 1950, often dramatically, almost all the growth was outside the United States, principally in the Third World. U.S. deficits and requirements increased by virtually any criterion. Of eighty-six materials Congress's Office of Technology Assessment reviewed, the United States was self-sufficient in twenty-two of them in 1984, while fifty came from diverse or stable sources. Fourteen absolutely vital materials, without which the United States literally could not function militarily and would be seriously hobbled economically, came primarily from central and southern Africa as well as the USSR.

Indeed, by the early 1970s, U.S. experts on raw materials issues had reached a much higher level of understanding in assessing their importance, focusing not only on quantities and shares but also on the vital role of specific materials whose qualitative significance escaped crude numbers. To repeat, technologically advanced industries have a far greater need than ever for relatively small quantities, in dollar and weight terms, of certain materials, and chromium, cobalt, manganese, and the platinum group were probably the most important, and since 1950 these were almost entirely imported. Official experts increasingly measured their true value in terms of multipliers of twenty-five to thirty times: for example, $10 million worth of materials in technologically based industries made possible about $250 million worth of economic activity, and some estimates were even higher. "This approximately $32 billion [of raw materials]," the former director of the U.S. National Commission on Materials Policy told Congress at the end of 1973, "is the life blood of a $1,152 billion economy," and nearly half of it was imported.[1] The irony of all these data was that the United States' objective economic need to exploit freely the world's poorer nations was greatest at that time after 1945 that its power to control them was relatively the weakest.

Confronting the economic and political problems emerging from these statistics therefore preoccupied the Nixon Administration after 1973 to an extent it had scarcely imagined possible four years earlier, largely because, given the economics of the situation, a crisis between the United States and oil-producing nations was long overdue, for the United States no longer had the capacity, as in 1956, to pump sufficient oil to withstand concerted action from the oil-exporting nations to increase prices. The combined demand of all the industrial capitalist nations made the astonishing stability in oil prices that had persisted until 1970 too assailable. The large oil companies maintained their solidarity on prices until September 1970, when Libya demanded that Occidental Petroleum pay 20 percent over the world price. When the seven major oil companies refused to supply Occidental with alternative sources, it succumbed to Libyan pressures. Oil prices more than doubled in the three years prior to October 1973 as the OPEC nations began picking off other vulnerable companies. In January 1971 the Nixon Administration tried to thwart OPEC's refusal any longer to subsidize Western economic growth with cheap oil. But it found after sending a mission to the Middle East that its military surrogates in both Iran and Saudi Arabia were unwilling to forgo a far greater share of oil profits, and Saudi Arabia, indeed, began to link oil prices to U.S. policy toward Israel. Well before the October 1973 War, official American circles were publicly discussing an imminent conflict with the major exporters.

The oil shock following the October War was a historic turning point in the economic relations between the oil-producing Third World and the major industrial capitalist nations, the United States above all, and it strained traditional political alliances to the limit as nations rushed to protect themselves. From $1.26 a barrel in 1970, the OPEC price rose to $9.40 in 1974 and $24 at the end of 1979. The United States' bill for imports, which was $2.8 billion in 1970 and nearly doubled over the next two years as the crisis began, was $24.3 billion in 1974 and over twice that by 1979—an increase of twenty times! The Arab world cut off exports to the United States temporarily during the October War, but most of America's NATO allies and Japan ostentatiously distanced themselves from Washington's policies in order to escape the boycott and ruination in Arab hands. "It was not," Kissinger later recalled, "one of the finer moments of allied relations."[2]

With both the Shah of Iran and King Faisal of Saudi Arabia joining in the fray to exploit their new unity and leverage, the White House felt utterly betrayed, and its helplessness was reflected in occasional vague threats over coming months and years to invade Saudi Arabia should it prove necessary. The "oil weapon," as Kissinger called it, proved the most effective assault upon American interests since 1945, greatly accelerating a transformation of the world economy and the U.S. position in it that was already well under way.[3] The Gulf states became rich beyond imagination, imposing not only the energy question but also the threat of the use of the vast horde of petrodollars for political purposes as vital issues defining U.S. relations not merely with the Third World but especially with its allies. Oil also pushed Washington's military focus sharply toward the control of the Gulf and reduced its ability to cope with less dramatic and less costly but nonetheless vital challenges elsewhere in the Third World.

The crisis in oil also spilled over to other raw materials, and the price of metal ores about doubled between 1972 and 1974, even though most U.S. officials dealing with the problem during the early 1970s had already predicted an imbalance in supply and demand in the near future—and therefore higher prices. Responding to such issues preoccupied leading decisionmakers to an unprecedented extent, and an intensive and quite sophisticated focus on raw materials issues, and their policy implications, prevailed among them for the remainder of the decade. Greater use of stockpiling, reduction of consumption, and innumerable schemes were discussed widely throughout this period, creating much more interest in Africa as Latin America's share of U.S. minerals imports fell throughout the 1960s.

OPEC revealed that it was possible for the poorer oil nations to stop subsidizing the prosperity in the industrial capitalist nations, and producers of other raw materials made a concerted effort to revive commodity associations as effective bargaining tools to increase their share of the world's blessings—leading to an immediate confrontation with the United States. "The United States has always been lukewarm in its enthusiasm for commodity agreements," the assistant secretary for African affairs admitted in September 1972 with characteristic understatement, "and at times even formally opposed their use."[4] Diplomatic niceties alone had kept it from outright denunciation of nearly all of them, but its rare support for a few was essentially part of a maneuver to control them. In 1969, unable to manipulate the international sugar agreement that the United States had dominated since 1937, it dropped out of it. Expanded markets, more efficient production, and such slogans were ritual American responses to Third World demands for stable and fair prices. In the aftermath of October 1973, the bitter arguments between the United States and those seeking to raise prices revealed that what was at stake was the division of the world's wealth rather than equity, and that sheer power would dictate the outcome of disputes.

The State Department in January 1974 had concluded that the chance of raw materials' prices paralleling those for oil was unlikely in the short run save in copper and bauxite, but given that "the longer run U.S. dependence on foreign sources of raw materials is likely to increase . . . [w]e should consider appropriate steps to reduce the possibility and effectiveness of aggressive action by producers to deprive us of adequate supplies."[5] Mexico and Venezuela especially took the lead in promoting new commodity associations and resuscitating old ones, and the Nixon Administration responded brutally to these "tactics of confrontation," as Kissinger described them. The Latin nations were particularly anxious to develop united efforts because most had little oil relative to their population. "Such tactics are particularly inappropriate for the Western Hemisphere," Kissinger warned, "where they threaten to repudiate a long tradition of cooperative relations with the United States. . . ."[6] Those relations now were reduced to their barest economic essence.

In 1975 the United States therefore rewrote its trade act to "preempt" and provide "a deterrent against new commodity cartels" by denying nations joining them tariff preferences, notwithstanding its nominal traditional commitment to freer trade and commerce rather than aid.[7] The Administration had little to worry about in reality because it had ample alternative import sources in most cases, and aspiring cartel members were often disunited for a variety of reasons. At the end of 1975 it sought to modify its materialist, self-serving image by proposing convoluted schemes involving the World Bank and private investors to create a hodgepodge of cosmetic changes that would bypass Third World efforts and give a new World Bank institution a "facilitating role as third party with the host country and the foreign investor."[8] None of the schemes was realized.

U.S. militancy in defending its economic interests as a consumer was scarcely new, nor were the renewed threats to "bring to bear available political and economic influence to get a satisfactory resolution" of disputes over everything from trade to protecting its overseas investors.[9] American multinationals were also exporters of raw materials, and they profited enormously from post-1973 price increases. The exact extent of this gain is impossible to calculate, save for the oil companies. Suffice it to say that U.S. direct investment abroad in 1960 was $32 billion, with 35 percent of it in the Third World, while by 1982 it had risen to $185 billion, but only 21 percent of it was in the Third World. The profits from all foreign investments have been consistently far higher, usually two to three times, than those within the United States, and returns in the Third World have been, by far, the most lucrative of all. In 1982 they accounted for 39 percent of all profits from foreign investments.

INTERNATIONAL BANKS

Given the major changes occurring in the world economic structure damaging both the Third World and traditional U.S. power at the same time, it was inevitable that American leaders would seek to exploit far more systematically those international official banking institutions that the Eisenhower Administration and its successors had begun to shift to as more effective and subtle means for attaining their goals. Had the multilateral banks not existed as highly developed instruments by the mid-1960s, then it would have been essential for Washington to create them, but they stand out as a brilliant example of U.S. prescience after 1945 on how to seek to extend its hegemony over the world economy. Without them, America's economic power and its control over basic economic trends in the Third World would have declined much more than they did.

The United States effectively dominated both the World Bank and the IMF as well as their affiliates, and in 1974, a total of 41 percent of the bank's top managers were Americans, and the president was always a U.S. citizen. An official U.S. review in 1982 of its postwar ability to define major multilateral bank decisions concluded that it had succeeded in the great majority of cases where it exerted pressure. Its most celebrated triumph was in cutting all loans to Chile after 1971, but that was only one of many politically motivated decisions. The banks consistently linked the economic and financial reforms they demanded to U.S. political goals after 1956, especially during debt renegotiations, when borrowing nations were most vulnerable. They were completely candid regarding their general function, as an official American survey summed it up, to "use their loans as leverage to encourage positive economic performance and acceptance of market economy principles in recipient countries. Thus, the banks perform the difficult task of requiring performance standards of their borrowers, a task which the United States and other lenders may be reluctant to impose on a bilateral basis."[10] These included a strong export orientation, especially for "increased supplies of raw materials and other products needed by the U.S. economy," discouraging import substitution and tariff barriers—indeed, all those objectives that Washington had propounded since 1945.[11]

Actual World Bank/IDA loans through 1973 attached the highest priority to building an economic infrastructure essential for private, mainly foreign, investors, and the lowest to social programs, which received nothing before 1963 and less than a tenth of their funds over the next fifteen years. Other multilateral banks pursued the same strategy. The banks openly sought to influence national macroeconomic policies with their lending programs, and "the [World] Bank's reputation as an instrument of the developed economies," one U.S. official analysis observed with satisfaction, "seems justified."[12] By using what it purported to be "relatively apolitical economic policy expertise," the banks were "acting as a catalyst for private investment," a U.S. Treasury study said in summing up its experiences in 1982, "encouraging rational LDC economic policies under free market concepts and global economic efficiency."[13]

There had always been a consensus between the politicians and private banking and industry organizations that it was best to rely on multilateral banks where possible. In 1970, the Nixon-appointed Peterson task force recommended a yet greater emphasis on using the banks to impose "performance standards" on Third World nations, and its recommendations were accepted as a natural culmination of an older policy of shifting away from bilateralism.[14] After all, as Charles W. Robinson, the undersecretary of state for economic affairs observed in May 1975, "the Banks' contribution to development planning based on market-oriented economies" was generally accepted, for they could "offer hard economic advice in an apolitical context which is less offensive to national sensibilities," sparing U.S. officials the controversial task.[15]

Washington's growing emphasis on using multilateral banks as the key instruments of a neocolonial policy to integrate Third World nations into a United States-led and -guided world economy was the subject of frequent detailed internal official economic analyses, which made it clear that after decades of experience the banks' negative effects were both understood and desired, even though their authors personally sometimes also had other objectives in mind. In October 1972 the AID's Bureau for Program and Policy

Coordination circulated a background paper that concluded charitably that "Many practices and policies followed by multilateral and bilateral donors, including AID, have unwittingly made income distribution more unequal" by encouraging capital-intensive projects that "in some instances . . . may have even reduced employment." Many loans were channeled through credit institutions that provided funds "to enterprises which are large, located in the major metropolis, and/or owned by wealthy families." These, in turn, had "the greatest political power."[16] Yet the official desire to promote a development strategy "which encourages exports," particularly of "Raw materials . . . essential to the continuing vitality and non-inflationary expansion of our domestic economy," made such social and political consequences both axiomatic and intentional.[17] If some officials later argued for more labor-absorbing projects, the main thrust of Washington's goals remained the same: the banks advanced its general interests in the world and "they serve as vehicles for assisting countries favored by the United States and for influencing the economic affairs of countries with which the U.S. Government has international disagreements."[18]

The importance of multilateral official banks to the United States in regulating Third World economies increased after the late 1960s as the value of the dollar declined, and to a significant degree because of it. By 1970 virtually all major U.S. banking and investment firms strongly favored IMF leadership in rescheduling loans to Third World nations, especially when their funds were involved, because it had the ability to impose conditions that would have been denounced as imperialist had the private banks proposed them. With Europe's gradual shift away from the dollar, which had begun before 1968 and continued slowly until 1971, when it turned into a run and forced the Nixon Administration on August 15 to remove the dollar's gold backing and abandon the Bretton Woods system, which had prevailed since 1946, U.S. pretensions to economic hegemony were profoundly undermined. The pressure on the dollar did not cease, however, and with the October 1973 War and the sudden emergence of vast amounts of petrodollars and the beginning of huge U.S. budget and payments deficits, it was increasingly apparent that the multilateral banks had become America's most effective, if not only, nonmilitary means for shaping Third World economies to suit its interests. It was the weakening of the dollar, which became subject, like all other currencies, to world market forces and the consequences of irresponsible domestic economic policies, that ended U.S. hopes for shaping unilaterally the world economy to its desires. And this loss of mastery was, more than any other factor, the outcome of its protracted effort to save its credibility in Vietnam.

While the reliance on multilateral banks had a certain logic and was partially successful, it was both increasingly irrelevant and too late in coping with the new world economy that emerged after 1970. Ironically, the failure of official U.S. policy was to a large degree due to the avarice of American banks, which soon far surpassed corporate investors and official lending agencies in shaping the relationship of Third World economies to world capitalism, for the private banks offered many Third World nations a way around these traditional modes of control.

U.S. banks operating abroad were still of minor significance in 1960, when they had assets of only $3.5 billion. Five years later their assets had almost tripled, but their role as a source of credit was still marginal. By 1972, before the oil crisis had fully matured to produce huge sums of petrodollars that went into their coffers, their assets had grown to $90 billion, and by mid-1976 they were double that. With the growth of the immense world private credit system, which incorporated giant non-U.S. banks as well, Third World nations had an irresistible alternative to bilateral and multilateral official loans, with all their strictures, while the private banks, who were the largest recipients of OPEC's surpluses, were desperate to loan them money.

The share of the total profits of the thirteen largest U.S. international banks earned abroad rose from 17 percent in 1970 to 49 percent in 1976, for there was a much greater demand for their funds outside the United States. The combined assets of the twenty-one largest U.S. commercial banks operating abroad at the end of 1975 were twenty times the lending resources of the IMF and the EEC special facility combined. Compared to these banks, direct corporate investment seemed paltry as a source of capital, and in various ways state-sponsored economic projects in many Latin nations became means both of independent economic development and deeper entanglement with world capital. But for a relatively brief time some of the Third World nations could borrow freely without accepting strict limits on their use of funds or economic policies. The Latin debt to official creditors in 1979 was less than it was in 1960, but its total debt in 1979, most of it to private banks, was now far greater than ever. To some extent, the main beneficiaries of the dizzying rise in the price of oil were the banks that processed the largest share of the gains. From the U.S. government's viewpoint, all this meant that unless countermeasures were taken, its ability to define the Third World's economic policies was more in doubt than ever. And from the private banks' vantage, some regulation was essential if they were ever to be repaid the interest and principal owed to them.

The debt itself provided the United States with the handle it needed to attempt to reimpose its hegemony via the official banks. Brazil's debt as a percentage of its exports grew from 36 percent in 1973 to 61 percent in 1979, while Mexico's nearly tripled, to 64 percent. By 1976 both private bankers and U.S. officials began to converge on a solution for their common anxieties in the form of a greatly expanded critical role for the IMF in the lending activities of private banks, especially when they had to renegotiate more loans to bail out those nations inevitably falling into distress. Their goal, in the words of a U.S. Senate report, was to "give the IMF more clout in putting pressure on deficit countries to undertake the often painful and politically difficult adjustment policies required to bring their external accounts into balance," measures the banks were least able to impose without turning the political ire of the population of many states against them.[19] As the revised IMF charter assigned it new surveillance functions, IMF "conditionality" increasingly became the impetus for political crises and food riots in a growing number of countries as hapless nations attempted to meet its inflexible, ritual demands to cut social services of all kinds. This struggle remains central to the experiences of our own times.

CHANGING STRUCTURAL RELATIONS

Estimating accurately the structural relationships between the United States and the Third World by the latter half of the 1970s is at best a precarious undertaking, if only because by 1970 both had entered into a rapidly evolving, fluid phase of their economic history and each, in certain crucial ways, had become weaker. The extent to which the United States had declined was even more difficult to gauge because its vast political and military resources for compensating for its economic fragility still existed, though the potential price America might pay both at home and abroad should it employ its power, as Vietnam had shown, was a growing inhibition on its freedom to act. For since the late 1960s we have lived in an epoch of great change and transformation, astonishing in its rapidity and portentous in its implications for future generations of mankind, not only in the Third World but in America as well.

This context limits the U.S. relationship to the Third World to the extent that rationality still exists within the American political order, which at this point in time means largely the instinct of those who rule to preserve what they have rather than risk everything on persisting to attain the imperialist, hegemonic goals that inspired them after 1945. To an unpredictable extent, as with the case of Vietnam, the willingness of those outside the power and political decisionmaking system to protect their own interests against the recklessness of the dominant class will also weigh on the scale of factors shaping the course of events. The relationship of the United States to the entire international order depends to some vital extent on subjective elements still very much in flux, but capable in the worst case of immense destruction throughout the world, even nuclear war.

To some crucial extent as well, the equation between the United States and the Third World is being altered by the emergence of other capitalist nations with their own structural needs, far stronger currencies than the dollar, and increasing ability to serve as a counterpoise to American domination. The U.S. capacity to define events and economic trends in various Third World nations, short of the threat or use of its military, has declined with the rise of competition from other capitalist states, providing a number of key countries with crucial leverage to play off investors regarding prices and terms. Non-U.S. automobile producers have allowed Brazil, Mexico, and others since the late 1960s to rewrite completely the conditions under which American companies used to operate. Japan, which has a much greater raw materials deficit than the United States, has on every continent written contracts far more favorable than those of U.S. companies in order to assure itself of essential supplies.

Reflecting these new competitive forces, American control over the entire stock of foreign investment in the world has declined since it reached its peak of 59 percent in 1960. By 1971 it was 52 percent and less than half by the latter part of the decade. With Japanese overseas investment alone increasing at an annual rate three to five times that of the United States, all of the structural trends in the world economy eroding America's postwar hegemony intensified after 1970 to confront it with insuperable challenges—with which we live today.

Notwithstanding these countervailing factors, the objective position of the Third World, especially the low-income, nonoil-producing nations, has worsened dramatically insofar as external debt problems weigh upon them. By 1979 nonoil-developing-nation debt was at least $225 billion, five times its 1970 level, and the ratio of their debt service to exports rose sharply for the major borrowers within them, about doubling over that period. In large part because debt and IMF-private bank pressures have remained the determining factors in shaping their internal policies, positive economic changes within the Third World as an aggregate have been astonishingly slight, especially if oil producers are separated from the rest.

In terms of a share of the value of the world's exports, the developing countries' share fell consistently, from 30.5 percent in 1950 to 16.3 percent in 1972, and only with the rise in the price of oil increased to 25.2 percent in 1974, when it again began to drop. Given the terms of trade, the entire export-oriented emphasis the United States and its banks have mercilessly pressed upon these nations has relentlessly worked against their escaping from their poverty through foreign commerce. A few nations, such as Brazil, have been able sharply to increase their exports of manufactured and semimanufactured goods, but even in 1972 they comprised only 27 percent of Brazil's sales, and its main exports were still subjected to a fluctuating, unfavorable world market. For the low-income nations, the share of their gross domestic product that manufacturing generated was 14.7 percent in 1960 and 14.4 percent in 1981, while "other industry" (mining, utilities, and construction) rose from 5.9 to 8.4 percent. All developing economies combined, including the middle-income ones, had 17.2 and 19.5 percent in manufacturing over that period, and 9.0 and 15.5 in "other industry." Their situation had changed very little structurally or in its relationship to the rich countries. Much of the growth of Third World manufacturing exports, often produced by U.S. multinationals exploiting their cheap labor, was in fact oriented toward the developed capitalist nations, and it was simply another form of dependency. As long as the internal markets of these increasingly debt-ridden countries remained small, as the prevailing class structure and income distribution necessitated, such imbalanced, dependent development was inevitable.

In terms of per capita agricultural production throughout the entire Third World, far more significant for the masses, not until the early 1960s was the 1927 level exceeded, and by 1975 it was only slightly larger. Asia, mainly due to China, accounted for this progress; in the rest of Asia and Latin America, per capita output in 1975 was lower than it had been in earlier years.[20]

There had been, to be sure, much progress in certain domains, but many failures and difficulties in others, especially in those socially and demographically disrupted export-led, low-wage societies that no longer possess the possibilities of a more balanced economic development that existed before their thorough integration into the world market. To measure all these changes is impossible, for aside from its faults, the data are often inconclusive on face value. What *is* certain is that the United States' promise of serious progress in the Third World should it pursue those export-oriented economic goals Washington consistently both urged and imposed on it failed utterly to alter the fundamental structural problems involving human existence and to attain a minimum of decency and security. The inherited Wilsonian objectives based on the international division of labor had helped the United States to prosper enormously, but they did nothing for those nations, above all in Latin America, that applied them or that were integral parts of the neocolonial systems the United States endorsed in Africa and elsewhere. Instead, by the late 1970s there was hunger and turbulence in countless nations and far stronger revolutionary movements in many more places than had existed after World War Two. And much of it was the consequence of those wrenching transformations, ranging from IMF-dictated fiscal measures to uprooted populations making way for export-oriented economic development, that the United States had managed to impose.

The African Cauldron

*T*HE NIXON ADMINISTRATION'S POLI-
cies toward Africa mirrored those
preceding it. It shared the same am-
biguities and conflicting goals regarding the perpetuation of white regimes
and apartheid, and its strategic needs in Europe and their relationship to
European colonialism in Africa colored its thinking deeply. The new government also shared its predecessors' impulse to preserve what it believed to
be a stable status quo while also satisfying the demands of moderate nationalist forces. Most important, as with the Johnson Administration, its overwhelming distractions elsewhere and its relative indifference to the affairs of
the continent also caused it to opt for support for the existing order of things.

The Nixon Administration considered its Africa policy in a desultory way
throughout 1969, with the CIA and Pentagon urging closer, nonconfronta-
tional relations with the white-controlled regimes while the State Department
favored a continuation of the inherited eclectic, contradictory policies. When
the NSC finally presented its study of options in December 1969, NSSM 39,
the White House endorsed its synthesis of the conflicting bureaucratic positions that had become routine in Washington on African issues. NSSM 39,
later dubbed the "tar baby" option because, as a key official in charge of the
review later assessed it, "its only real result would be to mire the United
States deeper on the side of the oppressors," was nonetheless a remarkably
candid review of the permanent differences on Africa within successive
administrations since 1945. It described a confusion of priorities as well as
resignation to the perceived inevitable permanence of racist regimes, and it
concluded that U.S. policy satisfied no one. A new compromise endeavored
to establish a closer "limited association" with the racist regimes, extend

more aid to the black nations, and encourage moderation on everyone's part. Nixon had earlier decided to end "lecturing" Portugal in a way that risked access to its Azores bases, including relaxing the nominal arms embargo, and this, too, became part of the "less doctrinaire" new strategy.[1]

"Tar baby" allowed the Administration to tilt heavily toward greater collaboration with the white regimes while maintaining a pretense of support for some of the black nations' demands. The CIA continued its close ties with all the white security services; economic interests could pursue profits everywhere, ignoring the UN embargo on imports from Rhodesia; and the Pentagon kept its bases and tracking stations. This policy and its specific consequences remained secret until late 1974, when it was leaked to a journalist. With NSSM 39 the United States, as before, was firmly aligned with the existing forces of white domination in Africa on immediate economic and strategic issues involving power, even if it straddled the fence with symbolic rhetoric on such problems as racism.

This policy of reopening "communication" with racist regimes was partially the result of the Nixon Administration's conviction that they had the resources to endure, and thereby could satisfy practical U.S. economic and strategic demands.[2] NSSM 39 made it clear that while the United States had important interests in Africa, none was vital, and given the manner in which Nixon and Kissinger monopolized all key foreign policy questions, their own indifference to Africa, combined above all with their ignorance of it and monumental distractions elsewhere, precluded a stronger, clearer U.S. position. Moreover, despite periodic U.S. complaints that the French and British economic ties with their former colonies created closed trading blocs and tariff preferences that damaged U.S. interests, which Washington attempted partially to counteract, it nonetheless persisted throughout the 1970s in publicly acknowledging that there was "some justification" for the view that "Africa is largely a European preserve" and that "their interests and influence greatly exceed our own."[3]

Its deference to Europe's role notwithstanding, the United States was deeply conscious of the fact that southern Africa possessed a large majority of the world's reserves of chromite, the platinum group metals (both among its four most vital imports), and gold, plus major amounts of others. For practical purposes, Africa became synonymous with raw materials, especially after 1973, when awareness of their importance increased greatly. Economic aid was given in modest quantities to black African nations largely with an eye to maintaining goodwill for continued access to minerals developments involving U.S. firms. In this domain U.S. direct investments in sub-Saharan Africa grew from $824 million in 1960 to $2.3 billion in 1970 and then $4.1 billion in 1976, when it leveled off for at least six more years. The important trend in these figures was that while the share of American investment in South Africa as opposed to the rest of the continent declined from 49 percent of the total in 1950 to 32 percent in 1966, which many thought would compel the United States to be more sympathetic to black demands, it rose sharply thereafter and was 41 percent in 1976 and up to 47 percent in 1982—restoring the apartheid regime's significance to advancing U.S. economic interests.

The Rhodesian case revealed how decisive raw materials were in defining Washington's policies. The UN had sanctioned imports from Rhodesia in the hope of penalizing the tiny white minority, 5 percent of the population, ruling that nation, and while the Johnson Administration had opposed African demands for a UN-endorsed army to resolve the political problems there, as it had done in the Congo, it did approve sanctions. In May 1969 Union Carbide obtained from the White House previously refused approval to import chromium ore it claimed to have purchased before the boycott, and the Administration also eliminated some other restrictions on the white regime. Nor did the White House oppose Senator Harry F. Byrd's bill to permit raw materials imports that de facto circumvented the UN position. It became law in November 1971, making the United States along with Portugal and South Africa the only nations to violate the UN ban openly. While the United States had always preferred to follow Britain's lead in dealing with the Rhodesian crisis, it made an exception in this case, siding with Portugal and South Africa in the UN three times during 1973 to vote against the economic embargo and its enforcement.

In South Africa the United States was much more overt, despite the fact that it nominally retained the cautious position of its predecessors by opposing apartheid as well as any violence or active measures to end it. With the secret NSSM 39 as guiding policy, Washington openly worked with the Pretoria regime, encouraging U.S. investment and trade, selling computers, helicopters, and planes with military applications, and abandoning the practice of shunning South Africa's diplomats. By 1970, indeed, support for what was also the Democratic policy of working with the regime on a practical basis was so widespread within the foreign policy establishment that it can be said that Nixon was neither behind nor ahead of it. "The real state of mind of the South African native remains," putative liberal foreign policy critic George Kennan wrote in 1970, "a book with seven seals." As abhorrent as apartheid was, he urged, "let it be the task of those [white] rulers, who know their own situation better than any outsider can, to find the conceivable alternatives."[4] Nixon merely continued to apply the Democratic-Republican consensus with less pretense as to its practical meaning, but he introduced no new policies, and when he resigned the presidency in August 1974, his successor, Gerald Ford, continued on the same course until Kissinger transformed Angola into a significant crisis.

THE ANGOLAN CRISIS

America's policy toward Portugal's two main African possessions, Angola and Mozambique, had always been sympathetic to the colonialist cause, and in November 1963 it publicly made clear that "we have no desire to see the Portuguese forced out of Africa," even though it counseled reform in the face of growing black militancy.[5] Its greater commitment to maintaining bases on the Azores, which Salazar kept available to the Pentagon on a year-to-year basis, thoroughly inhibited the Americans. Salazar died in 1968 but Portuguese policy did not change, and although the United States desired peaceful change within the colonies, it also secretly continued its small subsidies to Roberto of the FNLA and offered aid to Jonas Savimbi of UNITA.

By 1970 the Administration believed Portugal's policy was improving, and it shared Kennan's public praise for Portugal's accomplishments, which allegedly made its territories "well ahead of most of the black-ruled countries" and produced no "great discontent with Portuguese rule."[6] In 1971 the United States decided to sell Lisbon military equipment, including napalm, capable of being used against guerrillas, to provide four hundred million dollars in credits, and to ignore, in effect, the UN prohibition on any aid which might help Portugal's colonial wars. Nixon from the inception had made it clear that he wanted access to the Azores bases, and American "neutrality" required it to keep silent on Portuguese actions. In the 1973 UN General Assembly vote to investigate Portuguese massacres in Mozambique it sided with Portugal, South Africa, and Spain in standing alone in opposition to it. After the October 1973 War the U.S. desire to use the Azores bases to resupply Israel led Kissinger secretly to pledge far greater weapons aid to Portugal. But the radical military coup that overthrew the Lisbon regime on April 25, 1974, also abolished the colonial empire. The United States' misplaced confidence that the Portuguese would rule indefinitely now forced it to confront the basic dilemma of its relations with Portugal's black successors.

Three main factions existed in Angola, two of which the CIA subsidized. The FNLA under Roberto, the son-in-law of President Mobuto of Zaire, was based among the Bakongo tribe spread along Zaire's border. It had the largest number of soldiers and received aid from China, Libya, and Romania as well as Zaire and the United States. Roberto's politics, like Mobuto's, were personal, and tribalism provided his mass base. UNITA in the south under Savimbi was based on the Ovimbundu tribe, and it was extremely antiforeign. The MPLA, with Agostinho Neto as its head, was a true party with active internal debate, and it was the only nontribally oriented force capable of both uniting and modernizing the country. Although it was Marxist-Leninist, the

Russians, who had earlier supported it, cut the MPLA off in 1973 for ideological reasons. It attracted most educated Angolans, and while its army was somewhat smaller than that of the FNLA, it was also more capable.

In May 1974, when the Portuguese had already scheduled the formal transfer of power to the blacks for November 11, 1975, the Chinese sent 120 military advisers and arms to the FNLA, and the CIA two months later also increased its funds to Roberto. In November 1974 the FNLA attempted to seize the capital of Luanda, an MPLA stronghold, and unleashed open war among the three factions. In early January 1975 they all agreed to share power when the Portuguese left until a national election could be held, but the accord was not to last long.

The main problem was that the MPLA was stronger and better able to rule Angola than its two rivals, and so in January 1975 the "40 Committee," over which Kissinger presided and that supervised the CIA's work, decided to give the FNLA significant aid. While the Administration later claimed it amounted to only three hundred thousand dollars, the fact that it systematically understated the value of its arms shipments throughout this affair makes this number doubtful. Encouraged by Mobuto and the United States, Roberto resumed his drive on Luanda the following month, upsetting the January accord and rekindling a civil war that was to continue until the end of the year. From the U.S. viewpoint, it was essential to maintain Africa as the only continent without any Marxist regime, so its initially relatively small involvement appeared to make sense to it. When the Soviets in response began to ship arms to the MPLA during March, however, for Kissinger the stakes in Angola immediately increased significantly to include the credibility of American power.

In April the MPLA, defensively fighting to retain control of Luanda, asked Cuba for aid, and 230 advisers joined it in July as Zaire also sent its troops to aid the FNLA. It was at this point that Kissinger overrode the objections of the State Department's—and some CIA—African experts to plunge far more deeply into the crisis. From this time onward the State Department was excluded from policy deliberations, but even the chief of the CIA operation felt as if "we were mounting a major covert action to support two Angolan liberation movements about which we had little reliable intelligence." As he understood it, "Uncomfortable with recent historic events, and frustrated by our humiliation in Vietnam, Kissinger was seeking opportunities to challenge the Soviets."[7] The idea of Soviet arms defeating American arms in the hands of its erstwhile friends again raised the specter of proxies and American prestige, which was in fact now integral to the credibility notion. In the United States' first major crisis after its final defeat in Vietnam, the Angola imbroglio revealed that its leaders were still wholly committed to assumptions and a mode of acting that made them as willing as ever to embark on dangerous adventures.

Coincidentally, U.S. relations with Mobutu had been extremely poor in the months preceding the July decision to deepen U.S. involvement, and this was also seen as a way of improving them. During July U.S. arms began to pour into FNLA hands, the first of a minimum of thirty-seven million dollars worth, and the FNLA also received large amounts of Chinese arms, and North Korean instructors began to train them. China and South Africa both began to arm UNITA. An alliance between UNITA and the FNLA, with strong CIA encouragement, now threatened to overwhelm the MPLA, and regular South African forces also joined UNITA's efforts. The tide of the war began to shift against the MPLA.

By late September the first of seven hundred Cuban soldiers began arriving, and they were installed in Luanda to help defend it against a drive led by four thousand to six thousand South African troops plus UNITA men to the south and FNLA and Zairian forces coming from the north. In the midst of what turned out to be an artillery battle between the two sides, on November 11, 1975, Angola became an independent nation, but it was to be one the MPLA ruled. Confronted with longer-range weapons, the far larger anti-MPLA armies were decimated and began to disintegrate. Over the next weeks Cuban troops, eventually numbering up to twelve thousand, helped the MPLA mop up resistance, and by March 1976 all that remained were stray UNITA bands in the bush, where they have lingered ever since, with U.S. and South African assistance.

It was after the catastrophic failure of the November offensive that the U.S. government divided in ways that revealed how profoundly Vietnam had affected its political ability to intervene in the Third World with the same impunity it had for over two decades. It had been split from the inception, but Kissinger's desire to appear, as the CIA saw it, "tough, even brutal," had prevailed until his utter ignorance and the weakness of the United States' aggressive proxies led to disaster and excluded them from participating in the political process on which the three sides had compromised in January 1975.[8] Its open alliance with the detested South African regime as well as China and North Korea had further isolated the United States in Africa, revealing it to be unprincipled and also irresponsibly adventurous and weak, with its credibility far more in doubt than ever. With all of his critics within the Administration leaking the details of his incompetence to the press, Kissinger asked the CIA to begin planning ripostes costing up to a hundred million dollars and employing mercenaries, but neither the CIA nor the Pentagon could or would provide him the money, and when the White House asked Congress for additional funding, the Senate and House by overwhelming majorities banned any covert aid to its Angolan clients. In effect, no

Executive could remain oblivious to the deep changes that had occurred in American political life since 1968 without further compounding Washington's symbolic weaknesses in both confronting and guiding the world to suit its designs.

Kissinger responded to the Angola debacle by moving in several directions. To reverse the global implications of the defeat of a proxy the United States had enthusiastically backed, he began to warn Cuba of unspecified but dire consequences should they intervene elsewhere in Africa, including the possibility of an American invasion of Cuba itself. And he let it be known to the Russians that events such as Angola could affect the entire range of U.S.-Soviet relations, including détente, blithely ignoring the fact that both Cuba and Russia had consistently responded to American initiatives in Angola rather than provoking the crisis.

Even as Kissinger blustered, his ability to continue attacking the MPLA and preventing it from consolidating power was undermined not only by Congress but also by U.S. business interests operating in Angola. The most important of these was Gulf Oil, whose fields produced five hundred million dollars in revenue annually for Angola, and at the end of 1975 it proposed to pay royalties of two hundred million dollars owed to Luanda, now controlled by the MPLA, thereby greatly aiding the MPLA to consolidate control. The MPLA, Marxist or not, wanted Gulf to continue operations as they had under the Portuguese, but it also hinted that should they fail to do so, then eager French bidders would be welcome. Indeed, Neto at this time in a *Le Monde* interview made it clear that the MPLA was an independent Marxist movement that took orders from no one, Moscow included—an assertion that was later repeatedly vindicated as Angola's relations with Russia always remained cool, and its closest ties were with Cuba. What the MPLA needed, obviously, was an economic basis for its autonomy, and it was eager to do business with foreign capitalists. Despite Washington's strong pressure on Gulf, which forced it to put its royalties in escrow, the oil company lobbied strongly to protect its interests and even maintained contacts with the MPLA via Nigeria. Meanwhile, Boeing, which had been in the process of selling two 737s to the Angolan airline and was eager to expand its business, also lobbied for dealing with the MPLA. Kissinger managed to block Boeing, too, but by the end of February their combined pressure forced the Administration to allow them to resume normal business activities—which they have continued ever since. Yet the United States together with China alone boycotted Angola diplomatically for the next decade. A Marxist state in Africa had come into being, and it endured.

Kissinger's subsequent response to Africa and the Angolan debacle was based on his long-overdue realization that as long as the United States was ready to intervene continuously, as it had in Angola, great-power conflict was possible in Africa and that the traditional American passivity toward the unresolved sources of tension there could produce more disasters for it. In April 1976, therefore, he began a two-week visit in the hope of mending fences but especially to attempt to defuse the crisis in Rhodesia, a nation whose problems the United States had hitherto assigned to Britain to resolve. At the end of April Kissinger announced "a new era of American policy" toward southern Africa, ostensibly repudiating the "tar baby" policy, renewing U.S. support for UN economic sanctions against Rhodesia, and giving greater support to British efforts.[9] The following September he returned to southern Africa and attempted futilely to arrange a Rhodesian settlement that both forestalled violence and a leftward direction for national liberation movements, for "the consequences of the radicalization of Africa would be serious in many other parts of the world."[10] But the blacks rejected his proposal because it was still too close to the white position.

The United States' problem in Africa, ultimately, was to a large extent both definitional and the product of ignorance. By universalizing local into global issues, with symbolism that involved the superpowers, it was able to produce crises where none need to have existed. Worse yet, the United States was again transforming the Soviet Union into a diabolical causal factor in African social change and upheavals, as if they were the origin of troubles that in reality evolved principally from white resistance to decolonization, as well as from poverty. This mode of reasoning, however, incorporated three decades of U.S. thinking, with dominoes, regional linkages, and credibility all combined together to produce an ideological mixture that imposed no constraints on American actions or priorities; nor did it provide a rational basis for analyses. It was a formula that made interventionism itself synonymous with the pursuit of U.S. interests, threatening to guide its policy and conduct in ways that increasingly sapped the very health of American economic power as well as further erode domestic political and social cohesion. Ironically, in Angola the Ford Administration's lack of concern for Gulf's great economic stakes revealed how far symbolic calculations had begun to displace the purely materialist needs of American capitalism, intensifying an irrational potential always inherent in the interventionist premises of postwar U.S. foreign policy.

The dilemma intrinsic in Washington's assumptions was that they required a studied ignorance of facts to sustain them, for in Angola all the information it possessed undermined its rationale for action and hope for success, and so it was ignored and the people who took it seriously prevented from influencing decisions. Ideology, symbolism, and desires overcame intelligence, as they had in Vietnam and so many other places. This, obviously, was dangerous, and it revealed an inherent capacity for self-destructive behavior in foreign affairs that was by no means unique but that in this case is far better documented than is normal by virtue of discontented insiders who were able and ready to expose it. Less than a decade later the Iran-contra affair replicated it exactly, bringing to the fore the same kinds of destructive and irrational adventurers and calculations that had become increasingly endemic to U.S. foreign policy in the Third World since 1945.

Yet even in Africa it was not too long before the mild shift Kissinger had initiated in southern African policy soon became just an aberration in the older, more consistent U.S. role in the region. Under Carter the emphasis on raw materials predominated, and despite an initial awareness that there was some Angolan justification for retaining Cuban troops to protect themselves against a UNITA-South African resurgence, it did not take long for the Carter Administration also to reimpose Cold War definitions on local issues, fearing that Soviet aid and influence would entrap various nations and pose a long-term threat to American interests. Zbigniew Brzezinski, Carter's national security assistant, convinced the flaccid president that he should ignore the State Department's persistently more restrained analyses that "underestimated the Eastern bloc connection in the region . . . underestimating its strategic implications."[11] Credibility and opposition to radicalism, along with a covetous desire for the continent's riches, remained the cornerstones of American policy in Africa, and the United States was again unequivocally ranged on the wrong side of the major conflicts there. All that had changed since 1945 was that the U.S. imposition of the Cold War context on African issues had become much more intense, while radicalism had become a far greater political factor almost entirely because of those European and racist policies it had endorsed since 1945.

The Philippines: Creating a Revolution

*T*HE 1969 ELECTION THAT RETURNED Ferdinand Marcos to power in one of the most manipulated and violent, and surely the costliest, electoral campaign in Philippine history exhausted the nation both politically and economically and marked a turning point in its development. The economic difficulties it brought to a head were the logical culmination of years of error and neglect, but the political crisis was a qualitatively new phenomenon, the outcome of a far greater public awareness that both the nation's traditional oligarchic politics and leaders were unable to resolve the massive problems of the society—and thereby ceased to be relevant. It was also the result of an incipient civil war within the traditional elite between those nationalist economic constituencies demanding more than conventional opportunistic politics to protect and advance their interests, and the dominant politicians who since 1946 had treated the state simply as a vehicle for self-enrichment—between those who were eager to serve U.S. interests and those ready to cut the economic cords that still bound the nation. It was this merger of structural economic problems with a new political consciousness that was to cause the Philippines to veer away from inherited methods of confronting problems and toward radical alternatives. These trends presented the United States with altogether new challenges in its Asian neocolony.

The enormous cost of the 1969 election to the Philippine treasury accelerated the massive deterioration of the economy, but it did not initiate it. Structurally, the economy was weak by virtue of its export dependence and strategic U.S. control over it, which would have caused the nation's debt to rise dramatically even if there had not been spectacular corruption. The 1969 election expenses did, however, produce a sharp inflation of 15 to 20 percent annually over the next three years, running up huge government deficits and forcing it to borrow, and the external public debt nearly doubled over the next year and rose sharply every year thereafter. The country was beginning to fall into the standard Third World debt trap, with all of its consequences. To cope with his problems, Marcos had no alternative but to call upon the World Bank to help him, and to get funds from the consultative group it set up to manage the debt. He accepted the bank's advice to devalue the peso again in February 1970 by 60 percent to stimulate exports. Given the sharp drop in the prices of its main raw materials exports on the world market over the next two years, the bank's cure only aggravated the nation's troubles, inflation included, and compounded the political difficulties Marcos confronted at the very point he was facing a new form of political opposition.

The economic foundations on which Marcos imposed these new problems could no longer absorb them without galvanizing opposition from both the nationalistic businessmen and, even more ominous, elements among the masses who had been quiescent for years. Income distribution in the Philippines had not altered significantly since 1945, with the richest fifth of the population receiving about 56 percent in 1970. Manufacturing's share of the gross domestic product did not grow throughout the 1960s and actually declined for most of that time, and given the failure of agriculture to absorb labor or increase income, the consequences of these trends showed up in a sharp growth in poverty. In 1971 the proportion of the nation below the already minimal poverty threshold level increased to 57 percent compared to 48 percent in 1965, and by 1975 it was at least 64 percent.

Politically, the dangers confronting both Marcos and the United States grew enormously after 1969 as an ad hoc informal alliance emerged comprising nationalist businessmen, radicalized sectors of the Catholic lower clergy and laity, and student protesters who gravitated toward a New Left politics that embraced diverse elements, including nominal Maoists, the intelligentsia, and others. Their common denominator was anti-Americanism. During the first quarter of 1970, often violent demonstrations against Marcos and the United States mobilized new constituencies outside the framework of the pro-Soviet Communist Party, and their rallies were larger than any either of the two major parties had held for years. Soon the Liberal Party and some of its ambitious leaders, including Benigno Aquino, Jr., sought to form a de facto alliance with these elements to defeat Marcos in future elections, an effort that may have succeeded if given time. In June 1971, as well, the first constitutional convention to rewrite the 1935 constitution began to meet, and nationalist business elements were strongly represented in it, greatly increasing the likelihood that the anti-American legislation that had been accumulating since 1959 would be institutionalized. The convention even talked of banning foreign bases. Worse yet from Marcos's viewpoint, it was certain to renew the existing ban on more than two terms for the president, which would have forced Marcos to vacate the office in December 1973. Marcos soon spread the word that Communists controlled the convention. With opposition mounting from every direction and on many levels, the issue increasingly became whether Marcos would relinquish power gracefully.

The first hints that he would not came in Marcos's repeated public assertions after 1969 that "I would not hesitate to declare Martial Law if the situation demanded it."[1] On August 21, 1971, at a huge Liberal Party rally in Manila's Plaza Miranda gathering nearly all its senatorial candidates for the forthcoming November election, two grenades were hurled on the stage, killing nine and injuring nearly a hundred. Virtually the entire Liberal leadership was wounded, some seriously, and while Marcos tried to blame the Communists, the U.S. embassy knew it was the work of his loyalists in the army. Yet the Liberals won six of the eight Senate seats in the election, and Marcos now concluded that he would have to take drastic action.

From the American viewpoint the trends were ominous also, for the nationalist upsurge that threatened to throw Marcos out embodied everything in Philippine politics that had menaced its interests since the late 1950s. More to the point, in August 1972 the Supreme Court handed down two rulings, the so-called Quasha decisions, which struck a profound blow at the whole web of past and future U.S. investments, invalidating the 1955 Laurel-Langley Agreement allowing U.S. citizens to own land (and hence natural resources) as well as operate certain kinds of business. It was clear now that Laurel-Langley would not be renewed when it expired in July 1974 and that U.S. investments with a book value of $640 million in 1970 (but a market value estimated at three times that) would be jeopardized. "We could wake up tomorrow and find a revolt under way—under the banner of nationalism," a "Western official" told *U.S. News & World Report.*[2]

Nationalism rather than the Left remained the origin of Washington's immediate problem. Estimating the state of the Left in April 1972, American experts dismissed the Huks as inconsequential, with most now mere criminals operating near U.S. bases. The Maoist New People's Army (NPA) of the newly formed Communist Party (CPP) had gone from 390 hard-core members in 1969, with an equivalent number of supporters, to 379 in 1971 and perhaps 10 times that many supporters—in a nation of 37 million people. While this figure was so small as to appear ludicrous, the Americans did note that the NPA, unlike the Huks, had managed to spread teams to a sufficiently larger number of islands to pose greater logistic challenges than the Huks had been able to do, and that they "have a much better reputation than the Philippine Constabulary who have been cited for stealing, intimidating and taking what they need without reimbursement."[3] It was perfectly obvious from such information that the tiny Left's only hope in 1972 was not in its own forces but rather in the intensification of the structural and organizational deficiencies of the existing society—over which it had no control. The system's demise, if it came, would at least at its beginning stages be the result of its own internal contradictions.

It was in this context that Marcos moved toward martial law and an end to the ambiguities of Filipino politics, because, unable to co-opt his opponents, he could only suppress them or relinquish power. Public discussion of martial law increased after the summer of 1971, and American officials either favored it or remained neutral. "The Philippines needs a strong man, a man on horseback to get the country organized and going again," the embassy's political officer during the post-1969 years wrote.[4] In the weeks preceding the proclamation of martial law on September 23, 1972, it was widely believed that Marcos would use alleged "Communist" actions and plots, linking them with his Liberal opponents, to abolish the nation's precarious period of constitutionalism. It was fully evident by this time that the main political trends emerging from Filipino democracy were more threatening than at any time since 1960. If Marcos lost power, then American strategic, economic, and political interests would suffer greatly. It was scarcely conceivable, given its readiness to act in nations where the stakes were far smaller, that Washington would passively accept such an ignominious end to its colonial experience and its long endeavor to show the world how its beneficent efforts could build a model Third World society.

THE UNITED STATES AND MARTIAL LAW

The U.S. view of its interests in the Philippines prior to September 1972 had not altered since 1945, and it involved retention and uninhibited use of two major and six small bases, "to avoid injury to established U.S. enterprise, i.e., to foster an orderly transition from the special relationships embodied in Laurel-Langley, and to promote to the maximum feasible extent the continued participation of American enterprise," as well as stability within the Philippines itself. "Moderating Philippine economic nationalism" was far more important than any other immediate American concern, and Washington clearly preferred that "technocrats" administer economic policy.[5] No American official working on the Philippines in 1972 believed there was a danger from Communists. The embassy regarded Marcos highly because while he was both described in the U.S. press, as well as known to be, extremely corrupt, he had also proved himself to be the most receptive of all major political leaders, notwithstanding a certain populist flamboyance and bouts of opportunism. But most important of all in the summer of 1972, top American leaders had their hands full elsewhere, above all with Vietnam and the U.S. presidential race, and they were indifferent to the fast-moving developments in Manila. It was left to the U.S. ambassador, Henry Byroade, to cope with the issue, and when he was informed during August that martial law would soon be declared, he simply told Marcos that it would be far more palatable in Washington were it justified as essential to cope with Communists. By mid-September its imminent announcement was public knowledge, and the CIA even obtained its text. Marcos decided to check by phone with a preoccupied Nixon, who told him, depending on the account, either to go ahead or raised no objections. Marcos saw Byroade the day before proclaiming martial law and told him that he would now be able to reverse the Quasha decisions and protect U.S. economic interests.

Marcos exploited his opportunity to the hilt, closing down all opposition papers and arresting Liberal and nationalist leaders as well, of course, as those leftists who had not already used the ample advance warnings to escape. All told, about fifty thousand people were detained, not including those under house arrest, and by 1975 there were still six thousand in Marcos's prisons, including Aquino, his most redoubtable Liberal opponent. No one in Washington objected to this wholesale suppression of civil liberties—a long-familiar, welcome procedure in the U.S. conception of how best to run Third World regimes.

Marcos had arranged for his executive secretary, Alejandro Melchor, to arrive in the United States just as martial law was declared, and after briefing Washington officials and the World Bank on Marcos's plans to help both U.S. business and introduce some overdue reforms, he obtained a pledge of far greater World Bank aid and met with most important American companies involved in the Philippines, assuring them that there was no more danger from nationalist legislation and Supreme Court rulings. On October 3 Marcos issued a new foreign investment decree aimed at attracting oil and mining capital. U.S. oilmen waxed enthusiastic, and *The New York Times'* Manila correspondent in late October concluded, "The American business community in the Philippines has greeted with relief the results of the Sept. 23 declaration of martial law."[6] It would mean the end of economic anti-Americanism, at the least, and Marcos's subsequent declarations for free enterprise and foreign investment, and abolition of unions and strikes, sustained this glow of mutual admiration over the next years. The honeymoon, however, assumed that both sides would help each other, and Marcos very much needed aid at this point in time.

In essence, the U.S. relationship to the authoritarian regime changed from a defensive to a dominant one after twelve years of anti-American agitation. The economic aspect of this restoration was crucial, given the immense debts Marcos had run up, and Washington's responsibility for influencing the economy, in accordance with its global policy, was transferred mainly to the World Bank and the IMF. U.S. bilateral economic aid dropped from $125 million in 1973 to $72 million (mainly as loans) in 1979, while military aid during 1973–76—essentially a rental payment for use of the bases—was twice as high as the average for the preceding four years. Political relations with Marcos during these years were excellent, his qualities—corruption notwithstanding—much appreciated, save for one gnawing concern that was to remain in the background throughout this period but that was later to emerge as a serious problem: his wife, Imelda.

The United States had no experience with such a person anywhere in the Third World. When William H. Sullivan replaced Byroade in spring 1973 he raised the first alarm regarding a woman he regarded as shrewd, consummately ambitious, and astonishingly corrupt and incompetent. It was clear she wished to succeed her husband eventually and establish a dynasty, but for the moment that danger was more abstract than real. For while Ferdinand could perform services in aborting the nationalist momentum that was gathering, Imelda might wreck everything that had been accomplished. This problem was all the greater because of the highly personalized nature of the regime Marcos was creating.

Marcos in his own way remained enigmatic, pursuing many diverse and essentially conflicting policies at the same time—above all, the aggrandizement of his own power. Ready to evoke nationalist, populist, and even neutralist rhetoric if it suited his purposes, he also retained a sufficient amount of economic protectionist legislation to preserve the national bourgeoisie. Yet he opened the door wide to foreign investors in fact, if not always with comprehensive legislation, at the same time allowing pliable technocrats to play an unprecedented new role in conjunction with World Bank and IMF advisers. This technocratic impulse, which the United States especially encouraged despite its readiness also to tolerate Marcos's venality, he more than counteracted with what was later called "crony capitalism," the transfer of huge private and public funds and privileges to his family and allies, as well as probably the greatest amount of personal corruption (in absolute rather than relative terms) in any Third World nation since 1945.

In the short run Marcos was America's puppet, granting it economic privileges and base rights, but he also ignored much that it desired to see accomplished. But in the long run he so traumatized Filipino life and society, creating all of the essential preconditions for the emergence of a powerful Left opposition, that the problems facing the United States, though very different, were far greater by the end of his regime than ever. And it was the threat of his wife continuing the rape of the nation that eventually compelled Washington to distance itself somewhat from him. For while Marcos was ready to make a tactical alliance with the United States, ultimately he was acting on behalf of his own account, and this was the most recurrent of all the U.S. dilemmas in relying on Third World dictators. America wanted puppets, but efficient ones, and it was never to find them anywhere.

While income distribution became somewhat more inequitable after 1970, reaching 59 percent for the richest fifth in the early 1980s, it was the decisive shift within the elite itself that comprised the most significant change in the economy and power. Marcos decided to reduce drastically the economic holdings of his premartial law political enemies, especially among the Liberals, and he transferred these to his family and closest political allies. Members of the traditional oligarchy who were ready to collaborate with him, and there were many, were left in peace. And, more generally, he allocated immense contracts, concessions, and cash subsidies, amounting to virtual gifts, to his cronies. Suffice it to say that in the year after Marcos's fall in February 1986, the new government sequestered 181 companies of his 5 closest cronies, 2 of them relatives, and nearly 100 companies of his other assorted allies. Together they possessed 56 radio and TV stations, as well as immense tracts of land, buildings, and much else. Government loans to just 10 of his cronies amounted to at least $2.4 billion. Marcos's own fortune is still not fully assessed, but estimates run up to $15 billion, and $5 billion is a conservative figure. Attempting to provide an analytically coherent description of this system defies structured categories because its capriciousness and contradictory nature makes it too convoluted, for Marcos's "New Society," as he called it, was anything but a stable, rationalized, and predictable order. The net effect of such "gangsterist" systems, which existed in China until 1949 and Latin America later, is that they traumatize already fragile societies and accelerate those social and economic developments that produce a strong Left opposition, putting revolution on the agenda where it might otherwise not be.

In the case of the Philippines, while Marcos levied a direct charge on the fortunes of the politically ambitious rival oligarchs, the greatest cost was indirect, and the people paid it. It was here that the United States to some extent lost control of the process, for while it sought primarily to protect its own economic and strategic position, using Marcos as a tool to do so, it scarcely realized that he, like so many like him elsewhere, would further pauperize the nation and foster a far more powerful Left challenge to American interests.

Marcos also basically and permanently altered the framework of power that existed in the nation since 1946 by transforming the military, which had always been relatively small and apolitical, into a personal instrument, in the process creating a crucial new arbiter of power and politics such as existed in many, even most, Third World nations. One of his first acts after declaring martial law was to promote officers he could trust, increase the pay of all of them, and raise living allowances for the lower ranks. He systematically doubled the size of the army by 1977, advancing loyal officers from his home province of Ilocos Norte, and recruiting soldiers from there as well. Far more important yet was his dramatic enlargement of officers' administrative and judicial responsibilities in normally civilian posts, making them key political executives also. The United States welcomed this trend in the Philippines as it did everywhere in the Third World, believing that since they had trained thousands of these officers they presumably would also become technocratic "modernizers" and advance American goals. Marcos, however, had far better control over them at the inception, but his own crony officers created a split within the officer corps that later further eroded the stability of his regime. In this role the military also became key corruptionists, habituated to the perquisites and exercise of state power. Measures initially intended to strengthen Marcos's authority soon created a potential countervailing force and military rivals for power—an enduring legacy for those who were to follow him.

THE WORLD BANK TRACK

The World Bank's role in the Philippines before 1973 had been relatively modest compared to other Third World nations its size, although the IMF's influence over the currency, balance of payments, and foreign borrowing was significant after 1970. With martial law, at the United States' behest the World Bank embarked on a comprehensive effort to restructure the Philippine economy along those classic lines it advocated everywhere, one that was to affect the economy profoundly. But Marcos always pursued several economic strategies in tandem quite eclectically, amassing the immediate advantages and long-run liabilities of all of them. He welcomed World Bank intervention insofar as it provided funds and helped obtain private loans to advance his crony capitalist strategy, and when the destructive consequences of bank policies and his own corruption demanded remedial measures, he accepted yet greater bank control. At the same time, he never wholly abandoned earlier protectionist legislation.

The World Bank's approach was both familiar and simple, stressing export-led development, primarily via traditional raw materials and labor-intensive industrialization, and in principle it discouraged import-substitute industrialization as inefficient. This standard formula also called for increased investment from both foreign and domestic sources, the latter requiring a restructuring of the local banking industry to mobilize sufficient funds. To implement this policy as well as cope with its failure later, it compelled Manila to devalue the peso whenever required—first in 1973, again in 1975, once more in 1981, and of course thereafter. Three export-processing zones with special labor, tariff, tax, and other exemptions were created to help execute the strategy.

The World Bank's leverage was its ability to obtain, in cooperation with the IMF, access to private borrowings from the world's main banking centers as well as lend its own funds, and this it did in the Philippines as in dozens of other nations. The Philippines' external debt to public and private sources stood at $2.3 billion in 1973 and rose to $3.8 billion in 1975, $8.4 billion in 1979, and over three times that by 1986. Servicing the interest on this debt amounted to 8 percent of export earnings in 1972 and rose to 31 percent by 1982, making the Philippines by far the most deeply indebted Asian nation. Worse yet, the World Bank's strategy never worked, partially because of various obstacles Marcos created but mainly because it was irrelevant and mistaken by any criterion, its own included. By 1979 it considered 63 percent of its programs as "problem projects."[7]

The main dilemma was that the Philippine economy's orientation toward a world market made it vulnerable to all those external forces it could not control, and while the terms of trade favored its exports through 1974, by 1977 they were nearly half the 1970 level. To a growing extent to provide essential imports for its export processing zones as well as pay for oil, the balance of trade, which had never exceeded a $300 million deficit before and was positive in 1973, shot up to a negative $418 million in 1974, nearly tripled the following year, and reached almost $2 billion by 1980—forcing the nation to go more deeply into debt. With all these mounting problems, World Bank and IMF influence over economic policy increased.

Although there were many examples, the classic case of sugar reveals what happened to export-led primary materials development. Here Marcos obeyed the World Bank prescription to expand exports, assigning responsibility to his closest cronies, who were given much of the land of his Liberal rivals in the process. Production grew, mills were constructed, and complex marketing and funding mechanisms were imposed upon the industry, in part with IMF funds. But with a dramatic fall in world prices for sugar in 1975 and a global decline in world demand thereafter, the Philippines found they were merely one cog in a grossly overexpanded world sugar industry, partially the consequence of too many nations pursuing the same World Bank-endorsed strategy. Twenty-eight percent of the value of all of its exports in 1974, sugar fell to a scant 5 percent by 1979—and the economy was stuck with a largely useless industry that Marcos then proceeded to subsidize so his cronies could continue making money.

The World Bank/IMF plan was also unable to cope with the growth of protectionism throughout the world by the later 1970s against Filipino garments and textiles employing the cheapest labor in Asia and the lowest-paid among U.S. firms operating anywhere abroad. Business interests in rich nations threatened by cheap imports did not share the World Bank's and the United States' ideology on the international division of labor, a reality even Marcos understood. Moreover, foreign investors installed or expanded operations in the Philippines, like everywhere, by borrowing the vast bulk of their capital needs locally and then shipping their profits home, and the pattern of decapitalization that existed in the 1960s persisted throughout the 1970s, so that the foreign capital outflow far exceeded the inflow during the latter part of the decade. Given the obvious complexities of relating to the world economy, Marcos ignored World Bank and IMF suggestions that he smash the indigenous manufacturing sector. Manufacturing's share of the gross domestic product remained constant throughout the decade, and toward the end of it Marcos began to formulate major industrialization plans over World Bank objections, and his toleration of the existing industrialists and plans to have his cronies move into these sectors became sources of deep dispute between the two sides. Although most of his schemes were never implemented, they revealed that Marcos was reluctant to follow World Bank advice unreservedly.

Neither Marcos nor the United States thought a renewal of Laurel-Langley per se essential, and it expired in 1974. American officials were confident that Marcos would find loopholes if necessary, as with a March 1973 foreign investment law that guaranteed investors new rights and went a considerable way to assuage their anxieties. Moreover, many mechanisms for getting around the foreign ownership restrictions continued on the books, and Japanese firms preferred joint ventures with local entrepreneurs, while Marcos's cronies especially welcomed the opportunity to link up with them—something most American companies were loath to do. Marcos granted U.S. investors a grace period after 1974, in effect to avail themselves of these loopholes, and they were never forced to divest ownership. But he also tried to bargain to gain access to protected American markets—thereby pursuing policies pleasing to local nationalists as well as to the Americans. Such contradictory programs soon became a bone of contention, though World Bank pressures often forced Marcos to alter them to conform to its plan to attract new foreign investments.

Yet U.S. companies did not rush to invest in the Philippines, despite all the concessions, cheap strike-free labor, and tax benefits, because there was more money to be made elsewhere in Asia, and the Philippines' share of U.S. capital in the region fell from 46 percent of the total in 1950 to 28 percent in 1970 and 11 percent in 1982. U.S. firms still controlled thirteen of the thirty biggest companies in 1973 and accounted for roughly half of all foreign investments during the 1970s (about twice as much as Japan's), but the larger scale of U.S. multinational operations and opportunities in neighboring states led them to go there. U.S. businessmen remained important as a political constituency interested in the nation, and they supported Marcos throughout the decade, but the relative stability of their economic role made strategic and political influences on American policy greater than ever. The United States still remained the nation's largest trading partner, though Japan in 1970 equaled it and was only marginally behind it during the decade. But U.S. control of a quarter of all trade in 1980 was still a far cry from a share three times that in 1950.

For all these reasons, especially their use of local capital, overseas investors never performed the role the World Bank's theory assigned them. Economically, the Philippines was subjected to exploitation from many directions, both local and foreign, only deepening its already grave social problems.

THE CONSEQUENCES OF REFORM

Land, above all, remained the key to the Philippines' future, for most of the nation lived in rural areas, and a majority of the labor force was in agriculture. The movement off the land, while important, has still not altered the basically agrarian nature of the society, and it has only reflected the fact that the Philippines ranks with Bangladesh, Indonesia, and Afghanistan as the four poorest nations of Asia. Since the end of World War Two its per capita food production had remained constant, and in 1969–71 the average Filipino consumed only 86 percent of the daily required energy supply—the rural population even less. By 1971 the percentage of the rural population living below the poverty threshold was dramatically higher than in 1965, reaching 64 percent and making the Philippines the second-poorest nation in Asia. Its rice and corn yields per hectare, the two basic staples, were the lowest in Asia after the war. Even if the organized Left was unprepared, the countryside was objectively ripe for rebellion when martial law was declared.

Marcos's "New Society" also embodied a distinctly populist dimension, and he immediately proclaimed his intention to implement land reform in rice and corn lands only—some 5.7 million hectares, or slightly more than half of all cultivated land. CIA analysts noted skeptically at the inception that sufficient reform legislation had been on the books for years and that Marcos had done nothing about it because of his "unwillingness to alienate the smaller landowners, many of whom are civil servants and military officers. . . ."[8] They frankly doubted that he would do better in the future.

The World Bank allocated a large portion of its loans to agriculture, both directly and to create an infrastructure, and especially favored propagating the "Green Revolution" employing better seeds, fertilizers, machinery, and the like. It was in this domain that it was to have its greatest social impact after 1972. The bank's own projects had little to do with land reform, since its emphasis was on increasing productivity rather than redistribution, a standard American position elsewhere as well, but the fact that it made credit available to recipients of new land helped commercialize the program—with dire consequences. It preferred to stress export crops, which were exempt from land reform and which increased in hectarage twice as quickly as food crops between 1970 and 1985, so that the proportion of all land devoted to food dropped over that period. The bank's effort, in effect, to commercialize smaller peasants bypassed entirely, as did land reform, the landless rural laborers, who numbered about half of the entire rural labor force but whose lives would be hurt by any form of modernization that reduced the demand for their labor. Indeed, combined with the near-landless tenants, these marginal sectors comprised 81 percent of the entire rural labor force in 1978—and their problems were ignored from the inception.

The land reform operation was quite simple underneath its usual bureaucratic jargon. It exempted landlords possessing less than seven hectares from reform, as well as certain categories of holdings between seven and twenty-four hectares—so that the tenants who worked for them, or a majority of the total number, were automatically ignored. Numerous loopholes reduced the land available for reform to a theoretical maximum of 1.5 million hectares, slightly over a quarter of the rice and corn lands, and of this only half was designated for actual land transfer to 400,000 tenants. The remainder was to be assigned to 600,000 tenants as protected lessees only, presumably with lower rents. In effect, slightly more than an eighth of the rice and corn lands was targeted for redistribution, though in practice less than a twentieth was affected. But to get a full title of ownership required the tenant to pay 15 annual installments to a land bank that had already compensated the landlord, and while they could get a certificate of land transfer before that date, the final transfer required full payment. Some 240,000 peasants obtained their piece of paper by 1980, but only 1,600 peasants (receiving 1,459 hectares) had become true owners. U.S. experts by that time concluded that the exceedingly modest program, which was unraveling, "has suffered from implementation problems to date. The reform has not yet achieved the tenure objectives originally set forth."[9]

Marcos' land reform had many other problems, the most obvious being credit for its ostensible beneficiaries. Smaller ones had access to none, and the large majority of them failed to make their required annual compensation payments. Many simply fell back into debt to former landlords and traditional usurers. More important yet was that the Green Revolution's reliance on commercial inputs, in the Philippines as everywhere it has been applied, increased farm costs more quickly than income, further magnifying the important role of lenders and usury in rural areas. Tenancy therefore increased rather than declined from 1971 to 1980 by about a third for all forms of agriculture, so that in 1985 about a quarter of the agricultural labor force was composed of tenants, while half were landless laborers. Tenancy even in rice and corn lands increased over this period, for reform without adequate credit could not alter the process of dispossession long under way in the agrarian society.

Indeed, by the end of the 1970s the emphasis on export agriculture and the Green Revolution had begun to effect profound changes in the countryside, making it possible for the New People's Army to expand greatly with them, transforming it into the powerful and growing force it is today. Population growth required greater emphasis on food for domestic use rather than export crops, and eventually it became necessary to import cereals. The use of herbicides and machinery reduced the need for labor in rice and sugar dramatically, increasing both underemployment and unemployment sharply. By the late 1970s American officials had begun to notice this alarming trend and the impact of land reform in widening the gap between the rich and the poor and helping to create growing numbers living in the most abject poverty. With the labor force after 1960 growing at a rate two and a half times faster than labor demand in nonagricultural sectors, and both Marcos and the World Bank opposed to labor-intensive industrialization for its own sake, all these seemingly abstract numbers comprised a recipe for hunger—and revolution.

The real wages of agricultural labor had begun to fall after 1960 as part of a long-term pattern. During 1976–78 they rose somewhat, but by the end of the decade and thereafter they were at a post-1960 low point. The same trend held true for skilled labor, both urban and rural. In the aggregate, according to an official estimate, those under the household poverty threshold in the entire nation grew from 42 to 58 percent between 1971 and 1985, the rural share being higher, though not qualitatively so. Always among the worst in Asia for public health standards, in the poorest provinces, such as Negros Occidental, 70 percent of the children seven years or under were malnourished in 1982. Nationally that year, fully 67 percent of all households were consuming less than 100 percent of their essential minimum energy needs, and 41 percent of all farmworkers earned incomes inadequate to buy 80 percent of their families' nutritional requirements.[10]

FROM NEW SOCIETY TO CONFRONTATION

Washington's main role in the Philippines after 1972 was to work through the World Bank and the IMF to seek to reintegrate it more thoroughly into a

United States-led world economic system—in effect, to undo the Filipino elite's unruly use of their independence. Wandering down the path of nationalist capitalism was even less tolerable from a former colony than from Latin American nations, but in reality they were both expressions of the same global impulse, for which the United States now had one solution: the multilateral banks. Marcos saw the World Bank's and the IMF's role, however, as simply another way of extracting more wealth for himself and his coterie and allies. He never accepted its ideological premises, and he himself had none in the true sense of that term. Neither Marcos nor those seeking to control him were to succeed to the extent that was essential for the final attainment of their goals, and both sides opportunistically exploited each other for their own ends. The irony was that both the American and Marcos's strategies, either alone but especially in tandem, were predestined to do irreparable damage to the Filipino society and people, guaranteeing that in due course the monumental task of reconstruction would become the responsibility of others. In 1972 the Filipino Left was divided and small; a decade later it was a large and growing mass movement.

Marcos was consistently intractable in dealing with the United States insofar as money was involved. America's expulsion from Vietnam in 1975, however, gave the Philippine bases a greatly increased strategic but especially symbolic significance in its overall Asian calculations, and Marcos sought to exploit the situation to obtain more money, directly or indirectly, for their use. It would be an error to focus too much on these complications, which began under the Ford Administration and were resolved when the Carter Administration agreed to provide $500 million in military aid over five years as de facto rent. There was never any question but that the two sides would reach an accord. Throughout the decade successive administrations left the Philippines to relatively lower-level officials to handle, and they cultivated Marcos and studiously ignored his human rights violations during the Carter Administration's selective and ambiguous phase of expressing concern over the issue elsewhere. Washington always appreciated Marcos and loyally supported him, faults and all.

By far the most important dimension of America's policy in the Philippines was not its conscious designs or quite typical diplomatic relations but rather the immense structural consequences, both intended and unintended, of the economic institutions and policies it sought to impose on the nation along with its important (but not decisive) aid to sustaining the Marcos regime. And regardless of the administration, Washington never resolved the question of who would fill the vacuum the Marcos era was creating. Ultimately it preferred to wait for the inevitable crisis to arrive before it turned its concerted attention again to the Philippine problem, only to support Marcos until it was certain he was about to be destroyed anyway. The dilemma was that the older nationalist elite and oligarchs could not function in the extraparliamentary environment that Marcos imposed, and the economic forces and malaise that Marcos, the United States, the World Bank, and the IMF created transcended their programmatic resources to cope with. Even after power returned to the traditional oligarchy in February 1986, it could not solve the legacy of difficulties Marcos and his predecessors left, nor undo the new power dynamics inherent in the large, politicized army. Both before and after Marcos's demise it was clear that the ultimate challenge to the United States in the Pacific would come from the resurgent Left, now the CPP and its NPA, as well as radicalized sectors of the Catholic Church and broad constituencies that reflected the ideological diversity of radical forces no longer committed to older Russian, Chinese, or social democratic doctrines—groups whose very pluralism was a measure of their health and adaptability. This alone guaranteed that the Philippines would end as it began: the most important nation in Southeast Asia for the United States, one of continuing and deep significance—but with a far greater challenge from the Left than before.

The Philippines remains a classic example of the United States' sustained dilemma of living with the consequences of puppets whom it aids and on whom it is dependent, men who both accelerate and preside over structurally conditioned crises that create social forces and movements that eventually challenge America's hegemony even more decisively. The decade of the 1970s, after all of Washington's efforts to develop military power and doctrines appropriate to the Third World, was increasingly to become the preeminent period for such structurally induced crises and organizations, posing a myriad of challenges to it in all the regions of the world. It was clear that the key issues defining the future of the Third World were neither military nor political but social and economic, and if arms and diplomacy could not cope with them, they were still capable of tempting the United States to intervene in new situations in which it could only lose when confronting able opponents. America's own social and economic program, as in the Philippines, only aggravated already grave existing economic, social, and political problems. There, as elsewhere in the Third World, U.S. policies in the 1970s revealed how impotent as well as dangerous American power had become as it sought to relate to the main trends of our times.

Iran
and the Eclipse
of American Power

*S*UPPLANTING BRITISH POWER IN
IRAN in 1954 was the single most crucial aspect of the United States' post-
war policy of penetrating the Middle East, leaving it with both enormous
rewards and responsibilities. While the magnitude of its gains were easy
for Washington to calculate in terms of oil, it never contemplated seriously
the unpredictable full extent to which it would also have to confront troublesome changes within the region, ranging from rising middle-class nationalism to resurgent Muslim fundamentalism. As Washington's attention
in the Middle East after 1954 moved principally to the states closer to the
Mediterranean, all its objectives and policies in Iran were focused both on
and through the Shah. With the Shah now an absolute monarch, it could
not have been otherwise. No other nation in the entire postwar era illustrated better the risks to America's power wherever it relied on proxies to
advance its interests.

The Shah was a complex, aloof man ruling over a troubled nation coping
with major social changes yet still under the heavy yoke of traditional Islam.
Although he was later sentimentalized in the United States, as Kissinger
described him, as "that rarest of leaders, an unconditional ally, and one
whose understanding of the world situation enhanced our own," he possessed his own agenda for action.[1] Pro-American in large part because he was
anti-British, he had a keen geopolitical sense of U.S. goals in the region and
was eager to exploit his alliance to reinforce his power—but on his own terms
if possible. He knew American backing had helped to save his throne, yet he
harbored qualms about the new oil conditions resulting from the 1954 agreement displacing the British, and he was always skeptical that Washington

would intervene to save him from military threats from the USSR or his other neighbors.

The Shah relied on the military as the basis of his power throughout his career, for the army's role during the 1954 coup was far more crucial than the CIA's, and he carefully filled its upper ranks with loyalists and permitted them to share generously in the corruption that was endemic to his regime. The nationalist middle classes that had supported Mossadegh were antagonistic toward him, and he did nothing to court their favor. As a Baha'i, he was also hostile to Shiite traditionalism, by far the largest religion in Iran, and he was prepared to challenge their most sacrosanct beliefs on the inferior status of women. By 1961, when Kennedy came to office, it was clear to the few American officials dealing with Iran that his political base was too narrow, and for several years they actively advocated efforts to reach out to the middle-class intelligentsia that had also supported Mossadegh: junior civil servants and officers, teachers, professionals, and the like. The most immediate threat, they concluded, came not from Russia but from internal upheaval, and until mid-1962 the Shah tolerated a reformist group within his weak cabinet, when he fired his pro-American premier and assumed virtually total power, initiating profound changes reflecting his own ideas and interests.

The Shah's most important action was to implement a land reform law, one that was ultimately to prove the most serious error of his entire career. The reform offended the Muslim religious leaders deeply, in part because they owned large tracts and underwrote much of their work from their revenues, but also damaged an important sector of the urban bourgeoisie with land-holdings. At the same time, while abolishing virtual serfdom among the peasants, he did nothing to provide the credit and infrastructure essential for them to benefit from the reform, so that usury, insecure tenure, and commercial relations typical of so many other poor nations replaced the relative stability of virtual feudalism for many peasants. The reform, above all, touched only a small minority, and was inconsistently and corruptly applied, with richer peasants gaining most and poorer peasants least, and the state superceding the landowners in many areas as the prime villain for the masses. Agricultural productivity declined, and many peasants were forced into the cities to survive, a trend the Shah encouraged because he believed it would aid industrialization. Land reform helped to shatter the cohesion of a traditional order, traumatizing the countryside. Above all, it made the Shah new and implacable enemies among the religious leaders and intensified middle-class hostility toward him.

From 1963 onward the main threat to the Shah came from the mullahs, the religious leaders, and riots they led in the major cities in June 1963 resulted in well over a thousand deaths and brutal repression. It was at this time that the Ayatollah Ruhollah Khomeini was arrested and later sent into exile, and control over the activities of Islamic leaders intensified. They in turn rightly saw U.S. hands behind the Shah and his reforms, and anti-Americanism became integral to their politics. But while the United States had encouraged reforms, the Shah had implemented them according to his purposes and limited, corrupt administrative abilities, and American analysts thought he had handled land reform badly, dispossessing the traditional elite and fanatical clergy while failing to mobilize the peasantry behind him. They saw that he was now more dependent than ever on the military, but for the remainder of the decade they concluded there was nothing more they could do except help the Shah retain the officers' loyalty. Although the Johnson Administration initially tried to impose some contingencies on aid, the Shah established greater leverage in his dealing with the United States by successfully pressuring the oil consortium for greater revenues and by threatening to turn to the USSR for sophisticated arms if America refused to sell them. U.S. attempts to define his basic policies ended. The key to America's strategy remained the monarchy: "The Shah, therefore," the NSC concluded in 1965, "remains a linchpin for the safeguarding of our basic security interests in Iran," and Iran was essential to protect NATO and Pakistan on its flanks, assure the flow of oil to Europe, and maintain a barrier to Russia.[2] While the U.S. rationale altered, its fundamental assumptions and goals remained constant.

Although the Shah was unable to mobilize broad public support for his program to modernize Iranian society from the top downward, rapid economic growth throughout the 1960s and thereafter provided him with ample resources to co-opt much of the potential opposition leadership among educated elements, and those he could not buy out he simply repressed. With a political order under his absolute power, he began to change a backward rural society economically and socially, especially strengthening the military, upon whom he lavished increasing amounts of equipment but, more important, privileges. His devotion to the army was intensified after 1965 when the United States distanced itself from Pakistan, their mutual ally, during its war with India, and by this time his priorities had shifted from a concern with Russia to coping with his hostile neighbors, especially the radical Iraqis. The Shah after the mid-1960s was ready to collaborate loyally with the United States when their interests coincided, but he never became its obedient servant.

Britain's decision at the end of 1967 to leave the Persian Gulf by 1971 cemented relations between the United States and the Shah irrevocably because now their mutual needs in the region coincided more than ever. The Nixon Administration's decision to make Iranian power in the Persian Gulf a surrogate for its own was inevitable given its own inability to fill the potential vacuum vulnerable, above all, to Iraqi-backed radicalism thrusting into the conservative but unstable oil-rich Gulf. From this time onward the United

States courted the Shah, who shrewdly encouraged Kissinger's geopolitical fears to advance his own goals. For nearly a decade he cultivated American dependency on himself, and Washington's earlier concerns about his internal policies were forgotten altogether as it attributed glowing personal virtues to him not only in public statements but also in private analyses. He was integral to U.S. power in the Middle East and, realizing it, he exploited the situation to the hilt.

The Shah wanted modern arms from the United States as well as from other nations, but since he had ceased to be a recipient of military aid the Nixon Administration was willing to sell him what he could afford, especially after 1971. Iran, Washington calculated, would be better able to play the role of an effective proxy but also to help reverse the rising deficit in the American balance of payments, not to mention augmenting its weaponsmakers' profits. But in 1969 and 1970 the only way the Shah could get the huge sums he needed for arms was to increase his oil revenues, and given the shift in the world oil market in favor of producers he made the most of it. He initially extracted more money from companies in Iran, but in 1971 he took the lead in organizing the Gulf states to raise their prices sharply, and in January 1973 he announced he would not renew the 1954 agreement when it expired in 1979, in effect nationalizing the oil industry and accomplishing what Mossadegh had unsuccessfully attempted earlier. Much to American distress, the Shah was a leader in raising oil prices until 1976, when demand for Iranian oil fell—but by that time the damage to Western interests had been done. His arms purchases were always linked to oil prices, and ultimately Western consumers paid for them. Meanwhile, he further traumatized Iranian society.

The Shah ordered $135 million in arms in 1970, almost three times that the following year, and $4.3 billion in 1974 after oil prices exploded. In 1977 he ordered $5.7 billion more, or $20 billion for the 1970–78 period, making Iran the purchaser of one-quarter of all American arms sold abroad during that period. Arms salesmen poured into Tehran after 1972 and paid huge commissions to officers who arranged the purchases of their wares, intensifying both corruption and conspicuous consumption. The Shah paid the high prices demanded because he craved arms, and they kept his generals happy, but the arms were far too complex for the military to maintain and operate despite the fact that a large share of the country's skilled labor was diverted into servicing them. To remedy the problem, American military personnel and contract employees, numbering seventy-two hundred by 1977, poured into the nation and became a visible new elite, further testifying to the Shah's dependence on Yankees.

Like every nation undergoing rapid changes, there were economic winners and losers. The biggest gainer of all was the Shah himself, who through state funds and family corporations was estimated in January 1979 to be worth at least a billion dollars and probably much more, and his family at least twice that. Next came the top officers and those industrialists and construction interests with access to state funding, as well as senior civil servants. The life-style of such elements was luxurious and highly noticeable, and it deeply alienated the losers, who comprised the vast majority. Iran's inflation doubled to over 20 percent annually between 1971 and 1975, reaching 50 percent the following year, and expensive food had to be imported in ever-larger quantities because the Shah did nothing to stanch the growing misery in the rural areas—still 58 percent of the population in 1972. On the contrary, he wished to see peasants move to the cities, where they became typical Third World urban poor—unemployed, disoriented, and more miserable than ever in their vast slums. The lower ranks of the military, too, were underpaid and alienated, and the petit bourgeoisie was also unable to maintain its standard of living. All of these increasingly marginalized elements fell under the influence of the mullahs, who excoriated the Shah, modernism, and American predominance with a fearless wrath the Left could never imitate.

The Shah's word was law, and he repressed those who opposed him, not only through SAVAK, the umbrella security organization the CIA had created and Israelis trained, but by systematic control over the press, labor, universities, and any institution capable of undermining his absolute power. SAVAK operated a vast system of informers and agents and used torture routinely, and in 1974–75 had, at the least, some thousands in its prisons—although the opposition claimed twenty-five thousand to a hundred thousand. After 1971, when resistance to the Shah's policies from especially middle-class and educated constituencies began to increase, SAVAK was especially active and brutal, and its close relationship with the CIA further identified the United States with their oppressors in the minds of the population. This linkage actually involved a division of labor: SAVAK told the CIA about Iranian internal affairs, becoming its nearly exclusive source of information, while the CIA agents in Iran concentrated on gathering data on Russia and training SAVAK in a variety of techniques essential to its political work, including torture. The CIA also reported to SAVAK on politics among Iranian students in the United States. In early 1977, after the Carter Administration began proclaiming its adherence to "human rights" abroad, the Shah made cosmetic changes in SAVAK's work but nothing more, and its ties with the CIA continued until his fall.

By 1977 Iran was institutionally inflexible and devoid of any ability to reform itself short of complete upheaval, yet its compounded economic and social problems had become grave, and the mounting pressures from below to do something about them had been completely frustrated politically. Profound economic and social innovations since 1954 had deepened class divisions and led inexorably to a total revolution, and this was all the more likely because the United States had helped the military to abort a relatively open political system in 1954 because it feared both the Left and the national bourgeoisie but not the militant mullahs. But even eliminating the absolute monarchy could not undo the structural transformation that had occurred since then. The Shah had already extensively upset an agrarian nation and wholly alienated deeply rooted Islamic forces that he could never extirpate. The Iranian impasse was a situation largely of America's own making, from reinstalling the Shah to power in 1954 to endorsing everything he stood for and its vital help in implementing his destructive policies. It left U.S. strategy in the Middle East wholly dependent on one man, guaranteeing that its next major conflict—and loss—would be with passionately anti-American Islamic fundamentalism. The seeds of this confrontation had been planted, both in Iran and the Middle East, over two decades earlier.

THE FALL OF THE SHAH

The Carter Administration was unable to reverse this situation when it assumed office, even though it immediately assigned Iran the same role in the region as the Republicans had done, depending entirely on the Shah both to remain in power and to dictate Iranian policy. But even if Carter had opposed all the Shah had done and was doing, he could not have reversed the confrontational nature of the struggle within Iran, one that pitted virtually an entire nation against one man, his army, and their satraps. For the Shah had no class basis independent of the small privileged order he autocratically presided over, and by 1976 hatred of the United States was synonymous with opposition to the Shah and, most important, the kind of society he had constructed.

During 1977 the Carter Administration supported the Shah unequivocally, resisting strongly Congress's objections to Iran's purchase of AWACS advance warning planes because of the Shah's notorious human rights violations. It exempted Iran from nominal restrictions on arms sales the Administration proclaimed for other countries, and to reassure the Shah of its sincerity, invited him to Washington in November 1977, and Carter went to Tehran the following month. "Iran is an island of stability in one of the more troubled areas of the world," the effusive president proclaimed: "This is a great tribute to you, Your Majesty, and to your leadership and to the respect, admiration, and love which your people give to you."[3] The problem was that official Washington really believed what the president was saying.

CIA analysts as late as September 1978 were predicting that the Shah would remain in office for another decade, though in January of that year the first bloody struggles between Muslims and the authorities had begun, some involving large numbers in the major cities. Indeed, the United States sent crowd-control equipment and tear gas to the Shah in August just as he slightly relaxed press censorship. Much more important than bad intelligence, however, was that "Our decision-making circuits were heavily overloaded" during the fall of 1978 until the crisis became very grave, as Brzezinski later recounted, and everyone's attention was "riveted on other issues, all extraordinarily time-consuming, personally absorbing, and physically demanding."[4] Such physical limits exist often and illustrate vividly the managerial difficulties of trying to run an empire. Yet it would not have made any difference had intelligence been accurate and had there been abundant time to think about it. Apart from the irreversible consequences of past errors, neither the Shah nor Ayatollah Khomeini, who emerged as the leader of the opposition, were going to pursue American advice unless they had their own valid reasons for doing so. The United States could never be a decisive participant in Iran, whatever the retrospective speculations of Brzezinski, unless it was ready to send potentially unlimited manpower to fight there indefinitely. But this was never even contemplated, and the Carter Administration remained an engrossed but impotent spectator, incapable of altering the course of events.

From late October onward the State Department and Brzezinski related to Iran by fighting with each other, for by this time the ambassador in Tehran, William Sullivan, while arguing for support to the Shah, was also advising "thinking the unthinkable" about options should he or the military fail.[5] The Shah had broached the option of a military government, which might then unleash the unlimited violence at the command of four hundred thousand soldiers, but rather than give advice, the White House simply assured the Shah of its unequivocal support for whatever he chose to do. While the Shah opted for a military cabinet, he hesitated to use full force. Brzezinski, on the other hand, wanted the Shah to employ as much repression as necessary before the opposition got out of hand, and he preferred a tough military without the Shah to a moderate one with him. Those who thought the Shah should be given time to weave through the maze he confronted, without exact advice from Washington, prevailed, but the highest officials were profoundly, bitterly divided, and their acrimonious struggle dissipated crucial weeks. In this context Carter favored a time-consuming strategy, and both the Shah and the president vacillated.

Meanwhile, mobs mainly under the influence of the mullahs took over the streets, and both the Shah and Secretary of State Cyrus Vance, among many others, came to realize that if the army were ordered to shoot at the priests and their followers, the poorly paid conscripts from the villages, themselves devout, would refuse to do so and the army would instead fight among itself. At this point the United States and its proxy ceased to have any hope of reversing the largely uncontrollable forces at work within Iran. Whether or not the Shah remained, Carter and all his advisers agreed that to destroy the military would eliminate Iran's future value in the region. Even Brzezinski, forever lusting for the military's use of an iron fist because, as he warned Carter, "world politics was not a kindergarten," concluded that the military's unity was even more crucial.[6] The worst scenario, from the American viewpoint, was for the military and mullahs to destroy each other and thereby open the door to a resurgent Left walking into power over their remains.

The resolution to this impasse came at the end of 1978 when the British urged the Shah to designate a civilian head of the government who was capable of dealing with the opposition, and then to leave Iran for two months. On January 2 he appointed Shapour Bakhtiar, a veteran of Mossadegh's National Front, as prime minister, but carefully left all control over the military with the generals, foredooming his chances for success. Several days later both the Carter Administration and the French also urged the Shah to leave, and while the Americans wanted Bakhtiar to succeed, they also urged the military to be ready to restore order if he could not. On January 16 the Shah left Iran, hoping it would be temporary and that during his absence the situation would improve. Instead, Khomeini returned from exile on February 1 and the military began to disintegrate. More and more military units joined Khomeini or abandoned their arms after he declared a new government on February 5. The remnants of the Shah's regime quickly disappeared, the officers included, and over the next weeks militant Islam consolidated control, presenting the United States with the greatest challenge to its power in the Middle East since World War Two.

FROM PROXIES TO RAPID DEPLOYMENT FORCE

The U.S. confrontation with Islam in Iran was the logic of the realities of Middle Eastern history and represented the failure of a policy that had ignored the dominant facts of religion and nationalism to focus on a fear of Communism—which was unable to organize significant domestic support in any Middle Eastern nation before 1978—and the Soviet Union, which in fact was much exploited for its arms but unable to dictate internal or external policies to any Middle Eastern state. No less significant, Iran once again revealed that Washington could not rely on regional surrogates as an effective substitute for its own troops and that the policy Nixon had made into a doctrine in 1969 was doomed to failure. Its dilemma was that surrogates still remained essential to the United States because of its domestic political and economic constraints as well as the sheer physical impossibility of playing the role of the policeman of the world.

The basic problem was that the United States could not depend on its proxies unless their societies were also stable and able to weather those structural crises increasingly flourishing everywhere in the Third World, from the Philippines to Iran to Central America. But the United States' very support for willing dictators ready to play the proxy role to advance their own fortunes and power invariably deepened these crises and undermined further the viability of the men and social and economic forces it was relying upon.

Iran compelled the Carter Administration to confront the failure of two decades of policy assumptions in the Middle East, but it did so in such a way as to perpetuate them. In large part this was inevitable because, like its predecessors, the White House instinctively transformed local challenges and their causes into issues of Soviet-American relations and global geopolitics, making it impossible to deal with situations such as Iran or Central America realistically on their own terms. And insofar as tangible U.S. economic stakes were involved, as they increasingly were in so many countries, it was impossible for Washington, in any case, to accept the main political trends because even though their origins were indigenous, they still conflicted with its basic interests and goals.

During 1977 Brzezinski had begun to propose the idea of a "rapid deployment force" of U.S. troops that could intervene directly wherever needed, and although the complex situation in the Horn of Africa gave rise to the idea, it was obvious they could also be employed elsewhere. Carter approved the principle in August, but some of his advisers were skeptical, and it took the Iran crisis a year later to stimulate action. For Brzezinski, who intuitively transformed regional questions into global ones involving Russia and who ached to use force, the object of the RDF would be to protect the "arc of crisis" in the Persian Gulf against Soviet meddling, projecting American power toward Africa, South and Southeast Asia, and the Middle East as necessary.[7] As it eventually developed, the RDF was to comprise about a hundred thousand troops throughout the world assigned to it and with the airlift and logistical ability to reach the Middle East quickly, where prepositioned equipment and bases were to be waiting for them. The RDF concept downgraded, if not eliminated, the role the United States assigned to proxies in policing the region. Nations like Saudi Arabia expressed concern that such a force might be used against them also should their oil policy damage the United States, but the main driving force during 1979 was not only Washington's loss of its Iran surrogate but also its desire to look "credible" once more, a mood that Iran's seizure of fifty-two hostages in the American embassy on November 4, 1979, deeply intensified.

It was in this context, months before the Soviet invasion of Afghanistan in late December 1979, that the Carter Doctrine was formulated as a policy for all occasions—and by virtue of its ambiguity, practical for none. The Carter Doctrine was proclaimed on January 23, 1980, and warned that any "outside force" seeking "to gain control of the Persian Gulf region" would be attacking the United States' "vital interests," and it would use all of the means it thought necessary to repel it. Over subsequent weeks various Administration spokesmen elaborated the Carter Doctrine by letting it be known that "the terrain or the tactic or the level of our response" was entirely open, and might include anyplace in the world the Soviets were vulnerable.[8] Like Dulles's January 1954 massive-retaliation doctrine "by means and at places of our choosing," the Carter Doctrine opened the door to World War Three over local and relatively marginal issues. The Administration welcomed the opportunity to focus on Russia, and its implied threats were aimed at Moscow, but the White House did not come to grips with the pressing regional challenges of nationalism that Iran personified.

The Carter Doctrine was not a policy but a stance, and apart from its slighting the realities of the area it ignored domestic inhibitions, for the 1973 War Powers Act affirmed Congress's right to prohibit troops from fighting longer than sixty days without its approval, and it was most unlikely by the 1970s that either Congress or the American public would endorse actions risking global conflagration. More to the point, the doctrine failed to acknowledge precisely those military constraints that since the Korean War had compelled various administrations repeatedly to rely on proxies, covert warfare, and the like as substitutes for local, much less nuclear, war involving U.S. forces directly. Nor could it recognize that there was no way to deal with local Arab nationalism by engaging in limited wars in the desert sure to lead to world oil boycotts and economic crises. Rather than overcoming its credibility gap, the Carter Administration only deepened it further.

It did not take long for senior Administration officials to admit that what really was at stake in the Middle East was the possibility of being "deprived of access to those resources," for then "there would almost certainly be a worldwide economic collapse of the kind that hasn't been seen for almost fifty years, probably worse."[9] After all, while its geopolitical role could be debated, the ultimate asset of the region in 1980 was the same as it had been in 1945—oil—only now it was much more important. It was this overwhelming fact that had goaded Washington to challenge British mastery over the area and eventually to supplant it. But time had not stood still, and the Arab world had become stronger. If the rewards of success in dominating the area had grown, so, too, had the difficulties of mastering it, and unlike the British, the Arabs were there to stay. The instabilities of the region that had so exhausted the British partially changed their forms but only intensified during the era of American preeminence. Having taken on the immense task of policing and controlling the Middle East, by the end of the 1970s the United

States had no means for doing so, and as with the British it, too, saw its efforts were producing mounting failures, each more serious to its aspirations than the preceding one. Like Britain before it, the United States was now staring at defeat in the Middle East, and its short but troubled period of success was drawing to an ignominious end.

The Central American Maelstrom

*L*ATIN AMERICA WAS THE ONE REGION of the Third World that irresistibly intruded into the harried, distracted time of Washington's key decisionmakers throughout the late 1970s, despite their desire to concentrate on serious challenges elsewhere, above all Europe. What had been a lesser concern and priority after World War Two now became among the most pressing and threatening in the Third World because of the accumulated legacies of the postwar years and the massive structural changes occurring within all the hemisphere's nations, above all in Central America. U.S. leaders hoped that the 1973 coup in Chile would lay to rest troubles in the hemisphere. But as the region closest to it, with large investments and of the greatest strategic importance, it was inevitable that the mounting problems within the economic and political systems of so many Central American nations would generate grave challenges to the stability of the United States' informal empire.

These difficulties were, above all, the direct consequences of those policies both U.S. private investors, the Alliance for Progress, and multilateral banks imposed upon the nations of the region. Central America was to become the leading example of how the very success of U.S. economic integration and its strategy for economic development created traumatizing structural changes that fatally undermined the military and dictatorial regimes on which the United States depended both to implement its plans and protect its interests. During the 1970s events revealed how the United States invariably created revolutionary conditions and revolutionary movements wherever it profoundly affected social and economic systems—thereby ushering in the end of its own hegemony. After amassing the profits of the region, the

United States was now also to harvest the political consequences of the profound traumas that export-oriented development and dictatorial, extremely hierarchical societies had created over three decades.

THE ECONOMICS OF REVOLT

The basic economic trend in Central America after 1950 was the intensification of an export-oriented agriculture that recast the demography of the region, changed the land distribution system dramatically, and transformed the economic context in which traditional politics had functioned until then. In largest outline, cotton and then beef production for export altered profoundly the rural societies, above all of Guatemala, El Salvador, Honduras, and Nicaragua, the four most populous nations, beginning in the late 1950s. Cotton is a capital-intensive crop, efficiently grown only on large farms, employing mainly seasonal labor, and far more profitable than the food staple of the poor, corn. Cotton production in the region increased sixteen times between 1952 and 1978, and while part of the vast acreage it required came from opening new croplands, much also came from cornlands generally employing small peasants. In El Salvador, for example, cotton expanded from a fifth to over a half of the croplands in the two decades after 1950, but corn fell from half to a third. At every stage in this growth, rural labor and small peasants lost access to better ground, either legally or by outright fraud and intimidation, and they either moved into marginal mountain regions or to cities, subsisting as seasonal migratory labor and on the economic fringes of urban society. In Nicaragua under 4 percent of the growers in 1977 accounted for 38 percent of the harvest, and the next 10 percent for 32 percent. Cotton produced desperation, and it affected the displaced peasants profoundly.

By the late 1960s, a world cotton surplus and rising sugar prices led to the diversion of some cottonlands into sugar, which also relies on wage labor rather than small farmers, and even large-scale corn production. But the principal new thrust was toward cattle production, primarily to provide cheap beef for the U.S. fast-food industry, and it in turn required much less labor but far more land than cotton. From 1966 to 1979 beef exports increased eleven times, eventually occupying more land than all other forms of agriculture combined. Although most cattle land was cut from forests, it, too, displaced peasants and deprived them of fuel and other resources. All of these changes toward export agriculture, wage labor rather than peasant-based food-oriented production, and urbanization transformed rural conditions in Central America, above all in the most populated states.

While the most profound changes occurred in the attitudes of the masses and were only later to express themselves politically, there are the usual statistical measurements dealing with material conditions. Despite the already high concentration of land in the hands of a small elite, their shares increased in general. In 1970, one-fifth of the region's population received 61 percent of the income, the poorest half 13 percent. Per capita food production fell slightly from 1948 to 1969. In Latin America as a whole, the nations in Central as opposed to South America were, in the aggregate, worst off. In 1970 Honduras had the highest share of households, 65 percent, living below the poverty line, and the same was true for its 45 percent living in destitution. The region's basic services were among the worst in the Western Hemisphere; its hospital facilities were among the lowest, and its illiteracy was among the highest.

While there is a great similarity among the development of the Central American nations, particularly the four largest, there are important nuances that cannot be slighted, though after the 1973 rise in oil prices they all faced comparable difficulties in coping with its economic consequences. In Nicaragua, where about 70 percent of the population lived on the land, cotton provided work, such as it was, for over a third of those with jobs, but the cities especially confronted the human and employment problems that export agriculture created. There, the Somoza family, which had taken over the nation in 1936, as well as their close cronies, owned 21 percent of all the land (the best, of course), nearly all mining, and their combined holdings accounted for 41 percent of the gross national product. In El Salvador, with the greatest population–land density, there was more landlessness and dependence on wage labor than elsewhere in Central America, and the subsequent strength of the guerrilla movement corresponds closely to those regions the cotton and beef boom affected most. Between 1961 and 1980 landlessness among rural households in El Salvador increased from 12 to 65 percent. There is a surfeit of comparable numbers, and they all point in the same direction.

To a critical degree, this transformation of Central America was the outcome of both U.S. policy as well as the logical culmination of the region's historic role, to a greater extent than any other area in the hemisphere, in servicing Yankees with its exports. No other region was so much in its sphere of influence economically, and given its population of 12 million in 1960, virtually any U.S. decision profoundly affected these nations. While the Alliance for Progress, more than any other postwar event, intensified export agriculture, U.S. control over the export of bananas and other crops since the nineteenth century, and its domination of transport and utilities, also played a major part.

The United States' belief in specialization and export expansion as part of a desirable international division of labor suffused the Alliance as it has everything else it has advocated throughout the Third World since 1945. The Alliance aided the development of exports in every way possible, from preinvestment surveys for U.S. firms but especially to roads that opened fresh lands to cotton and beef production. Loans from the IADB and the World Bank, where the United States also shaped policy, also reinforced the Alliance's emphasis on developing an infrastructure, so this effort continued after the Alliance ended. Funds usually were given to states to administer, and these governments in turn greatly accelerated the construction of modern packing plants able to process beef to U.S. health standards, making the cattle lands profitable. Political favorites benefited most from this arrangement, but so, too, did U.S. multinationals working with local interests, and their investments in food processing rose spectacularly. While this Alliance-backed focus on exports was to upset much of the region profoundly, some areas were affected more than others. In northern Guatemala, the AID, the World Bank, and IADB especially concentrated on developing not only beef but also rich oil and nickel deposits. The generals running the country joined personally in these ventures, confiscating huge amounts of land from peasants, and the area later became a stronghold of the guerrilla movement.

It was in Honduras, however, that U.S. economic control was the greatest, with U.S. firms owning forty-one of the fifty largest companies. Here bananas, which once were virtually the exclusive export, were equaled during the 1960s by coffee, cotton, and cattle, and the land was concentrated into fewer hands. It was in Honduras, too, that the two main U.S. banana companies began to return a portion of their lands to government-sponsored cooperatives, continuing to sell the output as the marketer, an arrangement that combined a measure of reform with good business, since they controlled prices as well. It was not too long before the coops, like all agrarian reform efforts under the auspices of military-led governments, fell into the usual pattern of corruption and misuse.

The economic policies of the Central American states were not one sustained list of unmitigated disasters, and they created a common market during the 1960s until it was disbanded after the Honduras-El Salvador war of July 1969. On the whole, however, they greatly aggravated the structural economic problems of the region, inevitably creating an increasingly crisis-prone political context within which U.S. policy had to operate.

U.S. POLICIES TOWARD CENTRAL AMERICA

Washington's policies toward Central America had always been infused with a measure of cynicism, one its contact with successively corrupt regimes over seven decades instinctively reinforced. Internationally, however, its ability to count on the region's loyal UN votes caused U.S. diplomats to reciprocate when it came to overlooking many of the foibles of the successive dictators and flamboyant characters who ran these nations. By the time Eisenhower chose to support the military and dictators in all of Latin America out of choice rather than necessity, the basic pattern of U.S. endorsement of the local oligarchies and military juntas had already become traditional practice; for dictators always welcomed U.S. interests, because by doing so they invariably gained personally.

A major U.S. activity before, during, and after the Alliance period was to make certain that the military and police, as an AID-sponsored consultant put it in 1973, "can serve as a reliable instrument of constituted political authority."[1] Events in Guatemala until 1954 alone would have made this fixation inevitable. U.S. officials dealing with the region did not want to see a repetition of it, and their stress on perfecting instruments of control and repression supplemented private investment and trade activities in defining the U.S. role in the region. U.S. training of military personnel therefore prospered, with Somoza's National Guard, some thirty-six hundred of them during 1950–68, the largest number for the region. Assistance to the police forces in various forms also flourished, ranging from training in U.S. police schools to donating equipment to resident police missions. Here Guatemala was the main recipient during the 1960s, and the police program was primarily a political one: "investigating and controlling subversives," as the AID's police advisers there defined it.[2] It included, as well, providing those in power with skills to handle all political opponents, whatever their ideology, should it prove necessary.

Agrarian reform played no role in the U.S. strategy under the Alliance. Those few U.S. officials who favored it in principle saw no point to it in the region, believing that corruption was certain to accompany any program. Most preferred to stress what they regarded as a rational restructuring of the land system toward greater productivity and exports. This was the basic U.S. policy throughout the hemisphere, above all where lands its citizens owned were extensive. Almost no nominal reform rhetoric was generated in favor of land redistribution, but much reform phraseology was evoked when the American Institute for Free Labor Development (AIFLD) entered the region shortly after the AIFLD was created in 1962.

Chaired by Peter Grace of the Grace Lines, whose company was deeply involved in the region, the AIFLD was nominally the responsibility of the AFL-CIO, which provided social democratic slogans and organizers, although the U.S. government paid nearly all its expenses. It was essentially a concentrated effort to stem the growing Cuban influence by organizing workers and peasants in ways that preempted more radical groups, including Catholic-led peasant and labor organizations, which grew up in this decade, but it soon found that its official status inhibited its reform ideas decisively as well. AIFLD activities ranged from discouraging labor agitation on U.S.-owned banana plantations to signing formal agreements with the El Salvador government in 1965 to organize militant peasants who might otherwise have been attracted to the opposition. But also, as in Honduras, it created a peasant organization that was taken over by leaders who participated in land seizures during the late 1960s. There can be little doubt that while Washington maintained a tight control over the small minority of its employees sympathetic to a greater identification with reforms, and its resources went overwhelmingly to support the status quo, the United States also found it helpful to maintain a pretense of sincere interest in social change. However, policy itself never wavered.

The dilemma the United States ultimately confronted, however, was that events in Central America were not the intended outcome of its conscious policies or those of the leaders and ruling classes it sustained loyally. The sheer impact of the vast economic changes altering the rural social system, within a context of corruption and repression as the elites' principal response to massive, growing social and economic problems, made inevitable a collision between the people and the status quo. These traumatizing forces were cumulative but also irreversible, the undesired but by now predictable consequences of the United States' economic development strategy. It was plain even before the early 1970s, when the disastrous 1972 Managua earthquake and punishing Honduras hurricane in September 1974 and the Guatemala earthquake in February 1976 only compounded the already grave problems in place, that the masses' ability to suffer quietly would inevitably end and that revolutionary upheavals would transform the region. By the 1970s the vast majority simply had nothing more to lose.

THE UNITED STATES CONFRONTS CENTRAL AMERICAN REVOLUTIONS

The natural disasters' effects on the already impoverished masses merged with the economic consequences of the post-October 1973 oil price hikes and world inflation to bring the crisis in Central America to a head. Throughout this period peasant resistance to land seizures and popular demands for access to vast holdings in local and foreign hands gathered momentum, and while some of it was spontaneous, it was also the result of the changing role of the Catholic Church in the region. Priests and nuns as well as Christian base communities led by laity in remote areas began to apply the liberation theology that was beginning to influence profoundly Church thought in the hemisphere, arousing the wrath of the various regimes. In Honduras, the peasant movement took on major proportions by 1975. Most of the priests who worked with the peasants were foreigners, and in June 1975 two priests were killed along with thirteen peasant leaders, the murder of the latter being a common occurrence by then. Peasant organization and repression went hand in hand throughout the turbulent region, but a combination of Church activism, leftist efforts, and spontaneous peasant actions unsettled the poorest nations, and it created a confrontation between them and their dictatorial rulers that could not be kept out of the U.S. headlines. Central America quickly became intertwined with the new mood of anti-interventionist politics that was emerging in Washington and the nation after the Vietnam trauma.

When Carter took office the question of ending U.S. support for repressive regimes was high on the liberal, antiwar wing of Congress's agenda, which had already written mandatory legislation into military aid measures, and Carter's political tacticians suggested that if he did not co-opt the issue he would end up fighting a continuous battle with the politically most potent section of his own party. Moreover, cutting aid to human rights violators was popular with a large segment of both the public and the press, and in a desire to appear "refreshing," as the architect of the strategy explained it, Carter became an advocate of human rights.[3] The fact that the policy was devised with an eye mainly to domestic politics and opinion soon mired the Administration in contradictions, opening it to criticisms of hypocrisy, though in fact Carter was no more cynical than successful politicians are wont to be. The White House showed this immediately when in early 1977 it opposed mandatory "no" votes on loans to nations violating human rights, a bill that was proposed in Congress. Moreover, when Brazil preempted a possible U.S. condemnation of its human rights record by refusing to accept military sales credits, the Administration realized its symbolism was unlikely to have an impact in curbing repression, and this made its domestic function all the more important. Argentina, El Salvador, and Guatemala then rejected military aid as well, and modest reductions in aid to Argentina, Ethiopia, and Uruguay only brought U.S. business interests into the picture to oppose the policy.

Since Carter never regarded it as anything more than one of many elements in shaping diplomacy, he decided that in order to avoid complicating U.S. relations with strategically and economically key countries that violated human rights—Iran, Korea, Indonesia, and the Philippines above all—he would focus on that region that presumably could do less damage to U.S. interests should pressures on nations there lead to a deterioration in relations. Guatemala, El Salvador, and Nicaragua therefore became the main targets of official human rights efforts, less to alter the regimes in those nations than to satisfy the exigencies of American politics. Indeed, Honduras, whose military leaders were scarcely better than those of their neighbors in respecting the rights of their citizens, saw its aid increase dramatically, so that by 1979 it was the leading recipient in the region. Guatemala and El Salvador merely turned to Israel and Western Europe for its arms. While the United States' human rights policy was a factor complicating the Administration's policy in Central America, it did not alter its basic objectives, which remained exactly the same as they had been under its predecessors. That it coincided with the upheavals in the region was accidental, but it scarcely caused them. By 1977 the Central American crisis was locked into an irrevocable track, one the ruling regimes were certain to lose.

WASHINGTON CONFRONTS THE NICARAGUAN REVOLUTION

The most obvious case was Nicaragua, where the Somoza family had ruled and bled the nation for over forty years. Their public image made it difficult for any administration to defend it. Organized opposition to the Somozas had been minor until the late 1960s, but it was the aftermath of the 1972 earthquake which greatly accelerated it at just the point that the disaster profoundly added intolerable suffering to the already miserable lot of the masses. Somoza's corruption in the wake of that calamity diverted at least half of the U.S. relief aid, deeply alienating the middle class and the Church, and when they attempted to use the normally rigged 1974 election to mobilize against him, he outlawed their parties and arrested their key leaders. The only option was armed struggle, and this brought the Sandinista Front for National Liberation (FSLN), founded in 1962 and largely inspired by the example of the Cuban revolution, into the picture after its earlier inconclusive efforts to organize peasants.

The Sandinista revolution was ultimately to be the outcome of a conjunction of factors, the most important being the economic transformation that had taken place since 1960 and the way the Somozas themselves related to it. Throughout the 1970s, but especially after 1977, the standard of living of the population fell, and this, too, conditioned the people to revolt, even where the FSLN and the Church offered no direct leadership. In terms of mobilized forces, the FSLN was principally a student movement, without strong roots among the peasants, who listened to the FSLN organizers and frequently assisted them but never joined the FSLN in large numbers. This fact caused it to split during its early career but later to reemerge with a united front strategy that gathered all anti-Somoza forces around a minimum platform of destroying the dictatorship. The FSLN was by then strong enough to pose an alternative, and the Carter Administration opted to ship Somoza arms quietly in late 1977 as the guerrillas began a modestly successful military offensive. Yet until January 1978, when Somoza had the editor of the major opposition paper assassinated, the FSLN remained an elite rather than a mass movement. The death of Joaquín Chamorro brought the urban masses out to the streets to fight the National Guard in what was largely a spontaneous upheaval, one that was savagely suppressed, but it gave the FSLN a largely self-directing mass base everywhere in the nation, including much of the countryside, as the people quite informally became the organization itself. It capitalized on this to renew the struggle in September 1978, when the population again took to the streets to fight the National Guard, with over three thousand civilian deaths, while the FSLN provided only as much guidance as its still relatively overextended numbers allowed. By then it was clear that the United States had a major challenge on its hands.

The Carter Administration now began to confront the Nicaragua crisis in earnest, and Brzezinski proposed sending more arms to Somoza secretly. Instead, Carter sent the dictator a secret letter praising his improved human rights record, hoping he could be cajoled into adopting a flexible political position that might win much of the middle classes away from an alliance with the FSLN. Somoza was in no mood after the September uprising to make concessions, and his brutal suppression of the opposition convinced the Administration that an orderly transition to replace Somoza was essential to head off an FSLN victory. With ample arms and training from Israel and Brazil, and support from Argentina, El Salvador, and Guatemala, Somoza spurned U.S. mediation efforts during the fall of 1978, causing it to stop all economic and military aid, though not the training of his notoriously brutal National Guard—which the United States saw had an important role to play even after Somoza. Meanwhile, the dictator began to double the size of his seventy-five-hundred-man National Guard to confront at least two thousand FSLN guerrillas and, for practical purposes, much of the population. Over the next months the Carter Administration, preoccupied with the Iran crisis, had to consider the real possibility of dominos falling throughout Central America, for successes in Nicaragua had already begun to inspire an upsurge of opposition to the neighboring dictatorships. The Administration's quite justifiable fear was to increase with time, and it considered the orderly replacement of Somoza by non-Left elements as even more imperative.

On May 29, 1979, just after Washington had endorsed Somoza's request to the IMF to replenish his treasury emptied because of arms purchases, the FSLN began a carefully prepared offensive, aided with arms from Costa Rica, Mexico, and Venezuela, as well as Cuba. Within weeks it was clear that it would win because of its popular support, and the United States, whose policy was now being dictated largely by the hawkish Brzezinski, convened the OAS in Washington on June 21 in a last-ditch effort to forestall its victory. "We must not leave a vacuum," Secretary of State Vance warned the meeting, and he proposed sending an OAS delegation to Managua immediately that would arrange a transitional government excluding Somoza but retaining his party, the National Guard as the principal armed force, and all those anti-Somoza conservative elements not aligned in the broad coalition the FSLN had formed—the FSLN to become only one of many groups.[4] It was a plan to preserve, in effect, an oppressive regime without its leader. The United States also called for an OAS peacekeeping force in lieu of its own purely unilateral intervention (which it threatened vaguely at the same time), to police Nicaragua until a new regime was able to do so. For the first time in the OAS's history, the United States both encountered a strong opposing resolution sponsored by thirteen of its twenty-seven members and watched its own basic position rejected entirely. The OAS had escaped its control, eliminating its traditional usefulness in clothing U.S. policy in multilateral garb. It was clear that states like Mexico and Venezuela wanted to see the end of Somoza's system as well as the man. The United States did not, and although it extracted some minor concessions, it was defeated ignominiously.

In a final desperate effort to save the situation, the Administration then sent officials to Nicaragua to seek an accord acceptable to itself directly with Somoza and the FSLN. It was able to persuade Somoza to agree to resign if the FSLN would consent to the preservation and incorporation of a reformed National Guard into the new government, as well as other less audacious but no less obvious and unacceptable efforts to contain, and later destroy, the FSLN. The issue was finally resolved as the National Guard's forces began to disintegrate, and on July 17 Somoza went into exile to spend the estimated $100 million fortune he had accumulated, leaving the Nicaraguan treasury with $3 million in cash and $1.6 billion in foreign debts. The United States' leaders understood full well that unlike Chile, where Allende won office but had no control over the military, the FSLN was now capable of establishing complete power, thereby inflicting the United States with its most important defeat in the hemisphere since January 1959.

The last U.S. hope for success now rested with the diverse members of the Government of National Reconstruction, which took power in July. While the FSLN dominated the five-member ruling junta and retained ultimate control, the ministries went mainly to middle-class political leaders, and even an ex-National Guard officer became minister of defense. In reality, of course, the FSLN had led the revolt from the inception without organizing the masses who participated in it into formal membership, but to them the FSLN was both the founder and the symbol of the struggle, and it had both legitimacy as well as a radical social program far more responsive to their aspirations. While the United States drew encouragement from the pluralistic nature of the cabinet, the FSLN went about the task of mobilizing the people who had spontaneously participated in the conflict, providing the bulk of its fighters, into mass organizations firmly committed to its principles. And the Sandinistas never relinquished control of the army. It was after July 1979 rather than before that the FSLN transformed itself from a vanguard organization (with very real differences within it) into an organized mass movement.

The FSLN's relation to the middle class, however, was not feigned, and maintaining a united front has been an integral aspect of its program to the present, one involving a high economic and political price. The final U.S. effort to save a pro-U.S. regime in Nicaragua and prevent the FSLN from consolidating power was based on the ingenious plan, as the assistant secretary of state for inter-American affairs described it, "that it is essential to supply aid to keep the monetary/economic system viable and enmeshed in the international economy, and to support the private sector. Failure to do so would leave the private sector abandoned and unable to compete with the currently stronger Sandinista structure."[5] In the three months after Somoza left office the United States gave the new government twenty-six million dollars in food and medical aid as a bait, and the FSLN leadership, despite disagreements, was ready to bite a yet larger hook. Other Western governments joined the strategy, along with the multilateral banks. During the fall of 1979 members of the junta breakfasted with Carter, and a congressional delegation went to Nicaragua after the Executive submitted a bill proposing seventy-five million dollars in economic aid. After adding a proviso that 60 percent of this sum was to be made available to private business, as well as comparable ideological amendments, Congress finally took nine months to pass the bill and appropriate the money. Meanwhile, the new government negotiated with private banks and rescheduled six hundred million dollars of Somoza's debt, preferring more debt rather than to renounce access to the capitalist money market. During its first years the FSLN remained enmeshed, as the United States would have it, but it also staved off more aggressive U.S. actions and gained a respite. Whatever the economic and political wisdom of its decision, which only time will tell, the revolution endured, and with each year became more likely to survive U.S. hostility.

THE CENTRAL AMERICAN BALANCE

Once the magnitude of the crisis in Nicaragua became clear, it was obvious to the Carter Administration that the regimes in the neighboring states, all with comparable problems and with guerrillas active in El Salvador and Guatemala, had to be strengthened quickly lest the entire region go the way of Nicaragua. In Nicaragua the United States had improvised from the beginning of the revolt after decades of support for Somoza, and its humiliating inability to mobilize the OAS, and the virtual impossibility of its acting unilaterally without creating a political explosion at home, finally compelled it to rely on nothing more ingenious than sheer bribery in its attempt to reverse events in Nicaragua. Its policy was confused and unsuccessful, and it sought to avoid similar mistakes in El Salvador.

El Salvador, in certain ways, was objectively more ripe for upheaval than Nicaragua, but compared to the FSLN, its four armed opposition groups in 1979 were far less able, and they were bitterly divided. Nonetheless, there were important parallel urban movements linked to them, and the long record of human rights abuses and repression of labor, especially via "death squads" that terrorized the country, combined with the population's misery to keep renewing the opposition despite its errors. These infamous squads had forced the Carter Administration to cut off military but not economic aid to El Salvador's military regime under General Carlos Romero, and in the fall of 1979 it sought to compel it to create a military and social context better able to head off an imminent guerrilla victory. A young officers' coup on October 15, 1979, very likely encouraged by U.S. officials, greatly eased the U.S. efforts and was used to justify the resumption of military aid and a fivefold increase in economic assistance—while support to Honduras doubled. But the new leaders were both unwilling and unable to contain the cycle of killings that had become routine for the state, and in January 1980 reactionary officers replaced them as well.

What this new group possessed was a superior sense of the reform rhetoric the Americans wished to hear, and three months later they agreed, if only on paper, to a United States-devised land reform program, but they, too, were rightists when it came to practice. On March 24, 1980, to make clear who had the power, death squads assassinated Archbishop Romero, and the murderer, a graduate of the police academy in Washington, was never brought to justice. In a cycle of intensifying violence, it was plain that there would be no reform and that armed struggle would eventually end in a victory for the Left, which in January 1980 had managed to unite its military efforts and greatly improve its performance. A mounting struggle continues in El Salvador, but one whose ultimate outcome, like those of the nations around it, has already become highly predictable. The Carter Administration left this legacy for subsequent administrations to confront, but it also made the basic commitment to plunge into the maelstrom as never before.

Nicaragua, like Cuba before it, was of profound significance in the United States' relationship to the hemisphere, and both confirmed that it had irrevocably lost its ability to control the main political developments that grew irresistibly out of the economic policies and social forces it supported. Nor could it stem the political consequences of United States-endorsed structural changes or define alternatives to them, for these impinged on its own basic economic needs and interests as well as those of the classes with which it was aligned. Its Nicaraguan defeat was, ultimately, structurally induced, as was the crisis in El Salvador, and despite the ineptness or confusion of the Left and its problems on the road to power and thereafter, these still did not reverse the main implications of their victories to U.S. hegemony over the hemisphere. Washington's reform pretensions, as the Alliance showed, were hardly more than shibboleths it scarcely believed itself, but they failed to halt the basic radicalization occurring in the hemisphere. In Central America, on the contrary, the very success of its development plans accelerated the destruction of traditional orders, their accumulated effects bringing multiple problems to a head. The United States could exploit the hemisphere's nations, helping to traumatize them, but it could not build stable societies. Nor could it utilize its own military power to undo the successes of the opposition forces, in all their diversity, which had begun to grow out of the social misery that abounded. Whatever its temporary achievements, it now confronted defeat close to home. It was neither politically, economically, nor militarily capable of fighting another protracted war in any nation, nor able to rely on its surrogates and allies to do so. By 1979 it had even lost its capacity to win the acquiescence of the other states in the hemisphere for whatever it wished to do, and there was no question that the resistance to intervention that Vietnam evoked would inevitably repeat itself again both at home and abroad should any administration seek to repeat that experience.

The Sandinista triumph in 1979 and its persistence since then was an event of historic proportions for the U.S. role in the hemisphere because it repeated its failures in Cuba, revealing it could not change its basically exploitive economic relationship to the nations of the hemisphere or discover how to avert the revolutionary consequences of its effects and that of the oppressive societies it sought to sustain. Nor could it find the resources—military, economic, and political—to undo liberation movements once the United States was expelled from a nation. Whether the process would be a short or a long one, Nicaragua confirmed that the Cuban revolution was not an isolated and accidental event but part of an ongoing process—one growing out of irreversible and cumulative structural changes that would increasingly confront the United States with the specter of revolution in the hemisphere.

CONCLUSION

COMPREHENDING OVER THREE DEC-
ades of intense U.S. activity in the Third
World is a major challenge precisely be-
cause the causes of America's conduct have grown in complexity. At the
inception of the postwar era, whether it was in terms of its relationship to
Western European power or its own direct interests, the United States possessed an essentially economic vision of its future role in the Third World.
Indeed, despite the serious risks of oversimplification in any monocausal
analysis that overlooks crucial nuances in each major region and other
sources of America's failures and contradictions, the economic component
remains the single most important factor in its postwar conduct in the Third
World, even if it is far from being a sufficient explanation.

The significance of economic causes is due not merely to the fact that U.S.
leaders have found it far easier to articulate their economic as opposed to
political goals. But whether a question of U.S. imports and investments, or
domino theories linking the stakes in one nation to the stability and control
over the surrounding region, economics, to varying degrees, suffuses their
policies and action everywhere. Both in practice as well as verbally, this
motive holds true with as much consistency today as it did forty years ago
because the Third World's intrinsic importance to American economic health
has increased since 1970. But assigning a precise weight to economic influences is complicated because the political and military prerequisites for the
attainment of its primary objective, which required that those in charge of
numerous countries be friendly to U.S. interests and its goal of an integrated
world order, had very definite economic but much vaguer and flexible political justifications. These quickly intensified the ideological obfuscation sur-

rounding Washington's purposes. It is essential, therefore, not to confuse the military and political effects of a policy with its basic causes, and sorting out such relationships is the crux to attaining an overall perception of the United States' postwar role in the major Third World regions.

The American commitment to advancing its essentially economic interests was revealed immediately after World War Two, above all in Latin America but also in the Middle East and the Philippines. In these areas the question of communism and the Soviet Union was nonexistent or, at most, marginal; its major problems were with those who, while ideological allies, were also economic rivals. Latin America's preeminent economic importance to the United States made it the single most significant test of Washington's basic goals and assumptions. The Open Door rhetoric of equal treatment for all, which the United States often employed in its statements of aims elsewhere, was irrelevant in explaining the special relationship it sought to build in this hemisphere. Throughout the postwar era, Washington's unwavering hegemonic objective of domination frequently pitted it against key, often ruling, sectors of the Latin American capitalists. Those who accept Open Door phraseology at face value as an adequate description of U.S. purposes ignore both the far deeper American devotion to its own interests in the most classically nationalist sense of that term and the role of its ideology not merely as a reflection of belief but also as a tool to neutralize its reticent allies.

The irony of U.S. policy in the Third World is that while it has always justified its larger objectives and efforts in the name of anticommunism, its own goals have made it unable to tolerate change from *any* quarter that impinged significantly on its interests. Much of its conflict with political forces in the Third World has arisen from this fact. Only in nations where there has been a strong Left has the United States sometimes allowed strategic and political considerations to define the form and even the ends of its policies and to minimize, at least temporarily, the central importance of its economic purposes.

More vital in causing the United States to waver from the systematic pursuit of its principal interests in the Third World has been its repeated inability since 1949 to reconcile the inherent tension between its diverse aims in every corner of the earth with its very great but nonetheless finite resources. America's formal priorities have generally reflected a relatively logical set of objectives. But its endemic incapacity to avoid entangling, costly commitments in areas of the world that are of intrinsically secondary importance to these priorities has caused U.S. foreign policy and resources to whipsaw virtually arbitrarily from one problem and region to the other. The result has been the United States' increasing postwar loss of control over its political priorities, budget, military strategy and tactics, and, ultimately, its original economic goals.

Until at least 1960, America's leaders always considered their most significant problems to be Europe and the USSR, yet by that time the Third World
had already absorbed much of their efforts and money and still was growing
in importance. Washington's ingrained unwillingness after 1950 to forgo intervention anywhere led to what has been a consistent but unsuccessful
effort to define a military doctrine that overcame the limits of both space and
its resources for realizing all its objectives simultaneously. Various concepts
of limited war and counterinsurgency were its responses to this challenge.
If the Vietnam War was the penultimate consequence of this dilemma, the
successive failure of every postwar administration to resolve the frustrations
inherent in America's arms and power led to a legacy of political and military
difficulties that have often appeared to overshadow the original economic
basis of U.S. policies in the Third World. The accumulated contradictions that
have emerged from such unresolvable quandaries have eroded persistently
the fundamental position of the United States as a world power.

The notion of the credibility of American power, which became increasingly influential in shaping Washington's calculations and actions after 1950,
intensified the United States' difficulties in its self-appointed role as the policeman of much of the world. The symbolism and essentially open-ended under-
takings inherent in its desire to sustain the confidence of its allies and the fear
of its putative enemies has caused the United States to stake its role in the
world on controlling events in relatively minor places. As soon as successive
administrations concluded that the logic of maintaining power in purely
narrow economic terms required it also to pay the necessary military and
political overhead charges of empire to keep those friendly to the United
States in office, they had no effective means to retain mastery over American
priorities and commitments. With the 1958 Lebanon crisis, credibility became a permanent aspect of U.S. strategic calculations, and while it emerged
unscathed from that episode and the 1965 Dominican invasion, in Vietnam
the unlimited risks intrinsic in such a dangerous approach to local problems
arose to produce the inevitable major crisis of American power. Its later
application in Angola showed how deeply credibility was embedded in the
minds of American leaders and how little they had learned from the Vietnam
experience.

Linked to the credibility obsession was the domino theory, which provided
a geopolitical justification for intervention and reintroduced an economic
rationale insofar as it judged the importance of a nation in its larger regional
context, which only made more defensible its involvement in seemingly
marginal countries. These two definitions of the nature of the world, more
than any others, became successive administrations' most consistent and
effective justifications to themselves as well as to the Congress, the media,
and the public. The problems inherent in the domino and credibility theories,

however, did not disappear simply because they were politically palatable at home. Their real test came not from their frequent successes but from occasional failures, which invariably forced the United States to persist in a futile policy or, as in Vietnam, escalate its efforts. It was at such a point that the dangers of its policy to the rational management of its global system produced the most profound economic and political contradictions in American power both at home and abroad, shattering those priorities for action it had initially believed essential to its success. The United States increasingly staked its future on places secondary to its direct interests but suffused, according to its thinking, with extraordinary symbolic significance.

Since all wars for the United States, if it does not win them quickly, become capital-intensive, imposing an economic and political price beyond its capacity to pay without sacrifices that divide the society, the main challenge confronting America's leaders after the mid-1960s was less the justification for interventionism, on which they agreed, but its viability. Korea and Vietnam both proved that the United States cannot fight a protracted war successfully but that given all of the assumptions, techniques, and goals in its foreign policy, it will not avoid fighting more in the future. America's inability to succeed with its fundamental policy was indisputable by 1969. But the high costs this fact imposed on the health of America's economy and society did not cause its leaders to abandon their global aspirations but only divided them on tactical issues rather than basic principles. The United States' postwar fixation on its credibility, dominos, and the like only produced more and more distractions over essentially extraneous issues and places, making it even less able to cope with the growing major challenges to its hegemony. Increasingly, by the late 1970s it was unable to reverse the successes of revolutionary movements, which grew, paradoxically, out of those exploitive social and economic conditions for which the United States was frequently responsible.

The extent of Washington's growing shortcomings and contradictions magnified as it tied its credibility in more and more nations to its need to maintain its surrogates and proxies in office. That the United States should sponsor and rely upon willing collaborators was essential for it to avoid stretching its own manpower far beyond their capacities. To varying degrees, the policy of aligning itself with cooperative military leaders, the Shah, or dictators in Nicaragua, Cuba, or South Vietnam became the rule rather than the exception early in the postwar era, and it was the inevitable outcome of Washington's belief that it had both the right and the ability to define the politics of any nation it deemed important to it interests. The fundamental, fatal danger of this policy for the United States is that it made its power no stronger than the men and regimes upon whom it depended.

The United States supported repressive constituencies and the socioeconomic conditions they fostered. Although these clients were generally most favorable to American economic interests, such a policy also virtually guaranteed that the United States not only would eventually help to mobilize a nationalist resistance to its local allies but also that such opponents, even if conservative in their social and economic goals, would, by necessity, also have to attack U.S. imperialism. Its intimate symbiosis with the inherently unstable forces of reaction, corruption, and repression in the Third World often resolved short-term challenges to U.S. interests. But in the longer run it compounded the extent to which its credibility would be placed at stake and its economic ambitions frustrated, for its economic hegemony never created political stability because the socioeconomic conditions emerging from export-oriented investment increasingly traumatized those nations in which the U.S. impact was greatest. The multilateral banks' austerity policies, which later paralleled and reinforced its influence, only deepened this pattern.

Ironically, the United States' confrontation with the inevitable political consequences of its surrogates' policies as well as its own economic penetration invariably strengthens the Left and anti-Yankee nationalism. But it has been incapable of perceiving its own role as a major catalyst of radicalization—and eventual challenge to itself. Although its economic and political interventions usually have no significant effect on the United States, which has literally dozens under way in various places at any given time, to a small nation of only minor interest to the United States its impact can be monumental and profoundly affect the quality of its life. But the failure of its efforts in a small country, and Washington's introduction of credibility and domino calculations to parallel its economic losses, potentially can transform only one of its many involvements into a major challenge to itself, such as a Cuba or a Nicaragua. It then opens the temptation to an intervention that, like Vietnam, eventually exacts a very high price from U.S. society and power also.

For innumerable small or poor nations, coping with the United States' real role and potential threat is a primordial issue to them as well as a precondition for obtaining the freedom to shape their own development. Each must tread a difficult path capable of bringing a society out of the institutional legacies that its own exploitive ruling classes as well as the United States or other colonial powers have imposed. At the same time, they have to avoid provoking a direct American intervention that can endanger all hope of change and even traumatize, as in Vietnam or Nicaragua, the entire social and economic fabric of a nation. For while Washington has never sought to allocate to the Third World the central place in its global foreign relations, in reality it has itself played such a role in the affairs of innumerable nations since the late 1950s. The problem of the United States is one of the most crucial obstacles confronting proponents of change in the Third World, and in many countries the single most important issue that they must face.

By the mid-1980s the major, growing challenges to U.S. power in Central America, the Philippines, Iran, and elsewhere were the direct outcomes of the contradictions and dilemmas it increasingly confronted throughout the post-war era. Washington's fatal dependency on its own dependent and extremely unstable clients, ironically, merged with the legacy of past failures in Vietnam and elsewhere, the persistent hypnotic spell of credibility and domino theories on the thinking of American leaders, and the economic imperatives that gave rise to U.S. involvement in much of the Third World, to leave America in a fundamental and essentially self-destructive impasse. This was true not only in its relationship to the Third World but also in the basic definition and conduct of its foreign policy. The United States has managed only to compound the social, economic, and political roots of crises in the Third World, and the efficacy of its military and political resources for coping with them are now fundamentally in question. Time will only increase the difficulties the United States faces, as it has over the past three decades.

The United States' role in the Third World has not only grown consistently since the early 1950s, but also both the forms its interventions take and the justifications its leaders have employed for them have become far more complex. The fundamental assumption that the United States retains the right and obligation to intervene in the Third World in any way it ultimately deems necessary, including military, remains an article of faith among the people who guide both political parties, and they have yet to confront the basic American failures in the past or the reasons for them. Indeed, the extent to which the United States has attained a measure of success until now has both goaded them and minimized their appreciation of the significance of its earlier defeats, causing them to believe they have the ability to triumph in the future. American leaders, in their congenital optimism, have ignored the extent to which their victories, as in Iran or the Philippines, have been transitory, and they have glossed over the potentially decisive costs of just one loss, as in Vietnam, to the health of their entire international position. Employing a logic that is ahistorical and irrational, the United States still holds the Soviet Union responsible for the dynamics of change and revolt in the Third World, refusing to see Communist and radical movements—the USSR included—as the effects rather than the causes of the sustained process of war and social transformation that has so profoundly defined the world's historical experience in this century.

Those who run American foreign policy have still to realize that inflation may affect a nation's politics more profoundly than all the radicals in it combined. They often ascribe astonishing powers to the Left despite its repeated failures or frequently inept political talents. The Nixon and Carter administrations increasingly sought to control trends in the Third World via the intermediary of détente and triangulation with China and Russia, as if these two states had the capacity to impose constraints on the dynamics of change in the Third World. But this strategy was testimony to their refusal after three decades of experience to comprehend the autonomous—and eventually more dangerous—nature of local rebellion. One can no longer attribute the origins of conflict and war in the modern era, and the factors that determine their eventual outcome, to the decisions of men and nations. Ultimately such events culminate the way they do because many of the same social and economic forces that created them in the first instance still play decisive roles as wars increasingly become struggles between rival social systems, their capacity to engage in extended struggle, and the political efficacy of the alternatives they present to the masses.

Whether our future will be as crisis-ridden as the past depends greatly on whether the United States can live in a pluralist world and cease to confront and fight most of the movements and developments that have emerged in the postwar era and have become more relevant since the irreversible collapse of Soviet and Chinese pretensions to lead international socialism. In addition to the many varieties of radicalism and socialism, it now faces all the forms of nationalism that are becoming more powerful in the Middle East, Latin America, and Asia. Can the United States end its purely negative role since 1946 in inflicting incalculably great damage on the many diverse parties of change in the Third World, and cease deforming them by constraining their choice of tactics in their legitimate struggle for power? The United States' role has increasingly become far less one of creating or consolidating those social systems in the Third World it believes congenial with its own interests and needs than in imposing often painful obstacles on the route toward social transformation there. Needed changes will come one way or another, but they would be immeasurably more successful, humane, and faster were U.S. backing for their surrogates and puppets not a constant menace to those seeking to end the poverty and injustice that so blights much of mankind.

At the present time it appears highly likely that America's responses to these questions will reflect its inherited ideology, immense vested interest in the status quo, and past failures, and that they will once again prove negative. The ability of the American political structure to adapt to the monumental changes occurring in international relations, not to mention its domestic needs (which ultimately are far more important to the welfare of its society), has not increased sufficiently despite the significant debate and the few measures of useful legislation the Vietnam War generated. Ultimately, the major inhibitions on the United States remain its incapacity either to fight successfully or to pay for the potentially unlimited costs of attaining its goals in the Third World, and these constraints have grown far more quickly than the process of reason among the leaders of both parties on the grave issues of war and change today. That America's policies and goals have increasingly failed on their own terms, eroding the quality of its domestic life and international strength in the process, has yet to penetrate seriously their thinking, much less their visions of alternatives and readiness to live with the dominant political realities of our era.

The Third World has more than enough problems to confront without also having to face the United States as well. No one nation can regulate the world, and it would be tragic were it to occur even if it were possible. History is full of accounts of those nations that have tried to impose their will and failed. Mankind's problem today is that while there have been many terrible wars between smaller nations, and the French, Chinese, and Russians have also engaged in a number of deplorable interventions against weaker states, only the United States among the major powers has embarked on a very large number of sustained interventions of varying magnitude and remains ready to do so in the future. More important yet, only the United States believes today that it still possesses sufficient material strength to play the role of the world's policeman. Whatever the impact of its failures in Korea and Vietnam but also in many other nations, America's political leadership has not abdicated the basic ideological principle that the United States has both the obligation and the right to intervene aggressively both covertly and, if necessary, overtly in the affairs of nations throughout the Third World. Astonishingly, unlike its allies whose imperialist ambitions have ended, the United States has never confronted seriously the increasing risks of its failure inherent in the sheer complexity and magnitude of its global aspirations and great but nonetheless finite resources, much less calculated carefully the ultimately immense costs of its persistence to long-run U.S. economic and political power and priorities both domestically and in the world.

We live constantly with the tensions and costs of the United States' aggressive foreign policy, which not only affects profoundly the likelihood of war or peace throughout the world but also imposes monumental constraints on urgently needed social and economic changes in the Third World today. To comprehend the origins and character of the events, forces, and decisions that have brought modern history to this dangerous state is not only to understand the recent past but also the causes of today's greatest problems and mankind's prospects for the future.

SOURCES AND NOTES

The following are a selection of general works, *in addition to* those given in the footnotes, that were especially valuable to me in preparing this book and that are not, for the most part, cited in them. Added to the books mentioned there, they constitute a list of basic references for those seeking more specialized readings.

For general works, see Cordell Hull, *Memoirs* (New York, 1948), vol. 2, for the World War Two background and U.S. postwar goals; Michael T. Klare's *Supplying Repression* (New York, 1977) and *American Arms Supermarket* (Austin, 1984) fully document military aid and sales; see also Miles D. Wolpin, *Military Aid and Counterrevolution in the Third World* (Lexington, Mass., 1972); Richard Nixon's *RN: The Memoirs of Richard Nixon* (New York, 1978), is important; Barry M. Blechman and Stephen S. Kaplan, *Force Without War: U.S. Armed Forces as a Political Instrument* (Washington, 1978), treats many crises also covered in this book.

For Africa, Thomas J. Noer, *Cold War and Black Liberation: The United States and White Rule in Africa, 1948–1968* (Columbia, Mo., 1985), is outstanding; see also Waldemar A. Nielson, *The Great Powers and Africa* (New York, 1969); Stephen R. Weissman, *American Foreign Policy in the Congo, 1960–1964* (Ithaca, 1974); Frederick S. Arkhurst, ed., *U.S. Policy Toward Africa* (New York, 1975); Henry F. Jackson, *From the Congo to Soweto: U.S. Foreign Policy Toward Africa Since 1960* (New York, 1982); Samuel Decalo, *Coups and Army Rule in Africa: Studies in Military Style* (New Haven, 1976).

For the CIA, consult David Wise and Thomas B. Ross, *The Invisible Government* (New York, 1964); Victor Marchetti and John D. Marks, *The CIA and the Cult of Intelligence* (New York, 1974). John Stockwell, *In Search of Enemies* (New York, 1978), remains the best book on the mind of the CIA; the reports of the U.S. Senate Select Comm. to Study Governmental Operations with Respect to Intelligence Activities are vital, especially *Alleged Assassination Plots Involving Foreign Leaders,* Nov. 20, 1975, and *Foreign and Military Intelligence,* bk. 1, April 26, 1976.

For economic data, the following are essential: U.S. Dept. of Commerce, *Selected Data on U.S. Direct Investment Abroad, 1950–76* (Washington, 1982), and *U.S. Direct Investment Abroad: 1982 Benchmark Survey Data* (Washington, 1985); regular AID volumes, "U.S. Overseas Loans and Grants"; U.S. Senate, Comm. on Foreign Relations, *Multinational Corporations in Brazil and Mexico: Structural Sources of Economic and Noneconomic Power,* Aug. 1975; Donald Sherk, *The United States and the Pacific Trade Basin* (Federal Reserve Bank of San Francisco, n.d. [ca. 1971]);

Raul Sosa-Rodriguez, *Les Problèmes Structurels des Relations Economiques Internationales de L'Amérique Latine* (Geneva, 1963); Inter-American Development Bank, *Annual Report, 1980;* AID, "Loan Terms, Debt Burden, and Development," April 1965; Shail Jain, *Size Distribution of Income* (Washington, 1975); World Bank, "An Anatomy of Income Distribution Patterns in Developing Nations," Economic Staff Working Paper no. 116, Sept. 23, 1971; annual issues of Asian Development Bank, *Key Indicators;* ADB, *Rural Asia: Challenge and Opportunity* (Singapore, 1977); C. Fred Bergsten et al., *American Multinationals and American Interests* (Washington, 1978).

For Indonesia, the best analysis of the period to 1965 is Jan M. Pluvier, *Confrontations: A Study in Indonesian Politics* (Kuala Lumpur, 1965); Richard Higgott and Richard Robison, eds., *Southeast Asia: Essays in the Political Economy of Structural Change* (Sydney, 1985), is very valuable. See also Hamish McDonald, *Suharto's Indonesia* (Melbourne, 1980); David Jenkins, *Suharto and His Generals: Indonesian Military Politics, 1975–1983* (Ithaca, 1984); and Richard Robison, *Indonesia: The Rise of Capital* (Sydney, 1986).

For Latin America, Samuel L. Baily, *The United States and the Development of South America, 1945–1975* (New York, 1976), is exceptional; Cole Blasier, *The Hovering Giant: U.S. Responses to Revolutionary Change in Latin America* (Pittsburgh, 1976), is a fine synthesis; U.S. Senate, Comm. on Foreign Relations, *United States-Latin American Relations,* Aug. 31, 1960, is informative; its *Survey of the Alliance for Progress,* April 29, 1969, continues its analyses. David S. Painter, *Oil and the American Century: The Political Economy of U.S. Foreign Oil Policy, 1941–1954* (Baltimore, 1986), is the best-informed survey of Latin America as well as the Middle East. The theoretical literature on the region is ably presented in James Petras and Maurice Zeitlin, eds., *Latin America: Reform or Revolution?* (New York, 1968) and Irving L. Horowitz et al., eds., *Latin American Radicalism* (New York, 1969). See also Fernando H. Cardoso and Enzo Faletto, *Dependency and Development in Latin America* (Berkeley, 1979); Guillermo A. O'Donnell, *Modernization and Bureaucratic-Authoritarianism* (Berkeley, 1979). On the U.S. and Guatemala in the 1950s, see also Stephen Schlesinger and Stephen Kinzer, *Bitter Fruit: The Untold Story of the American Coup in Guatemala* (Garden City, 1983); Blanche Wiesen Cook, *The Declassified Eisenhower: A Divided Legacy* (Garden City, 1981); Richard H. Immerman, *The CIA in Guatemala: The Foreign Policy of Intervention* (Austin, 1982). For Nicaragua, see Carlos M. Vilas' superb *The Sandinista Revolution: National Liberation and Social Transformation in Central America* (New York, 1986); Forrest D. Colburn, *Post-Revolutionary Nicaragua: State, Class, and the Dilemmas of Agrarian Reform* (Berkeley, 1986). For Central America in general, see the very valuable synthesis by Robert G. Williams, *Export Agriculture and the Crisis in Central America* (Chapel Hill, 1986), and Walter LaFeber's excellent *Inevitable Revolutions: The United States in Central America* (New York, 1983); also useful are Martin Diskin, ed., *Trouble in Our Backyard: Central America and the United States in the Eighties* (New York, 1983); Robert Armstrong and Janet Shenk, *El Salvador: The Face of Revolution* (Boston, 1982); Richard R. Fagen, "The Carter Administration and Latin America: Business as Usual?" *Foreign Affairs* 57 (1979), 652–70; and issues of *NACLA Report on the Americas* since its founding.

Elsewhere in Latin America, Jerome Levinson and Juan de Onis, *The Alliance That Lost Its Way* (Chicago, 1970), remains the best account of the Alliance for Progress. See also Willard F. Barber and C. Neale Ronning, *Internal Security and Military Power: Counterinsurgency and Civic Action in Latin America* (Columbus, 1966); James D. Cockcroft, *Mexico: Class Formation, Capital Accumulation, and the State* (New York, 1983); George M. Ingram, *Expropriation of U.S. Property in South America: Nationalization of Oil and Copper Companies in Peru, Bolivia, and Chile* (New York, 1974). For Chile, see Seymour M. Hersh, *The Price of Power: Kissinger in the Nixon White House* (New York, 1983); Theodore H. Moran, *Copper in Chile: Multinational Corporations and the Politics of Dependence* (Princeton, 1974); *NACLA Latin America Report,* Jan. 1973; Albert L.

Michaels, "Background to a Coup . . . ," in Claude E. Welch, ed., *Civilian Control of the Military* (Albany, 1976); Frederick B. Pike, "Aspects of Class Relations in Chile, 1850–1960," in Petras and Zeitlin, cited above; for Brazil, see especially Peter Evans, *Dependent Development: The Alliance of Multinational, State, and Local Capital in Brazil* (Princeton, 1979); Alfred Stepan, ed., *Authoritarian Brazil: Origins, Policies, and Future* (New Haven, 1973); Celso Furtado, *Diagnosis of the Brazilian Crisis* (Berkeley, 1965); Werner Baer, *Industrialization and Economic Development in Brazil* (Homewood, Ill., 1965); Nathaniel H. Leff, *Economic Policy-making and Development in Brazil, 1947–1964* (New York, 1968); Stefan H. Robock, *Brazil: A Study in Development Progress* (Lexington, Mass., 1975); Stanley E. Hilton, "The United States, Brazil, and the Cold War, 1945–1960," *Journal of American History* 68 (1981), 599–624; Albert Fishlow, "Flying Down to Rio . . . ," *Foreign Affairs* 57 (1979), 387–403; Helio Jaguaribe, "Political Strategies of National Development in Brazil" in Irving L. Horowitz, cited above. For Peru, see Carlos A. Astiz, *Pressure Groups and Power Elites in Peruvian Politics* (Ithaca, 1969); François Bourricaud, *Power and Society in Contemporary Peru* (London, 1970); E.V.K. Fitzgerald, *The State and Economic Development: Peru Since 1968* (Cambridge, Mass., 1976); Abraham F. Lowenthal, ed., *The Peruvian Experiment: Continuity and Change Under Military Rule* (Princeton, 1975); John Weeks, *Limits to Capitalist Development: The Industrialization of Peru, 1950–1980* (Boulder, 1985); Michael Locker, "Perspective on the Peruvian Military," *NACLA Newsletter,* Sept. 1969 and Oct. 1969; Barbara Stallings, "Privatization and the Public Debt: U.S. Banks in Peru," *NACLA Report on the Americas,* July–Aug. 1978, 2–19.

For the Middle East, David S. Painter, *Oil and the American Century,* cited above, is the single best account for the period to 1954; see also Michael B. Stoff, *Oil, War, and American Security: The Search for a National Policy on Foreign Oil, 1941–1947* (New Haven, 1980); John Marlowe, *Arab Nationalism and British Imperialism* (New York, 1961); A. J. Meyer, *Middle Eastern Capitalism* (Cambridge, Mass., 1959); Steven L. Speigel, *The Other Arab-Israeli Conflict: Making America's Middle East Policy, from Truman to Reagan* (Chicago, 1985). Three particularly useful books on Iran are Fred Halliday, *Iran: Dictatorship and Development* (Middlesex, 1979); R. K. Ramazani, *The United States and Iran: The Patterns of Influence* (New York, 1982); Barry Rubin, *Paved With Good Intentions: The American Experience and Iran* (New York, 1980).

For the military and society, see especially Gavin Kennedy, *The Military in the Third World* (London, 1974); Morris Janowitz, *Military Institutions and Coercion in the Developing Nations* (Chicago, 1977); Edwin Lieuwen, *Arms and Politics in Latin America* (New York, 1961); George A. Kourvetaris and Betty A. Dobratz, *Social Origins and Political Orientations of Officer Corps in a World Perspective* (Denver, 1973); Moshe Lissak, *Military Roles in Modernization: Civil-Military Relations in Thailand and Burma* (Beverly Hills, 1976); Catherine M. Kelleher, ed., *Political-Military Systems: Comparative Perspectives* (Beverly Hills, 1974); Liisa North, *Civil-Military Relations in Argentina, Chile, and Peru* (Berkeley, 1966); and Arturo Valenzuela, "A Note on the Military and Social Science Theory," *Third World Quarterly,* Jan. 1986, 132–43.

For the Philippines, Renato and Letizia R. Constantino, *The Philippines: The Continuing Past* (Quezon City, 1978), is a brilliant analysis of the 1940–70 era. Garel A. Grunder and William E. Livezey, *The Philippines and the United States* (Norman, 1951), remains useful. Carl H. Landé, *Leaders, Factions, and Parties: The Structure of Philippine Politics* (New Haven, 1964), is insightful, but should be compared to Willem Wolters, *Politics, Patronage, and Class Conflict in Central Luzon* (Quezon City, 1984). Resil B. Mojares, *The Man Who Would Be President: Serging Osmeña and Philippine Politics* (Cebu, 1986), captures the political mood ably. Also, Socorro C. Espiritu and Chester L. Hunt, eds., *Social Foundations of Community Development* (Manila, 1964); Luis Taruc, *Born of the People* (New York, 1953); Benedict J. Kerkvliet, *The Huk Rebellion: A Study of Peasant Revolt in the Philippines* (Berkeley, 1977); Edward G. Lansdale, *In the Midst of Wars: An American's Mission to Southeast Asia* (New York, 1973); Shirley Jenkins, *American Economic*

Policy Toward the Philippines (Stanford, 1954); Stephen R. Shalom, *The United States and the Philippines: A Study of Neocolonialism* (Philadelphia, 1981); David A. Rosenberg, ed., *Marcos and Martial Law in the Philippines* (Ithaca, 1979); International Documentation on the Contemporary Church, *The Philippines: American Corporations, Martial Law, and Underdevelopment* (New York, 1973). *IBON Facts & Figures,* Manila, is a vital continuous source of data. NEDA, *1986 Philippine Statistical Yearbook,* is a standard reference.

For Thailand, see Fred W. Riggs, *Thailand: The Modernization of a Bureaucratic Polity* (Honolulu, 1966); G. William Skinner, *Chinese Society in Thailand* (Ithaca, 1957); and Kevin J. Hewison, "The State and Capitalist Development in Thailand," in Higgott and Robison, cited above. For raw materials, Alfred E. Eckes, Jr., *The United States and the Global Struggle for Minerals* (Austin, 1979), is superior; also see Hans H. Landsberg et al., *Resources in America's Future: Patterns of Requirements and Availabilities, 1960–2000* (Baltimore, 1963); and Percy W. Bidwell, *Raw Materials: A Study of American Policy* (New York, 1958).

The "Declassified Documents Reference System" (Carrollton Press), an invaluable microfiche series reproducing key manuscripts from the CIA, the State Department, the Defense Department, the White House, the National Security Council, and others released under the Freedom of Information Act, is the single most important source for this book. To save space, it is usually cited by author, nature of the document, and date. The exact fiche reference is given as, for example, "R:325D," for those found in its "Retrospective Collection," and the year and fiche number for the annual sets beginning in 1975. For example, a document numbered "213C" in the 1977 set will appear as "77:213C."

Nearly all U.S. Agency for International Development manuscripts or reports cited here, including those of its police program, are found in the AID library in Rosslyn, Virginia.

The following code abbreviations are used in the notes:

AID – U.S. Agency for International Development.
CIA – U.S. Central Intelligence Agency.
DOD – U.S. Department of Defense.
DS   – U.S. Department of State.
DSB – U.S. *Department of State Bulletin.*
DT   – Minutes of telephone conversations of John Foster Dulles and Christian Herter, from the Eisenhower Library, Abilene, Kansas, reproduced on microfilm by University Publications of America.
FA   – *Foreign Affairs.*
FC   – U.S. Department of Commerce, *Foreign Commerce Weekly.*
FR   – U.S. Department of State, *Foreign Relations of the United States,* year and volume number.
ICA – U.S. International Cooperation Administration, predecessor to the AID.
IHT – *International Herald Tribune.*
JCS – U.S. Joint Chiefs of Staff.
NIE – "National Intelligence Estimates" produced by the combined U.S. intelligence agencies.
NSC – U.S. National Security Council. Where possible, references are to the NSC number assigned a document, plus the date.
NYT – *The New York Times.*

CHAPTER 1
The Wartime Image of the Future

1. Gabriel Kolko, *The Politics of War: The World and United States Foreign Policy, 1943–1945* (New York, 1968), 248, 251.
2. FR, 1945, I, 141.
3. Kolko, *Politics of War,* 478.
4. *FC,* Nov. 22, 1947, 4.

CHAPTER 2
European Priorities in Theory and Practice: From Africa to South Asia

1. U.S. Senate, Comm. on Foreign Relations, *Hearings: Reviews of the World Situation: 1949–1950,* 80:1, 2 [Historical Series, Executive Sessions], 292.
2. *FR,* 1948, I, 511. See also *FR,* 1945, VIII, 587–89; 1947, V, 531, 691–95; 1950, V, 1535.
3. *FR,* 1950, V, 1527.
4. *FR,* 1947, V, 492.
5. Ibid., 495, 514.
6. Ibid., 516.
7. *FR,* 1945, VIII, 11. See also *DSB,* March 23, 1947, 554–56; June 15, 1947, 1169–71.
8. *FR,* 1948, V, 11. See also *FR,* 1945, VIII, 10–12, 34–37; 1946, VII, 31–33; 1947, V, 520; memo of conversation, Joseph Grew and Nuri Pasha, May 29, 1945, Grew Papers, Harvard College Library.
9. *FR,* 1949, VI, 16–17. See also ibid., 10, 27; *DSB,* Feb. 27, 1950, 334–36.

CHAPTER 3
Confronting Turbulent Asia

1. CIA report, March 10, 1948, 4, 79:352C.
2. *FR,* 1946, VIII, 884. See also Ronald K. Edgerton, "The Politics of Reconstruction in the Philippines, 1945–1948" (Ph.D. thesis, Univ. of Michigan, 1975), passim, for the best documented account of U.S. policy.
3. *FR,* 1946, VIII, 874. See also DS, Research and Intelligence Service, "Recent Developments in Philippine-American Relations," R & A 3269, Oct. 5, 1945, passim.
4. U.S. Senate, Comm. on Foreign Relations, *Hearings: Reviews of the World Situation: 1949–1950,* 81:1, 2 [Historical Series, Executive Sessions], 156–57.
5. *FR,* 1946, VIII, 787.
6. Robert J. McMahon, *Colonialism and the Cold War: The United States and the Struggle for Indonesian Independence, 1945–49* (Ithaca, 1981), 311. See also *FR,* 1949, VII, 1131.
7. *FR,* 1948, I, 525. See also U.S. Senate, *Reviews of the World Situation,* 86, 160.
8. Dean Acheson, *Present at the Creation* (New York, 1969), 671–72.

CHAPTER 4
Latin America: The Nationalist Challenge

1. *DSB,* Sept. 22, 1946, 539–41.
2. *DSB,* Sept. 28, 1947, 642.
3. *DSB,* April 27, 1947, 770.
4. *DSB,* April 11, 1948, 471.

5. *DSB,* Aug. 11, 1946, 278. See also ibid., May 30, 1948, 714–15; *FR,* 1950, II, 594–99.

6. U.S. House, Comm. on International Relations, *Selected Executive Session Hearings of the Committee, 1943–50* (Washington, 1976), VI, 479.

7. *FR,* 1950, II, 600, 603, 607–8.

8. "On a Certain Impatience With Latin America," *FA,* 28 (1950), 572.

CHAPTER 5
The End of Postwar Optimism

1. *DSB,* March 2, 1947, 371.

2. *DSB,* Feb. 16, 1947, 291.

3. Dean Acheson, *Present at the Creation* (New York, 1969), 265. See also *FC,* Nov. 14, 1949, 4; *DSB,* Nov. 21, 1948, 627–28; Walter S. Salant, "The Domestic Effects of Capital Exports Under the Point Four Program," *American Economic Review* 40 (1950), 499–504.

4. *DSB,* March 19, 1949, 375.

5. *DSB,* June 12, 1949, 762–63. See also ibid., March 27, 1949, 376; Dec. 26, 1949, 976–77.

6. *DSB,* April 10, 1950, 553.

7. Quoted in Andrew J. Rotter, "The Big Canvas: The United States, Southeast Asia, and the World: 1948–1950," (Ph.D. thesis, Stanford Univ., 1981), 31–32. See also no author, "Point Four . . . ," *Yale Law Journal* 59 (1950), 1291–92.

CHAPTER 6
The Korean War: The United States Reassesses the Third World

1. DT, July 14, 1958.

2. Joyce and Gabriel Kolko, *The Limits of Power* (New York, 1972), 698–99.

3. DT, July 15, 1958. See also NSC minutes, Oct. 26, 1956, 13, 80:383C.

4. "Challenge and Response in United States Policy," *FA,* 36 (1957), 26.

5. Speech before 10th Inter-American Conference, March 4, 1954, DS press release no. 109, 5; DT, June 19, 1958.

6. DT, May 19, 1955.

7. DT, Jan. 22, 1953.

8. DT, May 18, 1954.

9. DT, April 19, 1954.

10. Transcript of Dulles remarks, March 27, 1958, IX, Dulles Papers, Princeton Univ. Library.

11. DT, June 19, 1958.

12. *DSB,* Sept. 13, 1971, 282. See also U.S. Commission on CIA Activities Within the United States, *Report to the President* (Washington, June 1975), 234–35.

13. U.S. Senate, Select Comm. to Study Governmental Operations, *Report: Foreign and Military Intelligence,* 94:2, April 26, 1976. Bk. 1, 21.

14. *DSB,* April 21, 1952, 626.

15. DT, June 24, 1954; William Y. Elliott, ed., *The Political Economy of American Foreign Policy* (New York, 1955), 224.

16. *DSB,* Nov. 28, 1955, 892. See also Dulles memo, n.d. [1954], 81:531A.

17. *DSB,* Nov. 16, 1959, 711.

18. *DSB,* Feb. 26, 1947, 300.

19. Senator Gravel Edition, *The Pentagon Papers* (Boston, 1971), I, 364.

20. Kolko, *Limits of Power,* 626. See also U.S. President's Materials Policy Commission, *Resources for Freedom,* June 1952 (Washington, 1952), I, 9; V, 110–20.

21. U.S. Senate, Comm. on Interior and Insular Affairs, *Report: Accessibility of Strategic and Critical Materials . . . ,* 83:2, July 9, 1954, 1. See also Harriman memo, Jan. 5, 1952, Harry S. Truman Papers, OF 335-B, Truman Library, Independence, Missouri.

CHAPTER 7
Asia and the American System

1. *FR,* 1951, VI, 34.

2. Ibid., 25. See also ibid., 35, 41, 59–61, 127.

3. Ibid., 1652, 1659.

4. *FR,* 1952–54, XII, 389, 391.

5. Ibid., XI, 1093.

6. Ibid., XII, 698.

7. Ibid., XI, 1092.

8. *DSB,* June 18, 1956, 1000.

9. Memo, Dean Acheson to the president, Aug. 31, 1950, 79:200A.

10. DS, Oct. 10, 1950, report, 78:102C.

11. *FR,* 1951, VI, 8–9, 24, 57. See also JCS memo, Sept. 6, 1950, 78:253A.

12. Joseph B. Smith, *Portrait of a Cold Warrior* (New York, 1976), 106.

13. R. A. Spruance to DS, March 6, 1953, R:728G.

14. Smith, *Portrait of a Cold Warrior,* 113. See also Renato Constantino, *The Making of a Filipino* (Quezon City, 1969), 194.

15. Smith, *Portrait of a Cold Warrior,* 250–52.

16. "USAID Reports . . . ," *AID Spring Review of Land Reform,* June 1970.

17. DT, Dec. 24, 1953. See also NSC 5413, March 16, 1954, 82:1219.

18. Smith, *Portrait of a Cold Warrior,* 254–55. See also minutes, Oct. 5, 1956, conference, 78:452B.

19. NSC 5813/1, June 4, 1958, 2–3, 10, 79:416B. See also updated NSC 5813/1, Nov. 26, 1958, 6, 81:343B.

20. Smith, *Portrait of a Cold Warrior,* 296, 312.

21. Ibid., 319.

CHAPTER 8
The Middle East: From Collaboration to Control

1. *FR,* 1950, V, 80, 91. See also ibid., 5, 76–77, 124, 190.

2. *FR,* 1950, V, 271.

3. *FR,* 1951, V, 2, 46.

4. NIE-26, April 25, 1951, 2, 82:15.

5. *FR,* 1951, V, 61, 70.

6. Dean Acheson, *Present at the Creation* (New York, 1969), 562.

7. Ibid., 565; *FR,* 1951, V, 259.

8. Acheson, *Present at the Creation,* 566. See also DS, Office of Intelligence Research, "Problems and Attitudes in the Arab World . . . ," May 19, 1952, 79:314A.

9. Miles Copeland, *The Game of Nations* (London, 1969), 55.

10. Grady to William Rountree, March 16, 1951, R:617E.

11. Acheson, *Present at the Creation,* 501. See also JCS to secretary of defense, Oct. 10, 1951, 80:376B; *FR,* 1951, V, 71, 295–99, 309–15.

12. Acheson, *Present at the Creation,* 682.

13. Robert H. Ferrell, ed., *The Eisenhower Diaries* (New York, 1981), 223.

14. Kermit Roosevelt, *Countercoup: The Struggle for the Control of Iran* (New York, 1979), 120.

15. NSC 175, Dec. 21, 1953, 2, 82:2141. See also Anthony Eden, *Full Circle* (Boston, 1960), chap. 9.

16. DT, March 17, 1954. See also DT, March 24, 1954; report on NSC 5402, April 15, 1954, 82:2140.

17. Manfred Halpern, *The Politics of Social Change in the Middle East and North Africa* (Princeton, 1963).

18. Selwyn Lloyd, *Suez 1956: A Personal Account* (New York, 1978), 27.

19. Harold Macmillan, *Tides of Fortune, 1945–1955* (London, 1969), 635.

20. DT, Nov. 29, 1955.

21. Lloyd, *Suez 1956,* 36.

22. DT, May 22, 1956.

23. Robert Murphy, *Diplomat Among Warriors* (Garden City, 1964), 377.

24. Anthony Nutting, *No End of a Lesson: The Story of Suez* (London, 1967), 11.

25. Eden, *Full Circle,* 512.

26. Nutting, *No End of a Lesson,* 52; DT, July 30, 1956.

27. DT, July 30, 1956.

28. DT, Oct. 30, 1956, 3:40 P.M.

29. Eden, *Full Circle,* 540. See also ibid., 634; DT, Oct. 30, 1956, 2:17 P.M. and 4:54 P.M.

30. Lloyd, *Suez 1956,* 78.

31. Nutting, *No End of a Lesson,* 53.

32. Murphy, *Diplomat Among Warriors,* 382–83.

33. *DSB,* Jan. 28, 1957, 128.

34. John C. Campbell, "From 'Doctrine' to Policy in the Middle East," *FA,* 35 (1957), 449.

35. U.S. Senate, Comm. on Foreign Relations, *Hearings: The President's Proposal on the Middle East,* 85:1, Jan.–Feb. 1957, 5, 41, 66, 776.

36. DT, June 14, 1958.

37. DT, June 18, 1958.

38. DT, July 14, 1958.

39. Murphy, *Diplomat Among Warriors,* 398. See also ibid., 399; DT, July 19, 1958.

40. DT, July 15, 1958.

41. DT, Aug. 23, 1958.

42. U.S. Senate, Comm. on Foreign Relations, *A Select Chronology . . . Relating to the Middle East,* 94:1, Feb. 1975, 12.

43. *FR,* 1952–54, XI, 151–52.

44. DT, Nov. 13, 1957. See also *FR,* 1952–54, XI, 154–55, 172–81; NSC 5614/1, Oct. 3, 1956, 81:177A.

45. DT, Nov. 14, 1957.

46. *DSB,* Jan. 13, 1958, 53. See also Dulles remarks, March 27, 1958, IX, Dulles Papers, Princeton Univ. Library; J. C. Holmes to Dulles, Feb. 6, 1958, 10, 81:182A.

CHAPTER 9
Latin America and the Challenge to U.S. Hegemony

1. Dean Acheson, *Present at the Creation* (New York, 1969), 330; U.S. Senate, Comm. on Foreign Relations, *Executive Sessions . . . Historical Series,* 82:1, 1951, vol. III, pt. 1, 346.

2. DS, "Latin America: A Study of U.S. Problems and Policy," Oct. 14, 1953, 53, 82:255.

3. NSC 144, March 4, 1953, 2, 77:107D.

4. *DSB,* Jan. 11, 1954, 51–52.

5. NSC report, March 6, 1953, 11, 81:331B.

6. *DSB,* Aug. 11, 1952, 211.

7. NSC report, March 6, 1953, 11; *FR,* 1952–54, IV, 6.

8. *DSB,* Nov. 23, 1953, 702, 709. See also *FR,* 1952–54, I, 72.

9. Joyce and Gabriel Kolko, *The Limits of Power* (New York, 1972), 416–17.

10. *Hispanic-American Reports,* March 1952, 30. See also contemporary issues of ibid.; *FR,* 1952–54, IV, 485ff.; Cole Blasier, *The Hovering Giant: U.S. Responses to Revolutionary Change in Latin America* (Pittsburgh, 1976), 134–39.

11. *FR,* 1952–54, IV, 304–5. See also NSC 144, March 4, 1953, 3, 77:107D; annex to NSC 144, March 6, 1953, 11, 81:331B.

12. Ronald M. Schneider, *Communism in Guatemala, 1944–1954* (New York, 1958), 186.

13. Ibid., 317–18.

14. DT, May 19, 1955. See also DS, "Latin America . . . ," Oct. 14, 1953, 42–43, 65; minutes of NSC meeting, Sept. 6, 1956, 3, 13, 80:382A.

15. *FR,* 1952–54, IV, 397.

16. Adolf A. Berle, *Navigating the Rapids, 1918–1971* (New York, 1973), 654.

17. *DSB,* June 9, 1958, 944.

18. John A. Calhoun, DS, memo, Jan. 30, 1959, 83:1932. See also report on NSC 5613/1, June 3, 1958, 3, 81:335A.

19. U.S. Senate, Comm. on Foreign Relations, *Executive Sessions . . . Historical Series,* 86:1, 1959, XI, 190.

20. *FR,* 1952–54, IV, 328.

21. Quoted in B. E. Matecki, *Establishment of the International Finance Corporation and United States Policy* (New York, 1957), 124.

22. Eugene R. Black, *The Diplomacy of Economic Development* (Cambridge, Mass., 1960), 53.

23. Milton S. Eisenhower, *The Wine Is Bitter* (Garden City, 1963), 230.

CHAPTER 10
Africa and the European System

1. *DSB,* June 19, 1950, 1002. See also *FR,* 1952–54, XI, 74.

2. *FR,* 1951, V, 1200.

3. *DSB,* Nov. 16, 1953, 656.

4. *DSB,* April 21, 1952, 623.

5. NSC 5719/1, Aug. 23, 1957, 7, 81:321A.

6. *DSB,* April 30, 1956, 717.

7. *DSB,* Nov. 28, 1955, 893.

8. *FR,* 1951, V, 1199.

9. *DSB,* May 19, 1958, 829; Nov. 28, 1955, 893.

10. NSC 6005/1, April 9, 1960, 3, 77:194C.

11. Thomas J. Noer, *Cold War and Black Liberation: The United States and White Rule in Africa, 1948–1968* (Columbia, Mo., 1985), 52. See also *FR,* 1952–54, XI, 73ff.

12. NSC 6001, Jan. 19, 1960, 8, 81:73A. See also J. C. Holmes to Dulles, Feb. 6, 1958, 7, 81:182A; NSC 5818, Aug. 26, 1958, 81:323A.

CHAPTER 11
Institutional Bases of the United States' Role in the Third World

1. *DSB,* May 31, 1954, 838.

2. *DSB,* Nov. 21, 1955, 848.

3. William Y. Elliott, ed., *The Political Economy of American Foreign Policy* (New York, 1955), 224.

4. *FR*, 1952–54, I, 78–79.

5. *DSB,* Jan. 3, 1955, 21.

6. ICA press release, Sept. 12, 1957, OF 116-B, Eisenhower Papers, Eisenhower Library, Abilene, Kansas.

7. Fleming to Eisenhower, Nov. 19, 1958, OF 116-J, Eisenhower Papers.

8. Douglas Dillon to Joseph M. Dodge, Sept. 16, 1958, misc. files, box 1, Dodge Papers, Detroit Public Library.

9. B. E. Matecki, *Establishment of the International Finance Corporation and United States Policy* (New York, 1957), 124.

CHAPTER 12
The Democratic Administration Confronts a World in Change

1. *DSB,* Aug. 7, 1961, 236. See also ibid., July 4, 1966, 12–13; NSC, "U.S. Overseas Internal Defense Policy," Aug. 1, 1962, 80:281A.

2. Senator Gravel Edition, *The Pentagon Papers* (Boston, 1971), II, 33.

3. NSC, "U.S. Overseas Internal Defense Policy," 1, 10.

4. See, for example, the program of the Foreign Service Institute, "Problems of Development and Internal Defense," Nov. 19–Dec. 21, 1962, AID Library, Rosslyn, Virginia.

5. *Pentagon Papers,* II, 34.

6. Ibid., III, 51; Foreign Service Institute, "Problems . . . ," 19.

7. Rostow in *DSB,* Aug. 7, 1961, 236.

8. ICA, "Report on the National Police in . . . Guatemala," April 9, 1956, summary, AID Library. See also ICA circular, Nov. 6, 1959, 81:133B; Chester Bowles to president, Sept. 30, 1961, 81:213A; Kennedy to Fowler Hamilton, Feb. 19, 1962, 80:372C; Frank M. Coffin memo, July 18, 1962, 81:1B; Ernest W. Lefever, [AID], "U.S. Public Safety Assistance: An Assessment," Dec. 1973, 11.

9. Martin L. Gross report, Sept. 9, 1960; Ray R. Baca report, Oct. 6, 1964; D. L. Crisostomo report, Dec. 9, 1965, to note but a few in the AID Library. See also Coffin memo, July 18, 1962; Foreign Service Institute, "Problems . . . ," 10; Jon P. Kindice and Edward R. Bishop, "Evaluation Report . . . ," Sept. 10, 1970, 13–16.

10. Samuel P. Huntington, *Political Order in Changing Societies* (New Haven, 1968), 222. See also John J. Johnson, ed., *The Role of the Military in Underdeveloped Countries* (Princeton, 1962); Institute for Defense Analysis, "A Study of U.S. Military Assistance Programs in the Under-developed Areas," April 8, 1959, 78:194B.

11. NSC, "U.S. Overseas Internal Defense Policy," 12, 16.

12. Foreign Service Institute, "Problems . . . ," 14, 18, 20.

13. Quoted in Miles D. Wolpin, *Military Aid and Counterrevolution in the Third World* (Lexington, Mass., 1972), 17, 29.

14. Komer to Kennedy, March 2, 1963, 80:281B.

CHAPTER 13
The Challenge of Latin America

1. Joyce Kolko, ed., "A Press Digest on United States-Cuba Relations, 1957–1961," June 1961, 1958-2 (copies of this comprehensive document are in the Harvard and Princeton libraries). See also Andrés Suárez, *Cuba: Castroism and Communism, 1959-1966* (Cambridge, Mass., 1967), 142–43.

2. DT, Sept. 20, 1957.

3. U.S. Senate, Comm. on Foreign Relations, *Executive Sessions . . . Historical Series,* 86:1, 1959, XI, 207.

4. Christian A. Herter to Eisenhower, Dec. 23, 1958, Whitman file, box 20, Eisenhower Library.

5. Richard E. Welch, Jr., *Response to Revolution: The United States and the Cuban Revolution, 1959–1961* (Chapel Hill, 1985), 35. See also ibid., 32ff.; Herter to Eisenhower, Dec. 23, 1958; John Dorschner and Roberto Fabricio, *The Winds of December* (New York, 1980), 152–54, 246; Luis Aguilar, ed., *Operation Zapata* (Frederick, 1981), x; CIA memo, Feb. 21, 1961, 76:9E.

6. "Press Digest," 1959-8.

7. Herter to Eisenhower, Nov. 5, 1959, Eisenhower Library.

8. "Press Digest," 1959-14. See also Herter to Eisenhower, Nov. 5, 1959.

9. Herter to Eisenhower, Nov. 5, 1959; Gordon Gray to Don Wilson, Dec. 3, 1974, Gray Papers, box 2, Eisenhower Library; Aguilar, *Operation Zapata,* x–xi; Dwight D. Eisenhower, *Waging Peace, 1956–1961* (Garden City, 1965), 533.

10. Adolf A. Berle, *Navigating the Rapids, 1918–1971* (New York, 1973), 737.

11. Delesseps S. Morrison, *Latin American Mission* (New York, 1965), 225.

12. "Report for Latin America," May 1964, 14, 77:99D.

13. DOD, International Security Affairs, Feb. 25, 1965, report, 50, 76:32B.

14. U.S. Senate, Comm. on Foreign Relations, *Hearing: Nomination of Lincoln Gordon . . . ,* 89:2, Feb. 7, 1966, 16, 67.

15. CIA, April 1, 1964, report, 4, 77:272C. See also Leonard Gross in *Look,* Aug. 28, 1962, 84–85.

16. Mann to Johnson, Feb. 6, 1965, 81:213B. See also CIA, Jan. 15, 1965, report, 77:272D.

17. Dillon to Kennedy, April 13, 1961, R:335F.

18. Gordon to Dean Rusk, March 28, 1962, 76:135E. See also NIE, Dec. 7, 1961, 76:3E; Gordon to Rusk, Aug. 13, 1962, 77:47G.

19. Gordon to Rusk, April 9, 1963, R:339A. See also William A. Brubeck to McGeorge Bundy, March 24, 1963, R:338E.

20. CIA, memo, July 2, 1963, 10, 76:4C. See also CIA, report, May 3, 1963, 76:4A; ibid., May 4, 1963, 76:4B; ibid., May 26, 1963, R:12F.

21. CIA, report, Aug. 26–27, 1963, R:13H. See also CIA, memo, July 2, 1963.

22. White House, memo, Sept. 30, 1963, 8, 81:599A.

23. George Ball to Gordon, Dec. 19, 1963, 76:262D.

24. Gordon to Mann, March 4, 1964, 75:84E.

25. CINCANTFLT to various commands, March 31, 1964, R:265C. See also consul, São Paulo, to Rusk, March 30, 1964, 76:49E; CIA, cable, March 30, 1964, 77:3F; teleconference minutes, April 2, 1964, 76:50C

26. CIA, memo, April 3, 1964, 75:233E.

27. Gordon to Rusk, April 5, 1964, 76:51E. See also ibid., April 4, 1964, 77:114D.

28. Ibid., April 10, 1964, 77:115C.

29. Rostow to Johnson, March 5, 1968, 82:1208. See also ibid., June 14, 1967, 81:599B; DS, report, Aug. 25, 1969, passim, 81:184B.

30. John Bartlow Martin, *Overtaken by Events* (Garden City, 1966), 131.

31. Ibid., 347.

32. Ibid., 661. See also U.S. Senate, Comm. on Foreign Relations, *Background Information Relating to the Dominican Republic,* 89:1, July 1965, passim.

33. Sept. 9, 1971.

34. Princeton N. Lyman and Jerome T. French, "Political Results of Land Reform," *AID Spring Review of Land Reform,* June 1970, 40. See also U.S. House, Comm. on Foreign Affairs, *Hearings: New Directions for the 1970's . . . ,* 91:1, March–May 1969, 661 and passim; U.S. Senate, Comm.

on Foreign Relations, *Survey of the Alliance for Progress,* 91:1, April 29, 1969, passim; IADB, Social Progress Trust Fund, *Seventh Annual Report, 1967,* 25–28.

35. "USAID Reports . . ." [Guatemala], *AID Spring Review of Land Reform,* June 1970.

36. Data taken from U.S. House, *New Directions for the 1970s,* 105–6, 149, 661, 740, and passim; U.S. Senate, *Survey of the Alliance,* 172–74, 779, 786, 812; Merilee S. Grindle, *State and Country-side: Development Policy and Agrarian Politics in Latin America* (Baltimore, 1986), passim.

37. Social Progress Trust Fund, *Seventh Annual Report,* 25.

38. World Bank, "Multilateral Debt Renegotiations: 1956–1968," April 11, 1969, 2.

39. Lyndon Baines Johnson, *The Vantage Point* (New York, 1971), 351. See also CIA, memo, Jan. 15, 1967, 5, 13, 77:272D.

CHAPTER 14
The Other Southeast Asian Challenges

1. *FR,* 1952–54, XII, 1066.

2. DT, Sept. 12, Dec. 8, 1957.

3. Howard P. Jones, *Indonesia: The Possible Dream* (New York, 1971), 156.

4. Jones to Rusk, March 6, 1964, 75:117C.

5. Embassy, Djakarta, to DS, Nov. 30, 1963, R:580A.

6. Ball to Johnson, March 18, 1965, R:597C.

7. U.S. House, Comm. on International Relations, *Hearings: Shifting Balance of Power in Asia . . . ,* 94:1, 2, Nov. 1975–May 1976, 164. See also CIA, report, Jan. 5, 1965, R:26B; Jones to Rusk, Jan. 21, 1965, National Security file, Indonesia, v. 3, box 246, Johnson Library, Austin, Texas; CIA, report, Oct. 2, 1965, R:27F; Green to Rusk, Oct. 3, 1965, R:607C; embassy [E. E. Masters] to DS, Oct. 22, 1965, 15, 79:434B; CIA, memo, Oct. 28, 1965, 2, R:29C; CIA report, n.d. [1972], 58, 80:220G; Harold Crouch, *The Army and Politics in Indonesia* (Ithaca, 1978), 96, 106–7, confirms the existence of something like the "Generals' Council."

8. See Green to Rusk, Oct. 3, 1965; U.S. House, *Shifting Balance of Power,* 226–30; Crouch, *Army and Politics,* 80–84, 114–17; Benedict R. Anderson and Ruth T. McVey, "A Preliminary Analysis of the October 1, 1965, Coup in Indonesia" (Cornell Univ. Modern Indonesia Project, 1971), passim.

9. CIA, memo, April 29, 1966, 3, 77:90A. See also embassy to DS, Oct. 22, 1965, 28–32; CIA, memo, Oct. 28, 1965, 7–8; Crouch, *Army and Politics,* 107–13; CIA 1972 report, 58; U.S. House, *Shifting Balance of Power,* 226ff.

10. Green to Rusk, Oct. 3, 1965, R:607E. See also CIA, report, Oct. 7, 1965, 75:53D.

11. CIA, report, Oct. 8, 1965, R:29A.

12. Green to DS, Oct. 5, 1965, R:608A.

13. Green to Rusk, Oct. 9, 1965, R:608E.

14. Ibid., Oct. 14, 1965, R:609A.

15. Rusk to Green, Oct. 29, 1965, R:612C. See also Green to Rusk, Oct. 17, 1965, R:609C; Green to Rusk, Oct. 28, 1965, R:612A.

16. Green to Rusk, Nov. 4, 1965, 2d of 2 cables, 79:434E.

17. Ibid., Nov. 7, 1965, R:613A; ibid., Nov. 8, 1965, R:613E.

18. Embassy, Bangkok, to Rusk, Nov. 5, 1965, R:612G. To maintain secrecy, much of the negotiations regarding such aid were done in Bangkok. See also Rusk to embassies, Bangkok and Djakarta, Nov. 6, 1965, R:613B; Green to Rusk, Nov. 7, 1965; embassy, Bangkok, to Rusk, Nov. 11, 1965, R:614E.

19. CIA, memo, Nov. 12, 1965, R:30A; Green to Rusk, Nov. 19, 1965, R:615D.

20. *DSB,* Oct. 24, 1966, 640.

21. CIA, memo, April 29, 1966, 4. See also Green to Rusk, Dec. 4, 1965, 77:128F.

22. See CIA, report, April 1, 1966, 5, 76:16B; CIA memo, April 29, 1966; Jones, *Indonesia,* 372; CIA, 1972 report, 80; Crouch, *Army and Politics,* 155; Hamish McDonald, *Suharto's Indonesia* (Melbourne, 1980), 53.

23. CIA, 1972 report, 85; U.S. House, *Shifting Balance of Power,* 161; *NYT,* Nov. 30, 1975; Crouch, *Army and Politics,* 224–25.

24. Green to Rusk, Dec. 1, 1965, 77:128D. See also Green to Rusk, Nov. 19, 1965, 79:435C; George Ball to Green, Nov. 23, 1965, 76:280D.

25. DS, summary, n.d. [early 1966], 76:282C. See also Green to embassy, Bangkok, Dec. 5, 1965, 77:128G; CIA, memo, Feb. 5, 1966, 76:16A.

26. DS, Policy Planning Council, March 25, 1966, paper, 39 and passim, 76:281F.

27. R. W. Komer to Johnson, Oct. 6, 1964, R:913G.

28. CIA, memo, Oct. 28, 1965, 77:273D.

29. W. W. Rostow to Johnson, Sept. 7, 1966, 77:357B. See also James C. Thomson to Rostow, May 4, 1966, 78:253B.

30. Oct. 6, 1966, paper, 79:444C.

31. CIA, memo, April 18, 1967, 79:127A.

32. *DSB,* April 24, 1967, 660.

CHAPTER 15
The Problem of Sub-Saharan Africa

1. Robert C. Good, *DSB,* Dec. 10, 1962, 887.

2. Rostow to McGeorge Bundy, May 13, 1961, 76:298D.

3. DS, "Guidelines . . . ," March 1962, 17, 78:392B. See also DS, paper, n.d. [1965], 4, 76:171E.

4. Arnold Rivkin, "Lost Goals in Africa," *FA* 44 (1965), 114.

5. DS, paper, June 28, 1962, 10, 77:207A. See also Samuel E. Belk to McGeorge Bundy, June 29, 1961, 76:135B; Rostow to Kennedy, July 16, 1961, 76:135D; Paul Sakwa, memo, Jan. 17, 1962, 81:575A; Thomas J. Noer, *Cold War and Black Liberation: The United States and White Rule in Africa, 1948–1968* (Columbia, Mo., 1985), passim.

6. DS, paper, June 28, 1962, 19. See also Noer, *Cold War and Black Liberation,* chap. 6.

7. DS, paper, n.d. [ca. late 1967], 4, 84:1604.

8. Joseph Palmer to Rusk, May 7, 1965, 76:172B.

9. Arthur J. Goldberg to Johnson, April 23, 1966, 80:393A.

10. David J. Gould, *Bureaucratic Corruption and Underdevelopment in the Third World: The Case of Zaire* (New York, 1980), xii.

11. *DSB,* April 12, 1965, 535–36.

CHAPTER 16
The Nixon Administration Confronts the Third World

1. Henry Kissinger, *White House Years* (Boston, 1979), 950.

2. *Public Papers of the Presidents of the United States: Richard Nixon, 1969* (Washington, 1971), 549, 555.

3. *DSB,* March 22, 1971, 344.

4. Ernest W. Lefever, "U.S. Public Safety Assistance: An Assessment," Dec. 1973, 13.

5. *DSB,* Sept. 13, 1971, 281.

6. Kissinger, *White House Years,* 658.

7. *DSB,* March 22, 1971, 344. See also Raymond L. Garthoff, *Détente and Confrontation: American-Soviet Relations from Nixon to Reagan* (Washington, 1985), passim.

8. Kissinger, *Years of Upheaval* (Boston, 1982), 765.

CHAPTER 17
Latin America: The Limits of Reform

1. John W. Jones to Rusk, March 12, 1964, 77:339C. See also DS, memo, Feb. 7, 1964, 78:102B; CIA, report, April 1, 1964, 190–91, 77:272C; U.S. Senate, Comm. on Foreign Relations, *Hearings: United States Relations with Peru,* 91:1, April 14–17, 1969, 13–19, passim.

2. *Le Monde* [English weekly ed.], Sept. 24, 1969.

3. CIA, reports, April 20, 1973, 79:125B; July 13, 1973, 79:125D; Aug. 21, 1973, 79:126A; Aug. 31, 1973, 79:126C; AID, "Development Assistance Program-Peru-FY 1975," 1–2.

4. McGeorge Bundy to embassy, Nov. 12, 1965, 82:116. See also Gen. O'Meara to Robert F. Kennedy, April 16, 1965, 77:290B; memo of conversation, Jan. 11, 1966, 82:119; *NYT,* May 17, Oct. 6, 1964; U.S. Senate, Select Comm. to Study Governmental Operations, *Hearings: Intelligence Activities* ["Covert Action"], 94:1, Dec. 4–5, 1975, VII, 11.

5. Ralph A. Dungan to Lincoln Gordon, March 10, 1966, 82:134; Gordon to Dungan, July 1, 1966, 82:138.

6. Kissinger, *Years of Upheaval* (Boston, 1982), 377. See also U.S. Senate, *Intelligence Activities,* 20.

7. Kissinger, *White House Years* (Boston, 1979), 675. See also U.S. Senate, *Intelligence Activities,* 159–60; U.S. Senate, Select Comm. to Study Governmental Operations, *Report: Alleged Assassination Plots Involving Foreign Leaders,* 94:1, Nov. 20, 1975, 229.

8. *NYT,* Nov. 6, 1970. See also U.S. Senate, *Assassination Plots,* 225–42; U.S. Senate, Select Comm., *Supplementary Detailed Staff Reports . . . ,* 94:2, April 23, 1976, IV, 121–27.

9. U.S. Senate, *Assassination Plots,* 231n. See also Kissinger, memo, Oct. 21, 1970, 82:569.

10. U.S. Senate, *Intelligence Activities,* 184–86; U.S. Senate, Comm. on Foreign Relations, *Hearings: Multinational Corporations and United States Foreign Policy,* 93:1. March–April 1973, pt. 2, 940, 950, 971, 1009–10.

11. Kissinger, *Years of Upheaval,* 395, 403–7; *NYT,* September 27, 1973; U.S. Senate, Comm. on Foreign Relations, *Hearing: Vance Nomination,* 95:1, Jan. 11, 1977, 57; *Washington Post,* Oct. 21, 1973; U.S. Senate, *Intelligence Activities,* 186; *IHT,* Sept. 21–22, 1974.

CHAPTER 18
The Middle East: Toward Protracted Crisis

1. Zbigniew Brzezinski, *Power and Principle* (New York, 1983), 354. See also Henry Kissinger, *White House Years* (Boston, 1979), 1262–64.

2. U.S. Senate, Comm. on Foreign Relations, *Hearings: Multinational Corporations and United States Foreign Policy,* 93:2, Jan. 30, 1974, pt. 4, 85.

CHAPTER 19
The United States and the Changing World Economy

1. U.S. Congress, Joint Economic Comm., *Hearings: Resource Scarcity, Economic Growth . . . ,* 93:1, Dec. 19–21, 1973, 5. See also U.S. House, Comm. on Interstate and Foreign Commerce, *The Energy Factbook,* 96:2, Nov. 1980, passim; U.S. Depts. of Commerce and Interior [Vivian E.

Spencer], *Raw Materials in the United States Economy, 1900–1977* (Washington, 1980), 14, 19; U.S. National Commission on Supplies and Shortages, *Government and the Nation's Resources,* Dec. 1976, 4–5, 16; U.S. Office of Technology Assessment, *Strategic Materials: Technologies to Reduce U.S. Import Vulnerability,* May 1985, 41–43, 51–52; L. Harold Bullis and James E. Mielke, *Strategic and Critical Materials* (Boulder, 1985), 30–32, 41–43.

2. Kissinger, *Years of Upheaval* (Boston, 1982), 875. See also ibid., 858ff.; U.S. Senate, Comm. on Foreign Relations, *Report: Multinational Oil Corporations and U.S. Foreign Policy,* 93:2, Jan. 2, 1975, 127ff; Maj. John A. Berry, "The Growing Importance of Oil," *Military Review,* Oct. 1972, 2–16; *Wall Street Journal,* Jan. 30, 1973.

3. Kissinger, *Years of Upheaval,* 893. See also U.S. Senate, Comm. on Foreign Relations, *Hearings: Multinational Corporations and United States Foreign Policy,* 94:2, Feb.–May 1976, pt. 14, 428–29.

4. *DSB,* Oct. 30, 1972, 501.

5. DS, memo, Jan. 22, 1974. See also *Washington Post,* Feb. 8, 1974.

6. *DSB,* March 25, 1975, 365–66.

7. U.S. Senate, Comm. on Foreign Relations, *Hearings: U.S. Relations with Latin America,* 94:1, Feb. 1975, 111. See also *DSB,* April 21, 1975, 498–505.

8. *DSB,* May 31, 1976, 662.

9. *DSB,* Oct. 7, 1974, 481.

10. U.S. House, Comm. on Foreign Affairs, *The United States and the Multilateral Development Banks,* 93:2, March 1974, 5.

11. U.S. Dept. of the Treasury, "United States Participation in the Multilateral Development Banks in the 1980s," Feb. 1982, 3 and passim.

12. U.S. House, *Multilateral Development Banks,* 52.

13. U.S. Treasury, "United States Participation," 49.

14. U.S. Task Force on International Development, *Report to the President,* March 4, 1970, 23.

15. *DSB,* June 9, 1975, 776.

16. AID, "Employment and Income Distribution Objectives . . . ," Oct. 1972, 8, 10–11.

17. AID, "Growth of Exports and Income in the Developing World . . . ," Discussion Paper no. 28, Nov. 1973, 23; U.S. House, *Multilateral Development Banks,* 130.

18. U.S. House, *Multilateral Development Banks,* 131.

19. U.S. Senate, Comm. on Foreign Relations, *Report: International Debt, the Banks, and U.S. Foreign Policy,* 95:1, Aug. 1977, 62 and passim.

20. Data from UN [Unctad], *Handbook of International Trade and Development Statistics—1976* (New York, 1976), 37; *Finance & Development,* Sept. 1984, 49; Paul Bairoch, in *Revue Tiers Monde,* 20 (Oct.–Dec. 1979), 673; David Roberts, "The LDC Debt Burden," *Federal Reserve Bank of New York Quarterly Review,* Spring 1981, 34–37.

CHAPTER 20
The African Cauldron

1. Roger Morris, *Uncertain Greatness: Henry Kissinger and American Foreign Policy* (New York, 1977), 110–11, 113, 119. See also NSSM 39, Dec. 9, 1969, passim, 78:187A.

2. Anthony Lake, *The "Tar Baby" Option: American Policy Toward Southern Rhodesia* (New York, 1976), 133.

3. *DSB,* Dec. 31, 1973, 789; April 4, 1977, 319.

4. "Hazardous Courses in Southern Africa," *FA,* 49 (1971), 226–27.

5. *DSB,* Nov. 18, 1963, 784.

6. Kennan, *FA,* 232–33. See also Thomas J. Noer, *Cold War and Black Liberation: The United*

States and White Rule in Africa, 1948–1968 (Columbia, Mo., 1985), 242; Oliver S. Crosby to Newsom, Sept. 16, 1969, 82:1039; Ridgeway Knight to DS, March 18, 1971, 82:1886.

7. John Stockwell, *In Search of Enemies: A CIA Story* (New York, 1978), 43, 90. See also Raymond L. Garthoff, *Détente and Confrontation: American-Soviet Relations from Nixon to Reagan* (Washington, 1985), 503–7; *NYT,* Dec. 19, 1975, Jan. 20, 1976.

8. Stockwell, *In Search of Enemies,* 235. See also Garthoff, *Détente and Confrontation,* 508–14.

9. Noer, *Cold War and Black Liberation,* 244. See also *NYT,* Jan. 9, Feb. 22, March 23, 24, 1976.

10. Sept. 11, 1976, press conference, DS release. See also *NYT,* April 24, 1976.

11. Zbigniew Brzezinski, *Power and Principle* (New York, 1983), 143. See also *DSB,* Dec. 1979, 29.

CHAPTER 21
The Philippines: Creating a Revolution

1. Ferdinand E. Marcos, *Today's Revolution: Democracy* (Manila, 1971), 123.

2. June 2, 1972, 72.

3. Thomas M. Finn and James L. McMahon [AID], "Evaluation of the Public Safety Program—Philippines," April 1972, 40 and passim.

4. Raymond Bonner, *Waltzing with a Dictator: The Marcoses and the Making of American Policy* (New York, 1987), 93.

5. Finn and McMahon, "Evaluation," 45, 48–49.

6. *NYT,* Nov. 3, 1972. See also *San Francisco Examiner,* Sept. 28, 1972; Primitivo Mijares, *The Conjugal Dictatorship of Ferdinand and Imelda Marcos* (San Francisco, 1976), 81–85; minutes, Oct. 4, 1972, Philippine-American Chamber of Commerce, New York; Bonner, *Waltzing,* 95–109.

7. Walden Bello et al., *Development Debacle: The World Bank in the Philippines* (San Francisco, 1982), 184.

8. CIA, weekly summary, March 3, 1973, 6, 78:225D.

9. Fred C. Shaver [AID] to Fred M. Schwarzwalder [AID], Feb. 4, 1980, 4 and passim.

10. These conditions are described, in addition to the above citations, in World Bank, "The Philippines: Recent Trends in Poverty, Employment, and Wages," June 20, 1985, passim; "The Philippines: Agrarian Reform Issues . . . ," May 12, 1987, passim; *IBON Facts & Figures,* Sept. 30, 1986, Feb. 28, 1987; Ian Coxhead and Sisira Jayasuriya, *Asian Survey,* Oct. 1986, to mention but a few studies.

CHAPTER 22
Iran and the Eclipse of American Power

1. Henry Kissinger, *White House Years* (Boston, 1979), 1261.

2. NSC, memo, n.d. [ca. 1965], 1, 76:43A. See also DS, memo, Feb. 11, 1961, 78:80D; DS, paper, March 20, 1961, 78:81A; DS, memo, April 3, 1961, 82:1769; DS, memo, n.d. [ca. 1961], 82:1772; William H. Brubeck to McGeorge Bundy, Jan. 21, 1963, 79:80B; DS, memo, May 7, 1963, 79:226A.

3. Barry Rubin, *Paved with Good Intentions: The American Experience and Iran* (New York, 1980), 201. See also R. K. Webster, report, Sept. 19, 1977, passim, 79:361D.

4. Zbigniew Brzezinski, *Power and Principle* (New York, 1983), 358.

5. Cyrus Vance, *Hard Choices: Critical Years in American Foreign Policy* (New York, 1983), 329.

6. Brzezinski, *Power and Principle,* 380.

7. Ibid., 446 and passim.

8. Ibid., 445. See also Kolko, *Main Currents in Modern American History* (New York, 1984), 412.

9. *IHT,* Feb. 16–17, 1980.

CHAPTER 23
The Central American Maelstrom

1. Ernest W. Lefever, "U.S. Public Safety Assistance: An Assessment," Dec. 1973, 13.

2. D. L. Crisostomo [AID], "Report on Police Progress . . . Guatemala," Dec. 9, 1965, 9.

3. *IHT,* May 5, 1977. See also *Business Week,* March 14, 1977, 111.

4. Richard E. Feinberg, *The Intemperate Zone: The Third World Challenge to U.S. Foreign Policy* (New York, 1983), 51.

5. Viron P. Vaky, "Hemispheric Relations: 'Everything Is Part of Everything Else,' " *FA* 59 (1981), 622.

LIST OF ABBREVIATIONS

AFL-CIO	U.S. trade union (American Federation of Labor and Congress of Industrial Organizations)
AID	U.S. Agency for International Development
AIOC	Anglo-Iranian Oil Company
CIA	U.S. Central Intelligence Agency
CPP	Communist Party of the Philippines (1968 split from PKP)
FNLA	National Front for the Liberation of Angola
FSLN	Sandinista Front for National Liberation (Nicaragua)
GATT	General Agreement on Tariffs and Trade
HUKS	the Hukbalahap
HUKBALAHAP	People's Anti-Japanese Army (Philippines)
IADB	Inter-American Development Bank
IMF	International Monetary Fund
IPC	International Petroleum Company, Standard Oil of New Jersey's Peruvian affiliate
ITT	International Telephone and Telegraph Company
LAFTA	Latin American Free Trade Area
LDC	less-developed country
MNR	Nationalist Revolutionary Movement (Bolivia)
MPLA	Popular Movement for the Liberation of Angola
NATO	North Atlantic Treaty Organization
NPA	New People's Army, Philippines
NSC	U.S. National Security Council
OAS	Organization of American States
OPEC	Organization of Petroleum Exporting Countries
PKI	Communist Party of Indonesia
PKP	Partido Komunista ng Pilipinas (Communist Party of the Philippines)
PLO	Palestine Liberation Organization
SAVAK	Iranian secret police
SEATO	Southeast Asia Treaty Organization
UN	United Nations
UNITA	National Union for the Total Independence of Angola

INDEX

ABOUT THE AUTHOR

Gabriel Kolko has written eight highly influential books on American history and foreign policy, and his *Anatomy of a War* (Pantheon, 1986) has been widely reviewed as the best history of the Vietnam War. He received his Ph.D. from Harvard and is Distinguished Research Professor of History at York University in Toronto, Canada.